KU-612-401

Fundamental Economics

Neil Fuller BSc (Econ), MSc, MCIPS

Revisions by
Nigel Proctor BA, MA (Econ), PGCE

WATERFORD CITY AND COUNTY LIBRARIES
WITHDRAWN

TUDOR

330/011 86887

Published in Great Britain by Tudor Business Publishing Ltd.

First published 1987
Reprinted with revisions 1990, 1993

Second edition 1997

© Neil Fuller, 1987, 1997

All rights reserved. No part of this publication may be reproduced or
transmitted in any form or by any means, electronically or mechanically,
including photocopying, recording, or any information storage or
retrieval system without prior permission in writing from Tudor
Publishing at Stanton House, Eastham Village Road, Eastham, Wirral,
Merseyside L62 8AD.

British Library Cataloguing in Publication Data:
A catalogue record for this book is available from the British Library

ISBN 1 872807 52 6

1 2 3 4 5   97 98 99 00

Cover design by Elizabeth Rowe

Typeset in 10/12 pt Palatino by GreenGate Publishing Services,Tonbridge, Kent
Printed in Great Britain by the Athenaeum Press, Gateshead, Tyne & Wear

Contents

Contents

Introduction

For the second edition of this book it was felt that the structure required a substantial revision to meet the changes in teaching methodology which have taken place since the publication of earlier editions. As is always the case with a text of this nature it has also been necessary to completely revise the data which illustrates the applied aspects.

The period since the publication of the first edition has been an exciting one for economists. It has seen the ascendancy of market economics, from the privatisation programmes in the UK to the collapse of the command economies in the states of the former Soviet Union; a disenchantment with Keynesian economics and the policies of demand management and the growth of the neo-classical approach to macro economics. Ironically during this period of less government there has been increased concern with environmental issues which may be difficult to address without governments establishing some form of legal framework. In the field of micro economics managerial and technological innovations seem to have delayed the tendency of costs to rise in some organisations as the scale of operations grow. This new edition captures some of these developments and explains them in a way which is intended to be as helpful as possible to the reader.

This book, as with the earlier editions is intended for students studying economics for professional examinations, A Level, and the first year of degree courses. With the semesterisation of many business degree programmes the new structure of the book makes it particularly suitable for single semester courses in economics. The syllabi of the major professional bodies are covered, as are those of most A Level Boards and foundation courses for degree subjects. The approach is intended to be concise and to the point avoiding wherever possible the excess of wording which often tends to obscure the salient points of the subject, particularly for those students studying economics for the first time. The style of the book attempts at all times to clarify the issues whilst maintaining their academic credibility and this should enable it to be used both as a concise course text and as a revision aid. It should prove particularly useful to students on single semester courses who are new to the study of economics but need to progress rapidly to a reasonable level of understanding.

It is suggested that students consider the learning objectives and key words at the start of each section, read the following chapters and then test their understanding by attempting the self-assessment questions at the end of the chapter; these can all be answered from the material found within that chapter.

Mathematical proofs have been put into appendices to avoid confusing less mathematical students. The chapter on the IS/LM and AD models has been included mainly for the benefit of undergraduate students, and the final section on the UK economy should give all students an insight into the current state of the UK economy.

I am grateful for the help given to me by Nigel Proctor both in restructuring the material and giving it a new format and for his assistance in up-dating the contents. I would also like to acknowledge Richard Ledward of Staffordshire University for his advice and assistance with the data collection, and Mike Atingi-Ego of the Liverpool Business School and my colleague David Barnes for their assistance and comments.

Neil Fuller 1997

Section A

The basics of economics

Containing the following chapters:

Chapter 1 – Basic concepts

Chapter 2 – Production

Chapter 3 – Specialisation and division of labour

The study of how people can provide for their material well-being.

This section should enable students to:

- *Understand* the basic economic concepts
- *Explain* the factors of production and their role in the economy
- *Contrast* the different types of economy
- *Evaluate* the importance of specialisation and mass production in a modern economy.

Keywords to consider:

choice; scarcity; opportunity cost; land; labour; capital; enterprise; free market; planned economy; mixed economy; privatisation; consumption; saving; investment; production possibility curves; diminishing returns; specialisation; comparative advantage; division of labour; barter; money.

1

Basic concepts

1 Economics

Economics is the study of how the human race can provide for its material well-being. As such it analyses the ways in which people can apply their skills, efforts and knowledge to the available natural resources in order to produce those goods and services which will satisfy their wants.

2 Social science

Economics is a social science. Social because it studies mankind and society, although unlike other social sciences it studies only one aspect of mankind's behaviour; and science because of the method of study. Economics attempts wherever possible to adopt a scientific approach. Therefore it attempts to use only positive statements which are those which can be verified by appeal to the facts, rather than normative statements, which are frequently matters of opinion, or **value judgements**, about which we may all hold different but equally valid opinions. Value judgements are more a matter for policy makers to decide in line with their perception of society's preferences, whilst economists are more concerned with finding the most efficient, or lowest cost, method of achieving a given objective. It cannot be ignored however that inevitably economic decisions will be influenced indirectly by social and political considerations.

Unlike other scientists, however, the economist cannot experiment as it is not possible to have a controlled experiment. In order to compensate for the lack of control over other variables economists frequently include the expression ceteris paribus (cet. par.), meaning 'other things being equal', when they make a statement, which means that they believe the statement to be true provided other factors remain unchanged.

3 Opportunity cost

As resources are always limited in supply and human wants appear to be insatiable then we always require more goods than are available. As resources are limited and wants are insatiable mankind is continually forced to make choices. It is the making of these choices which is central to the study of economics. Every time we make a decision to produce something we choose to forego the alternative which we could have produced, the cost of this foregone alternative is known as the **opportunity cost**. Opportunity cost also applies every time we make a decision to buy something as consumers, and every time we make a collective decision as a nation; for example if we produce Concorde those resources will not be available to build roads or hospitals.

4 Scarcity and choice

Scarcity therefore forces us to make **choices**, and as we make choices we are forced to **sacrifice** other things, in other words we are forced to economise. Normally however the choice is not between one good or another, but how many more of one good should we have and how much less of another. Scarcity and choice are therefore central to the study of economics. Those goods which are produced from our scarce resources are referred to as **economic goods**, and as they are scarce they have a **price**; the price being relative to their scarcity. Goods or resources which are not scarce but are available in unlimited quantities do not have a price, e.g. air; there is no need therefore to economise with them, and so they do not enter the study of economics.

5 Wants

Wants can be satisfied by the production of either tangible goods or the enjoyment of services. In the study of economics anything which satisfies a want is said to have **utility**. Different goods however produce different amounts of utility, or the same good can produce different amounts of utility in different places or at different times, for example water has a different utility in a dry country than in Britain.

6 Goods and services

As goods are produced they are then consumed and the act of consumption provides the required utility, but in so doing creates a new want. There is therefore an endless round of production, consumption, and the creation of new wants leading to new production. The rate at which goods are consumed however differs.

Consumer goods are consumed over a relatively short time period and we receive utility directly from their use, for example shoes. 'Single-use' consumer goods are consumed immediately, for example an ice-cream.

Consumer durables yield utility over a longer time period, for example a refrigerator or washing machine . The utility received is not from the good itself but from the stream of services it yields over its lifetime.

Producer goods or **capital goods** do not directly satisfy wants, but do so indirectly. They are the plant and machinery acquired by firms for the purpose of producing other goods which may produce utility. As such they constitute the **assets** of firms and may be referred to as **capital assets**.

Services constitute intangible utilities, and may be further sub-divided into **personal services** and **commercial services**. Personal services satisfy needs through personal attention such as hairdressing, entertainment or medical treatment. Commercial services are not directly personal but act as aids to production, and include activities such as banking, insurance and communications.

7 The factors of production

The purpose of production is therefore to create utilities by providing a flow of goods and services to fulfil wants. In order to undertake production it is necessary to combine the resources available. These resources are known as the **factors of production**, and they can be combined in various proportions to produce economic goods. The factors of production can be classified as

- land
- labour
- capital

The activity of combining these factors of production is referred to as **enterprise**, which is sometimes included as a fourth factor of production. Enterprise is undertaken by the **entrepreneur** who accepts the **risk** of producing in advance of sale and in return receives **profit**, the rest of the revenue from sales going in payments to the other factors of production.

8 Choices

The problem of society forcing us to make choices is actually the problem of how to allocate existing resources to different uses and how to allocate the resulting goods and services to different members of society. Different societies may have different approaches to resolving these problems, but the problem remains the same everywhere. The three basic problems which all societies are forced to resolve can be expressed as **what, how** and **for whom**?

- **What?** – refers to the problem of which goods should be produced and in what quantities.
- **How?** – refers to the method of producing the goods, making the best use of available resources.
- **For whom?** – refers to the way in which the total output is to be distributed amongst the members of the community.

All economies face the same problems although their approach to solving them may differ.

9 Types of economy

There are basically three alternative approaches a society may adopt in order to solve the problems of what?, how? and for whom?, the **free market**, the **planned** (or **command**) **economy**, and the **mixed economy** although in reality it is more like a spectrum with differing degrees of mixture between the two extreme forms of a completely free market economy and a totally planned economy, with few examples of the extremes and most being at some intermediate point between the two extremes.

10 The free market

In a free market, or private enterprise economy, all the factors of production are owned by private individuals and the decisions of what, how, and for whom, are made unconsciously by the interaction of market forces. We must assume here that consumers are rational and always attempt to maximise the utility they receive from their incomes, and that entrepreneurs are also rational and always attempt to maximise their profits. Given these assumptions, consumers are free to purchase whatever they wish in the market place. This is sometimes expressed as 'consumer votes' in the sense that they will spend more of their incomes (votes) on goods they favour. As the demand for these goods increases their prices will rise, making them more profitable, and entrepreneurs seeking greater profit will respond by entering into production of these goods, thereby increasing their supply. Hence more of those goods for which consumers have expressed a preference are produced. Production is therefore said to respond to the 'price signals' which indicates those goods which should be produced, and **consumer sovereignty** is said to prevail over the market.

The technical problem of 'how to produce' is determined by competition between producers which forces each to adopt the least-cost method of production.

The problem of 'for whom', the problem of distribution, is determined by relative incomes, which in turn are determined by supply and demand in the markets for productive services. If labour is scarce relative to its demand then wages will be higher and a greater proportion of output will go to wage earners; the same is true of owners of land and capital.

The concept of consumer votes should not be equated with any concept of 'fairness' in the accepted sense; some people have far more 'votes' than others, and if this is seen as a problem then it is one of income distribution not the price mechanism in itself. (See Chapter 27 for more details on this).

We are now in a position to list the main advantages and disadvantages of the three main types of economy.

11 Strengths of the free market economy

- Because goods are produced in accordance with consumers' preferences then society's resources are also allocated in line with the preferences of consumers.
- Because production responds automatically to the 'price signals' of the market, there is no need for the activities of thousands of manufacturers to be co-ordinated as this happens autonomously.
- Only those goods which are wanted by consumers are produced.
- People are free to spend their money in whichever way they choose.
- The free market economy offers the opportunity for those people with sufficient drive and initiative to enter production and create wealth.

12 Weaknesses of the free market economy

- Luxury goods for some may be produced before others have the basic necessities of life.
- During periodic recession valuable resources stand idle.
- The free market may not operate efficiently because of the existence of monopolies, and competition may therefore be lacking.
- Essential goods and services may not be provided or at least not be provided in sufficient quantities by the market. Some of these goods are referred to as 'merit goods' as they are thought to be so beneficial to society that they should be available to everybody. Others which are referred to as pure public goods, can only be adequately provided by government from tax revenue, for example defence.
- The free market does not allow for the 'social costs' of the entrepreneur's activities, e.g. pollution of the environment.

13 The planned economy

The **planned** (or **command**) **economy** is characterised by the collective ownership of the means of production and hence the price mechanism does not operate. The decisions of what, how and for whom are made by a central planning body who make their decisions in view of what they perceive as the needs of society.

14 Strengths of the planned economy

- Necessities for everybody will be produced in advance of luxuries.
- Resources need not stand idle during recession.
- Goods can be distributed according to need rather than income.
- Social costs and benefits can be incorporated into the decision making process.

15 Weaknesses of the planned economy

- The problem of co-ordinating thousands of different production decisions in the absence of price signals. For example, the decision to build 5,000 tractors will require the co-ordination of the production of hundreds of thousands of components, and an incorrect decision can hold up the production of the whole 5,000.
- Goods may be produced which consumers do not want, or goods may not be produced in sufficient quantities, the result being shortages of some goods and surpluses of others.
- The lack of personal involvement may result in a lack of incentive.
- The central planning body develops bureaucratic self interest and becomes insensitive to those it is supposed to be serving.

16 The mixed economy

The **mixed economy** is characteristic of most modern economies, and whilst leaving much production in private hands it allows for a substantial role for the government in the production of certain goods and services, and controls the worst excesses of the market place. To some extent it attempts to gain the better aspects of both the previous systems. Today the concept of the mixed economy is generally accepted by UK governments although there may be disagreement over the extent of the government's role. The Conservative government, which came to power in 1979, made attempts to reduce the role of the state in the economy by 'privatising' some sectors of production and reducing the amount of intervention elsewhere.

The advantages and disadvantages are not listed here as they are self-evident from the advantages and disadvantages of the previous two, but we have listed here the main reasons for the involvement of the government in the mixed economy.

- To provide those essential goods and services which would **not be adequately provided by the free market**, in particular those referred to as '**merit goods**' such as education and health, or pure public goods such as defence.
- **Where market failure occurs**, i.e. monopoly; in order to protect the interests of the consumer and prevent the worst excesses of monopoly.
- **Where production, if left to the market, would be inefficient** due to duplication of plant and capacity, or if produced by large private monopolies would lead to excess

power over the consumer, e.g. electricity production and supply.

- **To maintain services** which are important both strategically and economically and which may otherwise be in danger of collapse, e.g. Railways, Rolls Royce Aero Engines.
- **To regulate the activities** of the private entrepreneur to prevent the worst aspects of private production, e.g. environmental pollution.
- **To regulate the economy** in order to maintain the level of demand, employment, balance of payments and inflation. The simultaneous control of each of these variables is difficult and they may in fact conflict, different governments emphasising the importance of different variables; however, most government involvement in the economy is aimed at the control of one or more of these macro-economic variables.

As an act of political belief governments may assume ownership over some areas of the economy. Generally, Labour governments tend to favour the extension of the role of the state by nationalisation, whilst Conservative governments prefer a less interventionist role. Although when threatened with massive job losses through the loss of a firm at the forefront of technological development and a major exporter, in the form of Rolls Royce Aero Engines Division, the Conservative government took it under the control of the public sector. Nationalisation may therefore be just as likely to occur as a result of economic and political expediency as of political dogma. As mentioned above, the Conservative government elected to office in 1979 was more strongly in favour of the private market than other recent governments and has undertaken the sale of many state assets in order to return them to the control of the private sector, in the belief that they would be operated more efficiently and require less support from the taxpayer.

17 Privatisation

The sale of state owned industries to the private sector is referred to as **privatisation**. In several instances this privatisation of state industries has been considered by many to be a highly radical move with the actual and proposed transfer to the private sector some industries which were formerly believed to be natural state monopolies (see Chapter 27) such as telephones and electricity. The main aims of the policy of privatisation are as follows.

- To improve the efficiency of the industries involved by exposing them to the competitive forces of the market.
- To make the industries less bureaucratic and more responsive to the wishes of the consumer and in turn more accountable for their own performance.
- To reduce the amount of government borrowing (public sector borrowing requirement) which was necessary to finance the deficits of many of the state industries. Over recent years privatisation has also proved to be an important source of revenue for the government. Table 1.1 lists the industries privatised since 1980.

The Trustee Savings Bank although not strictly a state industry was also sold to the private sector. The most controversial privatisations are of those public utilities such as electricity, gas and water which were previously considered as natural monopolies best maintained under state control so that they could be operated in the interest of the consumers. How they perform in the private sector will be evident in the course of time.

Table 1.1 Nationalised industries privatised 1980–96

1980	Britoil
1982	Amersham International
1983	British Aerospace
	Associated British Ports
	Cable and Wireless
1984	British Telecom
	Jaguar Cars
1986	British Gas
1987	British Airways
1987	British Petroleum
1987	British Airports Authority
1987	Rolls Royce
1988	British Steel
1989	Water supply industry
1990	Electricity supply
1991	Electricity – regional boards
1992	PSA
1994	British Coal
	Railtrack
1995/ 1996	Rail franchises

Self assessment questions

1 Why might 'merit goods' not be provided in sufficient quantities by a free market economy?

2 Why is the statement 'a free market economy is better than a planned economy' by itself a 'value judgement'.

3 Give an example of a 'social cost' resulting from private production.

4 Explain what is meant by 'privatisation'.

2

Production

1 Sectors of production

As a starting point for considering the act of producing goods, or **production**, it is useful to sub-divide production into three broad categories:

- The **extractive** (primary) industries, refers to organisations involved in the extraction of basic (primary) materials, and includes industries such as mining, quarrying, farming, forestry and fishing. The outputs of these industries frequently form the raw materials inputs for other industries.
- The **manufacturing** (secondary) industries, are involved in the processing of materials or assembling of components to produce goods such as cars, food, chemicals, and engineering equipment.
- The **distributive** industries complete the chain of production by distributing the finished goods through the channels of distribution, through the wholesaler to the retailer and to the final consumer.

These industries however cannot operate effectively without the assistance of another sector of industry, the service industries.

2 The service industries

The service industries provide essential aids to those involved in production and include banking and insurance, advertising, general administration, transport and communications.

The UK economy has large numbers of people employed in each of these categories, Table 2.1 showing the size of the labour force in each sector and recent employment trends.

A characteristic of the UK economy in recent years has been the relative decline in the importance of manufacturing industry and the growth of the service sector. Figure 2.1 illustrates the percentage change in employment for each sector between 1955 and 1996. These changes are discussed further in Chapter 46.

Table 2.1

| | Employees 000's | | | | Changes 1971–1996 | |
	1971	1979	1986	1996	000's	% Change
All industries & services	22 138	23 173	21 594	22 156	+16	+0.07
Agricultural, forestry and fishing	450	380	329	278	−172	−38.2
Manufacturing	8065	7253	5239	4015	−4050	−50.2
Construction	1198	1238	992	825	−373	−31.2
Energy and water supply	798	722	539	208	−590	−73.9
Service industries	11 627	13 580	14 495	16 830	+5203	+44.75

Civilian employment (excluding self-employment) in Great Britain, 1955 and 1996

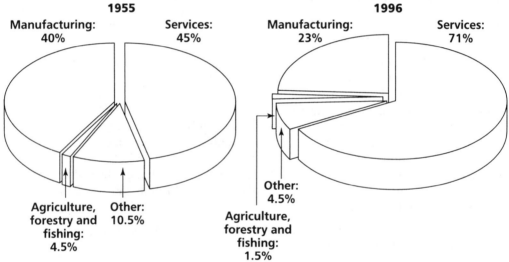

Figures for 1955 on estimated industrial classification 1980

Figure 2.1 Civilian employment (excluding self-employment) in Great Britain, 1955 and 1996

3 The firm

When we refer to the **firm** or **enterprise** we refer to the unit of ownership or control. A firm may consist of an individual unit or a parent company with several subsidiary firms. An **industry** is usually defined according to the physical and technical characteristics of the output produced and consists of all the firms producing those goods.

4 Factors of production

As mentioned in Chapter 1 the **factors of production** are essential for production to take place. They can be combined in various proportions, according to their relative prices, in order to achieve the least-cost combination. The least-cost combination will however change over time as factor prices change according to their demand and supply, and also with changes in technology. It is however not only the quantity of a factor of production which is important but also its quality. We will next consider each of these factors more closely.

5 Land

Land in this context is a wider concept than its everyday meaning, and includes all the natural resources available to man which can be utilised for productive purposes and which are provided freely by nature. It therefore includes building land, farming land, minerals, rivers and seas.

The supply of land is of course relatively fixed, the important point in the study of economics however, is that land can be used for different purposes. Land can be transferred between different agricultural uses or from agricultural to building, and will tend to be transferred to that use where it can earn the greatest yield (income). The location of land cannot be changed however and this is particularly important in town centres where land may have a high site value, no matter how much the demand for such sites increases the supply cannot be increased and such sites may earn what is known as **economic rent** (See Chapter 22).

6 Labour

In order to produce goods the entrepreneur will need to hire the services of labour in return for a wage. As a productive resource both the quality and quantity of labour are important. The quantity of labour will depend upon factors such as the birth rate, average age of the population, total population size and the number of hours worked. Labour quality is an important factor in productivity and this is dependent upon education, training, the possession of appropriate skills, willingness to accept changes in working practices, and the extent to which the labour force is motivated. Also important are its aptitude and intelligence, its willingness to acquire new skills and to adapt to new technology.

7 Capital

Capital should not be confused with money. Capital is anything which is created, not for its own use but for the purpose of further production. It therefore has the effect of making the process of production less direct, in that labour utilises capital equipment in the act of production.

Capital can be subdivided into two types, working capital and fixed capital. Working capital is used up during the course of production and consists of stocks of raw materials, work in progress, and finished goods. Fixed capital is not used up in the production process but is retained within the organisation and includes premises, machinery, fixtures and fittings, and vehicles. Another way to consider it is that working capital consists of items acquired for the purpose of re-sale whilst fixed capital consists of items not bought for re-sale but retention within the business. Items of capital are generally referred to as **capital assets**.

The nation's stock of capital can be sub-divided into social capital, private and public sector industrial capital and private industrial capital. Table 2.2 identifies these with examples.

Table 2.2 Capital stock			
Private individual capital	Private sector industrial capital	Public sector industrial capital	Social capital
E.g. Housing stock.	E.g. Factories, . machines, equipment	E.g. Nationalised industries.	E.g. Schools, hospitals, roads.

Capital goods can only be created by foregoing **current consumption**, i.e. **saving**. Current consumption is foregone in order to increase **future consumption**. However merely the act of saving will not create a capital good, the saved resources must be utilised in order to create a **capital good**.

The creation of a capital good is often illustrated by reference to Robinson Crusoe on his desert island. He catches 5 fish each day by using a line. He decided to spend three days constructing a net. After constructing the net he can now catch 5 fish in one hour and spend the rest of his time growing other foodstuffs and enjoying a more interesting diet. The cost of his net was the 15 fish he did not catch whilst constructing the net. He had to forego present consumption in order to create a capital good which enabled him to have a higher level of future consumption.

8 Investment and depreciation

During the act of production each year some of the stock of capital is used up, i.e. machines wear out. This is referred to as **depreciation**. The total amount of capital produced each year is referred to as **gross investment**, and any addition to the stock of capital as **net investment**. Thus the act of just replacing worn out capital will not increase the stock of capital, so there can be gross investment without net investment, but only net investment will increase the productive capacity of the economy.
therefore

Gross investment – Depreciation = Net investment

9 Production possibility curves

We can usefully illustrate both the problem of scarcity and choice, of which the conflict between current consumption and capital formation is a prime example, by the use of **production possibility curves** (PPC).

In order to illustrate the concept we will assume that our economy is capable of producing two goods, good X and good Y. It has the choice of devoting all its resources to the production of good X and having none of good Y, devoting all its resources to good Y and having none of good X, or choosing some intermediate point and having some of both. This is illustrated in Figure 2.2. At point A society is producing all good Y and none of X, and at point B all of X and none of Y. At point C some of both are produced. Note that the shape of the PPC is concave to the origin; this is because as we move along the curve from A toward B and factors of production are transferred from the production of one good to the other, as successive units of the factors of production are transferred they will be less and less efficient in their new use due to **diminishing returns**, and for each unit of Y sacrificed we will gain smaller and smaller quantities of X, i.e. the opportunity cost increases. This illustrates that in an economy which is fully utilising its resources **substitution** is inevitable, and wherever there are scarce resources society must always make choices. At point U society's resources are under-utilised and we can have more of both goods by moving on to the PPC. Point Z is unobtainable and can only be achieved by a shift of the whole curve upwards and outwards; this can only occur as a result of technological change, increased productivity or an increase in available resources.

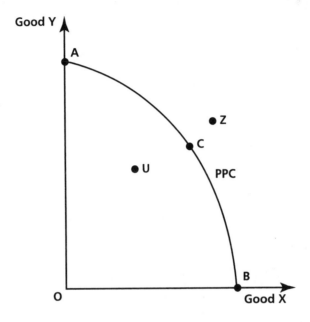

Figure 2.2

Figure 2.3 illustrates a society which in the current time period (t) has chosen a high level of consumption and a low level of production of capital goods.

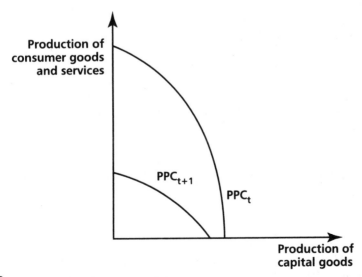

Figure 2.3

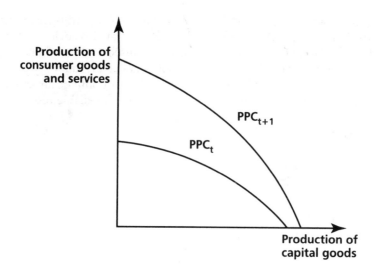

Figure 2.4

In the next time period (t + 1) the PPC has shifted towards the origin to PPC_{t+1} producing less of both goods and therefore a lower standard of living. Figure 2.4 illustrates a
society which in the current time period has chosen to have a high level of production of
capital goods and a relatively lower level of production of consumer goods for current
consumption. In the next time period (t + 1) however, the PPC has shifted outwards to
PPC_{t+1} and is enjoying a higher level of consumption and a high level of capital formation – by foregoing some current consumption they enjoyed a higher future 'standard of
living'.

10 Diminishing returns

It cannot be assumed however that because we have more of a factor available we can
always gain proportionate increases in output, as inevitably the returns from additional
units of factors of production will tend to decline. This is referred to as the **law of diminishing returns** or **declining marginal productivity**. This states that as we add additional
units of a variable factor to a constant factor then the product (output) of the variable factor will first of all rise but will eventually start to decline.

The theory assumes that all the units of the variable factor are identical in terms of productivity, and the techniques of production remain unchanged. In Table 2.4 **total product**
refers to the total output of the variable factor, in this case labour. **marginal product** refers
to the increase in Total Product from each additional unit of labour, and

$$\text{Average product} \quad = \quad \frac{\text{total product}}{\text{quantity of labour}}$$

In Table 2.3 we illustrate the example of a smallholder with one acre of land growing
potatoes employing at first a single unit of labour and then employing more and more

Table 2.3

Labour	Total product (Tonnes)	Average product (AP)
1	2	2
2	10	5
3	21	7
4	36	9
5	55	11
6	63	10½
7	70	10
8	72	9
9	72	8

labourers and keeping the amount of land constant. This is represented graphically in Figure 2.5.

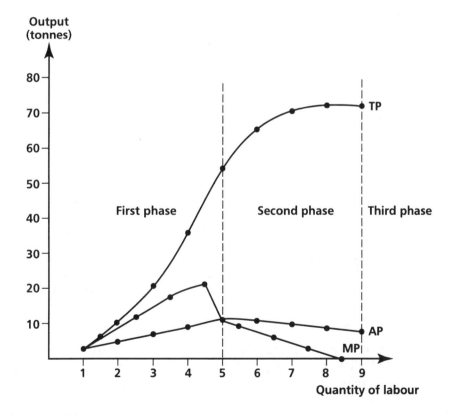

Figure 2.5

e first phase as additional labour is added to the fixed factor (land) each suc-
nit raises output and total product (**TP**), marginal product (**MP**) and average
t (**AP**) are all rising. This continues until the fifth man is added when MP reaches
k and falls sharply cutting AP at its highest point after which AP also declines.
ring the second phase, after the addition of the fifth unit of labour, the **rate of growth**
TP declines and both AP and MP decline, MP declining more sharply than AP. Up to
the fifth man total product increases at an **increasing rate** and there are **increasing
returns**. After the fifth man the rate of growth of total product declines and **diminishing
returns** set in as the marginal product declines. In the third phase at the point where total
product begins to fall, after the ninth man, marginal product becomes negative.

The normal relationship between marginal product and average product is illustrated
more clearly in Figure 2.6.

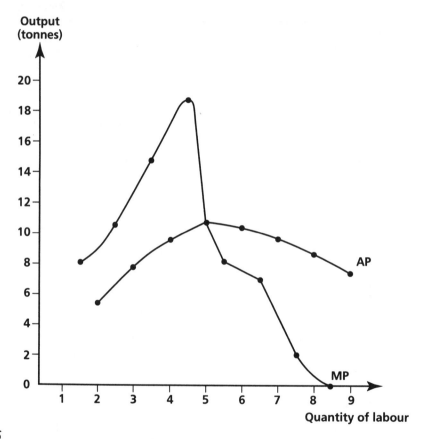

Figure 2.6

The law of declining marginal productivity assumes that one factor, in this case land, is
held constant. In the long run however all the factors of production can be varied so the
law of declining marginal productivity is really applicable to the short-run. Over the long
run it is possible to increase the amount of land available or labour efficiency can be
improved through training or improved equipment. In this way the effect of diminishing
returns can be offset. This would represent a change in the **scale of production** and is

dealt with later. The law of diminishing returns has important implications for the costs of production and will be referred to again later.

Self assessment questions

1 Distinguish between gross and net investment.

2 How is a capital good created?

3 What is meant by 'the law of diminishing returns'?

4 Identify the factors of production.

5 Why is the production possibility curve concave in shape?

6 How did the structure of employment in the UK change between 1955 and 1996?

3

Specialisation and the division of labour

1 Subsistence living

In a primitive society where individuals attempt to produce all their own requirements for living, life will be very basic and is referred to as **subsistence** living. Output will be very low and each individual will be producing just sufficient to survive. Each individual will be attempting to do their own hunting, fishing, building shelter, farming and making utensils and other requirements. Such production is extremely inefficient as an individual person is unlikely to possess equal talents in each of these activities; they may be good at some and very poor at others. It also means that they must be continually changing from one task to another or leaving some tasks whilst another one is completed.

2 Specialisation

The single most important element in allowing a society to advance economically is the act of **specialisation**. Specialisation occurs when each member of a society specialises in that task at which they are most talented. If each individual does this they become more productive and total output is increased. The person who is good at hunting devotes all their time to hunting, the person who is skilled at making bows and arrows makes them all the time. Each person now however produces a **surplus** over and above their own requirements, and the essential point is that they can **trade** this surplus for those goods which they do not produce.

3 Comparative advantage

The gains from specialisation can be achieved even if one person is better at all activities than another, provided one specialises in the activity in which they are most efficient and the other in the activity in which he or she is least inefficient. This is referred to as the principle of **comparative advantage**. If a person is better at all activities they are said to have an **absolute advantage** but they may still have a **greater comparative advantage** in the production of some goods and another person will have the **least comparative disadvantage** in the production of others. To illustrate this point, imagine there are two persons, A and B, both of whom manufacture pans and earthenware pots. Their output per day assuming they both divide their time equally is as follows:

A manufactures   either 40 pans or 40 pots per day.
B manufactures   either 37 pans or 16 pots per day.

Prior to specialisation actual output per day is:

A manufactures	20 pans and	20 pots per day
B manufactures	15 pans and	8 pots per day
Total output:	35 pans and	28 pots per day

Note that A is more efficient at producing both but is comparatively more efficient at producing pots, i.e. 40:16, whilst B is least inefficient at pans, i.e. 40:37. As a result, specialisation will raise total output.

After each specialising in the task at which they are most efficient, output per day is as follows:

A manufactures	0 pans and	40 pots
B manufactures	37 pans and	0 pots
Total output	37 pans	40 pots per day

Total output has increased by 2 pans and 12 pots per day.

Specialisation is not only the key to how society can raise its output and therefore its standard of living, but is also the precursor of trade.

4 The division of labour

Division of labour refers to the practice of breaking a complex task down into a number of simpler tasks and an individual can then specialise in one of these simple tasks. This is specialisation as most of us know it today in a factory setting where complex tasks, such as building a motor car, are broken down into many thousands of simple tasks, and individual workers specialise in one of them. Specialisation here is a narrower concept with the worker being used where he is most productive rather than most skilled.

A frequently quoted, but nevertheless relevant example, is the observation of a pin factory by the 18th century economist Adam Smith. He noted that the practice of making pins had been broken down into about 18 different operations: one man drawing out the wire, another cutting it, another putting points on, another grinding the heads, another fitting the heads, and so on. The output per head of the factory was about 5,000 pins per day, whereas if each person had to make the whole pin, Smith estimated that output would have been no more than a few dozen pins per day.

Specialisation and division of labour also occurs with the management functions of a business. As a firm grows it becomes impossible for a single person to have the necessary knowledge of all the functions, and to attempt to perform all of them, it would be extremely inefficient and time consuming. The firm will therefore employ specialists such as accountants, sales managers, engineers, buyers, production managers, and so on.

5 Mass production

Once division of labour has taken place and a process has been broken down into a number of simple tasks, it becomes easier to apply machines to the tasks. Machines can generally only perform a single task, i.e. they are inflexible, however when the process is broken down into its component tasks, machines can be applied more easily. This is the way in which **mass production** is facilitated.

The process of mass production, which carries specialisation and division of labour to its extreme, can be illustrated by reference to one of the earliest examples. Prior to the end of the 18th century muskets had always been individually produced by craftsmen who produced all the components and assembled them. All the components were unique and would fit only one weapon. At the end of the 18th century Eli Whitney received the contract from the new American government to produce muskets for the American Army, and was given a year to produce them. Until a few weeks before the delivery was due he had not produced a single weapon; he had in fact been producing the tooling – jigs, dies, stamping machines and setting out the work flow in his workshop. He was then able to produce them within a couple of weeks and fulfil his contract. After that of course he was then able to produce them more quickly and efficiently than anybody else.

Not only did this method produce the muskets more quickly and cheaply, but had a further advantage: all the components would fit any musket as they were identical, i.e. they were **interchangeable** or **standardised**, which meant that assembly was faster, and also that spare parts were available.

This method of production was later developed further by Henry Ford in America, who was the first manufacturer of motor cars to utilise mass production methods with the Model T, which was produced so cheaply and quickly that it became the most popular car in America for nearly 20 years and made the possibility of car ownership a reality for millions of low income Americans.

In recent years mass production has taken a further step forward with the increased use of micro-technology and robotics in assembly processes.

6 The advantages of specialisation

The advantage of specialisation is the productivity gain, which results from the following:

- People rapidly acquire skills when repeatedly performing a simple task.
- Training times and costs are reduced when skills are narrow.
- There is no waiting, or 'queuing' time; waiting for machines to become available.
- Time is not wasted moving around the workshop to perform different operations.
- It enables people to perform those tasks at which they have most natural aptitude.
- It facilitates the use of machinery, as machinery is easier to apply to a simple task.

7 The disadvantages of specialisation

There are, however, a number of disadvantages to the process:

- Consistently performing routine tasks soon becomes tedious and boring.
- Specialisation tends to remove the skill from work, hence workers are not given the opportunity to take a 'pride in their work'.
- A combination of the two disadvantages above tends to lead to 'alienation' and as a

result poor industrial relations. Workers will tend to lack motivation.

- A narrow specialisation may result in an increased risk of unemployment, and if the whole of the industry is in a recession it may be difficult to find employment. Also skills may become technically obsolete, e.g. typesetters in the newspaper industry.
- Where specialisation is taken to extreme, factories themselves tend to specialise, e.g. component manufacturers for the car industry. As a result the whole of industry becomes more interdependent, and is vulnerable to a breakdown of any part of the complex chain of production.

8 Barter

As mentioned earlier, in Chapter 2, specialisation results in surplus production and therefore trade. Early trade took the form of barter, where goods were simply 'swapped' for other goods. Barter has a number of weaknesses, however, which make it difficult for an economy to develop.

Goods are **non divisible** – if a bow is worth 2½ pots, we cannot trade as breaking a pot makes it worthless

If we want to trade not only do we need to find somebody who has what we want but they must also want what we have to give in exchange – a **double coincidence of wants**. The possibility of finding such a person is made greater the more people we meet, hence the development of market places where everyone can take their surplus goods and trade. This still happens in many parts of the world.

The weakness of barter leads to the next vital step in the development of an economy, **money**. Money facilitates the growth of trade and economic development.

9 Money

Money overcomes the weakness of barter because it has the advantage of being:

- Divisible
- Generally acceptable

Hence the problems of divisibility and double coincidence of wants are solved. Anybody will accept money and it can be divided into many denominations. Money can in fact be any commodity, and historically cowrie shells, salt, dogs' teeth (New Guinea) and wampum beads (Red Indians), have all been used. The easiest way to ensure general acceptability of a monetary unit is to ensure that it has intrinsic value, hence the popularity of gold coins for so long. We now use paper money which has no intrinsic value, but whose acceptability is based purely on people's confidence. That part of the note issue based on nothing other than people's confidence is known as the **fiduciary issue**. Bank accounts also function as money. The characteristics needed by a commodity for it to function as money are:

- **Generally acceptable**
- **Homogeneous (same)**
- **Divisible**
- **Portable**
- **Scarce**
- **Durable**

In this context it is interesting to consider cigarettes, which functioned very efficiently as money in prisoner-of-war camps.

The functions of money can be stated briefly as follows:

- **A medium of exchange**.
- **A measure of value** – the goods can be expressed in terms of a standardised unit.
- **A store of value** – it is a convenient form in which to store wealth.
- **A method of deferring payments** – it facilitates the system of trade credit.

Money has further significance relating to production. The development of money makes wage payments possible; it therefore becomes possible to concentrate the production process into factories where specialisation and division of labour can be carried further, into the system of mass production.

10 The limits of specialisation

The limits to which specialisation and mass production can be carried are set by:

- The extent of the development of the monetary system.
- The size of the market.

In order to offset the limiting effect of market size countries may join large trading blocks such as the EU, or as in the case of Britain in the 19th century, by trading with an Empire, or by trying to export throughout the world as does Japan today.

Specialisation and division of labour are the pre-requisites for economic development and not surprisingly were described by Adam Smith as 'the source of the wealth of nations'.

Self assessment questions

1 Why does specialisation and division of labour raise output?

2 What are the disadvantages of specialisation and division of labour?

3 Why is barter inefficient?

4 What are the characteristics of money?

5 What limits the extent of specialisation and division of labour?

6 Discuss the links between specialisation, division of labour and mass production.

7 How does specialisation take place in a mass production factory system?

Section B

The market

Containing the following chapters:

Chapter 4 – Elements of demand

Chapter 5 – Elements of supply

Chapter 6 – Determination of market price

Chapter 7 – Elasticity

Chapter 8 – Market analysis

The interaction of buyers and sellers, in any context, that results in the sale and purchase of goods and services

This section should enable students to:

- *Understand* the factors affecting demand and supply
- *Explain* the relevance of elasticity to the market
- *Contrast* the different market conditions that can exist
- *Evaluate* the importance of the market in the present UK economy.

Keywords to consider:

effective demand; contraction of demand; extension of demand; change in demand; diminishing marginal utility; substitute goods; competitive demand; complimentary goods; joint demand; regressive demand; contraction of supply; extension of supply; change in supply; joint supply; equilibrium price; price elasticity of demand; elastic demand; inelastic demand; point elasticity; income elasticity of demand; cross elasticity of demand; cobweb theorem.

4

Elements of demand

1 Market price

We consider next the factors determining market prices. Price, it should be noted, is not the same as value. Value is a subjective evaluation and is not necessarily the same as the price we receive for an item in exchange. We may place a value on an item for a variety of reasons, such as sentiment, but here we are interested only in the value the market places on a good which can conveniently be measured by its price. Market prices are determined by the forces of **demand** and **supply**.

2 Effective demand

When we refer to **demand** in economics we are referring to **effective demand**, not how much people would like to purchase but how much they can afford and are willing to buy at each price. Demand is, then, the quantity of a good demanded by consumers at a price in a particular time period.

3 Demand curves

At any period of time we can identify a definite relationship between the market prices and the quantity demanded of a good This can be referred to as a **demand schedule**. In Table 4.1 we illustrate a demand schedule for potatoes.

Table 4.1 market demand schedule for potatoes	
(1) price (£s per tonne)	(2) quantity demanded (000 tonnes per month)
30	25
20	50
15	75
10	125
5	200

Figure 4.1 is referred to as a **demand curve**, identified by the letters DD. From it we can read off the quantities demanded at each price. Note that as the price rises the quantity demanded falls and vice versa, the relationship between price and quantity demanded is therefore an **inverse relationship**. It is essential to note at this stage that changes in the quantity demanded, or movements along the demand curve occur as a result of **changes in price only**, all other factors remaining constant, i.e. it is an example of the ceteris paribus rule.

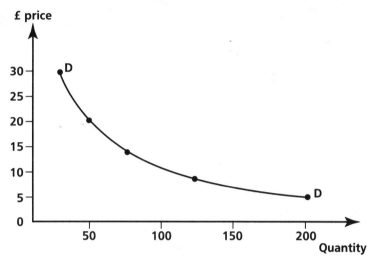

Figure 4.1

In Figure 4.2 a rise in the price of potatoes causes a movement along the curve, hence the rise in price to £20 reduces the quantity demanded to 50, a fall in the price increases the quantity demanded to 125. Changes in the quantity demanded may also be referred to as **extensions** or **contractions** in demand.

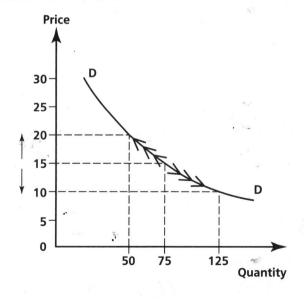

Figure 4.2

25

If other factors do change, i.e. the **conditions of demand**, then there is a shift of the whole demand curve. For example, supposing that there is a substantial increase in incomes so people buy more meat and less potato, this will cause a change in demand in that less will be demanded at each price. This change in the **conditions of demand** is represented in Figure 4.3 by a **shift** of the whole demand curve downwards and to the left, to D"D", and at the price of £15 instead of 75 being demanded, only 50 are demanded. An increase in demand is represented by a **shift** of the whole curve upwards and to the right to D'D' with 130 now being demanded at price 15 as a result of a favourable change in the conditions of demand; the same is true at each price, as essentially there is now a new demand curve.

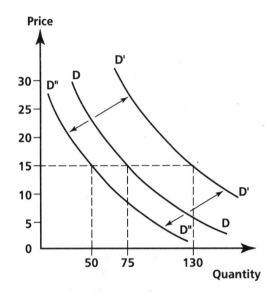

Figure 4.3

4 Summary

A change in the **quantity demanded** (or a **contraction** or **extension of demand**) is represented by a **movement along the demand curve**.

A **change in demand** occurs when the change occurs in the conditions of demand and are a result of **factors other than price**.

Changes in demand can occur as a result of:

- Changes in the price of a substitute good (see 7).
- Changes in the price of a complementary good (see 7).
- Changes in tastes or fashion.
- A change in incomes.
- Advertising.

5 Income and substitution effects

Demand curves are nearly always drawn as sloping downwards from left to right, consequently we refer to the **law of downward sloping demand**.
Demand curves slope downwards because:

- As the price of a good falls it becomes available to more people with lower income levels.
- As the price of a commodity falls it will be substituted for other commodities which have become relatively more expensive (substitution effect).
- As the price of a commodity falls it increases the **real income** of the consumer who can then buy more of all goods (income effect).
- As we obtain more of a good the additional utility (satisfaction) we receive from the extra units consumed tends to decline, we will therefore value it less highly and will only be prepared to buy it at a lower price. This is referred to as the law of **diminishing marginal utility**.

6 Marginal utility

Although there have been many attempts to measure utility it remains a subjective concept. To illustrate the concept, imagine a consumer who had not had a bar of chocolate for many years; if he now received a chocolate bar he would enjoy a high level of satisfaction, or utility, from it and would therefore value it highly in terms of price. If he now received a second bar he would receive more utility but not as much as from the first; his **total** utility is increasing, but his **marginal** utility is declining, and he will place a lower value on the second and subsequent bars than on the first. Eventually he may feel quite ill from consuming chocolate and place no value at all on further bars. Figure 4.4 illustrates the marginal utility from each additional bar of chocolate declining whilst total utility increases at a declining rate. In Figure 4.5 the marginal units are plotted separately and the smooth line A-B drawn through them is identical to a demand curve. The concept of diminishing marginal utility underlies the slope of the demand curve and is useful in explaining other aspects of consumer behaviour.

7 Substitutes and complements

Not all goods are completely independent in demand and the change in the price of one good may affect the demand for other goods.

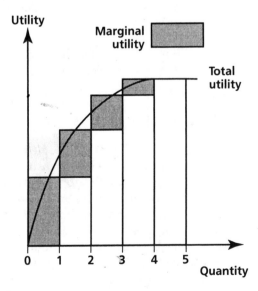

Figure 4.4

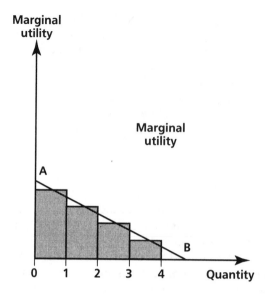

Figure 4.5

Substitute goods (competitive demand). An example of a substitute good is margarine and butter. Margarine (the **inferior good**) will be substituted for butter (the **normal good**) if the price of butter rises and vice versa if the price of butter falls. When the price of coffee doubled after the crop failure in 1976, there was a substantial increase in the demand for tea.

Complementary goods (joint demand). These are goods which normally go together such as shoes and laces, cars and tyres, bread and butter.

We can summarise the effect of changes in one of the two goods as follows:

- A rise in the price of a good will result in a fall in the demand for that good and an increase in the demand for its substitute. A fall in the price of a good will reduce the demand for its substitute.
- A rise in the price of a good will result in a fall in the demand for that good and therefore a reduction in the demand for its complement. A fall in the price of a good will increase the demand for its complement.

8 Exceptional demand curves

There are a few exceptions to the law of downward sloping demand, which are sometimes referred to as **exceptional demand curves** or **regressive demand curves**.

Figure 4.6 illustrates the case of regression at the upper end of the curve and may occur with **goods of ostentation**, such as jewellery, antiques or paintings. An increase in the price from P to P' increases the quantity demanded from Q to Q'. People attribute status to such goods and if sold too cheaply people will not feel they are receiving something providing the necessary status. This has certainly been found to be the case with imitation jewellery and it is not uncommon for antiques dealers to find they can sell certain items more easily when the price is raised.

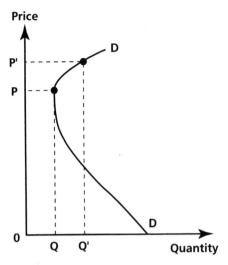

Figure 4.6

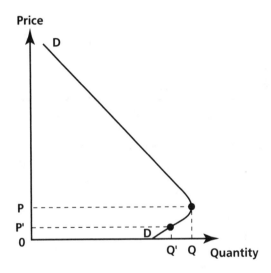

Figure 4.7

Commodity dealers who take a price increase as an indication of even higher prices in the future will increase the size of their current purchases in the hope of avoiding the highest prices.

Figure 4.7 indicates regression at the lower end of the curve. A price fall from P to P reduces the quantity demanded from Q to Q'. This may occur with certain inferior goods, in such cases these goods are referred to as 'Giffin Goods'. When a high percentage of household income is spent on such goods, any substantial price reduction will increase household income and the additional income will be used to purchase more of the superior good and less will be bought of the inferior good, potatoes and meat being the classic example. It is in fact a case of the income effect outweighing the substitution effect.

Commodity buyers who take a price fall as an indication of even lower prices in the future will reduce the size of their current purchases hoping to re-enter the market when the price has reached its lowest point.

The vast majority of goods however follow the law of downward sloping demand and are referred to as **normal goods**.

9 Market demand

Each consumer has their own individual demand schedule and demand curve for the commodities they purchase, and in order to derive the market or industry demand, i.e. the total demand for the output of the commodity, we merely sum horizontally each individual's demand curve at each price.

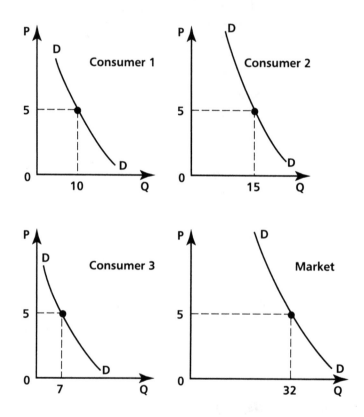

Figure 4.8

In Figure 4.8 each consumer's demand at price 5 is added to give one point on the market, or industry, demand curve. This can be done at every price to give a complete market demand curve. Market or industry demand curves always slope downwards because if the industry as a whole increases or lowers price, then the quantity demanded will decrease or increase. However, for each individual firm in the industry this may not be the case.

Self assessment questions

1 What is meant by 'effective demand'?

2 Why do demand curves generally slope downwards?

3 Distinguish between a movement along a demand curve and shift in a demand curve.

4 Give one example of an exception to the law of downward sloping demand.

5 What is meant by diminishing marginal utility?

6 Distinguish between an individual consumer's demand curve and a market demand curve.

7 What is meant by:

(a) A substitute good;
(b) Complementary good;
(c) A good of ostentation?

5

Elements of supply

1 Supply

Supply refers to the quantity which a producer is willing and able to put on to the market at a particular price during a particular time period.

Supply is ultimately determined by cost and costs tend to rise as output is increased (see Chapter 13). If we imagine a farmer producing potatoes, if he is to expand output of potatoes he will first of all need to replace other crops, such as barley, with potatoes, which he will only be willing to do if the price of potatoes is sufficiently high to yield him a higher return than the alternative crop. If he wishes to expand output further he may need to utilise marginal land which is not normally used. Such land will require the application of more labour and fertiliser and will therefore be more expensive to cultivate; a higher price will therefore be required by the farmer before the use of such land is considered. The law of supply therefore, says that **more of a good will be supplied at a higher price than at a lower price**, cet. par.

2 Supply schedule

In order to illustrate the relationship between price and supply we will utilise the example of the quantity of potatoes a farmer is willing to put on the market at different prices, and Table 5.1 is an example of such a supply schedule.

Table 5.1 Supply schedule for potatoes	
(1) Price (£s per tonne)	(2) Quantity Supplied (000 tonnes per month)
30	150
20	100
15	75
10	50
5	0

3 Supply curve

By plotting the data we produce the **supply curve** as illustrated in Figure 5.1, identified by the letters SS. From it we can identify the quantity which will be supplied at each price. As the price rises the quantity supplied also rises. Note that the curve slopes upwards to the right and we therefore refer to the **law of upwards sloping supply**. Supply curves therefore in general slope upwards and to the right. Like the demand curve, the supply curve is drawn on the ceteris paribus assumption – that no factors other than price change. If other factors do change, then there is a shift of the whole supply curve.

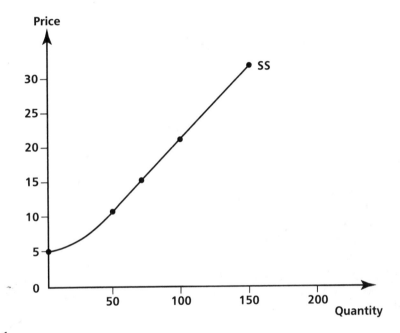

Figure 5.1

4 Movements along the supply curve

Movements along a supply curve occur in response to **price changes only** and are referred to as a change in the **quantity supplied** (or a **contraction or extension of supply**).

5 Changes in supply

A **change in supply** occurs when the change occurs in the conditions of supply and are a result of **factors other than price**.
Changes in supply can occur as a result of

- **Technical change**, i.e. changes in productivity as a result of technical innovation.
- **Changes in working practices.**
- **Weather** – important for natural commodities
- **Changes in taxes or subsidies.**
- **Changes in the prices of the factors of production affecting costs.**

6 Supply graphs

Figure 5.2 illustrates the effects of price changes on the quantity supplied, an increase in the price raising the quantity supplied and vice versa.

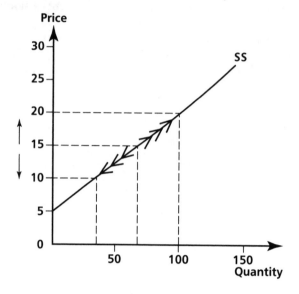

Figure 5.2

Figure 5.3 illustrates a change in supply, resulting from a change in the conditions of supply, represented by a shift in the whole supply curve. An **increase in supply** is represented by a shift of the entire curve downwards to the right from SS to SS', with a greater quantity supplied at each and every price. A **reduction in supply** is represented by a shift of the entire curve upwards to the left, from SS to SS'', with a smaller quantity supplied at each price.

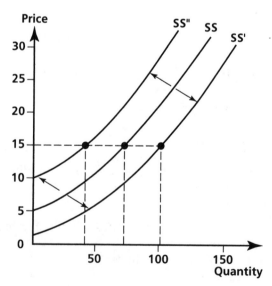

Figure 5.3

7 Joint supply

When some goods are produced it automatically results in the production of other goods, i.e. they are in **joint supply**. For example, an increase in beef production increases the supply of hides. An increase in the supply of petrol increases the supply of all oil derivatives produced in the refining process.

8 Exceptional supply

One exception to the law of upward sloping supply is the case of the backward sloping supply curve for labour, illustrated in Figure 5.4. An increase in the wage rate (the price of labour) from W to W' actually reduces the number of hours worked from Q to Q'. The supply curve is normal up to W then slopes backwards. This is because at higher wage rates some labour may prefer additional leisure to work once wages rise above W.

Most goods however follow the law of upward sloping supply.

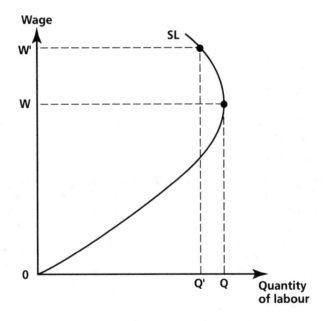

Figure 5.4

Self assessment questions

1 Why do supply curves slope upwards?
2 Distinguish between movements along a supply curve and a shift in the supply curve.
3 What effect would improved machinery have on the supply curve?
4 What effect would the abandonment of a restrictive labour practice have on the supply curve?
5 Under what circumstances could an increase in the wage rate reduce the supply of labour?

6

The determination of market price

1 Market prices

Having considered both demand and supply, we are now in a position to analyse the way in which market prices are determined.

The price of a commodity is determined jointly by the interaction of demand and supply. In order to illustrate this we can now combine the demand schedule (Table 4.1) and the supply schedule (Table 5.1) in Table 6.1 below.

TABLE 6.1 Combined supply and demand schedules for potatoes

(1) Price (£s per tonne)	(2) Quantity demanded (000s tones per month)	(3) Quantity supplied (000s tonnes per month)
30	25	150
20	50	100
15	75	75
10	125	50
5	200	0

By plotting both the demand and supply curves on to a single graph we can obtain the market equilibrium price. Market equilibrium price is that price at which demand and supply are equal, and in Figure 6.1 can be seen to be the point where demand and supply curves intersect. It is generally referred to as the **equilibrium price (E)**, and here the equilibrium price is £15 with quantity 75. This can also be found by inspecting the demand and supply schedules for the price at which demand and supply are equal. At any price below £15 demand will exceed supply and shortages will result; at any price above £15 supply will exceed demand and there are surplus stocks on the market.

2 Market equilibrium

For further analysis of equilibrium price we will identify prices by using P and quantity by Q.

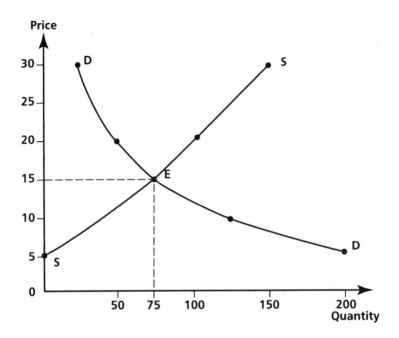

Figure 6.1

Market equilibrium price, or equilibrium price is therefore the price at which demand and supply are equal. Equilibrium price is the price at which the market will clear, i.e. the amount consumers are willing to buy is exactly the same as the amount suppliers will willingly supply: there are no shortages and no unsold stocks on the market. In Figure 6.2 demand and supply curves intersect at the equilibrium price Pe and quantity Qe. If at the commencement of the day's trading the price was set at P, there would be an excess of supply over demand and there would be an unsold surplus on the market of A–B. The only way in which these surplus stocks could be cleared would be to reduce the price, which would continue until the market equilibrium (E) was established, with demand and supply equal at price Pe and quantity Qe. If the price was set at P' demand would exceed supply by F–G and a shortage would prevail at that price. The excess demand would bid up prices and producers would respond by increasing supplies, which would continue until market equilibrium was achieved at price Pe and quantity Qe. Equilibrium price is therefore the **price to which a market will always return in the short run**, ceteris paribus.

This analysis of equilibrium price makes the 'ceteris paribus' assumption that all other factors remain unchanged, however over different time periods other factors may change resulting in different equilibrium prices. It is necessary next to examine more closely how changes in the factors underlying demand and supply may affect equilibrium prices.

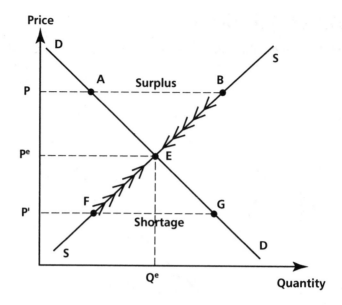

Figure 6.2

3 Changes in demand and supply

Figure 6.3 illustrates the market equilibrium for a good, for example butter, at price P and quantity Q. A substantial fall in the price of margarine would increase the demand for margarine and shift the demand curve for butter in the diagram downwards from D to D', with a equilibrium at E', a market price of P', and quantity Q'.

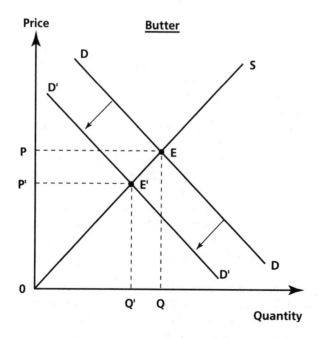

Figure 6.3

Less is now demanded at each price. A rise in the price of margarine would have caused a shift of the demand curve in the opposite direction, there would be an increase in the demand for butter as consumers' preferences switched to the commodity which had become relatively cheaper in order to maximise the utility they receive from their income. Similar shifts in demand can also be as a result of changes in consumers' tastes and preferences, for example if consumers became convinced that consuming too much butter was likely to be a health hazard. A similar shift from D to D' could also be the result of a heavy advertising campaign by the producers of margarine.

4 The interaction of markets

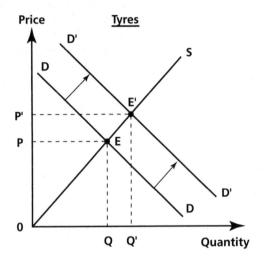

Figure 6.4

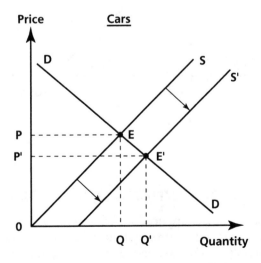

Figure 6.5

Figure 6.4 illustrates the market for tyres, and Figure 6.5 the market for cars, both of which are complementary goods. The car industry now introduces more productive technology such as 'robotics' which lower the costs of production, hence the supply curve shifts from S to S', and there is a movement along the demand curve DD to a new equilibrium at E', with lower price P and greater quantity Q'. As a result there is a change in the demand for tyres, with the demand curve shifting from DD to D'D', with higher price P' and quantity Q' with equilibrium at E'.

5 Partial equilibrium

Figure 6.4 can be referred to as a **partial equilibrium**. If the higher price P' persists for a substantial time period the tyre industry may attract more factors of production and become more productive, shifting the supply curve down to S' with new equilibrium at E" with lower price P" as illustrated in Figure 6.6. The final equilibrium price may even be lower than P. As the final equilibrium price in the long run after the factors of production have adapted to the new situation cannot be stated with certainty, it is said to be **indeterminate**: whilst the short run position in 6.6 can be stated with certainty and is said to be **determinate** which occurs before all factors of production have adjusted to the new market situation.

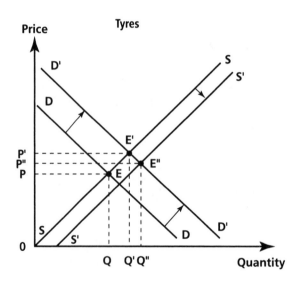

Figure 6.6

6 Applications of demand and supply analysis

In this section we consider some applications of demand and supply analysis.

If the government attempts to control rents and sets a rent ceiling of Rc below the market equilibrium E, then Q^0 will be demanded and only Q supplied leaving a shortage of rented accommodation of J–K.

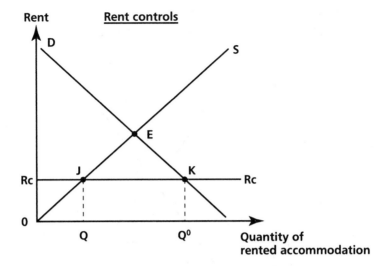

Figure 6.7

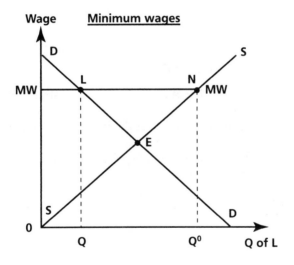

Figure 6.8

Attempts to force up wage levels by imposing a legal minimum wage, such as MW, results in a surplus of labour (more people wanting jobs than can obtain them at the prevailing wage rate). At MW, Q is demanded and Q^0 supplied, leaving a surplus of LN. An attempt was made in Costa Rica to raise wage rates in such a way with exactly the results predicted above.

In both cases there would have been no problem if the controls had been set so as to coincide with the market equilibrium price.

Figure 6.9 illustrates the attempt by a government to impose rationing.

As a result of an increase in demand from D to D' the equilibrium price rises to E'. The government attempts to control the price at CP, however at this price there is a shortage of EM. To achieve the ceiling price the government must reduce 'effective demand' back to DD by some form of rationing such as ration tickets. Even so some of the shortage will still be met illegally on 'black markets' at the market equilibrium, E' and price P'.

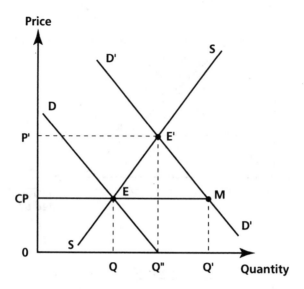

Figure 6.9

7 Taxation and the market

Incidence refers to who bears the burden of tax. Figure 6.10 illustrates the incidence of an indirect tax payable by a producer on each unit of sales. The tax is A–B, and shifts the supply curve upwards by the amount of the tax, but the price to the consumer increases by only P to P', i.e. C to E', whilst DC is absorbed by the producer. The amount which is passed on and the amount which is absorbed depends upon the relative demand and supply elasticities (see Chapter 7), in this case 50% each.

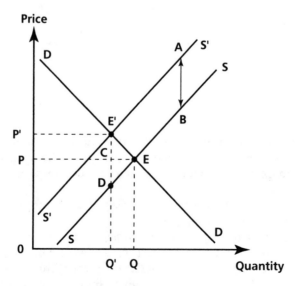

Figure 6.10

Self assessment questions

1 What is meant by 'equilibrium price'?

2 How does an increase in the firm's costs (cet. par.) affect equilibrium price?

3 What would be the effect of a legal minimum wage set below the equilibrium wage?

4 Distinguish between partial and full equilibrium.

5 Illustrate by the use of demand and supply diagrams the effect on the equilibrium price of coal of a substantial increase in the price of oil.

6 What is meant by 'the incidence of a tax'?

7

Elasticity

1 Total revenue

Total revenue (TR) refers to the firm's total receipts in monetary terms from its sales. It can be calculated therefore as **price** × **quantity**, i.e. TR = P × Q. This is also the area of the rectangle below the demand curve, shown as the shaded area in Figure 7.1.

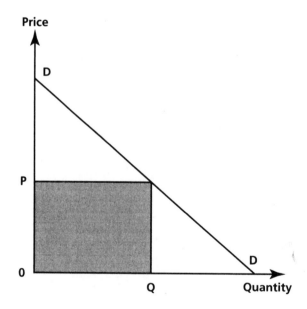

Figure 7.1

The area of this rectangle, and therefore TR will change as prices are changed, and of course firms will want this area of TR to be as large as possible. **Price elasticity of demand** (PED) refers to the way in which TR changes with variations in price.

2 Price elasticity of demand

Intuitively we can reason that a firm may reduce its price and by so doing sell so many extra units that its TR is increased, despite charging a slightly lower price per unit. Alternatively a firm may raise its price but in so doing lose so many units of sales that its TR declines. In both cases the opposite is also possible, i.e. reducing price may decrease TR, and in raising price TR may increase. This effect on TR of a price change is referred to as **price elasticity of demand (PED)**. A more precise definition is: **price elasticity of demand is the relationship between the proportionate (or percentage) change in price and the proportionate (or percentage) change in quantity demanded.**

3 Elastic and inelastic demand

Where the quantity demanded is highly responsive to price changes demand is said to be **elastic** and where it is unresponsive it is said to be **inelastic**. This can be illustrated by the use of demand curves, however with the exception of three 'special cases' **the slope of the demand curve is not a reliable guide to elasticity**, and extreme care should be taken in interpreting diagrams.

Figure 7.2 illustrates the concept of elastic demand over a given price range. A price reduction from £2.00 to £1.80 increases quantity demanded from 60 to 90, a 10% reduction in price has resulted in a 50% increase in demand, as a result TR has increased from £120 to £162. A price increase has the opposite effect and TR falls. Demand is very responsive to price changes in both directions over the price range £1.80–£2.

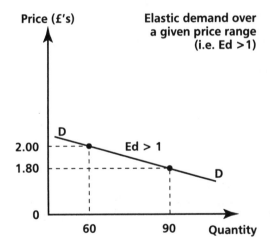

Figure 7.2

Figure 7.3 illustrates the concept of inelastic demand over a given price range. A price reduction from £2.00 to £1.50 increases the quantity demanded from 60 to 66, a 25% price reduction has resulted in an increase in quantity demanded of 10%, as a result TR has fallen from £120 to £99. A price increase has the opposite effect and TR increases. Demand is unresponsive to price changes in both directions. It is important to realise however that

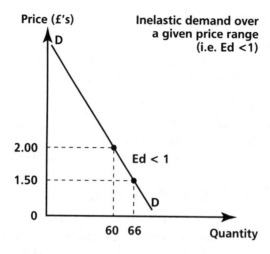

Figure 7.3

these diagrams only represent elasticity within the relevant part of the demand curve and in different parts of the demand curve elasticity will be different.

4 Visual interpretations

Visual comparisons of the elasticity of demand of two products can only be made when the following conditions apply:

- The scales are identical (note that in Figure 7.2 and 7.3 changing the scale changes the slope of the curve.
- Price changes are identical.
- The price at which the comparison is made is identical.

5 Measuring elasticity

Elasticity of demand, except in three 'limiting cases', varies at different points on the demand curve, and (except in the three special cases) there is no such thing as elastic or inelastic demand curves because measurements of elasticity are relative measures, which depend upon percentage changes taken at a particular point, whilst diagrams represent absolute changes. For this reason it is preferable to measure PED by the use of formulae. The formula which is most commonly used to measure PED is

$$PED = \frac{\text{percentage (or proportionate) change in quantity demanded}}{\text{percentage (or proportionate) change in price}}$$

For percentage changes this can be represented in notational form as

$$PED = \frac{\%\Delta Q}{\%\Delta P} \qquad \text{(where } \Delta = \text{a small change)}$$

The formula can also be represented as follows:

$$PED = \frac{\Delta Dx/Dx}{\Delta Px/Px}$$

Where:

ΔDx = the change in the quantity demanded of good x
Dx = the original quantity demanded of good x
ΔPx = the change in the price of good x
Px = the original price of good x.

The formula measures the degree of change in quantity demanded to a small change in price over a small area on a demand curve; and either percentage or proportionate changes can be used.

Table 7.1	
Price (P)	Quantity
6	100
5	200
4	300
3	400
2	500
1	600

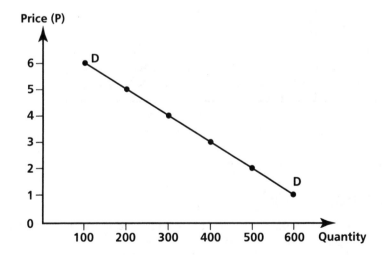

Figure 7.4

The resulting coefficient gives a measure of the degree of elasticity around a point on the demand curve. If it is < 1 demand is inelastic, > 1 demand is elastic, = 1 demand is unitary (see Figure 7.8) or 0 demand is totally inelastic (see Figure 7.6).

Table 7.1 is a simple demand schedule and Diagram 7.4 is its demand curve.

Using the formula to obtain an estimate of PED for a price reduction from 5p to 4p we have

$$PED = \frac{\%\Delta Q}{\%\Delta P} = \frac{100/200 \times 100}{1/5 \times 100} = \frac{50\%}{20\%} = 2.5$$

which represents a high degree of elasticity.

For a price reduction from 2p to lp we have

$$= \frac{100/500 \times 100}{1/2 \times 100} = \frac{20\%}{50\%} = 0.4$$

which represents an inelastic demand. This illustrates the fact that PED normally varies along a demand curve, and along a straight line demand curve will vary from 0 to ∞ (zero to infinity).

Figure 7.5 illustrates how a straight line demand curve passes from ∞ through an inelastic portion to the mid-point which is unitary, through an inelastic section to zero at the quantity axis.

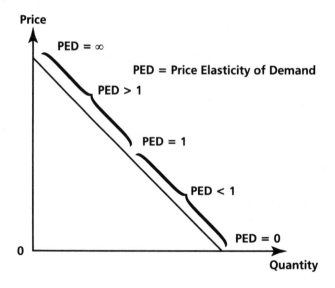

Figure 7.5

6 Extremes of PED

There are three special or 'limiting' cases of PED referred to earlier, and here the demand curve is a true representation of the PED

Figure 7.6 represents the case where PED = 0, quantity demanded will be totally unresponsive to price (within a relevant price range).

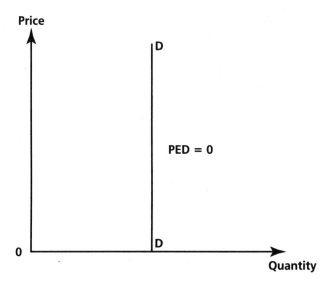

Figure 7.6

Figure 7.7 represents the case of the infinitely elastic demand curve PED = ∞ . Any increase in price will result in zero being demanded, any reduction in price will result in an infinitely large demand (this is the perfectly competitive case – see Chapter 14).

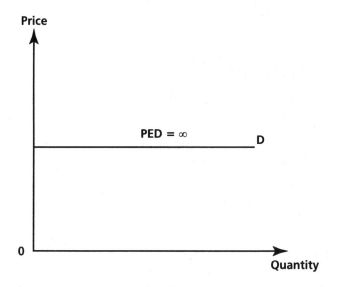

Figure 7.7

Figure 7.8 represents the unitary demand curve, PED = 1. As price is varied quantity demanded varies proportionately to maintain a constant TR. Mathematically it is a rectangular hyperbola.

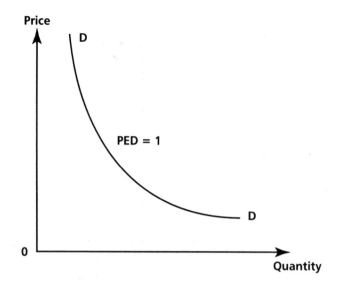

Figure 7.8

7 Determinants of PED

PED is determined by the following factors:

- The number and closeness of substitutes.
- The proportion of income the good accounts for.
- Whether the good is a necessity or a luxury.
- The influence of habit.

8 Applications of PED

An estimate of price elasticity of demand is an important element in a firm's pricing policy, particularly when it is considering price increases or reductions.

It is also important for the Chancellor of the Exchequer when selecting goods for the imposition of taxes or duties. It is preferable to select goods which are in inelastic demand in order to be certain of maintaining the tax revenue, e.g. petrol, spirits, beer and cigarettes.

9 Point elasticity

The measurement of elasticity used so far is referred to as **arc elasticity**. Arc elasticity measures the average value of elasticity over a small segment of a demand curve. An alternative measurement is **point elasticity** which measures elasticity at a single point on the demand curve and is therefore a more accurate measure, which unlike arc elasticity, is independent of the direction of the price change. The concept is illustrated in Figure 7.9, where point elasticity is given by the slope of the line A–B where it is tangential to the demand curve at the point under consideration, i.e. point x. The slope of the line A–B is given by $\Delta P / \Delta q$, therefore point elasticity can be defined as

$$PED = \frac{\Delta q/q}{\Delta P/P}$$

rearranging the terms gives

$$PED = \frac{\Delta q}{\Delta P} \cdot \frac{P}{q}$$

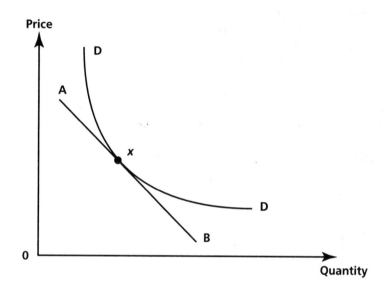

Figure 7.9

Where

P = original price
q = original quantity
Δq = an infinitely small change in quantity
ΔP = an infinitely small change in price

Point elasticity of demand therefore depends upon the slope of the demand curve, $\Delta q/\Delta P$ and the specific point on the demand curve at which elasticity is to be calculated, P/q. Those familiar with calculus will recognise that this process in fact amounts to using differentiation to find the rate of change of quantity with respect to price at a point on the demand curve. The smaller the changes taken in the calculation of arc elasticity the closer the result will be to the point elasticity value. In most instances, particularly for examination purposes, arc elasticity will be a sufficient measurement.

10 Income elasticity of demand (IED)

This measures the responsiveness of demand for a good to changes in income, and is calculated as

$$IED = \frac{\text{Percentage change in quantity demanded}}{\text{Percentage change in income}}$$

If the resulting coefficient for income elasticity of demand is greater than 1 then the good is **income elastic** and a rise in income would result in a **more than proportionate increase in quantity demanded**. This would be the case for all **normal goods**.

If income elasticity of demand is between 0 and 1 the good is said to be **income inelastic**, and a rise in income would result in a **less than proportionate rise in demand**. For example, there is a tendency for the demand for basic foodstuffs to rise less rapidly than income, referred to as **Engel's law.**

If income elasticity of demand is equal to 1 (unitary) the demand for the good **rises in exact proportion to the rise in income**. A positive relationship between income and demand would be expected for all normal goods.

The exceptions to the expected relationship between income and demand would be where income elasticity of demand = 0, i.e. a proportionate change in income results in no change in demand; and where income elasticity of demand is negative and increases in income result in a reduction in demand for the product, which would be the case for **inferior goods,** particularly those referred to earlier as Giffin goods. For example, as incomes grow, consumers may cease buying margarine and shift their buying preferences to butter.

The different measurements of income elasticity of demand can be represented graphically as in Figure 7.10 below.

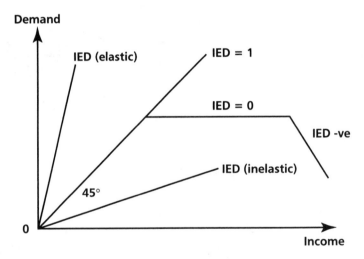

Figure 7.10

The concept of income elasticity of demand (IED) can be important for firms when forecasting the sale of their product during a period when incomes are changing. This can be illustrated with the simple example of a consumer good such as men's cotton shirts. In Figure 7.11 the pattern of demand for cotton shirts as income rises can be seen to pass through four phases. In phase A, income is too low for the purchase of cotton shirts and the consumer is restricted to nylon shirts, hence IED = 0. As income increases in phase B the consumer enters the market for cotton shirts and IED = > 1. Eventually the consumer's demand for cotton shirts is satisfied and in phase C further increases in income do not lead to any further increase in demand, hence IED = 0. Eventually at very high incomes the consumer enters the market for silk shirts and the demand for cotton shirts declines as income rises hence IED = negative. (< 1).

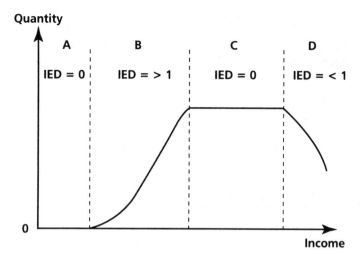

Figure 7.11

11 Cross elasticity of demand

Cross elasticity of demand measures the **responsiveness in the quantity demanded of one good to the change in the price of another good.** Where goods are close substitutes or complements cross elasticity is high. It is measured as:

$$\frac{\text{Cross elasticity of demand for X}}{\text{with respect to Y}} = \frac{\text{Percentage change in quantity demanded of good X}}{\text{Percentage change in the price of good Y}}$$

If the two goods are close substitutes then an increase (+) in the price of good Y will result in a transfer of demand to good X, (+) thus

$$Exy \ = \ \frac{+}{+} = +$$

and cross elasticity of demand is positive.

Alternatively if the two goods are consumed together, i.e. are complements, then an increase (+) in the price of good Y will reduce the demand for both goods (-) thus

$$Exy \ = \ \frac{-}{+} = -$$

and the cross elasticity of demand is therefore **negative.** If there is no relationship between the two goods then

$$Exy \ = \ 0$$

A practical example of cross elasticity resulted from the doubling of coffee prices in 1975 which followed the failure of the Brazilian coffee harvest due to frost and caused a transfer of demand to the closest substitute, tea, the price of which rose shortly afterwards as a consequence. Astute commodity buyers aware of the nature of cross elasticity entered the tea market shortly after the rise in coffee prices.

12 Elasticity of supply

The concept of elasticity also refers to **supply** and **elasticity of supply** can be defined as the **responsiveness of the quantity supplied to changes in price**.

$$\text{The formula for Es} \ = \ \frac{\text{\%age or proportionate change in QS}}{\text{\%age or proportionate change in price}}$$

Figure 7.12 illustrates different supply elasticities. It should be noted that any straight line supply curve passing through the origin is unitary. Elasticity of supply = 0 occurs when supply is fixed and cannot be increased, for example Rembrandt paintings.

13 Elasticity of supply and time

The time period involved is very important when discussing elasticity of supply. There are three time periods which are relevant to elasticity of supply; the momentary, the short run and the long run.

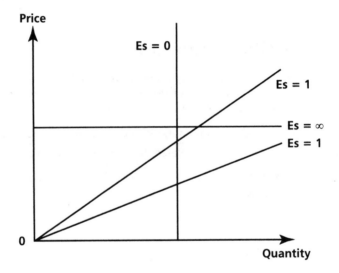

Figure 7.12

The momentary period is the period in which **no adjustments** of either fixed or variable factors of production can occur in response to a change in demand.

The short run is that period in which **variable factors** only can adjust to a new situation.

The **long run** is that period in which both **fixed** and **variable factors** can adjust.

In Figure 7.13(a) there is an increase in demand from D to D', but in the momentary period supplies are fixed at Q and supply is completely inelastic. For example, if demand for fresh fruit suddenly increases supplies at a fruit market cannot be immediately increased. After a period of time has passed supplies can however be increased as variable factors are used more intensively; in the example fruit farmers work longer hours and send more to market. As a result supply becomes more elastic, i.e. S' in 7.13(b), and the price falls to P², In the long run both fixed and variable factors have had time to adjust, fruit farmers will have increased their acreage, employed more labour and machines, and new farmers will have entered the industry. Supply has become more elastic, S^2 in Figure 7.13(c) with the long run price P^3 lower than P^2, with higher demand at Q^3. Whether the long run price P^3 is above or below the original price P depends upon how easily the industry has been able to obtain the additional factors of production it requires for expansion or whether the required factors had to be attracted from alternative uses by paying more for them. Also the extent to which the industry was able to gain economies of scale (see Chapter 13) from its expansion will affect the long run equilibrium price.

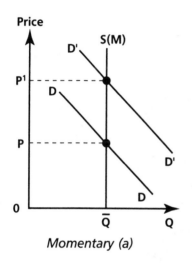

Momentary (a)

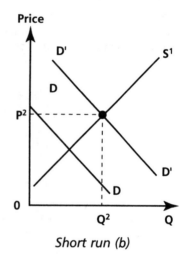

Short run (b)

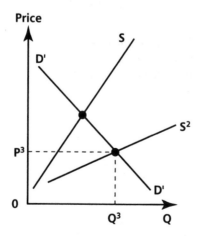

Long run (c)

Figure 7.13a, b, and c

Self assessment questions

1 Why is the gradient of the demand curve not a reliable indicator of price elasticity of demand?

2 With reference to Table 7.1 calculate the price elasticity of demand for a price increase

   (i) from 2p to 3p
   (ii) from 5p to 6p.

3 State the three limiting cases where the demand curve is a guide to elasticity of demand.

4 What are the three time periods relevant to Elasticity of Supply?

5 What factors determine the price elasticity of demand for commodity?

6 **(a)** Define each of the following terms:
   • price elasticity of demand
   • income elasticity of demand
   • cross elasticity of demand.
Describe briefly the factors that determine each of them.
(b) Below is the demand schedule for a product.

Price (£ per unit)	Demand (units per week)
10	400
9	500
8	600
7	700
6	800
5	900
4	1000
3	1100

Calculate the price elasticity of demand and comment on your results when
(a) the price is reduced from £9 to £8 per unit.
(b) the price is reduced from £5 to £4 per unit

8

Market analysis

1 Dynamic and static analysis

Incorporating demand and supply elasticities with the previous analysis of the determinants of market price makes possible the study of **dynamic models** of market adjustment, rather than the **static** analysis undertaken so far which simply describes the movement from one price to another. Dynamic analysis becomes necessary when the response of supply to changes in market price is characterised by considerable time lags, for example in agriculture where the **decision** to increase output is taken well in advance of any actual increase in output due to the time required for the crop to grow. One such simple dynamic model is known as the **cobweb theorem**.

2 The cobweb theorem

The cobweb theorem is best illustrated by the example of agricultural markets, particularly those where the actions of producers are uncoordinated with no central control and where no co-operatives exist. Such markets are characterised by substantial and frequent fluctuations in both price and output. The principle can be illustrated by referring to the production of coffee in South America. Given the correct climatic conditions, soil and altitude, coffee is a highly prolific crop and is certainly the easiest crop for the poor peasant farmers to grow, but with a time lag of between 3–5 years between the planting of the coffee tree and it bearing fruit. If in any particular year the price of coffee is high and growers receive a good return they will respond by increasing their acreage, of course they all respond in the same way with the consequence being that in the following period supply exceeds demand and the price falls. The response to the reduction in price may result in reduced plantings and shortages in the following period, hence there are alternating shortages and surpluses with corresponding fluctuations in price. An alternative response to the price fall following increased acreage may be that the individual farmer, unaware that the other farmers are doing exactly the same thing, actually increases his acreage in the face of a lower price in order to try to maintain his real income by increasing output, but because they all respond in the same uncoordinated way surpluses become ever larger and prices and therefore farm incomes continually decline. This is the situation in which Brazil's farmers found themselves in the period up to the 1970s. The same market characteristics however apply to most agricultural commodities, for example grain, sugar beet, potatoes etc. These price fluctuations may cause severe problems for the developing nations where incomes are dependent upon a narrow range of primary products.

3 The converging/stable cobweb

According to the cobweb theorem, therefore, the supply of a commodity in the current period depends upon the **price (P) which prevailed in the previous period (P$_{t-1}$) where-as the quantity demanded depends upon the price in the current period (P$_t$).**
Supply can therefore be represented as

St = f (P$_{t-1}$)

and demand as

Dt = f (P$_t$)

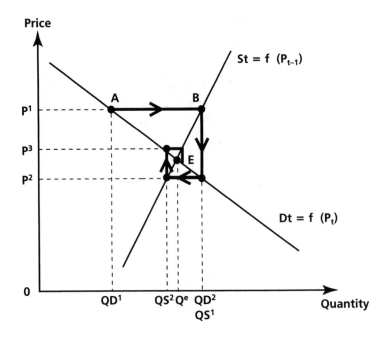

Figure 8.1

In Figure 8.1 the original price prevailing on the market is P^1 and growers respond to this price by ensuring that supply will be QS^1 or B, in the following period by appropriate planting. When this supply arrives on the market in the current year at the price prevailing in the previous period, P^1, only QD^1 will be demanded, which creates a surplus in the market of QD^1–QS^1 (or A–B). Because farmers must clear their existing stocks supply in this period QS^1 is totally inelastic consequently the surplus will drive the price down until there is sufficient demand to clear current stocks. Price therefore falls to P^2 where existing stocks are cleared. The price P^2 is now the price prevailing for the following year for which the appropriate supply is QS^2. At price P^2 however, demand is QD^2 resulting in a shortage of QD^2–QS^2. This shortage will push the market price up to P^3 which will clear the market. A similar sequence of events follows but with **successive surpluses and shortages becoming smaller and smaller until the market converges upon the long run equilibrium price at E.** The converging cobweb occurs when the supply curve is less elastic than the demand curve.

4 The diverging/unstable cobweb

The alternative model is the **diverging cobweb** where the market situation is **unstable** and departs further and further from equilibrium over successive periods. Such a situation occurs when the elasticity of supply is greater than the elasticity of demand. The diverging cobweb model is illustrated in Figure 8.2.

Analysis of the divergent cobweb model is identical to the convergent cobweb, however in this case the quantity supplied changes to a greater extent than the quantity demanded in response to any change in price. As a consequence **the market moves away from equilibrium over successive periods as surpluses and shortages become progressively larger,** the market is therefore unstable.

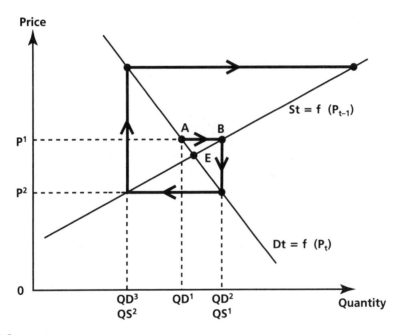

Figure 8.2

5 Buffer stocks

Because of the problems created by the large fluctuations in agricultural output and incomes, governments have introduced various agricultural stabilisation policies in the attempt to stabilise farm incomes and output. One policy which has been used in various countries is a **buffer stock** scheme. These schemes attempt to maintain farm incomes by means of a guaranteed or target price, which is maintained by means of a government agency which purchases surplus stocks and stores them, reselling them later during periods of shortage.

In Figure 8.3 if the **target price** is set at the average free market price Pe and in one particular year actual output is Q^2 the surplus Qe – Q^2 is withdrawn from the market by the,
government agency which enters the market as a buyer in order to maintain the target
price of Pe, this surplus is then added to the buffer stocks in government warehouses. In
the following year if actual output is Q^1 then the shortage, Q^1–Qe is eliminated by releas-
ing stock from the government warehouses forcing the price down from P^1 to the target
price Pe. Schemes such as this however rarely work smoothly, for instance there is no reason why shortages should automatically follow surpluses, and there may be successive
periods of surplus to be added to stocks with no opportunity for disposal Also the costs
of storage may be considerable with interest charges, deterioration and refrigeration for
meat and butter. Problems also arise with the setting of the target price, because of either
the difficulty of forecasting the average market price, or as the result of desire to boost
farm income or encourage greater output, the target price may be set above the equilibrium price, for example at P^1 in Figure 8.3.

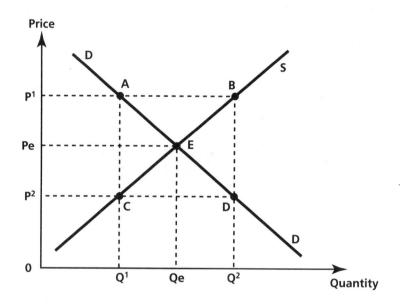

Figure 8.3

As a consequence farmers will be encouraged to increase output to Q^2 and the surplus of
Qe–Q^2 will have to be purchased and added to official stocks in every period. The knowledge that the minimum price is guaranteed and all production can be sold will encourage
producers to produce excess output. The continuous additions to stock can become a
financial problem for the government, but also the existence of vast food stocks being
unused may become a source of political embarrassment for the authorities. The financing of the stocks also becomes an issue, if they are financed from general taxation then
the incomes of the farming community are being subsidised by the non-farming community hence a non-voluntary transfer of income occurs. **The Common Agricultural
Policy (CAP)** of the EU is an example of such a scheme. The high intervention (target)
prices have resulted in the butter and beef 'mountains' and the wine 'lake' causing acute
embarrassment to the EU Commission. In order to off load the surplus stocks they were

sold off outside the EU at a price below the target price. This dumping of surplus stocks at prices below the target price constitutes a transfer of income from taxpayers in the EU to consumers outside it.

6 Price stabilisation

Schemes of the type outlined above stabilise prices at the target price but do not necessarily stabilise farm incomes. Total farm incomes are given by the target price (Pe) $\times$ output (Q) i.e. Pe $\times$ Q When output is Q^2 total farm incomes are Pe $\times$ Q^2 and when output is Q^1 incomes are Pe $\times$ Q^1, and Pe $\times$ Q^2>Pe $\times$ Q^1 .What in fact happens is that farm incomes vary in the same direction as outputs so when output is large incomes are large and vice versa. If the objective is to stabilise farm incomes then the demand curve for output will need to be unitary (=1) and the target price should be allowed to vary in proportion to output. As a consequence if output increases by 10% then price is allowed to fall by 10% and vice versa, which, given the unitary demand curve, maintains an unchanged income for farmers. Therefore, where the authorities wish to stabilise incomes they will seek to influence the demand side of the market but will need to be prepared to adjust target prices accordingly.

7 Buffer stocks in practice

Buffer stock schemes have generally met with the type of problems outlined above, for example in the attempt to maintain coffee prices the Brazilian government's intervention scheme resulted in having sufficient stocks in official warehouses to meet total world demand for several years, until the 1975 crop was depleted by frost. In the same year the crop of the world's second largest producer Angola was ruined by civil war. As a result of this combination of events the world price of coffee rose by almost 300% over the next two years. As a result of the higher world price for coffee, as the cobweb theory predicts, coffee planting increased substantially and by 1980 the real price of coffee had returned to the 1975 level as output increased.

8 Alternative approaches

There are various **alternative approaches to maintaining or raising prices and incomes** which may be used either independently or together with buffer stock schemes.

- **Quotas** on the production of a commodity whereby each producer is given a limit to the amount which can be produced.
- **Financial incentives to diversify** into alternative crops, for example the payment of a bonus to the farmer for every coffee tree replaced with cotton.
- **Export quota schemes** whereby each producer country is given a quota as to how much of a commodity they can export, for example the International Coffee Agreement (ICA), no longer in operation, which restricted the export of coffee.
- **Producer cartels** which are agreements between producer countries to withhold supplies from the world market in order to keep prices higher and thereby increase their revenues. This was done very successfully by the Organisation of Petroleum Exporting Countries (OPEC) in 1973/74 and 1979/80. It is difficult to maintain such cartels in the long run however because eventually it serves the interests of at least one member to

leave the cartel and undercut the other members; seldom is a cartel in the interests of all members at all times. Also the higher prices will eventually have some affect on demand which declines, for example in the case of high oil prices by economising on oil consumption and the development of alternative energy sources, which together with the reduction in demand resulting from the slow down in economic activity made it difficult for the OPEC cartel to continue to dominate world oil prices.

Self assessment questions

1 Distinguish between dynamic and static market analysis.
2 What is meant by:
   (a) Diverging cobweb price behaviour.
   (b) Converging cobweb price behaviour.
3 How do agricultural buffer stock schemes operate?
4 Why do cartels tend to break down eventually?

Section C

Business decisions

Containing the following chapters:

Chapter 9 – Growth of the business unit

Chapter 10 – Business units and sources of capital

Chapter 11 – Sources of capital

Chapter 12 – Location of production

Those economic decisions that influence the size, location and financial structure of the modern business unit

This section should enable students to:

- *Understand* how firms expand and the methods available
- *Explain* why firms decide to locate in particular areas or regions of the UK
- *Contrast* the different sources of finance available to a business
- *Evaluate* the influence of the government in the business sector

Keywords to consider:

internal growth; external growth; merger; acquisition; holding company, horizontal/vertical integration; conglomerates; limited liability; sole proprietor; partnerships; private limited company; PLC; public sector; nationalised industries; ordinary shares; preference shares; stock exchange; transport costs; sources of power; access to markets; industrial inertia; labour.

9

The growth of the business unit

1 Motives for growth

There appears to be an inevitable tendency for successful organisations to grow in size. The effect on the firm's costs will be one very important motive for growth, but there are other motives, and in this chapter we analyse what these various motives may be, and the form and direction that this growth may take.

The most frequent motives for growth can be identified as:

- To **gain the economies of scale** (see Chapter 13).
- To **gain dominance over the market** by gaining a larger market share, i.e. the monopoly motive.
- To **diversify into a wider range of products** in order to gain greater security, e.g. Imperial Tobacco now produce over 60 different products, as diverse as crisps, cigarettes and cardboard cartons.

2 Methods of growth

Firms may grow by either internal expansion or externally by merging with, or acquiring, other firms.

Internal expansion is most likely to occur in an industry which is relatively new and the market is still growing. Growth of this type usually takes the form of expanding the existing amount of plant and manufacturing units. The increase in capacity will enable the firm to:

- Increase the output of its existing products.
- Enter new markets with its existing products.
- Produce a wider range of products.

External growth refers to growth by means of either **merger** or **acquisition**.
Growth by **merger** occurs when two, usually similarly sized firms, decide to join together and merge their separate identities into one.

Growth by **acquisition** occurs when a business grows by taking over the plants or markets of an existing firm, sometimes referred to as a 'take-over'.

External growth by such methods may make use of a **holding company**. A holding company is formed specifically for the purpose of gaining a controlling interest (51% of the shares) in a number of other companies. The companies taken over may remain as separate units, but the main policy decisions will be made centrally by the holding company. Examples of holding companies include the Trafalgar House Group whose interests include insurance and shipbuilding, the Imperial Tobacco Company mentioned above and Sears (Holdings) Ltd. which has interests in activities as diverse as shipbuilding, footwear, engineering and retailing, and the British American Tobacco Co. whose interests include tobacco and insurance (Eagle Star Insurance). 1986 was a year of almost unprecedented merger activity with many large groups either merging or taking over other groups. The motive for these mergers was either to strengthen the firms market position in the face of the difficult trading conditions or to diversify into new product areas, generally for the same reason. Mergers included Habitat and British Homestores, Argyll and Distillers, and Amstrad and Sinclair. 1995 saw another record year with £66 billion of assets changing hands, the most significant being the takeover of Wellcome by Glaxo which created a drug company which now dominates the market.

3 Integration

Growth by acquisition or merger is also referred to as **integration**. Integration is normally classified according to the direction of the integration, which may be:

Horizontal:
The merging of two firms at the same stage of production.

Vertical:
* **backwards** towards sources of raw materials.
* **forwards** towards the final market.

4 Horizontal integration

Horizontal integration occurs when firms **engaged in the same stage of production** come under a single control. This is very common at the retail stage, for example the merger of Boots and Timothy Whites, and that between Habitat and Mothercare. Some of the UK's largest companies have been formed as a result of such mergers including: United Biscuits, Associated Biscuits, Associated Foods, British Leyland, and GEC. An illustration of a horizontal integration would be the merger of two woollen textile manufacturers. Horizontal mergers may occur in order to gain some of the economies of scale mentioned in Chapter 13. In particular the following economies may be gained:

* The establishment of a central purchasing department buying the combined requirements of all the companies in the group will gain better discounts for the bulk buying of components and raw materials. Centralised purchasing also facilitates the establishment of better buying and stock control systems, and can employ the expertise of specialist buyers. Large organisations pay considerably less for their supplies than do smaller companies. This is particularly important in retailing where these purchasing economies give a significant advantage to the large retail group over the small independent.

- Financial economies – see Chapter 13.
- Marketing economies – see Chapter 13.
- Technical economies – in addition to the points mentioned in Chapter 13, horizontal integration may create savings in research and development effort. Instead of competing and thereby reproducing costly research effort, research can be centralised, and the pooling of facilities, expertise and effort, can bring considerable savings. Also the combined output of the merged firms may justify the use of larger more efficient machines which would not be fully utilised by the output of a single firm. The same argument can be applied to new technology where robotic production systems and sophisticated computerised control systems can only be justified on the basis of large outputs.
- Managerial economies – see Chapter 13. Larger firms can afford to employ specialised management, and as there is more scope for division of labour the degree of managerial specialisation can be carried further than in small firms, with the subsequent benefits. Also larger firms can afford to pay the high salaries necessary to attract the most talented managers.
- The merger in 1986 between the rival electronics firms Amstrad and Sinclair provides an interesting example of a horizontal merger where the technical expertise and inventiveness of the Sinclair company was combined with the marketing expertise of Amstrad, to the mutual advantage of both groups.
- Some significant examples of horizontal integration in manufacturing industry have been: Allied Breweries and Showerings, GEC and English Electric, British Motor Holdings and Leyland, and the takeover of Jaguar by the Ford Motor Company.

5 Vertical integration

Vertical integration refers to mergers which take place between firms who are engaged in different stages of a production process. Forward vertical integration occurs when a firm merges with a firm at a later stage in the manufacturing process, for example a clothing manufacturer acquiring a chain of retail outlets. Backward vertical integration occurs when the merger takes place with a firm at an earlier stage in the manufacturing process, for example a woollen textile firm acquiring a weaving firm. When the entire manufacturing process from raw materials to distribution of the finished goods are under the control of a single firm the firm is referred to as 'fully integrated'. At the other extreme where all components are bought out and merely assembled by the firm, the firm is said to be 'disintegrated'. Ford of America was an example of a fully integrated firm. Growth by vertical integration has in the past been a characteristic of the motor car industry as motor car manufacturers attempted to gain control of component suppliers. Forward vertical integration in the motor car industry mainly occurs in the form of manufacturers attempting to establish distribution and dealership networks. In the brewing industry it is usually in the form of breweries taking over public houses. In fact the majority of vertical forward integrations are of this type, with manufacturing firms attempting to ensure retail outlets for their products.

6 The merits of vertical integration

Vertical integration may well achieve many of the internal economies of scale mentioned in Chapter 13. There may however be additional advantages to be gained.

Backward integration may be motivated by the desire to ensure the supply of materials which are relatively scarce. This is essentially a defensive motive but it may also be aggressive if these supplies are then denied to competitors.

Many modern manufacturing processes have very stringent quality control requirements for their components, and attempt to run their production on minimal stocks, they therefore have very tight delivery schedules for supplies. Vertical integration by acquiring component suppliers ensures closer control over the quality of supplies and their conformance with specifications, and also guarantees deliveries. The assurance of quality requirements brings savings in the form of lower inspection costs and lower reject rates during production. Guaranteed delivery performance by suppliers allows firms to reduce their stock levels of components and production materials which reduces their inventory carrying costs; which can be a considerable expense. Many large manufacturers favour such integration as it enables them, with the aid of micro-technology, to introduce techniques such as materials requirements planning, by which supplies are matched exactly with production requirements, resulting in considerable savings in stockholding costs. Such integration has been greatly favoured by the Japanese car and electrical industries.

The 'end-on' linking of processes is also facilitated by vertical integration, and if this is followed by the concentration of production into a single plant then there may be considerable technical economies. The integration of machines enables machine timings to be set in such a way as to avoid excess stocks of work-in-progress building up, or machines standing idle waiting for another slower part of the process to catch up. Modern steel works provide a good example of integrated production where the production of iron and steel, and the rolling of steel are combined in one continuous process.

Control over distribution networks is also a source of cost saving. Not only are outlets assured for the firm's products and the costs of distribution reduced, but the firm is also more able to match its production levels to current market demand, particularly where ownership extends to the retail level and market information can be readily fed back to the plant level where sales forecasts and production schedules can be updated in the light of the latest information. This avoids the holding of excess stocks of finished goods or lost sales as a result of shortages. Ownership of distribution channels and retail outlets also enables the firm to eliminate the wholesale function reducing costs and increasing profitability and, also assisting in the marketing and promoting of the product.

Product diversification may also result from vertical integration. This is the widening of the firm's product range and is a form of protection against the possibility of the failure of a single product putting at risk the survival of the firm. It is in fact one of the economies of scale; that of risk bearing. One example is the aquisition by BMW of Rover, the producer of the Land Rover, in order to gain access to the four-wheel drive market.

Tube Investments' acquisition of The British Aluminium Company who produced lightweight tubing, is an example of backward vertical integration, and the acquisition, also by Tube Investments, of Raleigh Industries is an example of forward vertical integration. Tube Investments then possessed a tube manufacturer and also a firm which utilised tubing in the manufacture of lightweight bicycles.

7 Recent trends

The majority of mergers in recent years have been of the horizontal type. These have been mainly defensive in character in order to consolidate market shares in the face of world recession and growing international competition. Despite this the opportunities to gain economies of scale remain one of the main motives for both types of merger, but are still only a single element in a complex decision.

Table 9.1					
	1965–73	1978	1982	1987	1994
Horizontal (%)	78	53	65	67	88
Vertical (%)	5	13	5	3	5
Conglomerate	17	34	30	30	7

8 Conglomerate mergers

Conglomerate mergers are mergers which are not strictly lateral or vertical but are between companies producing a product (or range of products) which are not directly related. The **objective** may be to reduce risk by diversifying or to enter a new market when the existing market offers little hope for further growth. They are frequently associated with **multi national companies** and **holding companies**. Examples are the Imperial Tobacco Group and Sears (Holdings) Ltd., mentioned earlier, and British American Tobacco which acquired Eagle Star Insurance, and Hanson Trust's acquisition of the London Brick Co. and in 1986 the Imperial Tobacco and United Biscuits Groups.

The year 1987/88 saw a very high level of mergers and acquisitions in the UK by industrial and commercial companies, however a second take-over boom emerged in 1995/96 with acquisitions reaching a record £67.7 billion. Internationally one of the most significant mergers was within the United States aircraft industry with the acquisition of McDonnell Douglas by Boeing which will give the combined company dominance over civilian and military aircraft production, including helicopters, and posed a severe threat to the European Airbus project.

Conglomerate mergers are currently less fashionable however, as the trend is for organisations to focus on their 'core activities,' due to the problems they have experienced in the management of diversified business activities. For example Hanson is breaking up into four separate business units, and recently Unilever sold its interest in chemicals and food flavourings to ICI.

9 Small firms

Despite the fact that economies of scale appear to offer substantial benefits to large firms many industries are still characterised by the survival of small firms. It is necessary to consider therefore why small firms survive and why they are so prevalent in some industries, and also why in some industries both large and small firms exist alongside each other. The main reasons are outlined below.

Where personal attention is involved and growth of the firm would involve loss of personal attention to detail. Examples are hairdressing and bespoke tailoring.

Where the total market is small, output will not be sufficient to achieve the necessary levels of specialisation and division of labour. Examples include retailing in isolated communities where only 'general' shops can survive because the limited demand prohibits specialised retailing. Garages tend to be small because the market is limited by the distance people are willing to travel for car repairs, and also the nature of the work does not lend itself to the achievement of economies of scale.

Some industries provide highly individualistic or 'exclusive' items. Such items are generally luxury goods and if produced on a large scale would lose their attraction as their appeal is their uniqueness. Such goods will frequently be the creations of talented, individuals and as the supply of such people is limited, the firm is unlikely to grow to large scale. Examples include designing, architecture and high fashion.

Small firms may survive in an industry by locating a **specialised segment of the market** which does not interest the large manufacturer who prefers longer production runs.

In the engineering industry many small firms survive by taking **work which is subcontracted** to them by larger firms who have no spare capacity and have too much work, or where the small firm provides a specialised service to the larger firms. Small firms may also undertake the highly specialised 'one-off' jobs that are of no interest to the larger firms.

Large firms may allow small firms to exist in order to **prevent investigation by the Monopolies Commission** (Chapter 19).

The fact that a firm is small may merely be due to the fact that it is in an **early stage of its growth** and is one of the large firms of tomorrow.

Economies of scale undoubtedly give advantages to larger firms, but there is little doubt that there will always be a place for the small enterprising firm, and it may be the case that such firms offer the greatest prospects for economic growth.

Self assessment questions

1 What are the two main methods by which firms grow?

2 Distinguish between vertical and horizontal integration.

3 What is meant by internal economies of scale?

4 What are the main motives for horizontal integration?

5 Give four examples of internal economies of scale.

6 Why do small firms survive despite the economies of scale enjoyed by large firms?

10

Business units and sources of capital

1 Business units and capital

The oldest and simplest form of business unit is the **sole proprietor**, a single individual providing all the capital, running the business, accepting all the risk and taking any profits which arise. The growth of specialisation and division of labour and the increased use of mechanised production however, increased both the demand for capital and the need for more specialisation within the management of businesses. The growing demand for capital in particular during the 19th century was a major factor in the development of **joint stock companies**. In joint stock companies the capital, for the acquisition of machines, premises and other assets, is raised from shareholders who each purchase shares in the business in return for a share of the profit, or dividend, at the end of the trading period. In this way joint stock companies are able to raise large amounts of capital to facilitate the growth of the business; by utilising the available reserves of numerous individuals, who individually may only be able to make a small contribution, but collectively the amount of available capital may be substantial.

2 Legal personality

Joint stock companies are a separate entity from the shareholders who own the business and in law have a **legal personality distinct from the owners**. This gives the firm all the rights in law of an individual, to sue or be sued etc. Such organisations are referred to as **corporate bodies**, hence joint stock companies are sometimes referred to as **corporations.** Because the shares are on sale to the general public they may also be referred to as **public companies**.

3 Limited liability

The ever growing demand for capital in the 19th century as production methods became larger, more complex, and therefore more expensive, meant that if firms were to develop the new technology and continue to grow then new sources of capital had to be found, in particular the funds of those with small amounts of wealth who were not prepared to take the risk of losing their investment in the event of the firms bankruptcy. This resulted in the mid 19th century in the introduction of **limited liability**. With limited liability companies the liability of the shareholder is limited in the sense that in the event of the firm going bankrupt they stand **only to lose the amount of their original investment and no more.** In this way firms are able to attract the small saver, who is more averse to risk taking, into investing in shares. As a result, corporations have access to far greater sources of funds than smaller business units. The owners of the business, the shareholders, however, have little control over the running of the business which is in the hands of paid managers.

4 Conglomerates

Established joint stock companies have a tendency to grow in size by acquiring, or merging with, other companies and may eventually become large **conglomerates** producing wide ranges of products or multinational with subsidiaries in many countries. The growth of companies is described in more detail in Chapter 9.

5 Business structures

The sole trader and the public joint stock company represent the smallest and largest of the business units and between their two extremes there are a number of intermediate forms through which business may grow. The actual choice of business unit will depend upon the financial, legal and organisational requirements of the firm. The main business units and their characteristics are outlined below, however it is frequently the case that a firm may start initially as sole proprietor or partnership and develop through the other stages into a joint stock company as the need for capital and more specialised management becomes greater as a consequence of the growth of the business.

6 The sole trader

The sole trader (proprietor) is the oldest and still the most common form of business unit. Many types of business find the sole trader a useful form of business organisation, for example shop-keepers and various services, such as; accountants, solicitors, window cleaners and painters. It is particularly prevalent in the retail trade.

The **advantages** of the sole trader are:

- The proprietor is their **'own boss'** and has complete control over the business.
- The **rewards of the business belong to the proprietor.** Therefore all profits belong to the proprietor.
- The proprietor is able to **choose all products they wish** to trade in and how they wish to trade in those goods, without consulting any other person.
- The sole trader can offer a **personal service.**

The **disadvantages** of a sole trader are:

- **Unlimited liability**, i.e. the debts of the business are not regarded as separate from the debts of the individual and in the event of financial difficulties, creditors will be able to claim the person's individual assets in settlement of their debt, e.g. house, car, etc.

- The sole traders **bear all the risks themselves** and are unable to have the benefit of spreading the risk of decision making amongst other people.
- The sole trader may be limited in the ability to expand owing to a **lack of capital**.
- One person may also be **restricted in the number of suitable business ideas** they are able to develop. Even if they have good ideas, time may be a constraint on development.

7 Partnerships

Partnerships can be of two types although the ordinary or general partnership is by far the most common. The two forms of partnership are:

- **The ordinary partnership**, which is governed by the Partnership Act 1890.
- **Limited partnerships**, governed by the Limited Partnership Act 1907.

The limited partnership is a rare type of organisation since it yields few benefits which cannot be more easily obtained through limited company status.

There must be between two and twenty partners, except for certain types of professional partnership such as firms of accountants and solicitors.

Partners' rights, responsibilities and rewards are normally specified in a legal document called **'the partnership deed'** In the absence of such a deed (which is not required by law), the rights rewards and responsibilities of each of the partners is determined by the **Partnership Act 1890.**

All partners may take part in the management and running of business in this type of organisation. As a result, the partners are 'jointly and severally' liable for any debts incurred by partnership.

Limited partnerships arise where a partner known as the **'sleeping partner'** or a limited partner wishes to invest in the business but has no desire to take part in the running of the business his only reward is to receive a proportion of the profits as determined by agreement. A limited partner is not allowed to take part in the management of the business by law (Limited Partnership Act).

The **advantages** of partnership are as follows:

- More than one person is able to make decisions and share in the decision making process.
- Normally there are a small number of people to consult when deciding on new products, or what products to trade in.
- Partnerships may also be able to offer a personal service, i.e facilitates a degree of specialisation within the management of the business. For example, one partner may specialise in finance and the other in marketing.

The **disadvantages** of partnerships are as follows:

- Partners may disagree.
- If one partner decides to leave the partnership, the partnership must be dissolved, i.e. there is no continuity.
- There may be a limit to the amount of capital available for expansion.

8 Partnership limitations

A partnership is not a legal entity, i.e. it is not recognised as a person in law, but it is regarded as an association of individuals. This has the following consequences:

- The firm cannot sue or be sued in its own name, any legal action must be taken by or against any or all of the partners.
- It cannot contract in its own name.
- On the withdrawal of a partner, either voluntarily or upon death or bankruptcy, the partnership is terminated.
- In the event of insolvency, i.e. the business going bankrupt, any or all of the partners can be held liable to contribute to the deficiency from his or her private estate.
- Any partner acting with authority as a representative of the business binds his fellow partners in contract.
- A partner may not transfer his share of the business without the consent of his fellow partners.

9 Limited companies

Limited companies (joint stock companies), have the following characteristics:

- **Limited liability**. A member's liability is limited to any amount unpaid on his shares i.e. a shareholder in the event of liquidation would lose only the amount paid or payable for the shares he owns, unlike a partnership or sole trader, his personal assets will not be used in the settlement of outstanding debts of the business.
- **Legal entity**. A company is regarded as a 'person' at law, i.e. the business is separate from the owners of the business (divorce of ownership from control). Thus a company may contract in its own name.
- **Continuity**. The existence of a company is not affected by any change in its members, no matter how much its ownership changes by the transfer of shares, the company remains unaltered.

10 Public and private companies

Public and private companies are registered companies and are the most common type of company in the UK. They have the following characteristics:

- Any company must have at least **two members,** there is no **maximum**.
- A public company must state in its **memorandum of association** that it is a public company and it must be registered as such.
- A private company is a company which is not a public company (cannot trade on the stock exchange).
- A public company may invite the public to subscribe for its shares and debentures. A private company may not.
- The shares of a public company are **freely transferable** whereas a shareholder in a private company may have to have **agreement of the other members**.
- A public company must end its name with the words **public limited company** or the abbreviation **plc.**
- A public company must have an authorised **minimum share capital of £50,000.**

- A private company may commence trading immediately it is registered. A public company must first have a **'trading certificate'** after it has proved that the authorised minimum share capital has been taken up.

The disadvantages are having to complete administrative documentation, such as memorandum and articles of association, filing company returns with the registrar and subjecting the business to an annual audit which is required by the Companies Act 1985, and other legal requirements specified therein. These disadvantages have to be weighed against the overriding advantage which is to limit the liability of the members.

11 Regulations for limited companies

Internal and external regulations for limited companies are:

- The Memorandum of Association establishes the legal identity of the company and determines and limits objects. Any activity of the company or its directors beyond scope of the objects is **'ultra-vires'** (outside the powers).
- The **Articles of Association** are the internal rules for governing the conduct of the company. They will include regulations establishing the powers, rights and obligations of members and directors. They may be altered within the bounds of the law, with the agreement of the holders of 75% of the voting shares.
- The **Companies Act 1985** consists of extensive legislation, supported by a considerable amount of case law. The 1985 Act consolidated the previous Companies Acts into a single Act and established the legal framework for the running of companies.
- The **Stock Exchange Regulations** regulate the dealing in shares on the Stock Exchange. Shares in public companies may be dealt in on the Stock Exchange only if they have been admitted to the listing. The 'permission to deal' granted by the Stock Exchange imposes on a company and its directors, regulations stricter than those required by law. The main purpose of this is to give additional protection to shareholders and investors.

12 Ownership and control

As a consequence of the fact the limited (or joint stock) companies have their capital subscribed by shareholders there is **a separation between the ownership and the running of the business by its management**. They are therefore:

- **Owned** by the shareholders.
- **Managed** by the directors.
- **Controlled** by those holding a majority of the voting shares because those shareholders can determine who are to be the directors.

13 Capital sources

Joint stock companies can therefore raise their capital by the sale of shares to the public. In the case of public companies shares may be traded on the **stock exchange** provided they have a Stock Exchange listing. Unlisted companies may have their shares traded on the **unlisted securities market**, which has undergone rapid growth over recent years; and is generally used by smaller companies. Shares may be purchased for two reasons; for a steady income from the dividends, or to make a capital gain by buying them at one price and re-selling them later at a higher price. As far as the firm is concerned, after it has raised its initial capital, it is of little consequence if its shares are later resold on numerous occasions, all it requires is the name and address of the current owner in its share register in order to send the dividend to the owner of the share. Shares may be purchased by individuals but are also purchased by various institutions such as insurance companies, unit trust companies, pension funds, finance houses etc. as part of their portfolio of assets. The trend in the UK has been towards institutional ownership of firms with over 80% of shares in 1995 owned by institutions and less than 20% by private individuals.

14 Nationalised industries

In the UK the government itself is responsible for a substantial proportion of output. This **public sector** activity may carried out directly by a central government department, or by local government. In some cases however, the type of activity may resemble more closely the activity and output of a private sector commercial enterprise. Where such industries, for either economic political, or strategic reasons, are owned by the state they are referred to as **nationalised industries**.

15 Organisation of public corporations

The nationalised industries in Britain were run by **public corporations** which were established by an Act of Parliament. These public sector corporations differed from those in the private sector mainly from the point of view of ownership and control. Public corporations had only a single owner which was the state, unlike the private sector corporation which is privately owned by shareholders. Each public corporation was slightly different in organisation of its internal structure but they were generally under control of a **chairman** and a **board** who were appointed by the appropriate minister, e.g. Secretary of State for Industry, Energy or Transport. The corporations were nominally free from interference by the minister in the day to day running of the industry which was intended to be left to the management, although governments sometimes found it difficult to resist interfering when they had some broader objective in mind, for example, dictating pricing policy during a period of inflation.

16 Control of public corporations

Public corporations were not subject to control through a meeting of shareholders at an annual general meeting in the way that a private corporation is; instead external control was exercised in three ways:

- **Ministerial control** through appointments to the board and general powers of direction. The minister also had the power to demand information and then control over specific areas designated under the act which nationalised the industry.
- **Parliamentary control,** indirectly through the minister and also parliamentary procedure, in particular the select committees known as the Public Accounts Committee and the Nationalised Industry Committee, which examined the financial reports and accounts of the nationalised industries.

- **Consumer councils** existed for each of the industries, they are intended to act as channels of communications for the opinions of the consumers of the industries goods and services regarding the standards of provision.

17 Control of the privatised utilities

The nationalised industries have since 1979 been returned to private ownership, as indicated in Chapter 1. The privatisation of these state owned monopolies leaves them with a structure similar to that for any public company as described above. In the case of the privatised utilities such as water, gas, electricity and telecommunications, however there are still the remaining problems which follow from the creation of a monopoly supplier of an essential utility. The problem becomes that of how to obtain the benefits of privatisation in terms of costs and efficiency whilst at the same time protecting the interests of consumers. It is for this reason that the concept of regulated companies was introduced. The activities of the privatised utilities are subject to a degree of regulation regarding the maintenance of quality and their pricing strategies. The major agencies in the UK are:

- Office of Telecommunication (OFTEL)
- Office of Water Services (OFWAT)
- Office of Electricity Regulation (OFFER)
- Office of Gas Supply (OFGAS).

The Monopolies and Mergers Commission (MMC) is also involved in regulation because of the monopoly position held by these utilities. The determination of prices by the regulatory bodies can be subject to appeal to the MMC.

Regulation, therefore, is intended to balance the requirements of ownership and efficiency with the public interest.

Self assessment questions

1 Distinguish between a private and public company.

2 What is meant by limited liability?

3 What are the main disadvantages of partnership as a business unit?

4 How do joint stock companies raise their capital?

5 In what sense does a company have a legal personality?

6 Distinguish between private and public corporations with regard to ownership and control.

7 What is meant by regulation and why is it considered necessary?

11

Sources of capital

1 Sources

Firms require fixed capital for the replacement or expansion of fixed assets such as plant and premises and working capital for acquisition of stock and meeting the costs of production. Sources of funds are therefore required which are **short term** and **long term** and may be generated from both **internal, external sources**.

2 Internal sources

Internal sources are the major source of funds for industrial and commercial companies in the United Kingdom. Internal funds are provided from retained profits and provisions for depreciation. In established companies these account for approximately two thirds of the total requirements and are therefore also the most important source of long term funds.

3 External sources

The major source of **external** funds for joint stock companies is the **shareholders' capital**. Shareholders' funds will include the funds raised by the company by the issue of shares at the commencement of the business. This is generally referred to as the issued share capital. Many companies when commencing however, will have **authorised share capital** which may be much higher than the share capital which is initially issued. If at some future date it should need extra funds to finance a major new project then it can issue the extra shares in order to raise the required capital. When the issue of new shares are restricted to the existing shareholders they are referred to as a **rights issue**, and may be issued at a price below the current market price. The shares of the public companies are traded on the **Stock Exchange** which is a medium for raising finance for the larger public companies with a Stock Exchange listing. Those companies unable to afford the high costs of a Stock Exchange listing and not wishing to meet the requirement to make a minimum of 25% of the company's share available to the public, may use the unlisted securities market where the costs of issue are much lower and only 10% of the company's shares need to be made available to the public.

4 Shares

Shares can be of several different types and a company will generally issue some, or all, of the following choices:

Ordinary shares (equities). This class of share bears the highest risk as they are entitled to a share of the profits as determined by the directors only when all the other classes of shareholder have been paid. They may receive no dividend if the directors deem it necessary to retain profit in the business for expansion or to create an accumulated fund as a precaution against bad years. On the other hand, ordinary shareholders may do very well in exceptionally good years. Ordinary shareholders have full voting rights at the annual general meeting and therefore have the right to appoint or dismiss the members of the board of directors.

Preference shares carry a fixed rate of dividend payable before the ordinary shareholders are paid. The preference shares can be classified into categories, each one indicating priority of payment. For example, Class A shares might be paid before Class B and so on. If the company has incurred arrears on preference shares because it had insufficient profits to pay in a previous year, then these must be paid before any ordinary dividends are paid. All preference shares are **cumulative** unless otherwise stated, i.e. if the firm is unable to pay a dividend one year, owing to insufficient net profits being earned, two years' dividends fall due in the next year. Preference shareholders do not have voting rights.

- Preference shares may be non cumulative.
- Participating preference shares carry a right to a fixed dividend plus a share of the profits available to ordinary shareholders.
- Redeemable preference shares are the only type of non-permanent share. The company gives an undertaking to redeem shares at a specified time, often at a premium.

5 Debentures

Debentures form an alternative source of long term external finance. Debentures are not shares but are more in the nature of a **long term loan** to companies in return for a **fixed rate of interest** which is irrespective of the profit made by the company. The debenture is a document issued by the company as evidence of the loan. It is redeemable after a specified period, for example 20 years; after which it must be repaid. Debentures are virtually free of risk because if the company is unable to meet its interest or repay the loan, the debenture holder can force the company into liquidation. Holders of **mortgage debentures** are in the position of **secured creditors** in that the loan is secured against specified assets of the company which the debenture holders can force the company to liquidate (sell) in order to meet its commitment. As debentures are loans rather than shares, debenture holders do not have voting rights. In the event of liquidation they are paid out before trade creditors and shareholders.

6 Loan finance

The major source of external loan finance for the short term requirements of most businesses is the banks. Bank borrowing accounts for approximately 60% of the external funds of UK industrial and commercial companies. Borrowing from the banks can either be by loan or by overdraft.

Banks are the major source of short-term finance for most businesses. Bank loans are generally used for specific purposes, and in particular for the acquisition of fixed assets, for example, plant and equipment. The bank will charge an arrangement or negotiation fee, and interest on the loan. Over the period of the loan, the charges made in interest will be greater than the arrangement fee. Loan interest is normally repayable on the capital or on the balance outstanding at between 2% and 5% above the banks base rate. All the major clearing banks' base rates, i.e. National Westminster, Barclays, Lloyds, the Midland and Royal Bank of Scotland, tend to move in line with each other. Most banks providing loans will require security, which is normally in the form pledging assets of the business; in other words, the loan will be secured against either what is called a fixed charge, that is a particular asset, for example, a motor vehicle, a machine, a factory; or a floating charge where the loan is secured against any asset that the firm holds. In the case of a floating charge, if the bank decides to call in its loan then it is entitled to recover the value of the loan and any interest due up to that date by means of selling any asset to the equivalent value that the firm has. In the case of a fixed charge, the bank has the right to sell the particular asset against which the loan is secured, take the amount that is due to the bank, and give the remainder back to the liquidator who is then able to repay other creditors.

Overdraft facilities are granted by negotiation with the firm's branch manager. Loans are normally for a specific purpose, whereas overdrafts are to meet any short term cash crisis. The overdraft facility is normally in existence for a long period of time. Interest on an overdraft is always paid on the amount of money actually borrowed, and this is calculated on a daily basis by the bank. Overdrafts are normally cheaper than loans because the interest rate charges are normally between 1½% to 4½% above the bank's base rate (i.e. the base lending rate plus 1½% to 4½%). From the borrower's point of view, bank overdrafts are a very flexible way of financing short term because the low interest rates are attractive. However, the danger is that the business becomes reliant on the overdraft, and furthermore from the banker's point of view, the overdraft is legally repayable on demand, therefore the bank could ask for repayment of the overdraft immediately. Normally, however, the bank will agree that an overdraft shall not be called in for a defined period of time and generally banks are prepared to continue financing a client whose business it considers to be profitable, and is showing a regular turnover of funds, but is in need of temporary finance owing to cash flow difficulties. From the bank's point of view, they would much prefer a self-liquidating loan, in other words, they would like to lend funds for a specific project which will yield a cash return which is able to meet their repayment. In order to obtain any form of loan from a bank, it will be essential that the business produces a cash flow forecast together with a profit forecast showing its ability to repay the loan or the overdraft in question.

7 Venture capital

In addition to the sources described above, there are also a variety of institutions which will provide venture capital for organisations, most of them being government sponsored. These bodies include: The Industrial and Commercial Finance Corporation (ICFC), Technical Development Capital Ltd., Finance For Industry (FFI), The National Research Development Corporation (NRDC) and Equity Capital for Industry. These organisations generally provide loans and advice, usually to smaller firms; and in particular where technological innovation is involved.

8 Loans and equity finance

The choice between loans and equity finance will be influenced by the relative costs of the two sources. Equity finance may be more expensive because equity holders who accept a higher risk (they may not receive a dividend in any particular year) will require a higher average rate of return than loan finance which would be considered to be more certain and therefore safer. Also the interest paid on the loan stock is an allowable expense on the company's tax liability. A further reason for preferring loan finance is that the issue of additional equity will result in a further dilution of the company's ownership. The ratio of debt to equity finance is referred to as **gearing** and is expressed by:

$$\text{Gearing} = \frac{\text{Debt}}{\text{Equity}} = \frac{\text{Long term debt and preference shares}}{\text{Equity capital}}$$

A highly geared company is one which has a high proportion of debt to equity and vice versa. The level of gearing affects the overall cost of finance to the firm, although under highly restrictive conditions, Modigliani and Miller have shown that the level of gearing is neutral regarding the firms cost of finance.

Self assessment questions

1 Distinguish between ordinary shares, preference shares, debentures.

2 What are the major sources of external finance available to a firm?

3 What is meant by the term 'gearing' in the context of a firm's financial structure?

References

1 Modigliani, F and Miller, M.H. 'The Cost of Capital, Corporation Finance and the Theory of Investment' AER Vol 48 (1958).

12

Location of production

1 Location decisions

The choice of site at which to locate may have a significant affect upon the firm's costs, and it is important, in theory at least, that the firm selects a site which minimises the costs associated with location. In reality however the choice of site may also be influenced by other factors which are not necessarily economic and modern industries may have a considerable degree of freedom in the decision as to the best site at which to locate.

2 Transport costs

Transport costs were considered to be an important factor in determining location, although they have less significance today than in the past. The transport of either raw materials or finished goods can have a considerable influence upon the final cost of a product. There are two opposing influences in this context, on the one hand the firm will desire to be as close as possible to its sources of **raw materials** but at the same time will wish to be as close as possible to the **market** for its final product and these two requirements may frequently oppose one another, being closer to raw materials may leave the firm more distant from its markets. This is sometimes explained in terms of '**weight gaining**' and '**weight losing**' processes. Some materials lose weight during the manufacturing process, for example, flour milling, iron ore refining and sugar beet refining. Others gain weight during processing, for example, prefabricated buildings, brewing and engineering. When a product loses weight during manufacturing it will tend to gravitate towards the source of raw material in order to minimise transport costs. An example is iron ore, which in the UK tends to have a low yield, has traditionally been smelted in the areas where it is quarried; in Northamptonshire and Lincolnshire. Flour milling is commonly carried out at ports for the same reason. In some cases the extraction or refining process has been shifted to the primary producing country; in particular the extraction of edible oils from seeds and palm kernel has shifted from the UK back to the producer countries such as Nigeria, where the oil is extracted and only the refined oil shipped to the UK. This reduces the transport costs but also gives a greater 'value added' for the producer country. Weight gaining processes are those where the product gains weight during the production process and in such cases the cost of transport will be minimised by locating closer to the market place. The extreme example would be prefabricated buildings which are assembled on site. Brewing was originally carried out in town centre breweries as it was more economic to distribute the finished product over as short a distance as possible to the largest market. Changes in brewing technology and transport have however considerably changed the location requirements of the brewing industry. Theoretically therefore the firm will choose an optimal location, which will be the one that minimises its transport costs given the extent to which its product gains or loses weight during the manufacturing process. This site may be at the source of the raw material, the final market, or some intermediate point.

The analysis of location according to the degree of weight gain or loss can be criticised on the grounds that it is the ratio of unit value to weight of the product which is more important than the actual weight. Where products have a low value to weight ratio then transport is likely to be a far more important consideration than for products with a high value to weight ratio. The example of beer brewing quoted earlier is a product with a low value to weight ratio hence transport constitutes a higher proportion of total cost, and the firm will attempt to minimise transport costs by locating as close to the market as possible. Where products have a high value to weigh ratio transport becomes a minor factor, as it is a low proportion of total cost, and location is less critical, for example, whisky can be distilled in Scotland and sold worldwide.

3 Sources of power

Proximity to sources of power was an important factor in determining location during the 19th and early 20th centuries. Early industry was located near fast moving rivers when water power was the prime source of power, later water power was superseded by steam power and nearness of a supply of coal became important hence industry became concentrated on the coalfields of the north of England. Since the widespread adoption of electricity which is available almost everywhere in the UK through the National Grid, it is no longer necessary for the supply of a power source to have influence over the location of the firm.

4 Declining influences

Improvements in transport and availability of power have mean that access to raw materials and power are now of minor importance in the firm's location decision and many industries are now described as '**footloose**', meaning that they can locate virtually anywhere they choose.

5 Access to markets

Access to markets is now one of the most important factors influencing the location decision. This has always been the case with goods where the ratio of value to transport costs is low or for goods which are perishable, for example, ice-cream has always been produced close to large centres of population. However, with the major changes which have taken place in the industrial structure and the methods of transport **market access has**

become a dominant factor. Much of UK industrial output today consists of lighter high value goods such as electronics, which are easily transportable and consequently has low transport costs, and transport is therefore a relatively unimportant factor. Ease of access to large markets such as the cities may figure more significantly in the location decision. This tendency has been accelerated by technical improvements in transport with larger vehicles, containerisation, improved mechanical handling, and the development of the motorway system. Many of the newer lighter industries therefore tend to be near to the big conurbations, in particular in the south east in proximity to London and in the Midlands. It is also interesting to note the proliferation of industrial estates around the access points to motorways in order to take advantage of the shorter delivery times and ease of access offered by the motorway system. Access to large trading blocks such as the EU may also be a factor in location, for example, the decision by the Japanese car manu-facturers Nissan to locate in the north-east of England was partly influenced by the desire to obtain access to EU countries for the marketing of their vehicles.

6 Labour

Labour requirements can also influence the firm's location, in particular the need for spe-cific types of labour. For example, a firm in the cotton textile industry would find the skilled labour it required by locating in Lancashire; this readily available skilled labour force would have the effect of reducing the firm's training costs. Much of industry is how-ever now much less labour intensive, utilising more capital intensive methods of production and requiring less skilled labour. Many firms now require unskilled or semi-skilled labour and do not want permanent commitments to the labour force. They may therefore prefer to employ part-time female labour, nearness to large urban areas is there-fore attractive to many firms, particularly those involved in light assembly work. As consequence, many industries are now 'footloose' regarding the labour requirements.

7 Industrial inertia

Originally the location of an industry in a particular area may have been due to certain natural advantages which the area could offer, for example the damp atmosphere of Lancashire was a attraction to the cotton spinning industry as it prevented the threads from snapping, steel making at Sheffield due to the availability of coal and iron. These factors may no longer be as relevant today as technology has superseded the original advantages, as in the case of artificial humidifiers in the cotton industry, however the industry may remain in the same area due to **industrial inertia**. Industrial inertia keeps an industry in an area long after the original advantages have been lost. This is due to cer-tain **acquired advantages** which offer **external economies of scale** to the industry, for example a skilled labour force or suppliers of components (see Chapter 9).

8 Non economic factors

If we assume that firms attempt to maximise profits then they will at all times select the site which offers the lowest overall cost; in reality however **non-economic factors** may weigh heavily on the decision. Once located in an area, senior management may be reluc-tant to move to another site which they find less attractive from the point of view of amenities, friends, housing, children's schooling and status. This can explain to some extent the reluctance of firms to move away from the south-east of England to the regions of higher unemployment in the north despite the attraction of government grants. There are also many examples of firms which are located at a particular site for no reason other than the personal preference of the original founder. Morris built his motor car factory at Cowley in Oxford, not for any particular economic advantages but because he happened to live there and the family cycle business was already located in the town.

9 Government policy

Government regional policy can be a further influence in the location decision. Governments offer a range of grants and other incentives to firms in order to attract them to locate in the regions where unemployment is highest. This is discussed in detail in Chapter 31.

10 Present trends

The major trend in location today is the increased freedom of firms in the choice of site. Technical developments in production, transport and sources of power have all contributed to making industry more 'footloose' than ever before. This trend has been accelerated by the tendency towards 'disintegration' in some large industries. Disintegration refers to the buying out from suppliers of components and assembling them rather than the firm manufacturing all its own components. This trend is particularly prevalent in the motor car industry where it gives the manufacturer more freedom in the location decision. For example, Ford at Dagenham closed their foundry for making engine blocks as this tied them to one source of supply. Ford and Vauxhall on Merseyside now produce cars from components brought in from plants in various European countries and assemble them on site rather than produce entire vehicles. Modern multi-national companies when looking at the location decision do not feel constrained to a single country but will consider the choice of alternatives on a world-wide basis. The opening of the Channel Tunnel will undoubtedly influence the location decisions of many UK firms in the future as they attempt to minimise their total distribution costs. This may be achieved by locating facilities, particularly distribution centres, either at a convenient point for access to the tunnel or even by establishing distribution centres in European locations.

Self assessment questions

1 How does the concept of weight gaining and weight losing materials affect the firm's location decision?

2 What is meant by an industry being 'footloose'?

3 Why is most industry more footloose now than in the past?

4 What is meant by industrial inertia?

5 How might the advent of the Channel Tunnel influence the location decisions of UK firms?

Section D

The theory of the firm

Containing the following chapters:

The accepted theoretical framework under which profit maximising firms are thought to operate, given the different market conditions

This section should enable students to:

- *Understand* the structure of a firm's costs
- *Explain* how different market structures produce different models
- *Contrast* the output and price decisions of the different models
- *Evaluate* the effectiveness of government legislation in controlling the activities of firms

Keywords to consider:

fixed/variable costs; marginal cost; internal economies of scale; diseconomies of scale; external economies of scale; marginal revenue; normal profit; profit maximising output; barriers to entry; price discrimination; kinked-demand curve; price leader; non-price competition; product differentiation; branded goods; managerial theories; behavioural theories; sales maximisation; mergers; restrictive practices; Office of Fair Trading

13

The firm's costs

1 The importance of costs

During the act of production the firm will incur certain costs and it is necessary to examine how these costs behave as output changes. It is necessary to consider how costs behave with a fixed set of plant and capacity, and also how they behave over the longer period when plant and capacity can be varied.

2 Costs

Costs can be classified as either **fixed costs** or **variable costs**.

Fixed costs (sometimes referred to as overhead costs) do not vary with output, they remain constant, or fixed. Examples of fixed costs (FC) include rent, rates, interest on loans, depreciation of plant and equipment. No matter to what extent the firm is utilising its capacity this group of costs remains unchanged. This should not be taken to mean that FCs never change, for example, rates may increase; but they do remain constant over fairly long periods, and more importantly, do not vary with output .

Variable costs (VC) are costs which vary directly with output. Examples of variable costs (also referred to as direct costs) may include wages, raw materials and power. When output is zero variable cost will be zero and they rise directly with output.

Total costs (TC) are the sum of fixed and variable costs, i.e.

$$TC = FC + VC$$

When output is zero TC = FC and as output rises TC increases with the increase in VC. Fixed, variable and total costs are illustrated in Figure 13. 1.

3 Average costs

In order to analyse the effect of output on costs however, it is necessary to identify costs more closely with units of production, i.e. the cost per unit. Total costs need to be converted into **average costs**. To achieve this all that is required is to divide FC, VC and TC by output (Q). Hence we obtain **average fixed cost (AFC)**, **average variable cost (AVC)** and **average total cost (AC)**.

i.e.

$$AFC = \frac{FC}{Q}$$

$$AVC = \frac{VC}{Q}$$

$$AC = \frac{TC}{Q}$$

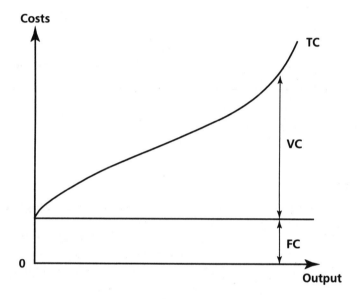

Figure 13.1

Figure 13.2 represents these average costs diagramatically. Because FC is constant but spread over an increasing number of units it falls over its entire length. AVC falls then rises slowly, whilst AC falls then rises in a U-shaped curve.

Mathematically AC = AFC + AVC.

4 The AC curve

The AC is typically a U-shaped curve, with average costs of production falling and then rising. The AC curve falls initially for the following reasons:

As fixed costs are spread over more units of production the average fixed cost per unit will fall, i.e. fixed costs are £50 and we produce 50 units, each unit carries £1 of fixed cost, if output rises to 100 units each unit carries only 50p and so on.

As more variable factors are added to the fixed factors (land and capital) there will be increasing returns, eventually however diminishing returns will set in, causing costs to rise again. After reaching a minimum the AC curve begins to rise because:

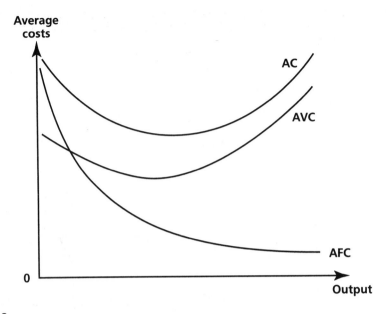

Figure 13.2

- As output increases we may have to employ less efficient labour, as we can assume that the 'best' labour will have been employed first.
- Less efficient machinery may be utilised which would not be used at lower outputs.
- Labour may have to work overtime at higher hourly wage rates.
- Machinery worked consistently at full capacity is liable to more frequent breakdowns.
- The managerial problems of co-ordination and control become greater at higher outputs.

The optimum (or ideal) output for the firm is where AC is at minimum, at the lowest point on the AC curve.

5 Normal profit

A further essential point about average cost is that in economics cost includes **normal profit**. Normal profit is that rate of return which is just sufficient to keep the factors of production in their current use and prevent them transferring to any alternative. It can therefore be considered as the cost to the entrepreneur of keeping the factors of production in their current use.

6 Marginal cost

Marginal cost is another very important concept in the study of the firm's costs. Whenever the term 'marginal' is used in economics it refers to the extra, or incremental unit. In the case of costs marginal cost refers to the **addition to total costs incurred by producing one extra unit of output**.

Table 13.1

Q	FC	VC	TC	MC
0	30	0	30	
				15
1	30	15	45	
				10
2	30	25	55	

7 The interaction of AC and MC

Table 13.1 illustrates the concept of marginal cost where it is shown against the mid-points of the increase in output (Q) because it is the increase in costs incurred by increasing output by 1 extra unit. As FC is constant MC is the same as the increase in VC. The derivation of the columns in Table 13.2 is straightforward and is explained in 2 and 3. The average and marginal cost data is plotted in Figure 13.3.

Table 13.2

Q	FC	VC	TC	AC	MC
0	30	0	30		
					15
1	30	15	45	45	
					10
2	30	25	55	27½	
					5
3	30	30	60	20	
					10
4	30	40	70	17½	
					30
5	30	70	100	20	
					50
6	30	120	150	25	
					95
7	30	215	245	35	

It can be seen that the MC curve falls then rises rapidly **cutting the AC curve at its lowest point**. Whenever MC is below AC, AC is falling and whenever MC is above AC, AC is rising, MC **always** cutting AC at its lowest point. This must be the case because of the relationship between MC and AC.

This can be explained by analogy with a darts contest. If a player had scored an average of 100 in ten games and then in his eleventh game scored only 90 then his average would fall to 99. If on the other hand he had scored 110 his average would have risen to 101. It is therefore the additional, or marginal, game which determines the average, and if the marginal score is below the average the average falls, and if the marginal score is above the average, the average rises.

It can be clearly seen from Figure 13.3 that the lowest per unit cost, or optimal output, is at the lowest point on the AC curve, which coincides with the point where MC crosses AC.

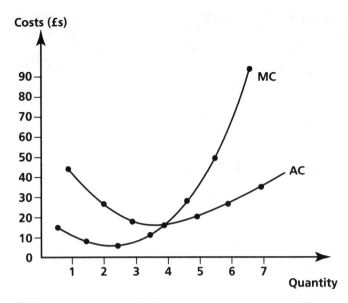

Figure 13.3

8 Short run and long run costs

All the costs mentioned so far assume that the firm has fixed plant and equipment, i.e. the firm is in a **short-run situation**. It is quite possible however, and indeed probable, that the firm will vary its plant over the longer period, particularly if it suffers rising costs from a given plant size it may well expand its capacity.

As the firm encounters rising costs it may decide to re-invest and expand its capacity. This new set of plant will have an entirely new AC curve with its optimal output higher than for the previous plant. This is referred to as changing the **scale** of production and it is necessary to consider the effect of such changes on **costs**, i.e. the behaviour of **long-run costs**.

Figure 13.4 illustrates the effects of changes in the scale of production on long run costs. The firm's first set of plant has short run average cost curve SRAC¹, but eventually costs rise so the firm invests in a new set of plant which has a greater capacity, with cost curve SRAC², this is repeated for scales 3 and 4, which may represent an overall period of 20 years or

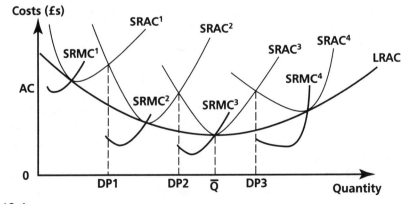

Figure 13.4

longer. Note that when the new plant is introduced, i.e. decision points 1, 2 and 3 its costs may be higher than the minimum point on the old plant, this is because its capacity may not be fully utilised initially, but as output grows it moves down its AC to the lowest point.

9 Economies of scale

It should also be noted in Figure 13.4 that the minimum point of AC for each successive plant size is lower up to Q̄ and then begins to rise again. This is because the **economies of scale** resulting from large scale production tend to reduce costs whilst after Q̄ **diseconomies of scale** set in and costs start to rise again. Q̄ is the optimal long run combination of plant and output but firms rarely recognise when they are at such a point and will more frequently have to attempt to move back to it, after encountering rising costs, by a process of rationalisation.

10 Long run average cost

By drawing a smooth curve which is tangential to each short run AC curve we can derive the **long run average cost curve (LRAC)**, sometimes referred to as the long run 'planning envelope'. The lowest point on this LRAC curve is the long run optimal output Q̄. This coincides with the lowest point on $SRAC^3$.

The long run average cost curve (LRAC) shown in Figure 13.4 may have to be modified in reality as it may not have the smooth U-shape described. This is because the economies of scale usually apply with some degree of certainty as the firm expands its capacity, however the diseconomies of scale are more imprecise and may be offset by skilful management until late in the growth of the firm. As a consequence the shape of the LRAC may be more like that illustrated in Figure 13.5. Up to output Q costs fall as scale increases but beyond Q there is a substantial range of operations where costs remain unchanged and there are constant returns to scale. Diseconomies of scale only become established as capacity expands beyond Q', and the actual point at which Q' occurs will vary widely between different firms and industries. It is therefore possible in some circumstances for firms to expand their capacity over a large range without encountering rising costs. However, at some point they will almost certainly encounter rising long run costs as diseconomies of scale set in.

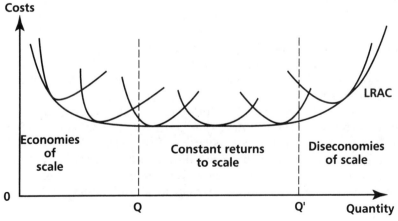

Figure 13.5

11 Internal economies of scale

Internal economies of scale are benefits to the firm which are generated internally and result from larger scale production. They have the effect of reducing the per unit (AC) costs of production. Such economies result from:

Purchasing economies: Larger firms buy their raw materials and other requirements in larger quantities and in return receive larger discounts from suppliers which contribute to cost reduction. Smaller firms are not able to take advantage of such discounts and therefore pay more for their materials.

Marketing economies: Larger firms are able to make more effective use of their salesforce. A salesman can negotiate an order for 500 units in almost the same amount of time as one for 100 units. Administrative costs also do not rise in proportion with order size and cost per item ordered are generally much lower. Larger firms are also able to utilise more effective advertising media such as television, and where the product range is wide the advertising of the brand name helps to sell all the firm's products.

Managerial economies: Large firms can afford, and justify, the employment of specialist managers such as accountants, production managers, sales managers, lawyers etc., whereas in the small firm the managers may have to manage all aspects of the business. The greater degree of specialisation in management leads to greater efficiency.

Financial economies: Large firms are generally able to raise capital more easily and cheaply than small firms. They have more substantial assets and with a sound trading record, financial institutions see them as representing a lower degree of risk, since they can lay claim to those assets if the firm defaults on payments on a loan.

Technical economies: Larger firms have greater scope for the division of labour, and specialisation can be carried to a higher degree. This facilitates the introduction of more machinery and specialised equipment which raises productivity. As output increases labour costs per unit of output tend to decline.

Indivisibility: Many production processes are either technically impossible, or not financially viable, on a small scale – they are indivisible in that they cannot be broken down into small scale production. Many chemicals can only be produced commercially on a large scale, the same is true of steel and cars. As firms become larger they are able to take advantage of these more efficient, large scale, manufacturing processes.

Risk-bearing economies: Larger organisations tend to produce a more diverse range of products; this creates a form of protection in that if one product fails the firm has others which will enable it to survive. Large firms can also afford to undertake high risk activities such as research and development into new products. High costs will be incurred during the development stage without any certainty of making an adequate return. When such activity is successful, however, it can be highly profitable, for example the drug industry's expenditure on research is vast but so too are the profits made on a successful new product.

The principle of multiplies: this is a further economy favouring large companies. Machines tend to have different operating speeds and it can be difficult to link them 'end-on' in a production process. This is particularly difficult with only a few machines as it becomes very difficult to ensure a balanced flow which ensures that each machine is being fully utilised. With more machines however, larger firms find it easier to organise them in linked processes which ensures that they are all fully utilised.

12 Diseconomies of scale

Diseconomies of scale will set in at some stage in the growth of the firm and result in rising per unit costs. These are more difficult to identify but tend to be more managerial in nature:

- As the firm grows the problems of **co-ordination and control** tend to grow rapidly after a certain point and the costs of employing more management (which is not directly productive) grows disproportionately .
- Problems of **communication** arise, both lateral and vertical communications become difficult, not only is it difficult to ensure that instructions are received, but also that they are carried out correctly.
- As organisations grow they may involve production at several separate plants, and the **co-ordination** of activities become less effective.
- Large organisations tend to become more **impersonal**, there is no feeling of 'belonging', hence attitudes of apathy tend to develop, and at worst the workforce becomes 'demotivated' or 'alienated'.

13 External economies of scale

The economies of scale discussed above are all **internal**, they are generated from within the firm as a consequence of its growth. Another group of economies referred to as **external economies of scale** are generated not as a result of the growth of the firm, but as a consequence of the concentration and growth of an industry within an area. Briefly the major external economies of scale are as a result of:

- A pool of labour with appropriate skills within the area.
- Shared research facilities.
- Appropriate financial facilities.
- The growth of component and other suppliers within the area.
- Appropriate educational courses at colleges and universities
- An appropriate infrastructure developing, i.e. roads, harbours and transport.

These factors tend to reduce the operating costs of all the firms in the industry.

14 Avoiding diseconomies of scale

The existence of large firms that do not exhibit dis-economies of scale suggests that they are not necessarily inevitable. The Toyota motor car company is now a vast multi-national manufacturer which despite its size seems to be enjoying ever reducing costs. An insight into how this is achieved through the adoption of 'lean production' techniques is described in detail in 'The Machine That Changed The World' (Womack, Jones and Roos, *Rawson* 1990). Some of the ways in which dis-economies appear to be off-set include:

- Modern computerised management control techniques such as manufacturing resource planning (MRP 11) may overcome some of the problems of co-ordination and control in large plants.
- Communication and control have been improved by modern flatter management structures in place of the old hierarchical structures.
- Prevailing management methods which involve employee participation or

empowerment which in turn involves giving people working in teams some control over their own decisions and immediate work activities. Some of the problems of decision making and demotivation are overcome in this way.

- Making greater use of suppliers who have assemblies or sub-assemblies sub-contracted to them. These 'first tier' suppliers then co-ordinate all the activities further down the supply chain. For example Toyota deals only with the supplier of seats and the seat supplier is responsible for the co-ordination of the supply of seat components, the assembly of seats to a given specification, and they deliver to the Toyota factory. In effect Toyota take advantages of their suppliers' skills and economies and build them into their own.
- The introduction of cost centres or small business units within the larger organisation so, for example, one product line becomes treated as a business unit responsible for its own costs, operations and profitability within the overall organisational structure.
- Strategies such as Just-in-Time (JIT) stock management and Total Quality Management (TQM) which have as their objectives the elimination of investment in stocks and the elimination of waste throughout the organisation. These 'lean' production methods give much tighter, more responsive, control over manufacturing operations with subsequent improvements in quality and reductions in operating costs.
- 'Outsourcing' non-core activities. These are activities which add nothing to the value of the product and should therefore be undertaken by an outside contractor who has a 'distinctive competence' in this specific area. For example a manufacturer may contract-out canteen provision to a specialist caterer.
- New technology provides opportunities for overcoming the tendency for costs to rise.

It may be that many firms have long run average cost curves that are quite flat at the bottom rather than the U-shape assumed above, giving constant returns over quite wide ranges of output. The question which must be asked however is can any firm enjoy permanently falling costs? The answer must be that they cannot or costs would fall eventually to zero which is illogical, hence it is really a question of where the firm actually is on its long-run cost curve.

Self assessment questions

1 Distinguish between fixed costs and variable costs.

2 Why do average costs fall and then rise?

3 At what point does the marginal cost curve intersect the average cost curve?

4 In what sense is normal profit a cost?

5 What is meant by internal economies of scale?

6 Explain the term diseconomies of scale.

7 What is meant by external economies of scale, and why do they occur?

8 How is the firm's long run average cost curve derived?

9 Why does the long run average cost curve initially fall and then rise?

10 Under what circumstances may a firm achieve constant returns to scale?

14

Perfect competition

1 Market forms

We consider next the various market forms, the first of which is **perfect competition**. In reality very few markets are perfectly competitive, examples being the Chicago Grain Market, the Stock Exchange, and some of the commodity markets; however the concept does provide a yardstick by which the degree of competition in real world markets can be measured. It is assumed here that firms compete on price alone and not the other forms of competition, such as advertising, which may be a characteristic of other market forms.

2 Market conditions

In order for a market to be considered as perfectly competitive, a number of conditions must be satisfied, these are:

- There must be a single **homogeneous** (same) **product**, i.e. each seller is offering an identical product.
- There must be **many buyers and sellers**, none of whom can alone influence the market price.
- All buyers and sellers must have **perfect information** regarding the market.
- **Perfect mobility of factors of production** to and from the industry. If profits are high, entrepreneurs can enter the industry, or leave if greater returns can be earned elsewhere.

Given these conditions, there can only be a single market price which cannot be influenced by the activities of any single buyer or seller. As competition is based purely on price, and the product is homogeneous, buyers will buy from whoever is the cheapest; therefore each producer is forced to adopt the least-cost method of production and all excess profits or losses will in the long run be eliminated by entry to, or exit from, the industry.

3 Perfectly elastic demand

We can illustrate the concept by using a simple diagram. In Figure 14.1 we have a buyer in a market place where there are six sellers all selling an identical product, say for example, bags of sugar. The buyer knows the price each seller is charging and we assume that the buyer behaves in a rational manner.

Assume that seller 1 raises his price while the others all keep theirs constant, clearly the buyer will buy zero from seller 1 and obtain his requirements from the others. On the other hand, if seller 1 reduced his price whilst the others kept theirs constant, the others would all sell zero and seller 1 would sell all that the buyer was willing to take. This is in fact another way of saying that the firm in perfect competition has an infinitely elastic demand curve (see Chapter 7).

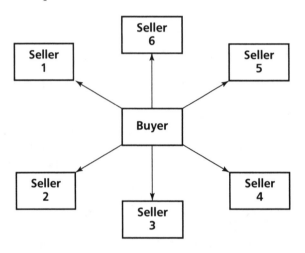

Figure 14.1

4 Revenue

Marginal revenue is the addition to **total revenue** which a firm receives from the sale of one extra unit of output.

The total revenue of the firm (TR) is calculated as **price × quantity**.

Average revenue (AR) is the same as price. This is obvious if we consider that Total Revenue is defined as **price × quantity**.

i.e. $\text{TR} = P \times Q$

therefore $\text{AR} = \dfrac{\text{TR}}{Q} = P$

if AR = P then the **average revenue** curve is the **same thing as the demand curve**.

5 MR=AR=D

In perfect competition as each unit is sold at the same price then both MR and AR are constant and are the **same as the demand curve**, this is shown more clearly in Table 14.1 where it can be seen that because price is constant, under conditions of perfect competition

P = AR = Dd = MR. This is illustrated graphically in Figure 14.2. (Marginal revenue under conditions of imperfect competition where the demand curve is downward sloping is illustrated in Appendix 1 on page 120.)

Table 14.1				
P	Q	TR	AR (TR) $\over$ Q	MR (Increase in Total Revenue)
5	1	5	5	
				5
5	2	10	5	
				5
5	3	15	5	
				5
5	4	20	5	
				5
5	5	25	5	
				5
5	6	30	5	

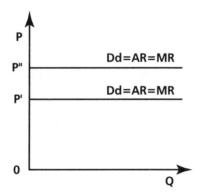

Figure 14.2

The firm's demand curve, as stated above, is infinitely elastic so it can sell all its output at the prevailing market price. The price, in this case P' in Figure 14.2, is determined by the market and cannot be influenced by the individual firm whose output is too small relative to the total industry output. The firm in perfect competition is therefore said to be a **'price taker'** rather than a 'price maker'.

6 Price determination

The equilibrium market price, which applies to each firm, is determined by the intersection of the market demand and supply curves for the **industry as a whole**. The industry demand curve slopes downwards because if the industry as a whole reduces its price it will sell more. The industry or market equilibrium price, P' in Figure 14.3, is at the point where the market demand and supply curves intersect. This establishes the price for every firm in the industry. Should the market price fall or rise for any reason, this new price will then apply to every firm in the industry. For example, an increase in industry demand to D' in Figure 14.3 increases the price for each firm in the industry to P''; in Figure 14.2.

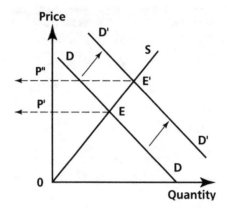

Figure 14.3

7 Profit maximising output

It is now possible to derive the competitive firm's **profit maximising output**. The competitive firm's Average Cost (AC) curve is the usual U-shaped curve, and is of course defined so as to include **normal profit**. The MC falls and then rises sharply cutting AC at its lowest point. In order to maximise its profits, the competitive firm will expand output to the point where MR = MC, at point E, in Figure 14.4. This is the competitive firm's equilibrium point with the profit maximising output at Qe. At lower outputs the firm is not maximising its profits, for example at output Q^2 MR exceeds MC by A–B and the firm

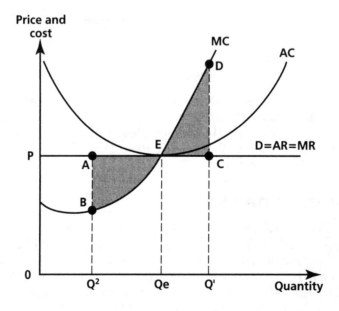

Figure 14.4

can increase its profits by the shaded area by raising its output to Qe. At higher outputs than Qe the firm can increase its profits by reducing output, for example at output Q^1 MC exceeds MR by D–C and the firm is therefore making a loss on each additional unit. Profit will therefore be increased by the shaded area if output is reduced to Qe. As the price is just equal to MC at the lowest point of AC, the firm is using its plant at peak efficiency, and is just covering its costs with no abnormal or super-normal profits being earned, only normal profits being made.

The two essential rules to remember are:

- that a firm's profit maximising output is where

$$MR = MC$$

and this is true of firms under any market conditions
- that under conditions of perfect competition, the firm's price is equal to the marginal cost.

$$P = MC$$

8 Super normal profits

Super normal profits (SNP) can only be earned under **conditions of perfect competition in the short run**, during the period of time which it takes for factors of production to enter the industry.

9 Long run equilibrium

We can now analyse the process by which super normal profit or losses, will be eliminated in a perfectly competitive industry in the transition to long run equilibrium.

In Figure 14.5a. a firm has a short run equilibrium output of Q^0 (MR = MC at E), and cost is only OL (Q^0 M) per unit, hence the firm making a super normal profit of PLME. These high profits will attract new entrants to the industry and supply will increase, prices will start to fall and the amount of super normal profit will decline as in 14.5b, however as long as SNP is being earned, entry to the industry will continue until all SNP's have been eliminated and all firms are earning only normal profits, as in 14.5c. This is the long-run equilibrium.

In Figure 14.5d a firm has a short run equilibrium output of (MR = MC at E), but the cost per unit is OS (Q^0R) and the firm making a loss of PERS, as is each firm in the industry. Firms will leave the industry in search of higher profits elsewhere, supply will fall and prices rise, reducing the size of the loss, as in Figure 14.5e. As long as losses persist, firms will leave the industry until eventually each firm which remains is a marginal firm making only normal profit, as in Figure 14.5c.

In the long run, all excess profits and losses are eliminated and each firm is a marginal firm selling at P = MC. (14.5c.)

A classic example of excess profits being eliminated by competition was the Rubic's Cube where entry to the industry by new firms brought the price down from £5 to £1 in less than a year. The same sort of competition now exists with micro-computers where competition is reducing prices and profit margins rapidly.

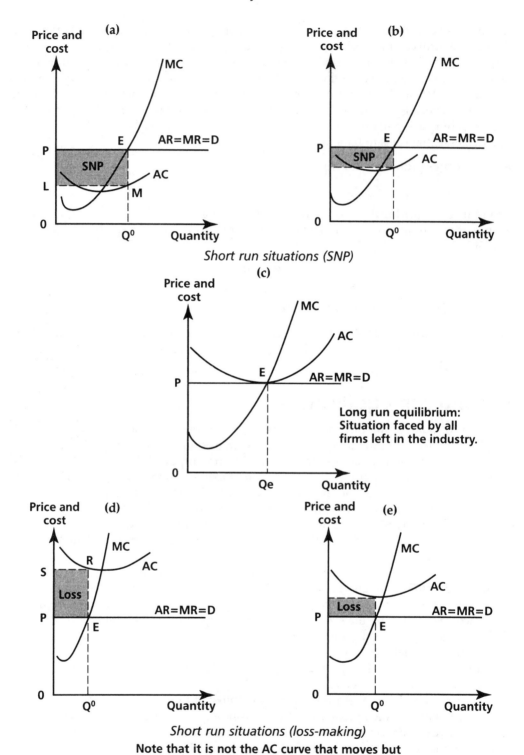

Short run situations (SNP)

Long run equilibrium:
Situation faced by all
firms left in the industry.

Short run situations (loss-making)

Note that it is not the AC curve that moves but
the price line AR which moves relative to it

Figure 14.5

10 Normal profit

Although normal profit applies throughout an industry, it is not necessarily the same between different industries. Normal profit can differ between industries due to:

- The degree of risk and uncertainty involved. High risk industries require high profits in order to attract capital.
- The nature of the production process involved. Capital intensive industries require higher rates of return in order to make investment worthwhile.
- Exceptional entrepreneurial ability enables some industries to earn higher profits by skilful management; sometimes referred to as 'rent of ability'.
- There may be quite substantial time lags before firms can enter an industry due to the shortage of skilled labour or the need to construct plant. Such temporary profits are referred to as **quasi rents**, and they occur whenever profits are earned as a result of a temporarily fixed supply of factors of production.

11 Shut-down point

Where firms have specific assets, in the sense that they cannot immediately be used to produce something else if the price of, product falls, they may in fact stay in an industry for a period even if the price falls below average cost. In Figure 14.6 the firm is in equilibrium at E with price P and quantity Q^3. If the price falls to P^1 the firm will move down the MC curve to the new equilibrium of MC = MR and produce Q^2, The firm will continue to produce until price falls to P^2 at which point it will cease production. Equilibrium point M is therefore referred to as the 'shutdown point'. The firm will therefore continue to produce at any price which covers its average variable costs of production, because anything over AVC makes a contribution to the fixed costs which have to be paid whether the firm produces or not, and will therefore reduce the size of its losses. However, if the price falls below its AVC by producing the firm will actually increase its losses, and the more it produces the greater the loss will be. In the short run, therefore, a firm with specific assets will remain in production as long as the price is greater than AVC.

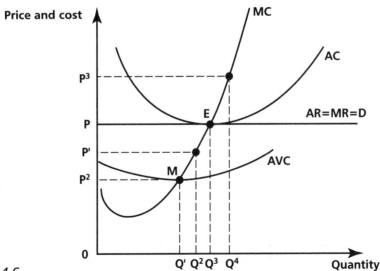

Figure 14.6

12 Marginal cost and supply

If we consider the firm's MC curve in Figure 14.6 it can be observed that the portion of it above M relates the price to the quantity the firm will produce, it is therefore the firm's supply curve. **The competitive firm's MC curve above AVC is its supply curve.** If the MC curves of all the firms in the industry are summed together we obtain the industry supply curve.

13 Imperfect competition

We consider next conditions of **imperfect competition**. The breakdown of perfect competition occurs when one firm introduces a cost saving innovation and is therefore able to produce more cheaply than its competitors. However, not only does it make the innovation, but it is able to keep information regarding the details to itself and permanently undercut its competitors.

Self assessment questions

1 What are the conditions necessary for the existence of a perfectly competitive market?

2 At what point will the perfectly competitive firm be in equilibrium?

3 Where will the perfectly competitive firm in equilibrium set its price?

4 What is meant by normal profit?

5 How are super normal profits eliminated from a competitive industry?

6 Describe the relationship between MC and supply.

7 Under what circumstances may a firm decide to produce and sell at a loss rather than cease production?

Appendix 1

(1) Price (=AR)	(2) Quantity	(3) Total Revenue	(4) Marginal Revenue
20	0	0	
			18
18	1	18	
			14
16	2	32	
			10
14	3	42	
			6
12	4	48	
			2
10	5	50	

Because price is not constant where the demand curve is downward sloping AR is not equal to MR. This is discussed further in Chapter 15.

Appendix 2

The firms' profit maximising output can also be determined by the use of **total concepts**. Figure 14.7 illustrates **total cost (TC)** and **total revenue (TR)**. The profit maximising output will be at the point where the difference between TR and TC is the greatest, which coincides with the maximum point on the **total profit curve (TP)**. This profit maximising output is the same as that obtained in the lower section of the diagram by following the MR = MC rule, i.e. OQ. This can be proved by drawing parallel lines at a tangent to TC and TR and these lines will be tangential (touching) TC and TR at the profit maximising output. At this point therefore the rate of change of TR and TC are equal, i.e.

$$\frac{dTR}{dQ} = \frac{dTC}{dQ}$$

and as $\frac{dTR}{dQ}$ = MR and $\frac{dTC}{dQ}$ = MC

then at that output MR = MC (note this proof is not essential for A level or professional students).

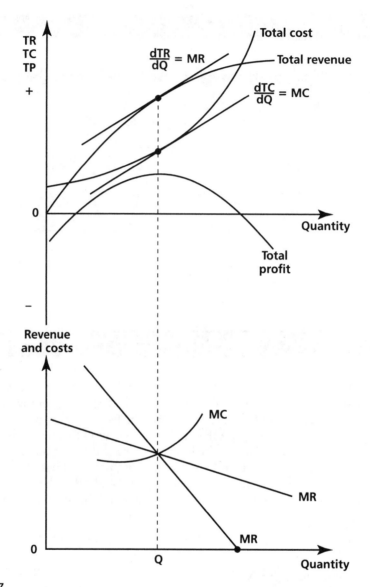

Figure 14.7

Appendix 3

The cost curves actually encountered by firms may not conform exactly to the U-shape predicted by economic theory. In many firms average costs may fall slowly as output increases up to the firm's normal operating capacity, with marginal costs almost constant over the range; as illustrated in Figure 14.8.

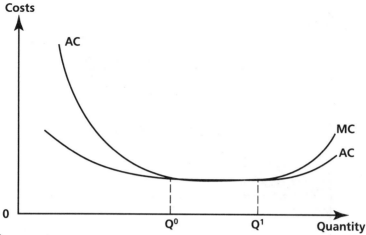

Figure 14.8

The 'normal' operating range is Q^0 to Q^1 and above Q^1 marginal and average costs both rise quite rapidly. Around the normal operating range of Q^0–Q^1, however, costs do not change very much and therefore fluctuations in output around the normal range of output do not have a significant effect upon costs. Also, the whole of the range Q^0–Q^1 can be considered to be the minimum AC, and MC does not cut AC at a single unique point. Cost will, however, be affected by operating at significantly reduced levels of output, or at very high levels of output. In practice, because of the expense involved and the difficulty of obtaining the information, most firms will only bother to estimate their cost curves for a product over a range of output which is relevant to their current level of activity. It is important however to note that the predictions regarding the relationship between average and marginal costs and the fact that they will initially fall and then rise over the total possible range of output are generally valid, although the actual shape of the cost curves may differ between firms.

The model used by cost accountants differs from that used by economists in a number of significant details; the two models can, however, be quite easily reconciled. For practical purposes the cost accountant is only interested in the behaviour of costs and revenue over the range of output which is significant to the firm, i.e. Q^0–Q^1 in Figure 14.8. The cost accounting model assumes that over this range of output variable costs increase proportionately with output, hence the total cost function is a straight line. It is also assumed that the selling price remains constant over this range of output so total revenue rises proportionately with output. Therefore, the total revenue function is also a straight line passing through the origin, as illustrated in Figure 14.9. In the diagram the firm is assumed to 'break-even' at the point where sales revenue is equal to total cost. Profit is the difference between total cost and total revenue, hence above output $\bar{Q}$ the contribution of each unit of output represents additional profit; below $\bar{Q}$ the contribution is insufficient to cover costs and the firm incurs a loss.

If the economic model is expressed in terms of total cost and total revenue functions as in Figure 14.10, the obvious difference from the accounting version is that these functions are not linear. The shape of the total cost function being influenced initially by increasing returns and then diminishing returns. The total revenue curve reflects the fact that total revenue increases more slowly than sales volume.

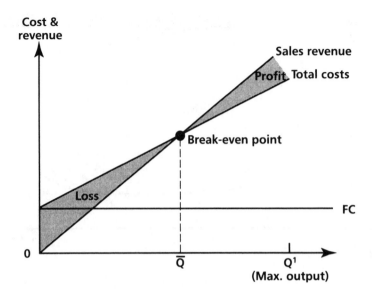

Figure 14.9

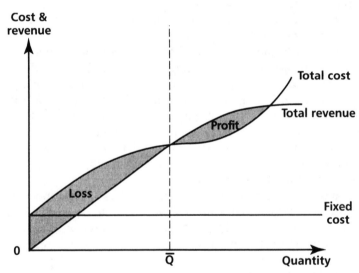

Figure 14.10

The main differences between the two versions can be summarised as follows:

- The cost accounting model assumes a constant marginal product, i.e. increasing and diminishing marginal returns are ignored, hence a linear total cost function is utilised.
- The accounting model assumes that all output can be sold at a constant price.

From the economic point of view both of these assumptions are dubious, however the economist is considering the situation over the whole range of possible output whereas the cost accountant is considering the behaviour of costs and revenue over a fairly narrow range of output which is relevant to the firm. The accountant's version provides a practical and simple approach to the determination of costs and output despite its theoretical shortcomings.

15

Monopoly

1 Monopoly market

Monopoly refers to a market where supply is under the control of a single supplier. In the case of perfect monopoly, this will be a single firm, however the effect will be similar if several firms act together in fixing prices, which is referred to as a **cartel**. In both cases buyer is facing a **single source of supply**.

2 Monopoly demand

As the monopolist is the sole source of supply in a market, the demand curve is also the industry demand curve; the monopolist therefore faces a **downward sloping demand curve**. If the monopolist wants to sell more the price must be reduced.

3 Average and marginal revenue

Figure 15.1 illustrates the downward sloping demand curve of the monopolist. It also illustrates another important difference between the monopolist and the competitive

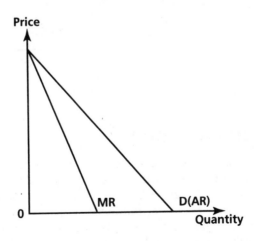

Figure 15.1

firm; the monopolists average revenue (AR) is not the same as marginal revenue (the MR is in fact less than AR.) This is because when the monopolist wants to sell more the price must be reduced, not only on the extra units he sold, but also on all of the earlier units. To illustrate assume that a monopolist is selling 10 units at £1 each, therefore TR = £10. In order to increase his sales to 11 units the price must be reduced to 99p each, and TR = 10.89, i.e. 11 × 99p. The increase in total revenue (TR) from the sale of the extra unit was 89p, despite the price being 99p. This is because of the 1p lost on each of the 10 units sold previously. Mathematically MR has twice the slope of AR (see appendix).

4 Profit maximising output

The monopolist, like any other firm, finds its profit maximising output where MR = MC, at point E in Figure 15.2, giving output O$\bar{\text{Q}}$. Price is however set above the marginal cost of production at M, the appropriate point on the monopolist's demand curve. At output O$\bar{\text{Q}}$ however, the average cost of production is only N, producing a **monopoly profit** (or **monopoly rent**) of PCNM. Unlike the super normal profits earned under perfect competition these monopoly profits will persist into the long run and will not be eliminated by entry to the industry.

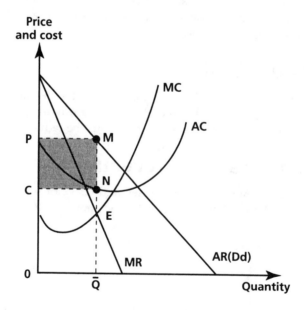

Figure 15.2

5 The case against monopoly

From Figure 15.2 is can also be seen that the monopolist, unlike the competitive firm, is not operating at the lowest point on the AC curve, and could in fact be producing more at a lower cost, but does not choose to do so. Instead the monopolist restricts output and sets price above the marginal cost of production. The monopolist's resources could be used more efficiently elsewhere, hence society's resources are being misallocated. The two arguments against monopoly are therefore:

- They exploit the consumer by setting a price greater than MC.
- They create a loss of efficiency by misallocating societies resources.

It is these two points which frequently lead governments to take action in order to control or curb monopoly power.

6 Taxing monopoly profits

It is sometimes argued that a lump sum tax should be levied upon monopolists equivalent to their monopoly profit which could then be redistributed (i.e. PCNM in Figure 15.2), this would leave their profit maximising equilibrium point E unchanged, and therefore their output. This suggestion however does not overcome the chief objection to monopoly – that of resource misallocation, as monopolist would still not be operating at the most efficient point on the AC curve.

7 Elasticity

Marginal revenue is related to elasticity. Whenever MR is positive demand is elastic, and whenever MR is negative, i.e. below price P in Figure 15.3, demand is inelastic. Monopolists therefore will never produce at a price where demand is inelastic, because the MR is negative and they can increase their total revenue by reducing output.

8 Monopoly power

The monopolist's power will depend upon two factors:

- The availability of substitutes. The greater the absence of substitutes, the greater the power of the monopolist to make profits.
- The ease with which the monopolist can erect **barriers to entry,** to prevent new firms entering the industry (see Chapter 16).

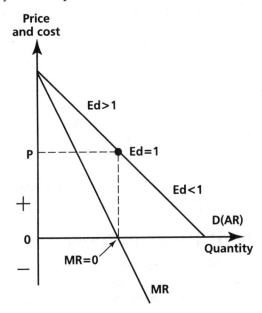

Figure 15.3

9 Limits of monopoly power

The monopolist's power however does not extend to the control of demand. Because the monopolist cannot control demand there are two options:

- Control supply and let demand determine price.
- Set the price and let demand determine the quantity supplied.
- It is not possible, however, to do both.

10 Price discrimination

The monopolist can make greater profits by practising **price discrimination**. Price discrimination refers to the charging of different prices in different markets. Price discrimination will be successful under the following conditions:

There must be no 'leakages' between two markets, i.e. consumers must not be able to travel between markets in order to buy in the cheapest, or buy in one market and re-sell in another, such **arbitrage** would eventually equalise the price in both markets. The **segmentation** of markets may be by either:

- **Time.** Usually used in the case of non-storable services, for example, peak and off-peak rail fares and telephone calls.
- **Geographical dispersion**. Where markets are widely dispersed geographically, price discrimination can be practised as long as the price differential is less than the cost of transport between two markets, e.g. the price differential between Rover cars in the UK and Germany was pushed to the point where it became cheaper for UK buyers to import them from Germany.
- **The status of the consumer** may also provide a basis for price discrimination. For example, the elderly may receive low priced fares on public transport or cheaper seats at the cinema or football matches. Children may be charged less for travel and holidays although they consume the same quantities as adults.

Where the elasticity of demand is different in two markets then charging different prices, a high price in the inelastic market and a lower price in the elastic market, will maximise profits. This can be illustrated by the example of a monopolist selling into two distinctly separate markets, A and B in Figure 15.4. In the absence of price discrimination the price in both markets would be Pe, where MR = MC at E in the combined market (A + B) this price however would be too low in market A and too high in market B. If the markets could be separated and prices set appropriate to their individual MR = MC intersections at M, a price of Pa would be set in market A where demand is **inelastic** and Pb in market B where demand is **elastic**. Because a high price is set in the market where demand is inelastic and a low price in that where demand is elastic, total revenue is maximised in both markets. Only a firm in a monopoly situation however, could exploit such a situation.

Price discrimination does not only occur under monopoly however, but may also occur under other forms of imperfect competition.

11 An argument for monopoly

The classical case against monopoly rests upon the assumption that they misallocate society's resources. The analysis so however, has been conducted in static terms, which assumes other factors, such as costs, remain unchanged when an industry is monopolised.

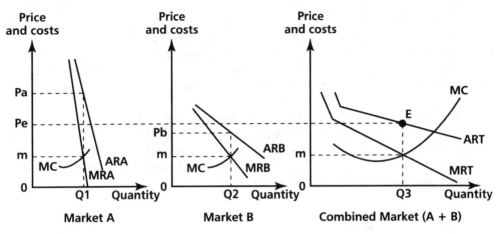

Figure 15.4

This may not however be the case and monopolisation may generate dynamic changes which produce benefits to society which outweigh the allocative costs.

12 Monopolisation

Figure 15.5 illustrates the monopolisation of a perfectly competitive industry. Original competitive market demand and supply curves give equilibrium at E at the bottom of each firm's AC curve, with output Qc. After monopolisation of the industry the industry

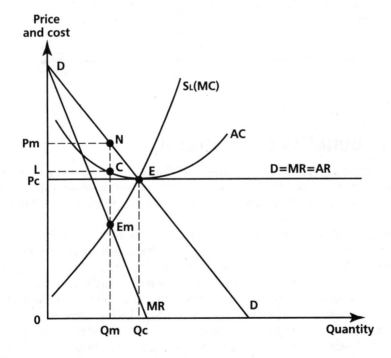

Figure 15.5

demand curve becomes the monopolising firm's demand curve with MR lying below it. Equilibrium of MR = MC is now at Em with output Qm, with price Pm and monopoly profit PmLCN. Output is lower and price higher after the industry has been monopolised. This analysis however assumes that the cost structures remain unchanged, whereas in reality they may well change. The concentration of the production of many small competitive firms may produce such substantial economies of scale that costs will fall as a result.

In Figure 15.6 the competitive industry output is Q with price P. Monopolisation could be expected to reduce output to Q_1 and raise price to P_1. If however monopolisation results in substantial economies of scale which shift costs down from MC to MCm, then the monopolist's output will be higher at Q_2 with the price lower than the competitive price at P_2 despite the existence of monopoly profits.

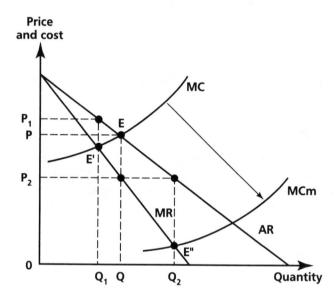

Figure 15.6

13 The benefits of monopoly

Whether monopoly is 'good' or 'bad' must also depend to some extent upon how monopolists actually behave and what they do with the monopoly profits. It is quite possible that the monopolist shares the profits with the workforce in the form of higher than average wage rates and working conditions.

Monopoly profits may also be reinvested within the firm in the form of research and development. An example of this is the drug industry where substantial profits are made, but at the same time the level of research and development into new drugs is high, and most new drugs are in fact introduced by firms with a high degree of market power. Monopoly also avoids the duplication of research and development effort making more efficient use of resources and more rapid technological advancement.

Some authorities such as Joseph Schumpeter and J.P. Galbraith suggest that technical innovation is closely linked to market form and that monopoly is most likely to create the atmosphere which is conducive to innovation. Only monopoly provides the stability in the market which will encourage firms to undertake innovation which is both risky and costly. Only firms making monopoly profits have the resources to undertake extensive research and development, and this will only be undertaken if firms can be certain of achieving a high rate of return on their investment which would by no means be certain in a competitive environment. Monopoly provides the stability and the returns necessary for such expenditures to be undertaken.

Joseph Schumpeter refers to the process of 'creative destruction' in which monopolies make innovations only to eventually have their profits destroyed by competitive activity as the monopolist's profits attract others to try to obtain some for themselves. The classical example of this being the ball point pen which was introduced by the Reynolds Company in 1946, who held a monopoly position at that time. The original price was $12.50 and cost 80c to make; however by 1948 competition had entered the industry and the price fell to 39c and cost 10c to produce, with very little profit left in their production. Patents will not prevent this process as they will be by-passed by the development of similar but slightly different products. Schumpeter estimated that losses due to resource misallocation amounted to no more than 2–3% of national income which was more than outweighed by the increased economic growth generated by innovation.

14 Some conclusions

It is therefore by no means certain that in all cases monopoly is harmful, and even accepting the harmful effects upon resource allocation these allocative costs may be outweighed by benefits of the types described above, a possibility which is reflected in UK legislative controls over monopoly and mergers (see Chapter 19).

Self assessment questions

1 Why is the monopolist's MR less than AR?

2 What are the two main arguments against monopoly?

3 State the conditions which make price discrimination possible.

4 Outline the arguments in favour of monopoly.

5 What factors will determine the market power of a monopolist?

6 What is meant by the process of 'creative destruction'

Appendix

Proof that for the monopolist the marginal revenue curve (MR) has twice the slope of the average revenue curve (AR). Recalling that **AR = Dd = P**. The equation for a downward sloping demand curve, or AR curve is:

(1) $P = a - bq$

where
   a = a constant
   b = the gradient of the curve
   q = quantity demanded.

Total revenue (TR), which is $P \times q$, is obtained therefore by multiplying (1) through by q.

(2) $TR = aq - bq^2$

Marginal revenue refers to a small change in total revenue, so by differentiating total revenue with respect to quantity we obtain marginal revenue.

$$MR = \frac{dTR}{dq} = a - 2bq$$

therefore MR has twice the slope of AR (the coefficient for the gradient is 2b rather than b).

16

Oligopoly

1 A definition

Oligopoly refers to markets which are **dominated by a few sellers** The entire output of the industry is produced by a few large firms and the contribution of each firm is sufficiently large to be significant in the market. Oligopoly is the prevalent market form in many areas of manufacturing in Europe and the UK. The tendency towards oligopoly is a result of the attempts by firms to gain economies of scale by amalgamation and merger. In the UK oligopoly is the characteristic market form in the detergents, car, chemicals and oil industries.

2 Interdependence

Oligopoly is not only distinguished from other market forms by the number of firms but also by a qualitative difference. When the number of competitors in the market are few, each seller becomes acutely aware of how his rivals are likely to react to any change he may make, particularly on price. Oligopoly is the only market form therefore where the firm's pricing and output decisions will also incorporate the perceived, or expected, reactions of competitors. Firms are therefore to a certain extent interdependent, the policies of one influencing the other.

3 Price rigidity

This interdependence helps us to understand one of the major characteristics of oligopoly markets – that of **price rigidity.** The prices charged by monopolists tend to be similar even if there is no collusion (i.e. price fixing). It is necessary therefore to analyse the nature of oligopolistic markets and attempt to identify why it is that the prices charged by the different firms tend to be similar even in the absence of a formal agreement.

4 'Kinked demand curve'

One explanation for this is the **'kinked demand curve'**. This solution suggests that firms in oligopoly potentially face two demand curves, one for price increases which is highly **elastic** and one for price reductions which is highly **inelastic.** In Figure 16.1 for price increases the firm is on the elastic curve dd and for reductions it is on the inelastic curve DD, and the firm's actual demand curve is dED; the demand curve has a 'kink' at E with price $\bar{P}$ and quantity $\bar{Q}$ all the firms in the industry being in a similar position. This is because if one firm raises its price and its competitor fails to follow suit then a large proportion of sales and therefore revenue will be lost, it is therefore on the elastic position of the curve dE. If one firm attempts to reduce price by itself its competitors have no alternative but to follow suit, and reduce price by at least as much and possibly more in order to retain their market share. Price is now lower but with the same market share, hence the firm is on the inelastic portion of the curve ED. Price reductions may even start a price war which may be disastrous for one firm, a possibility all will want to avoid; making any reduction below P unlikely. The actual demand curve is therefore dED with prices tending to be inflexible, or rigid, around the 'kink' in the curve at E. This is one explanation of why prices tend to be inflexible in oligopolistic markets, and once firms find themselves in this situation it becomes easier to enter more formal agreements on price fixing.

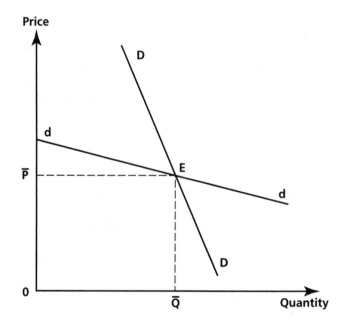

Figure 16.1

Such collusion reduces still further the risk of a price war, and in addition to price fixing may involve production quotas or other methods of reducing competition. These methods are however subject to legal controls (See Chapter 19)

In such oligopoly situations a **price leader** may emerge. The price leader is accepted informally by all those within the industry as the firm which gives the lead in price increases. When the price leader raises the price the others take it as the signal to raise their own prices to the same level.

5 Cost differences

Even where substantial cost differences exist between two firms this may not be reflected in market prices. The 'kink' in the demand curve at E in Figure 16.2 produces a vertical section or 'discontinuity' in the marginal revenue curve of both firms, indicated by the letters G-F. Irrespective of where the firms' cost curves intersect this vertical section of the marginal revenue curve price and output will remain unchanged. In Figure 16.2 there is a low cost producer with cost curves AC' and MC' and a high cost producer with cost curves AC and MC, despite the cost differences the price for both remains P with output Q. The weakness of this analysis is that it explains **how** the kink in the demand curve occurs but cannot predict **where** it will occur and may therefore be considered as an 'ex post' rationalisation.

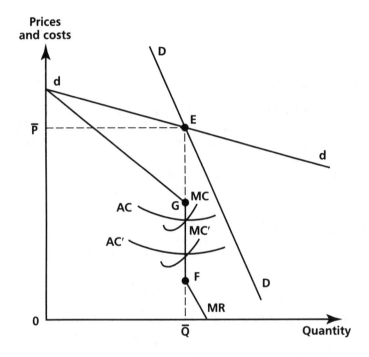

Figure 16.2

6 Non-price competition

Although firms in markets which are oligopolistic may not compete on price such markets may have the appearance of being highly competitive due to the prevalence of **non-price competition**. This non-price competition will occur because although the firms may not wish to compete on price they will still desire to increase their market share and hence their profitability. Firms will not compete on price but competition takes a variety of alternative forms.

7 Methods of non-price competition

Non-price competition may involve some, or all of the following methods:

There is usually a high level of competitive advertising. Advertising is used to emphasise minor real, or spurious, differences between products, a process referred to as **product differentiation**; and also in the attempt to establish brand loyalty.

- 'Free' gifts.
- Competitions.
- Coupons which can be collected and exchanged for gifts.
- Special offers.
- Guarantees and warranties.
- Sponsorship.
- After sales service.

An important point is that the consumer may prefer a lower price but is not given that alternative.

8 Barriers to entry

Monopoly power, whether pure monopoly or oligopoly, will depend in the long run upon how effectively potential entrants to the industry can be kept out. Measures to keep new entrants out of an industry are referred to as **barriers to entry.** The most commonly found barriers to entry are as follows:

Extensive advertising by existing firms in order to create brand loyalty and the high level of product differentiation in the form of branded goods makes entry by new firms difficult. Initially they would at least have to match the advertising expenditure of the existing firms but on the basis of a much smaller market share.

The **minimum efficient scale (MES)** production may be high relative to the market share of the new entrant. A high MES may be due to the technical economies of scale, where for example production on a small scale is possible only at a very high cost, which on the basis of the small market share which a new entrant would have would be impossible to sustain Where the MES is low, advertising may be used as a way of increasing costs, making entry more difficult. Also where existing firms may have substantial economies of scale of the type mentioned earlier, the new entrant with a small market share will be at a considerable cost disadvantage. In addition, existing firms adopt a pricing strategy which makes entry even more difficult. In Figure 16.3 the profit maximising price for existing firms is Pe, however this is above the minimum price for a new entrant enabling them to cover their average costs and charge price Pn. Instead the existing firm may settle for a lower monopoly profit and set price at PL, below the entry price for a new entrant.

- Existing firms may have a high degree of control over the channels of distribution and may deny new entrants the means of marketing their products.
- Legal barriers may exist such as patents which hamper the entry of new firms.
- High levels of expenditure on research and development may act as a further barrier to the entry of new firms.

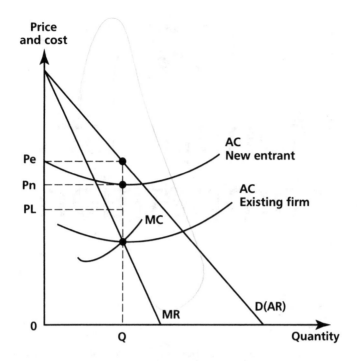

Figure 16.3

Self assessment questions

1 What is meant by oligopoly?
2 Explain the observed price rigidity in oligopolistic markets.
3 What is meant by non-price competition? Give examples.
4 Explain what is meant by barriers to entry.
5 What is the minimum efficient scale of an industry?

17

Monopolistic competition

1 The market

Monopolistic competition is a form of imperfect competition and such markets are characterised by the prevalence of **branded goods.**

The market consists of:

- **A product group**, e.g. cigarettes, and within each product group there are:
- **Brands**, e.g. Benson & Hedges, Players, Peter Stuyvesant etc.

Each producer sells a product which is slightly different from their competitors' products and will attempt to emphasise these differences, which may be real or artificial. Where no real differences exist the producer will attempt to create them by appropriate packaging and advertising. This process of creating differences is referred to as product differentiation, and its objective is to create **brand loyalty.**

2 Monopoly power

The essential point to note is that each firm has a monopoly over its own brand because nobody else can produce it, however all the brands in the product group are in competition. The more the producer can convince consumers that their brand is different to their competitors, the stronger their market position will be.

3 Short run profits

In the short run monopoly profits will be made and the short run equilibrium position will be the same as under monopoly. This is illustrated in Figure 17.1 where the short-run equilibrium is at E with output OQ and price P, making monopoly profit POMN.

4 Barriers to entry

If the barriers to entry to the industry are weak the monopoly profits will attract new entrants into the market with similar brands. This will result in a fall in the market share of each firm. In Figure 17.2 the firm's original demand curve is DD, but as new brands enter the market it is shifted to the left to D'D'

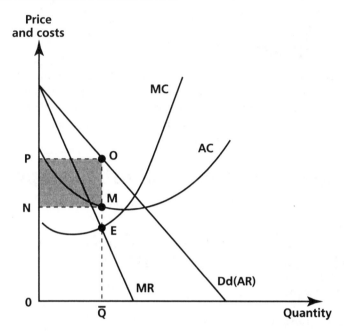

Figure 17.1

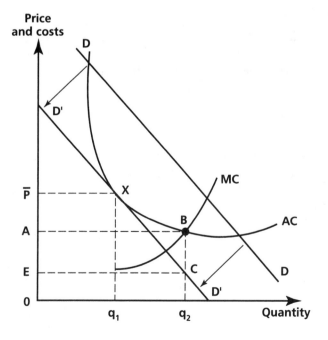

Figure 17.2

Entry to the industry will continue until all monopoly profits have been eliminated and only normal profit is being made. In Figure 17.2 this is at point X where the demand curve D′D′ is tangential to the AC curve, with costs just being covered, with price $\bar{P}$ and output q_1. Losses will occur at any other output as AC will be greater than AR, for example if output is increased to q_2 a loss indicated by the area ABCE will occur, the same will be the case if output is reduced. There is therefore a long run tendency for monopoly profits to be eliminated.

5 Excess capacity

A further important characteristic which should be noted from Figure 17.2 is that the firm is not operating at the lowest point of its AC curve, it has the capacity to produce more, but cannot do so; and q_1–q_2 represents the spare capacity of the firm. As each firm is in the same situation, one of the most important long run characteristics of monopolistically competitive industries is **excess capacity.**

6 Characteristics of monopolistic competition

The characteristics of monopolistic competition are therefore:

- A wide variety of brands.
- High level of advertising and other forms of non-price competition.
- A long run tendency, in the absence of strong barriers to entry, for super normal profits to be pushed down to zero.
- Excess capacity in the industry.

Self assessment questions

1 What is a product group?

2 Explain what is meant by product differentiation.

3 Explain how monopoly profits are eliminated under conditions of monopolistic competition.

4 Why do monopolistically competitive industries suffer from excess capacity?

18

Alternative theories of the firm

1 Profit motive

The theories of the firm discussed so far are all based on the assumption that firms will always be motivated purely by the desire to maximise their short-run profits. In many firms today however, there is a clear division between the ownership and control of the organisation. Ownership is spread amongst shareholders whilst control over day to day decision making is in the hands of paid managers, and although some of the senior management, such as directors, may also have a minority shareholding, the majority of shares are held by individuals who have little or no contact with the firm on a regular basis and may only wish to exert influence through their votes at the annual general meeting of shareholders – if they are sufficiently interested to bother voting.

2 Alternative motives

The division between ownership and control of the organisation allows for the possibility that **managers may pursue some alternative objective than profit maximisation.** The alternative theories of the firm fall into two categories:

- Those which assume that managers attempt to **maximise some objective other than profits**, referred to as managerial theories of the firm.
- Those which allow for the possibility that **managers do not attempt to maximise any variable** but are motivated by some **alternative objective**, referred to as **behavioural theories** of the firm.

3 Baumol model

Baumol[1] proposed a model of the firm based upon the principle that the primary objective of the managers of a firm is to maximise sales revenue. Managers may seek to maximise sales revenue for a variety of reasons but mainly because the status and salaries of managers are generally linked to the growth of sales, as their performance is frequently judged by the growth of sales rather than profitability. In this model the need to make profits is still recognised but they act as a constraint on managerial behaviour rather than as an objective. It is recognised that there is a minimum level of profit which is necessary to meet the expectations of shareholders hence sales can be maximised subject to the constraint of earning the minimum level of profit. Sales maximisation does not refer to the maximisation of sales volume but the maximisation of sales revenue.

4 Sales maximisation

The Sales Maximisation model is illustrated in Figure 18.1 In the diagram profit is maximised at output Q^1 where the difference between total cost and total revenue is greatest, coinciding with the profit maximising rule of MC = MR (see Chapter 14, Appendix 2). The line Pc represents the firm's profit constraint which is the minimum level of profit necessary to satisfy shareholders. The sales maximising firm will therefore increase output beyond Q^2 up to the point where rising costs reduce profits to the level of the profit constraint which is output Q^2 in the diagram. The model therefore predicts that the **output of the sales maximising firm will be greater than that assumed under the profit maximising rule**. The only way in which the two outputs could coincide would be if the profit constraint was set at the point of profit maximisation.

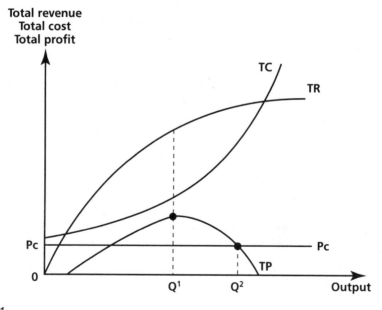

Figure 18.1

5 Objectives and the advertising budget

The Baumol model also suggests a **relationship between the firm's advertising budget and its choice of objectives**. This relationship is illustrated in Figure 18.2. In the diagram the shape of the total revenue curve assumes that the physical volume of sales can always be increased by advertising but eventually diminishing returns set in. It is also assumed that total revenue will vary in exactly the same way so any increase in physical sales volume resulting from increased advertising expenditure must always be accompanied by a proportionate increase in total revenue. The firm's other costs are assumed to be a function of advertising outlay and are added to advertising costs to obtain the total cost curve CC. The total profits curve TP is derived by subtracting total cost from sales revenue at each level of advertising expenditure. The line Pc is the profit constraint as described earlier.

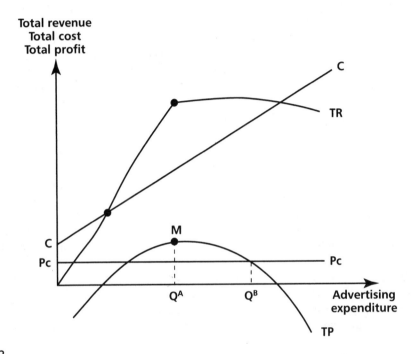

Figure 18.2

The advertising budget for the profit maximising firm is Q^A where total profit is maximised at M; however the constrained sales maximising firm will increase the advertising budget to the point where total profit just meets the profit constraint (Pc), i.e. advertising budget Q^B. The constrained sales revenue maximising firm will therefore advertise more than the profit maximising firm, because advertising will increase the sales volume and hence sales revenue, and advertising expenditure will increase to the point where the firm comes into conflict with the profit constraint.

6 Williamson model

O. Williamson[2] developed a **managerial utility model of the firm** based upon **managerial discretion** within large corporations. The model is based upon the assumption that shareholders do not exert direct control over the management of the firm and that the firm is not operating in a highly competitive market. Given these assumptions **managers pursue their own goals, subject to their being able to maintain control of the firm**. The goals of the firm therefore reflect the goals of the individual managers. The goals of the firm's managers are expressed in a managerial utility function which consists of three broad groups of expenditure:

- **Managerial salaries.**
- **Discretionary investment spending** on, for example, lavish offices and furniture.
- **Expenditures on the number of staff** reporting to a particular manager.

The greater the profits of the firm the more managers have the ability to undertake these forms of expenditure; hence **profits are important in the model.** However, the ability to undertake such expenditure also depends upon the ability of management to divert profits from shareholders. This is not a problem, however, as shareholders do not involve themselves in the management of the firm, and consist of a fragmented group which can be kept largely in ignorance of the detailed finances of the firm by the senior managements; which implies that **managers will enjoy a considerable degree of freedom regarding expenditures which enables them to maximise their own goals.**

7 Marris model

Marris[3] developed a model which emphasised **corporate growth as the main objective.** The model, as the others discussed so far in this chapter, assumes a separation between management and ownership (shareholders) and a sales market with a low level of competitive activity. It is also assumed in this model that **managers relate their salaries and status to the size of the firm;** any growth in the size of the firm therefore enhances their salaries and status within the firm. They therefore see the **growth of the firm as one of their major objectives.** On the other hand they fear takeovers by other firms as this may result in a loss of status and scope for salary increases. Takeover attempts are deemed to result from a depressed share valuation below the market valuation as judged by the firm considering the takeover. The main source of growth, through internal growth and diversification, depends upon a high level of retained profits for re-investment, however this creates a dilemma because a high level of retention implies a low level of dividend payments to shareholders which reduces the market valuation of the company. The management is therefore faced with a 'trade-off' situation between the dividend policy and retained profits and must seek the optimal balance between the two. The valuation ratio of a company is expressed as:

$$\text{Valuation ratio} = \frac{\text{Share price valuation}}{\text{Accounting valuation (book value)}}$$

and when the valuation ratio falls too low the firm becomes liable to takeover attempts. **The objective of the management can therefore be said to be to maintain the minimum valuation ratio consistent with deterring takeover attempts in order to maximise growth whilst retaining security.** Shareholders would prefer the maximisation of the valuation ratio through a higher dividend policy, management however will prefer a higher growth rate.

8 Managerial theories

The models discussed so far are generally referred to as **managerial theories** of the firm. These models stress the maximisation of some managerial objective although usually it is subject to some constraint. To the extent that they attempt to maximise an objective they have this feature in common with the profit maximising models. Another set of theories of the firm referred to as **behavioural theories**, which are based on the work of **H.A. Simon**[4] recognise that management faced with the complexity of the data and its imperfect nature recognise the impossibility of making the optimal decisions required for maximising behaviour and instead attempt to 'satisfice'. This means that a firm's management will attempt to set itself **minimal standards of achievement intended only to ensure the firm's survival and a level of profit which is acceptable to shareholders.** Satisficing behaviour is not necessarily static as it involves a learning process. If a firm easily achieves its given objective it will review its aspiration levels in the following period upwards; failure may result in the stabilisation or lowering of aspirations in the following period.

9 Cyert and March model

Cyert and March[5] built upon the work of Simon and developed a model in which the firm was viewed as a **coalition of different interest groups**, which includes managers, shareholders, employees, the government, and creditors. These interest groups form a **loose coalition** but each group within the coalition will have **differing goals which may conflict;** these goals will receive attention in sequence as the particular group finds itself in a position to promote its interests according to how important it is perceived to be in the coalition at a particular time. **The conflict between different interest groups is resolved by a process of continuous bargaining.** Where groups fail to have their goals satisfied they are compensated by **'side payments'** which may be in the form of higher salaries, a higher status in the management structure, or more of the trappings of status such as a larger office or more office furniture etc. Shareholders are seen as a passive group who are easily satisfied, whilst the 'active' management group requires more than just side payments, and this group has most influence on the organisation's objectives. Management does not attempt to maximise profits, or any other variable, but **attempts to achieve an acceptable level of performance for a number of operational goals.** These goals reflect the objectives of different groups in the coalition and frequently conflict. The conflict between groups is resolved by the bargaining process described above. The organisational goals can be briefly summarised as follows:

- **A production goal** – production should be relatively stable and should keep the plant fully employed.
- **An inventory goal** – stocks should be maintained at a level which avoids 'stockouts' but without tying up excessive amounts of working capital.
- **A sales goal** – in terms of both revenue and market share, should be increased.
- **A profit goal** – should be sufficient to finance investment for growth, dividends, and internal budgets.

The goals which are actually pursued will be a **compromise reflecting the way in which conflicts are resolved within the particular organisation.** Provided that goals are satisfactorily achieved within one period then the same goals may be pursued in the following period. This satisficing behaviour gives rise to the possibility of **organisational slack.** Organisational slack refers to the situation where the firm has **more resources available than are necessary to meet current goals**. This serves several functions, firstly more resources are available for making side payments in order to resolve unsettled conflict within the organisation, and secondly during unfavourable market conditions the firm can reduce the level of organisational slack in order to maintain satisfactory performance levels. **The presence of organisational slack enables the firm to remain stable and therefore viable.**

10 Some conclusions

Observation in the real world suggests that businessmen frequently have little knowledge of their marginal costs and are not therefore in a position to make the optimal price and output decisions necessary for profit maximising theories. The managerial and behavioural theories attempt to overcome these weaknesses by making a different set of assumptions about the ways in which firms actually behave, and the prediction of these models are frequently consistent with the actual behaviour observed within large companies.

Self assessment questions

1 Explain what is meant by satisficing behaviour.

2 Discuss the effect of sales maximisation with a profit constraint on the output of the firm.

3 Discuss growth as a corporate objective.

4 What are the means by which goals are established in the Cyert and March model?

References

1 Baumol, W.J., *Business Behaviour, Value and Growth*, Macmillan, New York, 1959.

2 Williamson, O.E., *The Economics of Discretionary Behaviour: Managerial Objectives in a Theory of the Firm* Prentice-Hall, 1964.

3 Marris, R., *The Economic Theory of Managerial Capitalism*, Freepress, Glencoe, ILL, 1964.

4 Simon, H.A., *Theories of Decision Making in Economics*, American Economic Review, Vol. XLIX June 1959.

5 Cyert, R.M. and March, J.G., *A Behavioural Theory of the Firm*, Prentice-Hall. 1963.

19

Competition policy

1 Efficiency and exploitation

Control over monopoly and restrictive practices is considered to be necessary in order to promote economic efficiency and to protect the consumer against exploitation. The economic arguments against monopoly are stated in Chapter 15, we will consider here UK legislative measures to promote competition and prevent the worst excesses of monopoly.

2 Aims of legislation

UK legislation relating to competition is directed towards:

- Dominant firm monopoly.
- Mergers which may create a monopoly position.
- Restrictive practices and resale price maintenance.

3 The UK approach

If there was a definite relationship between market structure conduct, and performance, as implied by economic theory then the solution would be to enact legislation to ban monopolies; or mergers which may result in a monopoly position. In reality however the evidence against monopolies is less clear, and in some areas gains in efficiency may outweigh the allocative costs (see Chapter 15). This has been reflected in the attitude contained within UK legislation towards monopoly and merger which is non-committal. There is no automatic assumption in law that monopoly is illegal per se (in itself) but rather is liable to case by case investigation, recognising that in some cases there may be benefits but at the same time attempting to control the abuses.

4 UK legislation

Relevant legislation, in chronological order, is as follows:

- 1948 Monopolies and Restrictive Practices Act.
- 1956 Restrictive Practices Act (Amended 1976/77)

- 1964 Resale Price Maintenance Act
- 1965 Monopolies and Mergers Act
- 1980 Competition Act

5 UK legislation in detail

The main details of the relevant legislation can be summarised as follows:

Monopolies and Restrictive Practices Act 1948. Established the Monopolies Commission to investigate cases of monopoly referred to it. Its major role was to investigate and find facts relating to cases referred to it by the Department of Trade and Industry (then Board of Trade). It was essentially powerless and could only report and not take controlling action. Monopoly was defined as control of one third of the market share.

Restrictive Trade Practices Act 1956. This act established the **Restrictive Practices Court** and a **Registrar of Restrictive Practices** to investigate agreements between firms. Such agreements covered prices and conditions of sale or supply. Restrictive practice agreements had to be registered with the Registrar and were considered to be illegal except where they could be justified through one or more of eight 'gateways' which indicated that they may be beneficial to the 'public interest'. Examples of these 'gateways' included: the agreement was protecting the public against injury, was maintaining employment or exports, made available other benefits or counteracted restrictive measures taken by another person. In a White Paper in 1989 the government proposed to strengthen this legislation by making price-fixing cartels illegal. Unfortunately a lack of Parliamentary time meant that this did not become legislation. A Green Paper in 1992, 'Abuses of Market Power' looked at the failure of existing policies to effect anti-competitive practices. This also failed to become legislation:

Resale Prices Act 1964. The practice of enforcing a retail price by a manufacturer on to a retailer was deemed to be illegal. The 1964 Act abolished the practice either collectively or individually, since the 1956 Act had still allowed the practice to continue on an individual basis. The Act allowed resale price maintenance to continue where the Restrictive Practices Court could be convinced that it would be in the 'public interest' and that abolition would cause the public to suffer in one or more of five ways, for example there would be a substantial reduction in the number of retail outlets, there would be a reduction in the quality or variety of goods available for sale or that there would be a danger to health as a consequence. Only certain drugs, books, and maps were initially exempt. Although recently the Net Book Agreement has been abolished and the Drug Agreement has been challenged.

Monopolies and Mergers Act 1965. The Act laid down that any proposed merger could be referred to the Monopolies Commission if it would result in one third of the market being controlled by a single firm or where the assets acquired exceeded £5 million (later raised to £15m).

Fair Trading Act 1973. Created the post of Director General of Fair Trading (DGFT) under whom competition and consumer law was codified and centralised. Legislation was extended to cover services such as insurance and estate agents, and the DGFT could enforce the prohibition of any practice adversely affecting consumers.

Monopolies and Mergers Act 1973. Amended the 1965 Act. The DGFT assumed responsibility for the operation of monopoly policy, and was empowered to refer monopolies to the re-named **Monopolies and Mergers Commission**. The Commission determined whether the case in question is, or is likely to be, detrimental to the public interest and to make recommendations as appropriate. Responsibility for the implementation of corrective action lies with the appropriate minister and may be by voluntary undertaking or by a binding statutory order. Monopoly was redefined as control of 25% of the market.

Competition Act 1980. The overall objective of the 1980 Act was to stimulate competition by controlling anti-competitive practices, and the legislation was extended to include the nationalised industries. The Director General was empowered to refer price issues and other specific activities to the Monopolies and Mergers Commission for investigation. Where the Commission find a practice is 'against the public interest', the Secretary of State may act to control it.. In 1981 the role of the Commission was expanded to include the efficiency of the nationalised industries. Investigations took place in 1994 into the cost of mortgage valuations and the price of compact discs and music cassettes.

6 Market concentration ratio

Monopoly legislation does not appear to have prevented the strong tendency towards market concentration in the UK. Market concentration can be expressed by means of a **market concentration ratio**. A five firm concentration ratio (CR^5) refers to the market share of the largest five firms, a two firm (CR^2) to the largest two firms, and so on, and is calculated as:

$$\text{Market concentration ratio } (CR^5) = \frac{\text{Sales of the largest 5 firms}}{\text{Total market sales}}$$

The average CR^5 rose from 55.4% in 1958 to 63.4% in 1968, and 65.1% in 1975, but declined to 42.4% in 1987, according to product group. The data also suggests a much higher level of concentration in the UK than in many comparable countries in Europe, and the USA.

7 Commission reports

The Monopolies Commission has reported on monopoly situations on a diverse range of products which has included detergents, brickmaking, brewing, breakfast cereals and solicitors services. Since 1994 criticism has been raised regarding the lack of firm remedial action by the government following publication of the Commission's reports, which have been thought to be rather timid.

Many of the reports of the Commission have criticised the restrictive practices followed by firms. For example it was critical of the practice of Roche products in charging excessively high prices to the National Health Service for the drugs Librium and Valium whilst other customers were paying much lower prices. It was also critical of Sega and Nintendo for controlling the market for video game software in 1995.

8 Restrictive agreements

Policy directed towards restrictive agreement appear to have had some degree of success. Of the 4,468 agreements which had been registered by the end of 1980, 3,295 had been disbanded and of these only 39 were as a result of a judgement by the Restrictive Practices Court, the vast majority being voluntarily disbanded. This is because a judgement applies to the whole product group and once the defence for a restrictive practice is over-ruled there is little point in anyone else proceeding. It is probable therefore that many more restrictive practices would be currently in existence in the absence of the measures taken.

9 Mergers

The control of mergers is intended to prevent monopoly situations from developing. During the 1970s there was a steady increase in the number of mergers falling within the criteria laid down by the Fair Trading Act as eligible for investigation. Since the '1965 leg-islation' more than 1500 mergers have been screened however of these only 53 were referred to the Monopolies and Mergers Commission, which could be taken as evidence that the official policy is not unfavourable towards mergers. Of the mergers investigated only 18 were prohibited as being against the public interest, and 18 were allowed to pro-ceed provided certain assurances were given, the other 17 being abandoned. Whilst the trend in the 1970s and 1980s was for mergers to create even larger business units, able to compete in the Single European Market and the global markets, the fashion in the 1990s has been for demergers. This trend has been emphasised by the success and greater share values of demerged companies such as Racal/Vodafone (formerly Racal), ICI/Zeneca (formerly ICI) and BAT/Argos/Arjo (formerly BAT Industries).

10 Office of Fair Trading

The Office of Fair Trading can only investigate those arrangements where firm evidence exists and in such cases can be said to have had a fairly high degree of success. However, many formal arrangements have probably been replaced by informal arrangements or 'gentlemen's agreements', for example trade associations circulating price lists and tacit agreements not to compete on price. Cases actually dealt with by the Restrictive Practices Court may not accurately reflect the actual extent to which such practices exist.

11 The effectiveness of legislation

The apparent ineffectiveness of monopolies and mergers legislation in the UK may reflect the flexible, or pragmatic, nature of the underlying philosophy. In particular the criteria for the investigation of mergers is quite restrictive (£ 15 million assets or 25% market share) and may not cover many mergers which do have adverse effects on competition and performance. In order to make the legislation more effective it has been suggested that an assumption should be made that certain categories of merger should be assumed to be illegal with the onus on the proposers of the merger to prove that the effects would be beneficial, others would be cat-egorised as beneficial and allowed to proceed. A further suggestion has been that a system of fines, as is the practice in the USA should be introduced for abuses of monopoly power and that the legal system should contain a stronger presumption against monopoly.

12 Some conclusions

Competition policy in the UK can therefore be considered as relatively mild, reflecting a flexible attitude towards monopoly with no automatic assumption against any particular monopoly or merger, each case being treated on its merits. Legislation has therefore prob-ably done little other than to remove the worst and most visible restrictive practices and abuses of monopoly power.

Dissatisfaction with existing restrictive practices legislation has resulted in the publi-cation of a White Paper (Opening Markets: New Policy on Restrictive Trade Practices, July 1989, Cm 727) which contained new proposals for the control of restrictive practices to be introduced during 1990. The new proposals represented a fundamental change of emphasis from the previous rules. Agreements and practices with anti-competitive effects were to be prohibited outright instead of being made subject to a requirement to register. The system of registering agreements was to be scrapped and instead time and resources were to be concentrated on dealing with agreements which did raise competi-tion problems. Also UK law was to be made compatible with European Community law and the legislation was to be extended to include the professional bodies which were pre-viously excluded. Under the proposed legislation the DGFT was to investigate cases arising and publish conclusions on them. Under the proposals a new Restrictive Trade Practices tribunal was to be established to reach decisions when those of the DGFT were disputed, to impose penalties on firms where warranted, and to consult with the DGFT when recommending exemptions.

Unfortunately these proposals never became legislation.

Self assessment questions

1 Why is it considered necessary to have legislation for the control of monopolies and mergers?

2 Explain what is meant by the term 'restrictive practices'.

3 What is the attitude towards monopolies and mergers which is reflected in UK legislation?

4 What is meant by a five firm concentration ratio?

5 How effective do you consider competition policy in the UK to have been?

Section E

Containing the following chapters:

The interaction of those elements that determine the rewards received by the factors of production

This section should enable students to:

- *Understand* the population structure of the UK.
- *Explain* how wage rates are determined.
- *Contrast* the way in which the rewards to the factors of production are allocated.
- *Evaluate* the effect that trade unions have on the wage rate.

Keywords to consider:

marginal productivity theory; marginal revenue product; derived demand; collective bargaining; differentials; rent of ability; quasi-rent; transfer earnings; economic rent; working population; dependency ratio; per capita income; ageing population; birth rate; death rate; optimum population; diminishing returns; marginal efficiency of capital; savings; normal profit; net profit; super normal profit.

20
Wages

1 Rewards to labour

Wages are the payments received in return for labour services and as such are the returns received by **labour** as a factor of production.

2 Wage rates

It is necessary however to explain why it is that the **wage rates** differ between occupations. In order to explain these wage differentials it is necessary to consider both demand and supply in the labour market.

3 Marginal productivity theory of wages

One explanation is the **marginal productivity theory of wages**. The law of declining marginal productivity was explained in Chapter 2. It will be recalled that the marginal product (MP) is the addition to total output or product which occurs when one additional unit of a variable factor is added to a fixed factor. It will be recalled that MP initially rises but then starts to decline as diminishing returns set in. Total product rises but at a declining rate. In this particular case the variable factor is labour and all other factors are fixed. The theory also makes a number of other assumptions:

- Conditions of perfect competition, therefore the firm can obtain all the labour it requires at the prevailing wage rate.
- Labour is an homogeneous factor, i.e. the productivity of each unit of labour is the same.
- Perfect mobility of labour between occupations.
- The entrepreneur's aim is to maximise profits, therefore the main concern will be the difference between the cost of employing labour and the revenue to be gained from the sale of the output of labour.

4 Marginal Revenue Product

Marginal revenue product (MRP) refers to the addition to total revenue received from the sale of the additional unit of output, and is calculated as the marginal physical product (MPP), e.g. tonnes of potatoes etc., multiplied by price, i.e. $MPP \times P = MRP$.

As under conditions of perfect competition price is constant the MPP curve will be identical in shape to the MRP curve. Under conditions of imperfect competition the MRP curve is obtained by multiplying the MPP by marginal revenue, i.e. MPP × MR = MRP. Note that as P = MR under perfect competition, then as a general rule MPP × MR = MRP in both perfect and imperfect competition.

5 MRP and ARP curves

In Figure 20.1 the MRP curve can be seen to rise and then fall cutting the average revenue product (ARP) curve at its highest point. The ARP curve represents the average return, in monetary terms, per unit of labour employed. As a result of the competitive assumption the supply of labour will be perfectly elastic at the prevailing wage rate, W^0, which is determined by the **market**. Recalling the assumption of profit maximisation it is evident that the entrepreneur will want to employ labour as long as the MRP is greater than the wage rate (cost of labour) in Figure 20.1 he will continue to employ additional labour up to $O\bar{Q}$ his will add more to revenue than to costs. Above $O\bar{Q}$ additional labour will cost more than its MRP and will not therefore be employed. The profit maximising entrepreneur will therefore employ $O\bar{Q}$ labour. If we consider the wage rate the marginal cost of labour we can see that the conclusion is another form of the MR = MC rule encountered under the theory of the firm, point E being the equilibrium point.

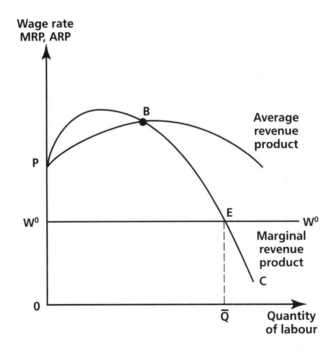

Figure 20.1

6 The demand for labour

The relevant section of the MRP curve is however B–C only. This is because no firm would employ labour when the wage rate is greater than the ARP as the profit maximising entrepreneur would never pay more to all workers than the highest ARP, as losses would result. The section of the MRP curve below ARP, i.e. B–C can be considered as the competitive firm's **demand curve for labour.**

MRP theory is therefore a theory of how the **demand** for labour is determined, but as the supply of labour is excluded it cannot be considered as a theory of how wages are determined as it says nothing about the determination of wage rates.

7 MRP theory

MRP theory however can be useful as a tool for analysing the effects on the demand for labour of the changes in the relevant variables. In Figure 20.2 an increase in the wage rate from W^0 to W^1 will result in a reduction in the quantity of labour employed from Q^0 to Q'. If however the MRP curve can be shifted upwards and outwards from MRP' to MRP'' then the quantity of labour can remain unchanged at Q^0.

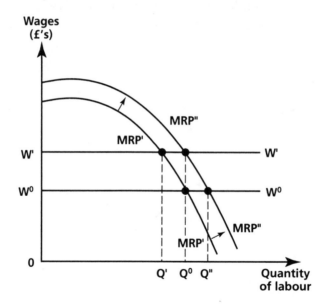

Figure 20.2

Alternatively if the shift in the MRP curve takes place with the wage rate remaining constant at W^0 the amount of labour employed would increase to Q'' or the existing work force Q^0 could enjoy the higher wage rate. Shifts in the MRP curve from MRP' to MRP'' can be brought about by:

- An increase in productivity brought about by the abandonment of a previously held restrictive practice.
- The adoption of new technology which makes labour more productive.
- An increase in the price of the product – which may be difficult given the competitive assumption.

8 Labour demand characteristics

The demand for labour has four characteristics which affect the extent to which the labour force can affect the wage rate.

- The demand for labour is a **derived demand**, i.e. The demand for labour is derived from the product it produces, the greater the demand for the product the greater the demand for labour.
- The elasticity of demand for labour is derived from the elasticity of demand for the product; the greater the elasticity of demand for the product the greater the elasticity of demand for the labour producing it.
- The proportion of total cost accounted for by labour – the lower this is the more scope labour will have to gain increases in wages.
- The extent to which capital can be substituted for labour in the production process, the easier this is the weaker will be the position of labour.

9 The labour market

The wage rate in a particular occupation is determined by the interaction of demand and supply in that particular labour market. The labour market is not a single homogeneous market but consists of thousands of different markets each with its own particular supply curve. The elasticity of the labour supply curve will depend upon factors such as the amount of training and skill required and the duration of the training period required. The supply curve may be more inelastic due to restrictions upon entry to an occupation, where for example, trade unions insist upon lengthy apprenticeships. Figure 20.3 represents the supply curve for a relatively unskilled occupation where an increase in the wage rate from W' to W" leads to a more than proportionate increase in the supply of labour from Q' to Q".

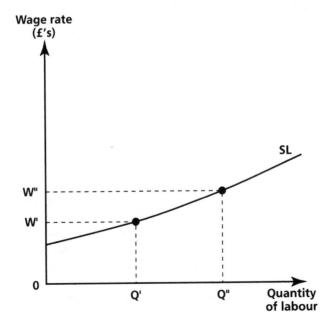

Figure 20.3

The same magnitude of increase in the skilled occupation, represented in Figure 20.4, has a far less significant effect upon the supply of labour, Q' to Q" due to the training period required to acquire the necessary skills, or restrictions placed upon entry.

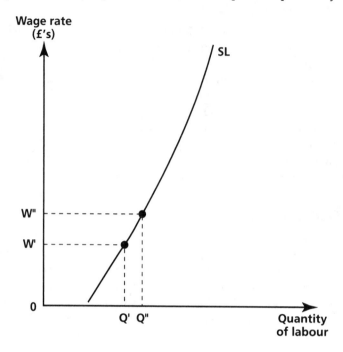

Figure 20.4

10 Wage theory omissions

Other points for consideration which wage theory does not incorporate, but may affect wages, include:

- Legislation such as the Sex Discrimination and Equal Pay Acts 1975.
- Incomes policies, under which governments have attempted to control the rate of wage increase according to some predetermined 'norm' .
- Government management of the economy and the effects of inflationary/deflationary measures, and tax policy.

11 The bargaining theory of wages

The bargaining theory of wages views wages as being the outcome of negotiations between two powerful monopoly groups, on the one hand the trade unions who monopolise the supply of labour, and on the other the employers' organisations who monopolise the demand. The relative bargaining strengths of the two parties will vary between different time periods according to changes in the economic climate. For example, during recession the employers will be in the stronger bargaining position and during economic boom when the demand for labour is high, the trade unions will be in a stronger position.

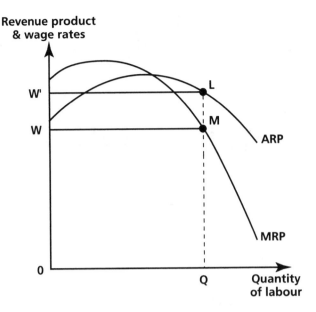

Figure 20.5

Bargaining theory can however be incorporated within marginal productivity theory. In Figure 20.5 the current wage rate is OW, and recalling that the entrepreneur will never pay a wage greater than the ARP of labour, we can see that the highest wage which would be paid is OW' (QL). LM is the surplus earned by the entrepreneur on each worker employed (OQ). A wage increase above OW would normally reduce the quantity of labour employed. If however the workforce is strongly unionised they may be able to resist the reduction in the workforce and persuade the employer to pay the increase out of the surplus L–M. The extent to which L–M will be shared with the workforce depends upon relative bargaining strengths at the time.

12 Some conclusions

Despite the criticisms of marginal productivity theory the principles it contains appear to be inescapable in the long run and it does appear that any wage increases which are considerably above the rate of productivity increase will result in a reduction in the size of the work force. Marginal productivity is therefore probably always present at the bargaining table, whether the parties to the bargain are aware of it or not; but there are so many other factors influencing wages that it is probably not a fully adequate explanation of any particular wage rate.

Self assessment questions

1 Which section of the MRP curve represents the firm's demand curve for labour?
2 How does the competitive firm decide how much labour to employ?
3 State the weaknesses of MRP theory as a theory of wage determination.
4 Outline an alternative theory of wage determination.
5 Discuss the factors other than MRP which may influence wages.
6 How relevant is marginal productivity theory in a modern economy?

21

Trade unions

1 The role of trade unions

The economic theory of wage determination is discussed in Chapter 20, however it is impossible in an industrial society to analyse the factors which determine wages without giving some consideration to the role and influence of **trade unions.**

Although we are mainly concerned here with the affect of trade unions on wages, it is important to be aware of the wider role of trade unions. The Donovan Report (1968) considered the role of trade unions under three main headings:

- Promoting the interests of their members.
- Accelerating the economic advance of the nation.
- Accelerating the social advance of the nation.

2 Collective bargaining

Wage rates and conditions are determined by the process referred to as **collective bargaining,** whereby the union officials bargain with employers on behalf of their members.

Collective bargaining generally occurs at the national level and the pay rates determined apply to a whole industry and are embodied within a national agreement. This agreement may be supplemented by additional payments or benefits negotiated locally at plant level. Nationwide collective bargaining has the advantage for both unions and management of reducing the costs of bargaining below what it would be if employers and employees negotiated individually.

3 Membership

Trade union membership in the UK grew throughout the 20th century, but with the main periods of growth being around the two World Wars, the late 1960s and the 1970s; but with membership declining in the 1980s and 1990s as a consequence of rising unemployment and government legislation. Table 21.1 indicates the pattern of trade union membership in the UK.

TABLE 21.1				
Year	Men	Women (millions)	Total	Total membership as a % of total employees
1951	7.7	1.8	9.5	45
1961	7.9	2.0	9.9	43
1971	8.4	2.8	11.1	49
1981	8.4	3.8	12.1	50
1986	6.8	3.7	10.5	44
1990	5.3	3.5	8.8	38
1991	5.1	3.5	8.6	37
1992	4.6	3.4	8.0	36
1993	4.4	3.4	7.8	35
1994	4.2	3.3	7.5	34
1995	4.1	3.2	7.3	32

4 Raising wage rates

It is often argued that unions can raise their members' wage rates only at the cost of reducing the number employed. Such analysis assumes that the demand for labour is competitive and the demand curve is static. In Figure 21.1, DD is the demand curve for labour and SS the supply curve.

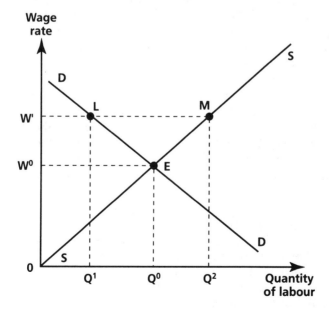

Figure 21.1

The equilibrium wage is W^0 with Q^0 labour employed. If the union now enforces a wage increase to W^1 which is the minimum wage at which union members are allowed to work, the demand for labour falls to Q^1 (L) as a consequence of:

- The higher price being charged for the product being produced, which is necessary to cover the wage rise.
- Factor substitution as capital is substituted for labour in the production process as it is now relatively cheaper.

The supply curve for labour is now W^1 M S with no labour supplied below the minimum wage (W^1) and an infinite amount up to $M(Q^2)$, the labour supply curve is therefore infinitely elastic along the portion W^1 L M, but the labour supply will not increase above $M(Q^2)$ without a higher wage rate. The new supply curve intersects the original demand curve at L, the new equilibrium point, with Q^1 labour demanded, whilst the quantity supplied at that wage rate is Q^2. The quantity of labour employed has been reduced by $Q^0 - Q^1$ and there is an excess labour supply of $Q^1 - Q^2$ (L–M) at the prevailing wage rate. This type of analysis however ignores changes in productivity and Chapter 20 shows how an **increase in the marginal productivity of labour can maintain the numbers employed.** Such increases in marginal productivity can be achieved through the adoption of new technology and more efficient working practices.

5 Trade union influence

The extent to which a union can influence wages in a particular industry also depends upon the elasticity of demand for labour. (This is discussed in Chapter 20).

Generally it is the case that the more inelastic the demand for labour the greater the scope a union will have for gaining a wage increase for its members. In any particular occupation the scope for gaining wage increases will also be influenced by supply factors, the more inelastic the supply the greater the scope for maintaining, or obtaining, high wage rates. Unions therefore have an incentive to restrict the supply of labour to any particular occupation by imposing entry conditions such as lengthy apprenticeships. Where there are few restrictions upon entry to an occupation, i.e. unskilled occupations, the union may need to substitute the threat of withdrawal of labour as a means of influencing wages.

The extent to which unions can raise the wage rates of their members may also depend upon a number of other factors such as the attitudes of the membership, the degree of geographical concentration, the stability of employment, and the degree of competition amongst employers. Studies, in the late 1980s, indicate that the hourly pay rate in an industry where the labour force was unionised and covered by a collective bargaining agreement was 8–10% higher than in a similar non-unionised industry. However in the 1990s the reduction in the power of the unions has in return reduced this differential.

6 Pay differentials

Trade unions, and relative demand elasticities are important factors in explaining the pay differentials which exist between occupations, a particularly important source of higher earnings being the length of training and level of education required. Adam Smith referred to **equalizing** and **non-equalizing** differentials and suggested that in a competitive labour market the **net advantages** of an occupation would **tend to equality**.

Equalising advantages were factors such as unpleasantness, dirt and discomfort, non-equalising differentials were wages. In an unpleasant occupation there would be higher wages to compensate and in pleasant occupations wages would be lower, and over a lifetime the net advantages between occupations will be equalised. In reality it is frequently the lowest paid occupations which are also the most unpleasant, as they are generally unskilled, entry to them is easy, and those in such occupations have no alternative available to them.

7 Factors creating wage differentials

Wages may also differ between people in the same occupations. One reason may be differentials as a reward for experience or length of service, or where pay scales are structured according to age. A major source of wage differentials is sex, as women even within the same occupation are frequently paid less than men. Women also tend to be concentrated into the occupations with the lowest rates of pay, such as catering and hairdressing. The combination of these factors means that on average women earn considerably less than men, and studies suggest that women's earnings are approximately 75% of men's despite the Equal Pay Act 1975. The main reasons suggested for this apparent discrimination against women are:

- Their weaker attachment to the labour force due to the convention that they look after children, and the need to be absent from work when having children.
- Absenteeism and labour turnover is higher for women than it is for men.
- As a consequence of the weaker attachment to the labour force women gain less experience and seniority in the work-place, and employers are less willing therefore to give training to women, which reduces their value in the workforce.
- Women tend to be concentrated in industries which consist of numerous small-scale establishments in which national wage rates tend to be lower than in the larger more concentrated industries. These also tend to be industries in which a lower proportion of the workforce belongs to trade unions due to the high costs of organising.
- Even within the same occupational group, women tend to earn less than men, for example, within primary school teaching women earn approximately 12% less than men, although the main source of this differential is not that women are paid less for the same job but that fewer of them occupy the higher paid teaching positions, due probably to the reasons given above.

If it is also considered that females work predominately part-time, (40% of total females in work compared to 5% for males) then the disparity in wages becomes even more pronounced. The anomaly of low pay for women has been only marginally influenced by Equal Pay legislation, despite the fact that this legislation together with the Sex Discrimination Act (1975) and the Employment Protection Act (1976) are now over 20 years old. If however, for the reasons given above, it is not discrimination but a reflection of a lower marginal revenue product which results in lower female wages then it may also be necessary to raise the marginal productivity of women by giving them more incentive to remain in the workforce; for example, better career prospects, training and a more appropriate educational structure.

8 Trade union reforms

The 1980s saw the largest programme of trade union reform ever. The motives were partly political but also to reduce the influence of the unions on the labour market (see Chapter 20). Many of these reforms were consolidated in the 1992 Act of Parliament and further measures were taken in the 1993 Act. The reforms have included the following measures;

- Trade unions must conduct a secret postal ballot before they can approve industrial action
- it is illegal to enforce closed shops
- picketing must be peaceful and is limited to the employees place of work
- union subscriptions can only be deducted from an employees wage after permission has been given. This process must be repeated every three years
- the abolition of the Wages Council
- Union officials must be elected every 5 years

The result of these measures, and others not listed, has been a weakening of the unions bargaining position and, some believe, a reason for the reduction of their membership. Figure 21.2 illustrates the decline in trade union membership between 1979 and 1995.

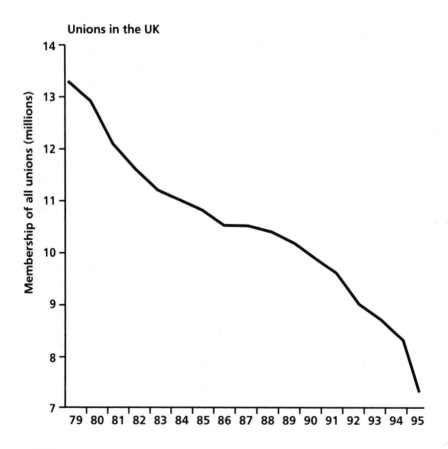

Figure 21.2

Self assessment questions

1 What is meant by 'collective bargaining'?

2 Under what circumstances can a trade union simultaneously raise wages and maintain employment?

3 Explain the differences in wage rates both between occupations and between males and females.

4 What is meant by equalising and non-equalising differentials?

5 Account for the decline in trade union membership in the 1980s and 1990s.

22

Rent

1 A definition

Rent in everyday terms refers to a regular payment made in return for the use of an asset, in economics however the term has a far more specific meaning. In economics rent refers to the **payment to a factor of production which is in fixed supply.**

2 Economic rent

The concept of economic rent was originally applied to land only. **David Ricardo** was one of the earliest economists to discuss the theory. Ricardo noted that as the supply of land was fixed, with no way of increasing or decreasing it, supply could not respond to changes in demand. If this was the case, what then determined the price of the land? The 'supply price' refers to the minimum payment which is necessary to keep a factor of production in its current use, and as the supply of land cannot be varied, it has no supply price. Any payment to a factor of production which is above the supply price is a surplus, and is referred to as **economic rent. Rent therefore is any surplus above the supply price.** As land is perfectly inelastic in supply, and therefore has no supply price, the whole of the return to the landlord for land is economic rent, i.e.

economic rent = current earnings – supply price

During the Napoleonic Wars grain prices rose to very high levels and many people blamed this on the high price, and therefore rents, of agricultural land. Ricardo however pointed out the flaw in this explanation. As the supply of land was fixed and therefore could not vary with demand, the price of land could not determine grain prices. The only demand for land is in fact a **derived demand**, derived from the demand for grain. If the demand for grain is high the price is high, which enables the landlord to charge a higher rent for grain growing land. Should the demand for grain fall however, the landlord would be forced to take whatever rent could be obtained as the land would still be there even if the return was zero. In reality of course land has alternative uses and at some point it may be more profitable to transfer it to some alternative use such as potatoes.

3 Pure economic rent

Figure 22.1 illustrates the concept of pure economic rent. The supply of the factor of production is fixed at $O\bar{Q}$ with demand DD and price P^0, the shaded area $OP^0E\bar{Q}$ economic rent. An increase in the demand for the factor to D'D' increases the rent by $P^0P^1E^1E$. As the supply has remained unchanged at $O\bar{Q}$ all of the additional factor income is rent.

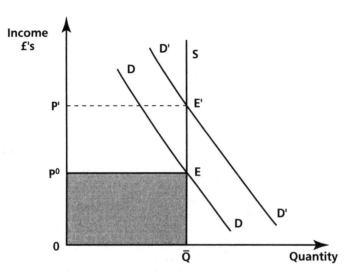

Figure 22.1

4 Rent of ability

Figure 22.1 could be used to illustrate the supply of individuals with unique talents, for example, certain entertainers, footballers and other sportsmen, great actors or skilful entrepreneurs. Such talents earn what is referred to as **rent of ability.**

5 Quasi-rent

When a factor is in temporarily fixed supply, for example a class of skilled labour, and economic rents will be earned in the short-run only, in this case until more people can be trained; then the rent is referred to as **quasi-rent.**

6 Transfer earnings

Although the amount of land, or any other factor, may be fixed, in reality it is unlikely to be specific to a single use only and may be transferred to alternative uses. For example, agricultural land may be used as building land, or transferred to alternative agricultural uses. The minimum payment which is necessary to retain a factor of production in its current use and prevent it from transferring to its next best alternative is known as its **transfer earnings**. Transfer earnings can be considered as the opportunity cost of keeping a factor in its current use. Where a factor has alternative uses **any payment made over** the factor's transfer earnings is economic rent. For example, a footballer earning £2,500 per week who has also trained as a plumber, and could earn £ 250 per week at plumbing. If his earnings as a footballer began to fall he would transfer to plumbing when his wages as a footballer fell below £250.

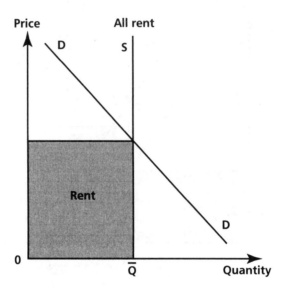

Figure 22.2

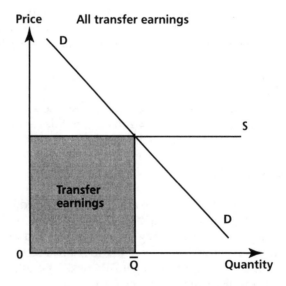

Figure 22.3

7 The importance of elasticity

Wherever a factor of production has an upward sloping supply curve, part of its earnings will be rent and part transfer earnings. The proportions of rent and transfer earnings depend upon the elasticity of supply of the factor. The less elastic is the supply the greater the proportion of economic rent, the greater the elasticity of supply the greater are the transfer earnings. In the extreme case of zero elasticity of supply, all the return is rent and where elasticity of supply is infinity it is all transfer earnings. The extreme case of all rent is illustrated in Figure 22.2, and all transfer earnings in Figure 22.3. In Figure 22.4 the factor earnings are equally divided between rent and transfer earnings.

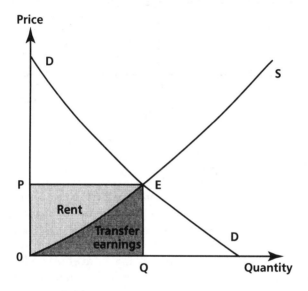

Figure 22.4

8 Alternative uses

City centre land sites are extremely expensive, which is a consequence of the highly inelastic supply. The supply of such sites is extremely restricted and each site has many competing uses. Demand is continually rising but the supply of sites for cinemas, restaurants, car parks, offices and shops cannot be increased. The high price of such sites results from the increasing demand and inelastic supply, however as the sites have many alternative uses the element of rent in the price for any particular use will be quite small, the greatest element being transfer earnings. The earnings in any particular use will have to be at least sufficient to prevent it from transferring to the next best alternative, for example, the high price of cinema tickets in city centres reflects the need for cinemas to earn sufficient returns to prevent them from being transferred to use as restaurants or offices. In Figure 22.5 demand curve DD represents the demand for an urban site for use as a restaurant, for which the price would be P^0 and D'D' the demand for the same site as a cinema, for which the market price which people are willing to pay is P^1. Only the shaded area $P^0P^1E^1E$, the surplus over the next best alternative use, is economic rent.

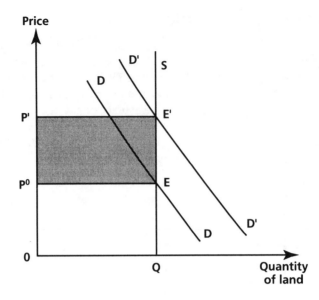

Figure 22.5

9 Economic rent a tax

It has been suggested in the past that the economic rents earned on land should be the basis for taxation. This suggestion is generally associated with Henry George, who advocated the use of such a tax in the USA during the 19th century. The land tax was to be the single source of taxation and was justified on the grounds that as the supply of land is fixed, the returns to the owner may rise without any extra effort on his behalf. It was this 'unearned increment' upon which the tax was to be levied, and as the supply of land was fixed the tax could not be avoided (i.e. the 'tax base' could not be eroded). The proposal to tax the economic rent on land has two main difficulties:

● How to distinguish between rent and transfer earnings.
● The problem of identifying the element of rent, recalling that the amount of commercial rent paid to the landlord is not the same as economic rent.

Similar arguments to those used in favour of the land tax have been used in support of the arguments to tax the rent element in the earnings of individuals with unique talents such as musicians, entertainers and footballers.

10 Essential points

The essential points to bear in mind are:

● **rents do not determine prices, it is prices which determine rents.**
● **rent is a surplus which becomes greater as the price of the product from which the demand for the factor is derived increases.**

Self assessment questions

1 Distinguish between economic rent and rent in its everyday context.
2 Outline the factors which determine economic rent.
3 Distinguish between rent and transfer earnings.
4 What is meant by quasi-rent?
5 Why are house prices in city centres higher than elsewhere?

23

Population

1 Introduction

Population refers to the number of people living in a particular area. In the study of population however, it is not only the absolute number of people which is of interest, but also the rate of change of the population size and also its composition. The study of population is important because of its economic implications, in particular the way in which change in the population can affect changes in the demand for goods and services, and therefore the allocation of society's resources.

2 Population growth

The total population of the UK, and the rest of the world, was characterised by a rapid growth throughout the 19th century and this growth has continued in the rest of the world throughout the 20th century, although in the UK since 1971 the total has remained fairly level with only slow growth projected to the end of the century. Table 23.1 shows the population growth for the UK. The size of the UK population is found from a census which has been held every 10 years since 1801.

3 Population composition

Although it is important to know the size of the total population it is also important to have details of the composition of the population, in particular an estimate is required of the following.

- **Working population** – the proportion of the population in the working age group 16 –65 (60 for females).
- **Age/sex structure** – Age structure refers to the number of persons in each of three groupings. (i) Young persons – below 16. (ii) Working age groups, 16–65. (iii) Men and women over 65.

Age/sex distribution refers to the number of males and females in each age grouping.

TABLE 23.1 UK population (millions)	
1851	22.3
1901	38.2
1921	44.0
1931	46.0
1951	50.2
1961	52.7
1971	55.5
1981	56.3
1991	57.6
1995	58.9
2001	(forecast) 59.8
2011	(forecast) 61.4

4 Standard of living

Both total population and the population structure have important implications for the nation's standard of living. Income per head or **per capita income** for a nation is calculated as:

$$\text{per capita income} = \frac{\text{national income}}{\text{population}}$$

From this equation it can be seen that even if national income is growing per capita income may fall if the rate of growth of national income is exceeded by the rate of growth of population, and it is this problem which faces many 'third world' countries.

5 Changes in the composition

Changes in the composition of the population alters the balance between producers and consumers over time. As stated above the age group 16–65 form the working population whilst those in the 0–16 and 65+ groups can be regarded as the dependent population.. An increase in the size of the dependent population relative to the working population, referred to as the dependency ratio, means that living standards would fall unless there is an increase in the real output of the working population as a result of increased productivity, for example; by the adoption of new technology. Changes in the composition of the population also affects the demand for age related goods and services, and for this reason has important implications for firms, local authorities and central government. An increase in the proportion of people in the 65+ age group, referred to as an ageing population, increases the demand for social provision for the aged, appropriate medical provision, and increases the burden of pensions on the working population. Although the UK population remained fairly level between 1971 and 1991 the proportion aged less than 16 fell and the proportion over 65 increased. Population projections up to 2011 show a rise in the numbers over 65 with the most significant increase in those over 85. Within the older age group females predominate as their life expectancy exceeds that of males. In 1994 women outnumbered men in the age group of 65 upwards, and in the 80 or over age group the ratio of women to men was over 2 to 1. Both females and males today however have a 50% chance of achieving a life expectancy of 70 years. This increase in life expectancy has been the result of the improvement in living standards, medical advances, and the extension of welfare services for the older age groups.

6 Population pyramids

The age/sex distribution of the population can be illustrated by the use of population pyramids as shown in Figure 23.1

The population pyramid illustrates the age/sex distribution of the population, the dotted lines showing the affect of an ageing population on the shape of the population pyramid.

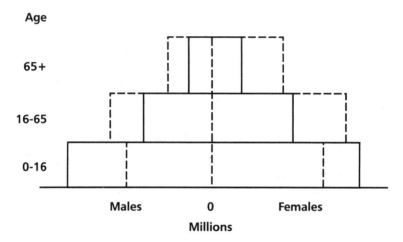

Figure 23.1

7 Birth and death rates

Births and deaths are usually expressed as crude birth and death rates. These are calculated as the number of births/deaths per 1000 population.

$$\frac{\text{number of births} \times 1000}{\text{total population}}$$

The crude birth rate is influenced by factors such as the state of medical knowledge, social and economic factors, social mores such as the attitudes towards family size, contraception, and religion.

The crude death rate is influenced by social and economic conditions, medical knowledge, hygiene and living standards, and the infant mortality rate (ie. the deaths of children below 1 year of age).

8 Life expectancy

The improvement in the average life expectancy in the UK to 70 years has been the result of the advances in medical care and the extension of welfare services for the elderly and in addition the affect of the general rise in living standards. The most significant fall in the death rate has resulted from lower infant mortality which has been a consequence of improved medical facilities, improvements in diet and housing, and the improvements in ante and post natal care.

9 Changes in population size

The overall size of the population is determined by the natural increase, ie. births minus deaths. In the UK during the 20th century the change in the birth rate is seen as being the major influence on population size as the death rate has remained fairly constant. The birth rate, despite its falling trend, is more liable to sudden variations. Unexpected increases in the birth rate, or 'baby booms', create population bulges such as those which occurred after the two World Wars and in the mid-1960s. Such bulges then pass through the population structure over time, creating an increased demand for age related goods and services which may not be required in such quantities when the bulge in the population has passed. For example, the 'baby booms' of the mid-1960s increased the demand for schools, but as the bulge passed into the older age group the demand for schooling fell resulting in falling school rolls and surplus school capacity. In the 21st century there will be an increase in the demand for pensions as the population bulge moves into the pensionable age group.

The major changes in population are of three types:

- **birth rate exceeding death rate** resulting in an **increasing population**.
- **death rate exceeding birth rate** resulting in a **decreasing population**.
- **exceptional increases** in the birth rate resulting in a **population bulge**.

Net migration which is calculated as **immigration minus emigration** has not seriously affected the UK population over the long term. Net migration is more likely to affect the quality of the working population, particularly if the most talented, healthiest, or skilled members of the workforce choose to emigrate.

10 Optimum population

The concept of the optimum population is central to the study of the economics of population. Optimum population can be defined as the population size which maximises the output (per head) of the economy. The concept of optimum population assumes that technology, trade and competition remains constant and only the population size varies. Given these assumptions, then as the population size increases output will initially increase, but eventually diminishing returns set in and as population grows further output per head declines. This is illustrated in Figure 23.2. Output per head is maximised at X with population OM.

Increases in population above OM cause output per head to fall and M–R can therefore be referred to as over-populated, with population OR giving a lower per capital income (OC) than population OM. Population ON fails to exploit the returns to scale and therefore also has a lower per capita income than OM; also having per capita income OC. ON can therefore be referred to as being under-populated.

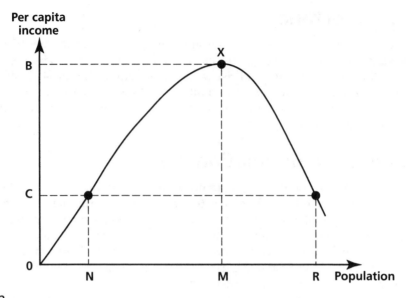

Figure 23.2

If the assumption that technology is fixed is dropped however, it may be possible for increased productivity through technological change to offset the effect of diminishing returns and the optimum population may coincide with the actual population as population grows. In Figure 23.3 as population grows from OM to OT technological change increases productivity per head offsetting the effect of diminishing returns shifting the most efficient, or optimum, point from X to S; the optimum population being the same as the actual population OT.

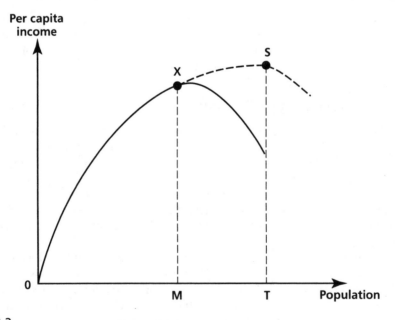

Figure 23.3

As population growth takes place, there could be a succession of points such as X and S each giving a higher per capita income and therefore standard of living.

11 Rev. Thomas Malthus – Essay on population

One of the earliest discussions of population size was that by the Rev. Thomas Malthus in his essay 'The Principle of Population as it affects the future improvement of Society' (1798), which was refined in a second essay in 1803. Malthus examined the relationship between population size and the means of subsistence; in particular the production of food. Malthus postulated that any increase in living standards would result in an increase in population size, however food production could not increase at the same rate as population growth. Population growth would therefore always exceed the growth of the means of subsistence and mankind was doomed to remain in poverty living at the subsistence level. According to Malthus the population was kept within its means of subsistence by the 'misery' of famine, war, disease, and pestilence. The only escape for civilisation from this vicious circle of poverty was through what Malthus referred to as 'moral restraint' by which he meant later marriage and therefore fewer children—a solution Malthus himself thought was unlikely.

Malthus' gloomy predictions proved to be incorrect—the population during the 19th century grew rapidly and so too did living standards. The weaknesses in Malthus' argument were as follows:

- The Malthusian argument is essentially one of diminishing returns with land as a fixed factor. In fact land was not a fixed factor as new food growing areas were developed overseas and food was imported, eg. wheat from the American prairies.
- Malthus did not foresee the rate of technological change which enabled living standards to rise alongside population growth.
- Improvements in methods of birth control and their general acceptance within society, and changed social attitudes towards family size.
- Malthus considered people only as consumers but generally each consumer is also a producer, therefore a larger population creates a greater output.

12 Neo – Malthusianism

The Malthusian doctrine can therefore be considered as a special case of the law of diminishing returns, the affects of which were offset in Britain by changes in other factors as listed above. The lessons of Malthus cannot however be totally ignored as it will always be necessary to relate finite resources to the demands of society and in many 'third world' countries where populations are growing more rapidly than the means of subsistence the principles advocated by Malthus are still relevant today. The application of Malthusian principles to the world situation is sometimes referred to as neo-Malthusianism.

Self assessment questions

1 What are the main causes of changes in the population size?

2 What is meant by the term 'optimum population'?

3 How does a change in the population structure affect the demand for goods and services?

4 What did Malthus predict about the future of mankind and why was he proved wrong?

24

Interest

1 Factor reward

Interest is the factor reward, or earnings, of **capital**. Alternatively it can be considered as the payment for the use of money. This money may be used for the purchase of capital equipment, but may also be used for alternative purposes. This source of finance will only be available if other people are willing to forego consumption and provide a pool of financial resources from which loans can be made. This supply of funds will only be forthcoming if those supplying the funds receive some reward for sacrificing their current consumption and are compensated for the risks involved; in particular the

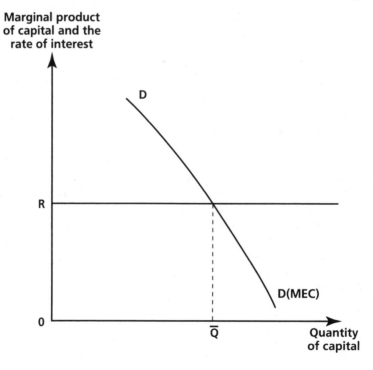

Figure 24.1

possibility of not getting their money back, or the possibility of a reduction in the value of their money due to inflation. Interest can therefore be considered as the price of borrowing money.

2 The demand for capital

The **demand for capital** can be analysed in a manner which is almost identical to the marginal productivity of labour theory of wages.

If the stock of capital is increased relative to other factors of production, diminishing returns will eventually set in as capital, like the other factors of production, is subject to the law of diminishing marginal productivity. The **marginal productivity of capital curve (MP)** in Figure 24.1 represents the firm's demand for capital curve. This is known also as the **marginal efficiency of capital curve (MEC)**. It slopes downwards due to diminishing returns and as the rate of interest is the cost of capital the capital stock will be expanded to just the point at which the cost is equal to the value of the marginal product. The firm will therefore employ O$\bar{\text{Q}}$ capital at interest rate R. Profitability is therefore maximised when: **mp of capital = rate of interest**.

As was the case in the analysis of wages, a change in either the physical productivity of capital or in the price of goods produced will bring about a shift in the MP curve and therefore the demand for capital.

Analysis is in fact more complicated than this as investment decisions are taken on the basis of anticipated returns from the investment over the lifetime of the capital compared with the current outlay. This approach requires the use of discounting to obtain the 'present value' of the investment's yield. This is discussed further in Chapter 42.

3 Classical theory

If the rate of interest is the 'price' of borrowed funds, then if we wish to formulate a theory of how interest rates are determined, we must also consider the supply of funds for lending. The theory that the interest rate is determined by the demand and supply for loanable funds is referred to as the **classical theory** of interest rate determination.

The supply of loanable funds for investment is determined by current savings. The supply curve in Figure 24.2 is society's savings function, the shape of which represents the **time preference** of individuals, i.e. the extent to which present consumption is preferred to future consumption. A rate of interest is necessary to compensate savers for the loss of current purchasing power, and is therefore necessary in order to induce savings. The intersection of the demand and supply curves gives the equilibrium rate of interest. If desired saving is greater than the demand for investment purposes there will be an excess supply of savings which will push down the rate of interest until equilibrium between demand and supply is re-established. If demand exceeds supply the rate of interest will rise until sufficient extra savings are forthcoming to re-establish an equilibrium.

- Classical theory is referred to as a 'flow theory' because it assumes that a continuous flow of savings is possible at the prevailing rate of interest.
- According to classical theory, savings are not assumed to be a function of (dependent upon) the level of income.

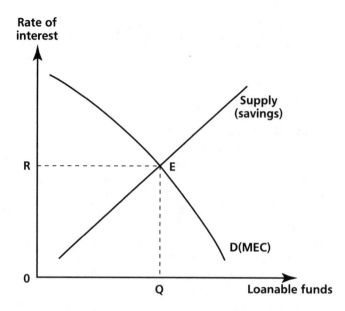

Figure 24.2

(There are other theories of interest rate determination which are discussed further in Chapter 42).

4 Determinants of saving

The major determinants of saving are as follows:

- The level of income. As incomes rise the proportion of income devoted to consumption tends to decline, hence in economies where incomes are high the proportion of saving tends to be higher.
- The extent to which the financial structure of the economy has developed thereby providing a range of institutions where savings can be safely deposited and where they can earn an adequate return with a minimum of risk.
- The extent to which a society views thrift as being a virtue or otherwise. This can vary between different societies, or within the same society over different time periods. In Victorian times thrift was seen as being far more virtuous than it is in the present day.

5 Types of savings

Savings can be of several different types.

- Personal savings consist of the money which households choose not to spend from their personal disposable incomes, which may be with the intention of acquiring some specific item, for example a car, or merely out of habit.
- Corporate savings consist largely of the retained profits of firms.
- Private savings consist of personal savings plus corporate savings.
- Government savings occur when the government gathers more in tax revenue than it spends, and is in a sense 'forced saving'.

- A large proportion of saving is contractual in that it consists of payments to insurance companies for life assurance or payments into pension funds.

It is unlikely that the rate of interest has any more than a marginal effect on any of these saving motives.

6 Savings behaviour

Experience of the 1960s and 1970s suggest that the growth of income is a significant influence upon savings behaviour. In 1969 the savings ratio (the ratio of personal savings to personal disposable income) was 8.1, this rose to 15.4 in 1980, before declining again as the rate of growth of incomes declined. Between 1986 and 1990 the savings ratio was negative, indicating that during this period of growing inflation household expenditure exceeded disposable income. After 1990 the saving ratio returned to a positive figure but during the period 1993 to 1994 it fell from 4.0% to 2.5%

Self assessment questions

1 How is the demand curve for capital derived?
2 What is meant by the 'time preference' of individuals and what is its relationship to the supply of loanable funds?
3 Describe the function of the rate of interest.
4 Outline the 'classical theory' of interest rate determination.
5 Discuss the factors which determine the level of savings.

25

Profits

1 Factor reward

Profit is the reward to the entrepreneur. This factor payment is the return to the entrepreneur for
- Co-ordinating and setting to work the factors of production.
- Taking the risk of losing capital.

2 Risk

Risk is always present in capitalist production as production has to take place in advance of sale and it can never be known with certainty that the goods will actually be sold. Profit is therefore the reward for uncertainty bearing and differs from interest in the degree of risk involved; interest is associated with investments which are virtually risk free.

3 Concepts of profit

At this stage it is useful to recall the different concepts of profit;

- Normal profit (Chapter 14).
- Super normal profit (Chapter 14).
- Monopoly profit (Chapter 15).
- The difference between profits and the other forms of factor income is that it is a **residual** which is paid after the other factors of production have been paid out, and may therefore be **negative**. Also because factor costs and sales cannot be controlled or forecast profit tends to **fluctuate** more than the other factor incomes.

4 Functions of profit

The functions of profit in a free market economy are as follows:

- To ensure a supply of individuals willing to accept the risks of uncertainty.
- Super normal profits indicate to entrepreneurs which industries should expand and which should contract. Therefore super normal profits reflect consumers' preferences

for a good, and encourages the increased output of those goods which are in demand by consumers.

- Profits provide the resources necessary for expansion, both by re-investment in the firm, and by enabling the firm to offer higher rewards to the factors of production and attract them away from declining industries.
- Profits overcome the technical problems of how goods are to be produced by ensuring that production is carried on by only the most efficient firms. In a competitive industry the firms making the largest profits are those with the lowest costs, if other firms are to survive they will be forced to adopt the same methods of production, otherwise their prices will be too high and they will not be able to compete. Eventually they will make losses and go out of business, or leave the industry.

5 Profit measures

For most firms the most practical measure of whether they are making adequate profit is the rate of return on capital. The rate of return on capital is calculated as

$$\textbf{Rate of return on capital} \quad = \quad \frac{\textbf{net profit}}{\textbf{fixed capital}} \times \textbf{100}$$

If this figure is too low then the firm would have to question either its profitability and how it could be improved or in extreme cases whether its capital could be invested more effectively elsewhere. Industrial investment which inevitably carries a degree of risk should for example, be making a better return than the capital would make on deposit with the bank where there is zero risk.

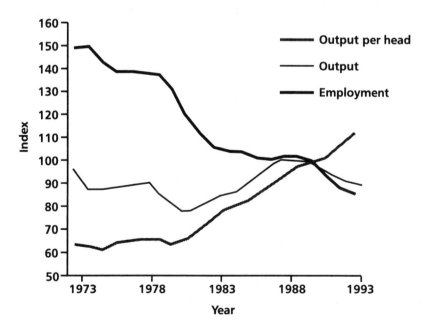

Figure 25.1

6 Profit in industry

The profitability of industry is a useful guide to the economic performance of a nation as this is an indication of how effective resource allocation has been in the past and to the potential of the economy for the future growth. Most countries experienced declining rates of return on capital since the mid 1960s, whilst the rate of return in the UK remained below that of its main competitors over the whole of the period. Following 1982 the UK experienced some recovery in profitability due particularly to the contribution of North Sea oil related industries and to a rise in the productivity of manufacturing industry which reduced costs.

The rise in manufacturing productivity which contributed to this improvement in profitability during the 1980s was greater in the UK than any other major industrialised country.

The recession of the early 1990s lead to decline in manufacturing output but output per head, productivity, continued to increase. The increase in productivity continued despite a fall in employment and a general contraction of demand for manufactured goods worldwide.

Self assessment questions

1 Distinguish between normal profit, super normal profit and monopoly profit.

2 In what sense is profit a residual?

3 What does the entrepreneur do in return for profit?

4 How does profit differ from interest?

5 What are the functions of profit?

6 What is meant by the statement 'profit is a residual of uncertain size'?

Section F

Consumers and the price mechanism

Containing the following chapters:

Chapter 26 – Consumer behaviour

Chapter 27 – The price mechanism

The behaviour of consumers within the market, and the inadequacies of the market system.

This section should enable students to:

- *Understand* how changes in a consumer's income will affect their purchases.
- *Explain* how individuals make choices between conflicting needs.
- *Contrast* the role of the consumer and the government in the market.
- *Evaluate* the effectiveness of the market in all situations.

Keywords to consider:

marginal utility; indifference curves; marginal rate of substitution; consumer preference; budget line; consumer equilibrium; income effect; substitution effect; income consumption curve; inferior good; price consumption curve; consumer sovereignty; welfare equilibrium; consumer surplus; producer surplus; Pareto optimality; allocative efficiency; public goods; merit goods; market failure; social costs; social benefits.

26
Consumer behaviour

1 Consumer satisfaction

Consumers will allocate their incomes between their chosen 'basket of goods' in a manner which maximises the utility (satisfaction) they receive from their expenditures.

Consumers compare the utilities they receive from various quantities of the goods they are considering buying to their prices. They will achieve the maximum satisfaction when the ratio of marginal utility to price between each good is equal, i.e.

$$\frac{\text{Marginal utility good 1}}{\text{Price of good 1}} = \frac{\text{Marginal utility good 2}}{\text{Price of good 2}} = \frac{\text{Marginal utility good 3}}{\text{Price of good 3}} \cdots \cdots \frac{\text{Marginal utility good N}}{\text{Price of good N}}$$

which can be alternatively represented as:

$$\frac{\text{MU good 1}}{\text{P1}} = \frac{\text{MU good 2}}{\text{P2}} = \frac{\text{MU good 3}}{\text{P3}} \cdots \cdots \frac{\text{MUn}}{\text{Pn}}$$

It can be intuitively reasoned that if a consumer could gain more utility by transferring expenditure from one good to another he would do so until the point where no further utility could be gained by re-arranging expenditures. At this point the MU to price ratios have been equalised.

2 Indifference curve analysis

In order to analyse the conditions for the consumer to be in equilibrium when faced with a given income and different relative prices we can utilise **indifference curve** analysis.

Indifference curves represent different combinations of goods available to a consumer, each combination yielding equal satisfaction to the consumer. As each combination of goods yields equal satisfaction the consumer is said to be indifferent regarding which actual combination is choosen. Table 26.1 represents different combinations of two goods A and B which will yield equal utility to the consumer. There would of course be many other possible combinations but here we have shown only four out of all those possible. As each of the combinations yield equal satisfaction the consumer will be indifferent as to which is actually choosen.

TABLE 26.1		
	Good A	**Good B**
1	35	5
2	20	10
3	10	15
4	5	35

These combinations are represented graphically in Figure 26.1. In Figure 26.1 the indifference curve I represents the four combinations of A and B shown in Table 26.1. Each point on the curve would be equally desirable to the consumer who would be indifferent to any combination available along the curve. The shape of the curve is convex when viewed from the origin, reflecting the 'law of substitution'. As one of the goods becomes scarcer as we move along the curve, the greater becomes its relative substitution value, and its marginal utility rises relative to that of the good which has become more plentiful; and the good which is becoming relatively scarcer requires larger quantities of the other good in return. The lines L–M represent the exchange terms at that point on the curve, i.e. 3:1. This is the **marginal rate of substitution** of A for B, which will maintain a constant level of utility along the curve.

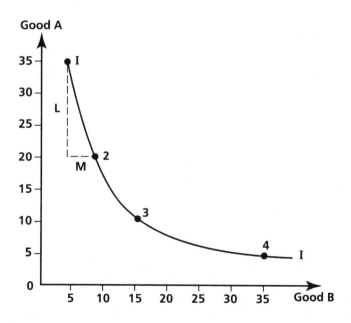

Figure 26.1

3 Indifference map

The indifference curve in Figure 26.1 is however drawn for a single level of income only, and as the consumers move to higher levels of income they will move to higher levels of satisfaction, and therefore a higher indifference curve. Figure 26.2 represents the **indifference map**, each indifference curve being relevant to a different level of income. The consumer will be indifferent between different combinations along any single curve, but as income increases can move to a higher curve. There is an infinite number of these curves, one for each possible level of income.

4 Consumer preferences

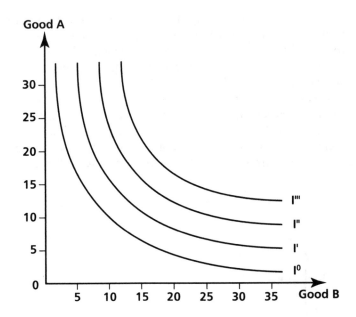

Figure 26.2

The indifference map refers only to **consumers preferences** if we are to establish which bundle of goods will actually be preferred, we need also to consider the relative prices of the two goods, and the consumer's income. If we assume that:

- consumer's income is £40
- the price of good A is £1 each
- the price of good B is £2 each

we can estimate the various quantities of each good which are available to the consumer given the income constraint and the prices of the two goods.

Table 26.2 illustrates some of the possible combinations of A and B. Clearly if 40 of good A are purchased there will be no income left for expenditure on good B, and vice versa if 20 units of B are purchased. Between these two extremes various combinations are available.

TABLE 26.2

Good A	Good B
40	0
30	5
20	10
10	15
0	20

5 The budget line

From the data in section 4 we can derive the consumer's **budget line**. This is illustrated in Figure 26.3 by the line D–F and represents all the possible combinations of the two goods which can be purchased assuming the entire income is spent on the two goods. The slope of line D–F is the ratio of the price of good A to good B. It is important to note at this stage that the budget line represents what is **available to the consumers not their preferences.**

6 Consumer equilibrium

In order to establish which combination will be preferred, or **consumer equilibrium**, it is necessary to combine the consumer's indifference map with the budget line. The £40 budget line from Figure 26.3 is combined with the indifference map from Figure 26.2. The point of consumer's equilibrium is at E in Figure 26.4 with 20 units of good A and 10 units of good B. The consumer is in equilibrium where the highest attainable indifference curve is just tangential to the budget constraint. The consumer cannot move to a higher indifference

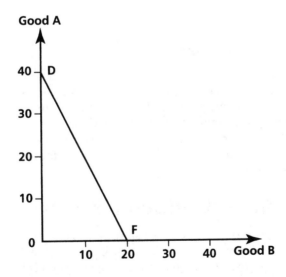

Figure 26.3

curve on current income, and will not move to a lower one as he will not be maximising his utility. At point E the consumer's marginal rate of substitution (MRS) of A for B is exactly equal to the ratio of the price of A to the price of B, from which it is evident that the condition for consumer equilibrium is

$$\text{MRS}_{AB} = \frac{P_A}{P_B}$$

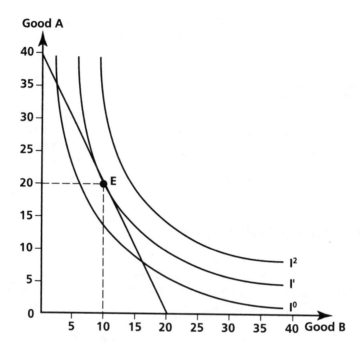

Figure 26.4

7 Changes of income

A reduction in income, or an equal rise in the price of both goods - which amounts to the same thing, will result in a shift of the budget line inwards towards the origin; the shift is parallel because the relative prices of the two goods are unchanged. In Figure 26.5 this is shown by the shift of the budget line D–F to NM.

Assuming both goods are normal goods, there will be a new equilibrium at E' where the new budget line is tangential to the highest attainable indifference curve I', with fewer of both goods purchased.

8 Income and substitution effects

An increase in the price of one good will shift the budget line in towards the origin. In Figure 26.6 the price of good B rises and the budget line shifts from DF to DM, the slope of the line changes because the relative prices of the two goods have changed. This leaves the consumer on the lower indifference curve I' with a new equilibrium at E'. As one good becomes cheaper relative to another, and provided both are normal goods, then more of the good which has become cheaper will be purchased in place of that which has become relatively more expensive. This is referred to as the **substitution effect**, and in the diagram it can be seen that at E′ more of good A is purchased than previously. Any price change also has an effect on **real income**, in this example the price increase reduces real

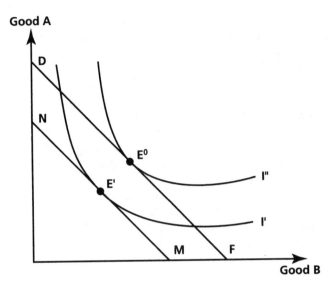

Figure 26.5

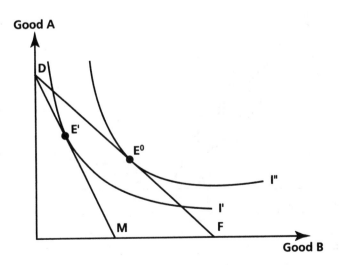

Figure 26.6

income and means that fewer of all goods can be purchased (and vice versa for a price reduction), this is referred to as the **income effect** of a price change. The substitution effect is represented by a movement along the indifference curve whilst the income effect is represented by a shift to another indifference curve. All price changes consist of both an income effect and a substitution effect and for all normal goods the income effect reinforces the substitution effect. However, for those inferior goods referred to as **Giffin goods** (see Chapter 4) a negative income effect may outweigh the substitution effect, in which case an increase in price may result in more of the good being purchased, and for a price reduction less being purchased. This provides a theoretical explanation for the regression in the demand curve for such goods, outlined in Chapter 4.

Figure 26.7 illustrates the method by which the income and substitution effects can be separated. The consumer is originally in equilibrium at E purchasing x of good B. The price of good B now rises and the budget line shifts in towards the origin to DG with the consumer now now in equilibrium at E' consuming x' of good B and more of good A which is now relatively cheaper. If now we keep the relative prices at their new level but alternatively give back to the consumer the amount of income by which the original price increase had reduced real income, we obtain the hypothetical budget line LM, parallel to the DG line because it faces the same relative prices but with the lower real income, we obtain equilibrium at E" with x" of good B consumed. The move from E to E" can only be as a consequence of the substitution effect. The movement from E to E' therefore represents the income effect. In the case of a Giffin good the new equilibrium position E" would lie to the right of E with more of good B consumed.

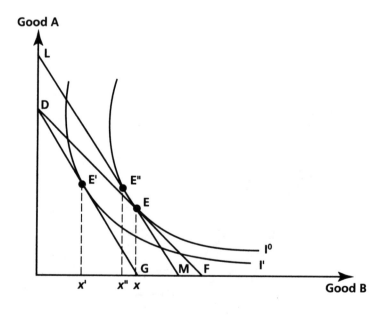

Figure 26.7

9 Income consumption curve

As household income changes, parallel shifts in the budget line occur and for each level of income there will be an equilibrium point at which each budget line is at a tangent to an indifference curve. This is illustrated in Figure 26.8 where successive increases in income are represented by the three parallel budget lines. In this example both goods A and B are **normal goods,** and by joining the equilibrium points for each level of income, the **income consumption curve (ICC)** is obtained. The income consumption curve shows how household consumption responds to changes in income with the money prices of the goods constant.

Figure 26.9 illustrates the ICC curve where good A is an inferior good and its rate of increase in consumption is very low relative to good B as income increases. Figure 26.10 illustrates the ICC for a **Giffin good**, where good A is so inferior that consumption declines as income rises.

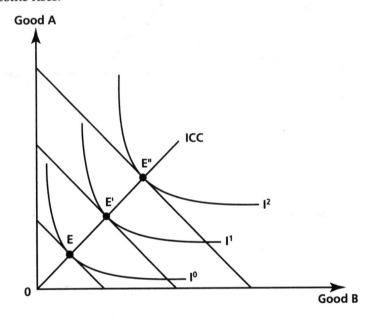

Figure 26.8

10 Price consumption curve

Changes in the relative prices of the two goods alter the slope of the budget line, as illustrated in paragraph 7. As the slope of the budget line changes, there will be successive points of tangency with the relevant indifference curves. Joining these successive equilibrium points as the **price of one good increases** produces the **price consumption curve (PCC).** The price consumption curve shows how household consumption responds to changes in the price of one good with the price of other goods and income constant. This is illustrated in Figure 26.11 where the price of good A is constant while the price of good B falls through three stages, P, P^1 and P^2. This analysis underlines the theory of demand discussed earlier, which stated that with incomes and the price of all other goods held constant, then a reduction in the price of a good will result in more of it being consumed. The PCC in Figure 26.11 conforms exactly to that prediction and provides an alternative derivation of the demand curve.

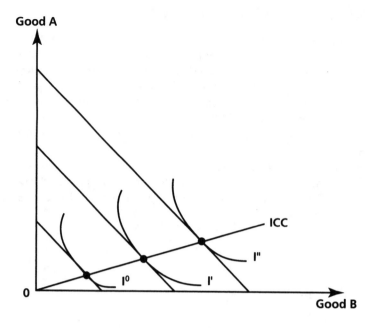

Figure 26.9

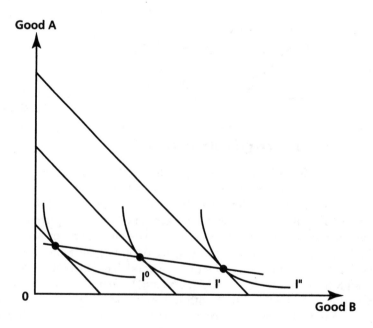

Figure 26.10

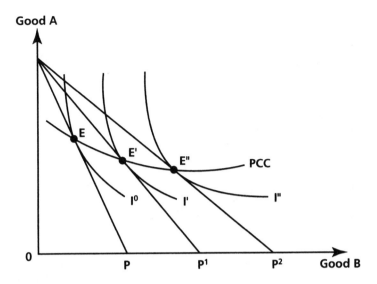

Figure 26.11

11 The demand curve

The alternative derivation of the demand curve by utilising indifference curves can be illustrated diagramatically using a similar analysis to that in 10 and Figure 26.11 above. Again we have the two goods A and B, the price of good A being held constant, while the price of good B is allowed to fall relative to it. This is illustrated in the upper segment of Figure 26.12 where the price of good B falls producing the three equilibrium points E, E′ and E″ with more of good B consumed as its price falls relative to good A. In the lower segment of the diagram the quantity demanded of good B is related to its price. Each of the equilibrium points in the upper segment produces one unique point on the lower segment where the price of the good is related to quantity. By joining the corresponding intersections, A, B and C, we can derive the downward sloping demand curve for good B. (This analysis ignores the income effect and more advanced study should allow for this by producing an income compensated demand curve).

Self assessment questions

1 What condition is necessary for a consumer to receive the maximum utility from expenditure?

2 Outline the method of construction and the significance of indifference curves.

3 What is meant by the consumer's budget line?

4 Using indifference curve analysis illustrate the conditions necessary for a consumer to be in equilibrium.

5 Illustrate how consumers' equilibrium is affected by:

(i) A fall in the price of one good

(ii) An increase in income.

6 Distinguish between the income and substitution effects of a price change.

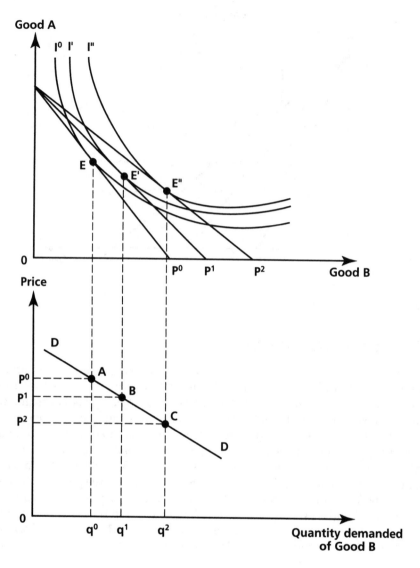

Figure 26.12

7 Illustrate the reaction of household consumption on two normal goods to a series of increases in income.

8 Illustrate diagramatically the distinction between the income and substitution effects in the case of a Giffin good.

27

The price mechanism

1 The basic problems

It will be recalled that the basic problems facing society are those of **what** to produce, **how** to produce it, and **for whom** the goods are to be produced. In a free market economy these problems are solved automatically by the interplay of market forces. According to Adam Smith 'each individual following his own self interest unknowingly brings about the general good', and the problems of what, how, and for whom are solved by what Smith referred to as the 'invisible hand' of the price mechanism.

2 Consumer sovereignty

Consumer sovereignty is said to prevail in a market economy because production and therefore resource allocation is in accordance with the preferences of consumers as expressed in the market place. If consumers prefer a good they will purchase more of it, i.e. it receives more 'consumer votes', as demand increases the market price will rise, and these 'price signals' indicate to producers which goods should be produced in greater quantities.

3 Welfare equilibrium

As the demand for goods changes so too do their relative prices, which results in a reallocation of the factors of production. In Figure 27.1, assuming goods X and Y are close substitutes, and there is a change in consumers' preferences away from X and in favour of Y. The price of X falls to P' and the price of Y rises to P'. The increase in Y indicates to entrepreneurs that Y is more profitable to produce and a transfer of resources will take place through demand and supply on the factor market and more of Y will be produced. Output and resource allocation has been in accordance with the preferences of consumers as indicated by the 'price signals'. In order to establish whether the price mechanism is capable of achieving an **optimal welfare equilibrium** it is necessary to consider next the concepts of **consumer's and producer's surplus.**

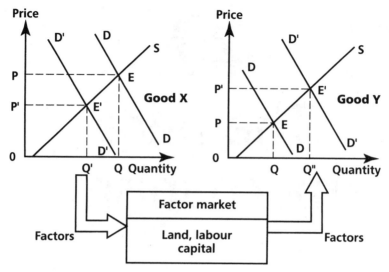

Figure 27.1

4 Consumer surplus

The concept of consumer's surplus refers to the **difference between the total utility from a given consumption level the consumer receives and the total expenditure at that consumption level.** This surplus arises because the consumer pays a uniform price on all the units purchased which is equal to the price of the last unit; however, we know from the

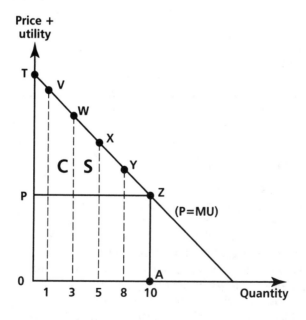

Figure 27.2

law of declining marginal utility that the earlier units are valued more highly than the last. Consumers will spend their budget on a good up to the point where **price = marginal utility (P = MU) only**; after this point they will purchase no more as they have maximised their utility. The concept is illustrated in Figure 27.2. The consumer pays price P for 10 units, however had only 1 unit been available the consumer would have paid price V, if 3 had been available price W, and so on. Only for the tenth unit is the P = MU, a surplus of marginal utility over price being gained by the consumer on all of the earlier units. The area of the triangle above P–Z is the **consumer's surplus**. At the tenth unit the consumer's evaluation of the marginal utility received from the additional unit is equal to the price, and total utility is area OTZA, but with expenditure only area OPZA.

5 Producer's surplus

Producer's surplus is the excess of market price over the minimum that would be necessary to persuade the producer to produce a given quantity. As the minimum return required to produce a given quantity is the marginal cost (MC), the **producer's surplus is the difference between market price and marginal cost.** As the marginal cost can be equated with the entrepreneur's opportunity cost then **producer's surplus is equivalent to the surplus over opportunity cost.** As the competitive firm's marginal cost curve is also its supply curve we can use the firm's supply curve to illustrate the point. In Figure 27.3 market price is P and quantity 10.

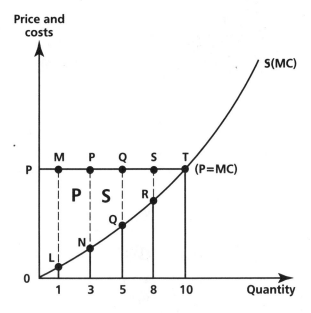

Figure 27.3

For the first unit however MC is L but price P is received, L–M is therefore the producer's surplus. For the third unit it is N–P, and so on. Only for the tenth unit is the market price exactly equal to the marginal cost, i.e. P = MC. The firm will not produce more than 10 because the MC would exceed the price received. Producer's surplus is therefore maximised at 10 units, and is represented by the triangle OPT.

6 Optimal output

If we assume a perfectly competitive industry it is possible to demonstrate that the competitive model can achieve optimal allocative efficiency. In Figure 27.4, the two previous diagrams are combined to illustrate a competitive market in equilibrium. We assume now that the demand and supply curves are market demand and supply curves. The market price $\bar{P}$ and quantity 10 maximises the total area of producer's and consumer's surplus. At this price each firm is operating at the lowest point on its average cost curve, **consumers are paying a price exactly equal to the marginal utility they receive from the last unit (P = MU) and producers are receiving exactly the marginal cost of producing that unit (P = MC).**

The situation is therefore optimal for society as a whole if all markets are in an identical situation. It is for the reasons outlined above that marginal cost pricing has been advocated as a rule for the nationalised industries to follow in their pricing policies.

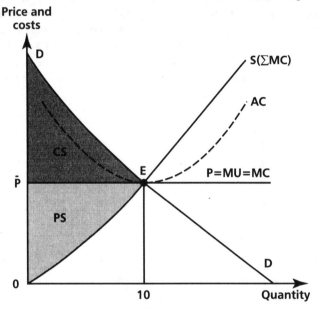

Figure 27.4

7 Consumer preference distortions

The concept of consumer sovereignty in the modern economy has been challenged by several writers, but in particular by J.K. Galbraith. Galbraith argues that consumer sovereignty is a myth and that the large corporations are in fact sovereign as they are able to create wants and impose them upon consumers by the use of advertising. Even if this overstates the case it is at least probable that advertising distorts consumers' preferences. Opponents of this view point to examples where consumers have resisted the attempts of large corporations to manipulate their preferences, in particular the failure of the Ford Motor Company to market their Edsel model in the 1950s.

8 Welfare economics

Given the existence of perfect competition in all markets it is theoretically possible for an allocation of resources to be achieved which is optimal for society as a whole. At the simplest level we can see that a competitive firm will produce at the lowest point on its average cost curve whilst the monopolist will not, also the competitive firm will produce a greater output at a lower price. It seems intuitively obvious therefore that competitive markets will be more beneficial to the consumer and anything which increases the competitiveness of markets will be to the benefit of the consumer. In order to reach this condition however we need a more objective criterion of what constitutes society's welfare, an area of study referred to as welfare economics.

9 Pareto optimality

In order to establish an objective criteria of social welfare, economists use the notion of **Pareto optimality**, named after the Italian economist Vilfredo Pareto (1848-1923) to whom the concept is attributed. A Pareto optimal allocation of resources is said to exist if it is not possible to reallocate resources so as to improve the well-being (or utility) of one person without making at least one person less well off (reduce their utility). To achieve a situation of Pareto optimality three conditions must exist within an economic system:

● **Allocative efficiency** – The economic system should ensure that the information regarding consumers' preferences are correctly conveyed to producers.
● **Technical efficiency** – The required output should be produced using the least possible resources or factors of production, i.e. the lowest unit cost method of production
● **Distributive efficiency** –The goods produced should be distributed precisely to those consumers desiring them.

10 Market failure

At this stage it may be worth reconsidering Figure 27.4. The conditions for Pareto optimality will exist when there is perfect competition in all markets. In the real world however, even if perfect competition could be established throughout the economy, there would still remain a number of conditions under which an economy would fail to achieve a situation of Pareto optimality. The situations in which perfect competition cannot achieve a situation of optimal efficiency are said to be situations in which **market failure** occurs. Three cases of market failure will be outlined here:

● **Natural monopoly**
● **Public goods**
● **Externalities**

11 Natural monopoly

This situation arises when the firm's long run average cost curve (LRAC) only reaches its lowest point at very large outputs, as illustrated in Figure 27.5. The firm has exploited all its economies of scale and is operating at its point of lowest cost at output Q^1. With such a cost structure the firm will be a natural monopolist because if faced with a competitor the firm can always exploit its cost advantage and temporarily lower its price in order to retain its dominance over the market. Natural monopolies tend to occur in industries where there are very high fixed costs which become less significant over high outputs, for example steel is impossible to produce viably on a small scale. Such industries are likely to be either regulated by government or taken into public ownership (nationalised) in order to control their monopoly profits. Such industries include steel, gas, electricity, and rail transport. It should also be noted that the marginal cost curve in Figure 27.5 lies below the long run average cost curve over most of its length, hence as long as market demand is consistent with output Q^1 the industry can operate the P=MC rule. However, if demand is below this level, for example DD, then the P=MC rule will produce a loss of A–B which will need to be subsidised from general taxation. Alternatively, the industry will be forced to set price = average cost (at C) and cover full accounting costs, which is not consistent with the P=MC rule for maximising society's welfare. (Note that output is also lower).

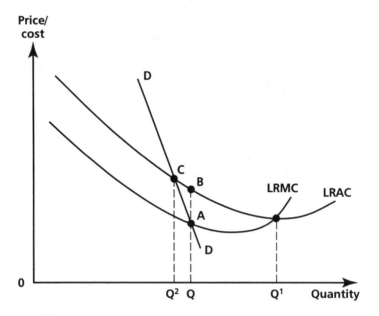

Figure 27.5

12 Public goods

Another class of goods which the price mechanism would fail to supply in adequate quantities are referred to as **pure public goods**. The essential characteristics of such goods are:

- They are **non-rival in consumption,** i.e. if one person consumes more, it does not mean that there is less for others as is the case with normal goods.
- They are in **joint supply,** i.e. if the supply is increased, it is increased to everyone.
- They are **non-excludable,** i.e. nobody can be prevented from consuming them.

The classical examples of such goods are: light from a lighthouse; law and order; and defence. The characteristics of such goods make it impossible to charge a user price. If rational consumers were asked to reveal their preferences for such goods and state how much they were prepared to pay for them, they would say zero because they would assume that they would receive all they wanted anyway. However, if each individual responded in the same way then there would be none provided, or at least there would be under provision, a problem referred to as the **'free-rider'** problem, which makes it impossible to make provision of such goods by a system of user prices. The only way such goods can be provided is collectively by governments through the tax system.

13 Externalities

Market prices fail to reflect **social costs** and **benefits**. Social costs may also be referred to as **externalities** or **spillovers**. Social costs occur when **actions by one party create costs which are borne by others**; or by society as a whole. For example, the act of production will involve private costs for the entrepreneur, but pollution in the form of smoke or effluent will impose costs upon the community at large. Conversely private expenditures, on for example health, education and housing may create social benefits not only to the individual but to society as a whole; for example, inoculations provide a private benefit to the individual but there is also the benefit to other individuals who will not now be at risk of catching the disease. **Market prices may therefore fail to reflect these external costs and benefits and will not bring about an optimal allocation of resources.**

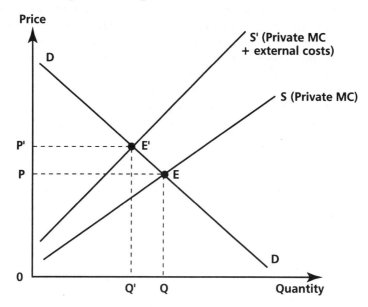

Figure 27.6

Externalities occur when a market has failed to emerge for a good because no-one is able to claim ownership of the good, hence there is a failure to allocate **property rights**, without which there can be no trading and therefore no price signals.

In Figure 27.6 when only private costs are taken into account, equilibrium price is P and quantity is Q, this does not however reflect the extra cost to society as a whole, or the marginal social cost. If social costs are included the supply curve, or marginal cost curve, becomes S^1 with the higher price P^1 and lower output Q^1. These external costs are unlikely to be incorporated in the decision-making of a private firm or individual as they will not be concerned with the effect of the marginal cost of their activities upon society as a whole, resulting in over-production of the good, i.e. Q instead of Q^1. The problem is therefore how to make individuals and firms incorporate social costs into their decision making or how to internalise them.

If, for example in the case of pollution of the environment by the emission of smoke from firms, a system of property rights could be established over the environment, and ownership given to the community, then bargaining could occur and firms would have to pay compensation if they wished to continue to pollute the atmosphere. In the absence of such an arrangement, firms will continue to pollute the atmosphere because it represents free disposal of waste, but by establishing property rights, a value is given to the resource of 'clean air' and a market begins to function, limiting the firms' use of it by putting a 'price' on its use.

Some commentators such as E.J. Mishan suggest the use of the tax system in the form of providing subsidies where there are external benefits, and taxes where there are costs, in order to bring about a level of output which is optimal for society as a whole. In Figure 27.7 market price is P and quantity Q. If there are external costs however the supply curve does not reflect the true marginal cost of production and the imposition of a tax raises the producer's costs to reflect both the private production costs and the external costs to society. As a consequence the price rises to P^1 and output falls to the optimal output for society, Q^1. Where there are external benefits private production costs do not reflect the benefits to society and the provision of a subsidy to the producer reduces costs, price falls to P^{11} and output increases to Q^{11}, with more of the socially desirable good produced. Provided the tax or subsidy is equal to the value of the externality the result should be optimal for society as a whole. In the diagram the tax would be A–B and the subsidy C–D in order to achieve the socially optimal outputs.

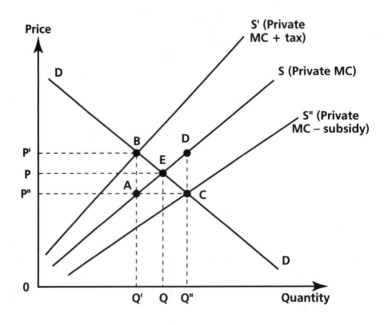

Figure 27.7

14 Merit goods

The market may fail to provide certain goods in sufficient quantities which society considers to be so essential that they should be provided free of charge. Such goods typically include education and medicine. Because such goods are considered to be so meritorious to society they are referred to as **'merit goods'**.

15 Pareto optimality – some conclusions

As mentioned in Chapter 1, criticism of the price mechanism on the basis of unequal income distribution is not valid, as the price mechanism and income distribution are separate issues. The definition of Pareto optimality has nothing to say about the **distribution** of economic activity.

In a modern economy it is unlikely that perfect competition could simultaneously exist in all markets and the conditions for the achievement of a situation of Pareto optimality cannot therefore be fulfilled. In reality there are imperfections in most markets, the majority of markets being either oligopolistic or monopolistic, as a consequence resource allocation in most markets will be less than perfect. This does not however mean that the competitive market has no relevance as it provides a useful yardstick for the measurement of the degree to which actual markets diverge from the competitive ideal.

Self assessment questions

1 What is meant by consumer sovereignty?

2 How does the market mechanism allocate society's resources?

3 What are the characteristics of 'pure public goods'?

4 Distinguish between private costs and social costs.

5 What is the 'free-rider' problem?

6 What are the market imperfections which prevent the price mechanism from achieving an optimal allocation of resources?

7 What are the conditions required for a situation of Pareto optimality to exist?

8 Outline three situations in which market failure may occur.

9 How could the tax system be utilised in order to internalise externalities?

10 Why are property rights important for the efficient functioning of a market?

Section G

The national economy

Containing the following chapters:

The workings of the system which aims to cure the problem of scarcity and the many difficulties encountered

This section should enable students to:

- *Understand* how an economy functions
- *Explain* how unemployment and inflation are caused.
- *Contrast* the effects of inflation and unemployment.
- *Evaluate* the effectiveness of regional policy

Keywords to consider:

national income; national expenditure; national output; consumption; investment; gross domestic product; gross national product; capital consumption; transfer payments; factor cost; retail price index; hyper-inflation; demand-pull; cost-push; incomes policies; quantity theory of money; structural unemployment, frictional unemployment; cyclical unemployment; regional unemployment; development areas; intermediate areas; enterprise zones; European Regional Development Fund; European Social Fund.

28

National Income

1 National product

National income refers to the aggregate, or total, income of the nation which results from economic activity. Income however depends upon how much output is produced and as output is a continuous process rather than a stock, we have to measure this output over a specified time period, usually one year. Total output is referred to as **national product,** and includes all the **goods** and **services** produced each year.

2 A definition

National income was defined by Alfred Marshall as '**the aggregate net product of and sole source of payment to, all the agents of production.'** If this definition is studied closely we can identify three components:

- Aggregate net product of, i.e. total output.
- Sole source of payment, i.e. incomes.
- All the agents of production, i.e. how the national product is distributed, and therefore the source of all expenditure.

3 Measurement of national income

From this definition we can identify three possible methods of measurement:

- **output**
- **income**
- **expenditure.**

Measurement by either of these methods will produce identical results because theoretically:

national income = national output = national expenditure

4 Circular flow

In order to understand the concept of income as a **flow** it is useful to study the **circular flow of income** in the form of a **flow diagram**. If Figure 28.1 is studied closely it can be seen that households provide the supply of productive services to firms and in return receive the factor rewards of wages, rent, interest and profit. These are the total of all incomes to households and will therefore form the basis of all expenditures. When expenditures are made with firms in the form of consumption then there must be an equivalent flow of goods and services from firms to households. It is therefore possible to measure each of these flows and achieve the same result, hence the conclusion that national income = national output = national expenditure. In reality the circular flow Figure 28.1 needs to be highly qualified, for example much of national expenditure is in the form of investment expenditure between firms, however it does illustrate the concept of national income as a flow.

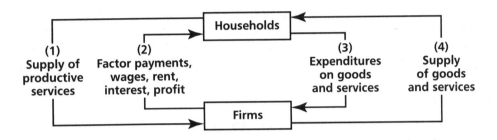

Figure 28.1

5 A summary

To summarise therefore national income can be regarded as:

- **the total value of the goods and services produced by all the industries and public services during the year.**
- **the total expenditure on final goods and services for consumption and investment purposes during the year.**
- **the factor cost of national output in terms of all the earnings in producing the national output.**

6 Real values

National income is estimated in money terms because money is the most convenient 'measuring rod', however care must be taken in comparing national income over time as a rise in the monetary value of national income does not necessarily imply a rise in living standards. The only real measure of whether national income has grown is whether the **real** value of output has increased, and it is possible that any apparent increase is a result of rising prices. For this reason data must be 'deflated' by a suitable index before comparisons of national income between different time periods can be made. One method of deflating data is to use the retail price index.

$$\frac{\text{national income at current prices}}{\text{RPI}} \times 100$$

This method produces national income at **constant prices**. If the index was based on prices in 1995, i.e. 1995 = 100 then the index could be said to be 'at 1995 prices'. As inflation has been removed from the data comparisons over time become more meaningful. National income and expenditure (The Blue Book) presents national income data in both current and constant prices. (See Chapter 29, Appendix I for example).

7 GNP and GDP

Gross **National** Product **(GNP)** and Gross **Domestic** Product **(GDP)** differ because some output produced within the UK is produced by foreign owned firms and the profits and interest are paid abroad to the owners. Similarly some productive resources overseas are owned by UK residents and the profits and interest are remitted back to them. The difference between payments made abroad and payments received from abroad is referred to as **net property income from abroad** and constitutes the difference between GNP and GDP. Gross domestic product as the name suggests, refers to the output of all domestically (i.e. UK) **located** resources, whilst GNP is the output of all resources **owned** by UK residents, i.e:

Gross National Product = Gross Domestic Product + net property income from abroad

N.B. domestic product is output produced within the UK.

8 Capital consumption

During the course of production assets become worn out and require replacement. This is referred to as **capital consumption** or more commonly, **depreciation**. This is a cost which must be incorporated within national income accounting and is deducted from gross national product to obtain the **net national product**; also referred to as the **national income**, i.e.

Gross National Product less depreciation = Net National Product = National Income

We can now consider the three methods of estimation separately.

9 The expenditure method

This method measures the total amount of final expenditures in the course of a year. It includes:

- Consumer's expenditure on goods and services.
- Investment expenditure by firms.
- Additions to stocks are included as nominal expenditure.
- Expenditure by public authorities on goods and services.

A number of adjustments must be made to the data in order to arrive at the final figure:

- Because the data collected is at market prices a number of adjustments have to be made in order to find the factor cost, i.e. market prices may be distorted by taxes and subsidies, and may not reflect the true cost. As subsidies artificially reduce the market price they are added back on, and as indirect taxes raise the price they are deducted, i.e.

Factor cost = market price + subsidies – indirect taxes

● An adjustment has to be made for the sale of output abroad (exports) and the purchase of goods from abroad (imports).

The expenditure method of calculation is therefore as shown in Table 28.1.

TABLE 28.1 The expenditure method	
	Consumers' expenditure
Plus	Public authorities current expenditure on goods and services
Plus	Gross capital formation (investment) at home including increases in stocks
=	Total domestic expenditure at market prices
Plus	Exports and income from abroad
Less	Imports and Income paid abroad
Less	Taxes on expenditure
Plus	Subsidies
=	Gross national product at factor cost
Less	Capital consumption (depreciation)
=	National income

10 The output method

This method measures the total output of all consumer goods and services, and investment goods, produced by all the firms in the country during the year. This measure can be obtained by totalling the **final** goods and services produced, or by taking the totals of **value added.** For example, imagine a firm which mines nitrates and sells the crude product to a chemical extracting company at £80 per ton. After refining it is sold to a fertiliser company at £100 per ton who produce and package garden fertiliser for sale to the retail trade at £150 per ton. The retailer sells it to his retail customers at the equivalent of £250 per ton. This is represented diagramatically in Figure 28.2.

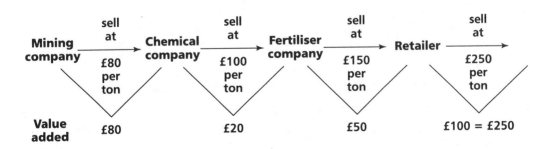

Figure 28.2

It should be noted that the sum of the value added (£250) is the same as the value of retail sales. Therefore either the value of the final goods or the total of value added can be used. What cannot be done is to add the value of output at each stage because this would involve counting the same item more than once, i.e. the £100 to the fertiliser manufacturer includes the £80 to the mining company. This error is referred to as **double counting** and can be a serious source of error in national income accounting.

The output of all industry is classified according to the official Standard Industrial Classification (SIC) and is added together to obtain total output.

A number of 'adjustments' have to be made to the output figures:

- Artificial increases in stock values due to inflation (stock appreciation) have to be deducted.
- Net property income from abroad.
- The 'residual error' (statistical discrepancy).

TABLE 28.2 The output method	
	Agriculture, forestry and fishing
Plus	Mining and quarrying
Plus	Manufacturing
Plus	Construction
Plus	Gas, electricity and water
Plus	Transport
Plus	Communication
Plus	Distributive trades
Plus	Insurance, banking and finance
Plus	Public administration and defence
Plus	Public health and educational services
Plus	Other services
Plus	Ownership of dwellings
	Total domestic output
Less	Stock appreciation
Plus/Minus	Residual error
Plus/Minus	Net property income from abroad
=	Gross national product at factor cost
Less	Capital consumption
=	National income

11 The income method

- This method measures the total money value of all incomes received by persons and firms in the country during the year. These incomes may be in the form of wages, salaries, rent or profit.
- Care must be taken to exclude **transfer payments** such as student grants, pensions and unemployment benefit. These are excluded because they do not represent payment for a contribution to output but are transfers of income from one group to another.
- Adjustments have to be made for the undistributed profits of companies and the surpluses of the nationalised industries which are paid to the government.
- Adjustments also have to be made for stock appreciation and net property income from abroad.

The income method of calculation is therefore:

TABLE 28.3 The income method	
	Income from employment
Plus	Income from self employment
Plus	Profits of private companies and public enterprises
Plus	Rent
=	Total domestic income
Less	Stock appreciation
Plus/Minus	Residual error
Plus/Minus	Net property income from abroad
=	Gross national product
Less	Capital consumption (depreciation)
=	**National income**

In theory the three methods must balance, but in reality they may differ due to errors and delays in returns; the residual error is added to ensure that they do balance. The source of some of these errors is found later and the figures are adjusted in subsequent years.

12 Problems of calculation

A number of problems are encountered in the calculation of national income, the main ones being:

- The problem of double counting (see 10).
- Transfer payments (see 11).
- Underestimates may occur where goods and services do not enter the market and are therefore unrecorded. For example, goods consumed by those producing them, as is the case with farmers; or farm labourers who receive part of their income in kind.

- Unpaid personal services are excluded, e.g. the work of housewives. Housework is an indirect contribution to output in that it enables others in the family to make a more direct contribution.
- Data collection may be inadequate due to firms failing to send in returns or making errors. Also much of the information is originally collected for different purposes, e.g. tax returns.
- The growth of the 'black economy'; in recent years it has been suggested that as much as 7½% of GDP may go unrecorded. The 'black economy' refers to that part of economic activity which is undeclared and therefore unrecorded for tax purposes, and is therefore deemed to be 'illegal'. Research suggests that there has been considerable growth in this sector over recent years.

13 International comparisons

International comparisons of national income as a basis for comparing 'standards of living' is subject to a number of qualifications:

- Whether or not a particular level of national income implies a high material standard of living also depends upon population size, and measurement requires an estimate of **per capita** income, i.e.

$$\text{NNP at factor cost } = \frac{\textbf{Per capita income}}{\textbf{Population}}$$

Therefore the growth of NNP must be greater than population growth in order for living standards to rise.
- 'Standard of living' is a subjective evaluation and other nations may put more value upon non-material aspects which do not enter national income accounting.
- Climatic differences may mean that although national income may be lower in some countries they have to spend less on fuel and clothing to keep warm.
- Transport in large countries where there are dispersed centres of population may absorb a higher proportion of national income.
- The use of exchange rates to convert national income statistics into a common currency unit may produce unreliable results for comparison purposes.

14 Living standards

Whether or not an increase in national income is the same thing as an increase in welfare is a matter of some discussion as national income measurements fail to include factors which many would suggest were an essential aspect of 'welfare', but which cannot be measured purely in terms of material goods. In particular they would indicate:

- 'Externalities' such as environmental pollution which may actually become worse as the rate of growth of national income increases.
- The level of provision of 'merit' goods such as education, health and welfare.
- The production of 'demerit' goods such as alcohol and tobacco.
- The level of provision of government transfers such as pensions, grants and social security benefits which are specifically excluded from the statistics in order to avoid double counting, but it could be argued that they cannot be omitted from any measure of welfare.

National income measurements do provide however an indication of whether or not output, and therefore incomes, is rising, and provided the qualifications are borne in mind during interpretation they do provide a useful indication of the trends in the economy.

The following page shows national income statistics for the UK 1995 measured by each of the three methods.

Self assessment questions

1 What is meant by the circular flow of income?
2 State the three methods by which national income can be calculated.
3 How does the problem of 'double counting' occur?
4 What are 'transfer payments'?
5 Outline the problems which occur in making international comparisons of national income.
6 Describe in detail one method of national income calculation.

TABLE 28.4	
UK National Income 1995 (millions £)	
Income	
Income from employment	377,900
Income from self employment	67,700
Gross trading profits of companies	91,000
Gross trading surplus of public corporations	4,600
Gross trading surplus of general government enterprises	600
Rent	62,800
Imputed charge for consumption of non trading capital	4,700
Total domestic income	609,300
Less stock appreciation	−4,800
Residual error	−200
Gross domestic product at factor cost	604,300
Net property income from abroad	9,600
Gross national product	613,900
Less capital consumption	73,300
National income (net national product)	540,600

(Continued)	
Output	
Agriculture, forestry and fishing	11,900
Mining, quarrying, including oil and gas extraction	14,600
Energy and water supply	15,800
Manufacturing	131,700
Construction	31,800
Wholesale and retail trade, repairs, hotels and restaurants	84,700
Transport, storage and communications	50,800
Financial intermediation, red estate, renting and business activities	158,200
Public administration, defence, social security	39,500
Education, health and social work	73,000
Other services	23,200
Adjustment for financial services	−30,700
Statistical discrepancy	<u>−200</u>
Gross domestic product at factor cost	<u>604,300</u>
Net property income from abroad	9,600
Gross national product at factor cost	<u>613,900</u>
Less capital consumption	73,300
National income (net national product)	540,600

(Continued)	
Expenditure	
Customers expenditure	447,200
General government final consumption	149,500
Gross domestic fixed capital	105,400
Value of physical increase in stock and work in progress	3,900
Total domestic expenditure	706,000
Exports of goods and services	197,600
Total final expenditure	903,600
Less imports of goods and services	−203,100
Statistical discrepancy	400
Gross domestic product at market prices	700,900
Net property income from abroad	9,600
Gross national product at market prices	710,500
Less taxes on expenditure	−103,600
Subsidies	7,000
Gross national product at factor cost	613,900
Less capital consumption	73,300
National income (net national product)	540,600

29

Inflation

1 A definition

Inflation refers to a **generalised and sustained rise in the price level,** or a **fall in the value of money,** both of which amount to the same thing - that a unit of currency will buy fewer goods. Inflation does not refer to the fact that some goods have become more expensive than others because **relative prices** change constantly according to demand and supply. Inflation refers to the fact that the price of **all** goods is rising.

2 The retail price index

It is not merely the fact that prices are rising which is important but rather the **rate of increase**. This is usually stated as the **annual rate of inflation** as measured by a **price index,** the most frequently quoted index of inflation is the **retail price index**. There are also manufacturing and wholesale price indices but the retail price index measures inflation as it affects the majority of people. The index is constructed from price data gathered in the **family expenditure survey** and is constructed from the prices of a collection of goods and services which enter a typical shopping 'basket', each item being weighted in accordance with its importance in the household budget. The 'basket of goods' is then revalued in each subsequent year at current prices, and inflation is represented by the increase in the index. The composition of the basket is changed periodically to keep abreast of changes in expenditure patterns. The index becomes outdated in its coverage eventually as the year upon which it was based becomes more distant in time. A further weakness is that during periods of rapid inflation the index may exaggerate inflation as consumers substitute those goods which are rising less rapidly in price and therefore become relatively cheaper. Index numbers represent percentage changes rather than absolute changes. For example in the base year the index will be 100; if in the following year the index is 120 then the index has risen by 20 percentage points. (See Appendix 1).

3 Real and nominal values

When comparing economic statistics over time it is necessary to **deflate** the data in order to eliminate the effect of inflation. For example, if incomes rise by 20% over a year but prices have risen by 15% the **real** increase in incomes is approx. 5% (actually 4.4%).

Money (or **nominal**) incomes (or wages) refers to income in terms of the number of pounds earned. **Real** incomes (or wages) refers to the actual increase in purchasing power after allowing for the effects of inflation.

$$\frac{\text{monetary income}}{\text{RPI}} \times 100 = \text{real income}$$

Increases in income may appear far more modest after allowing for the effects of inflation.

4 GDP deflator

It is also necessary to deflate the data when comparing GDP over different time periods in order to estimate the rate of growth of the economy. This is achieved in a similar manner to above by the use of the **implied deflator** for GDP. This is obtained by dividing the value of GDP at current prices by GDP at constant (1990) prices.

$$\frac{\text{GDP (nominal)}}{\text{GDP (1990 prices)}} = \text{GDP at constant prices}$$

5 Inflation trends

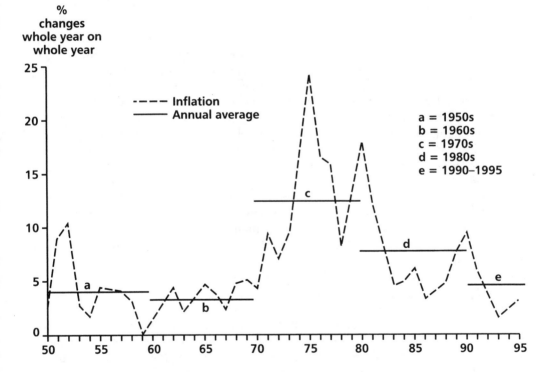

Figure 29.1 UK inflation 1950–95

Slow rates of inflation of 2–3% will always be present in a growing economy and may even be conducive to growth itself. When inflation rises to very high levels however the effects can be very damaging on the economy and is therefore unacceptable to most governments.

Sustained high rates of inflation, known as **hyperinflation**, have occurred several times in history, in particular the German inflation of 1923 and the Hungarian inflation of 1944. In Britain the 1970s saw higher rates of inflation than any other period in the twentieth century. Retail prices rose on average by 12.4% per annum between 1970 and 1979, compared with 3.5% between 1960 and 1969. Inflation in Britain reached a peak of 24% in 1975 before declining to an average of around 7% in the 1980s and 4% in the 1990s. Figure 29.1 illustrates the recent trends in inflation.

Although high rates of inflation are considered to be undesirable and most governments give priority to controlling it there are examples of countries enduring very high rates of inflation over sustained periods, in particular South American countries such as Chile and Brazil, but often only at the cost of foregoing democratic freedoms, and abject poverty for a large section of the population.

6 Causes

The causes of inflation are the subject of much controversy and academic debate, some of which will be discussed later; it is however common practice to classify inflation into two categories: demand-pull inflation and cost-push inflation.

7 Demand-pull inflation

Demand-pull inflation is defined as a situation where **aggregate demand exceeds aggregate supply at current prices,** hence prices are 'pulled up' by the total demand for goods and services exceeding what the economy is capable of producing. Inflation of this type is associated with the full employment of resources, where there is spare capacity of either, or, both labour and capital, an increase in demand may be achieved without a significant rise in the price level. If resources are fully utilised however it will not be possible in the short run to meet any increase in demand by increasing output and the excess demand can only result in an increase in the price level. An example of demand-pull inflation occurred during the Korean War (1950/51) when the western world was unwilling to forego its current consumption of goods following the austerity years after World War II but the western governments were engaged in a conflict in Korea which was demanding a high level of resource consumption. World demand for resources exceeded what could be supplied and prices rose substantially. Attempting to achieve high rates of economic growth during a period of full employment may also result in excess demand and rising prices.

8 Cost-push inflation

Cost-push inflation is a consequence of rising costs which tend to push up prices. It is **not** a consequence of excess demand for goods resulting in increased demand for factors, higher factor prices and therefore higher prices to the consumer. Cost-push inflation occurs when costs rise independently of an increase in demand. Cost inflation can result from some, or all, of the following:

- Increases in wages which are greater than the increase in productivity.
- A fall in the exchange rate which increases the cost of imported materials.
- A rise in the cost of imported materials due to other factors abroad, for example the

formation of the OPEC cartel and its effect on oil prices in the 1970s.
- Increases in indirect taxation (i.e. taxes on goods and services such as VAT).

Entrepreneurs tend to have a fairly fixed idea of the sort of profit margins they should be making, and as the costs of production rise they attempt to maintain these margins by marking up prices to the consumer.

9 Expectations

Expectations play an important role in the inflationary process. As inflation is experienced over a period of time employees tend to start thinking in terms of real wages rather than nominal (money) wages, i.e. they see through the 'veil of money', and begin to anticipate inflation. As a result union negotiators start to build a 'hedge' against inflation into wage negotiations. So, for example, if the union wants to gain a 10% increase in real wages for its members and anticipated inflation is 15%, and assuming 5% will be given away during the bargaining process, the union will bargain initially for a 30% increase:

30% (Union claim)
– 5% Lost during negotiation
– 15% Lost due to inflation
= 10% Increase in real wages

10 Sustained inflation

If we consider the causes of demand-pull and cost-push inflation we can see quite easily why they may result in a rise in the price level. They do not explain however how they can generate a sustained and generalised rise in the price level over a period of time, rather than a once-and-for-all increase. If however, we combine them with the effects of the expectations described above, and extend the effects to include the exchange rate and overseas trade we can see how a rise in the price level can start a **wage/price spiral,** resulting in a sustained period of inflation. Such a process is outlined in Figure 29.2 and it should be noted that in the example the process begins with a period of demand-pull inflation which becomes transformed into cost-push inflation, but the process could start just as easily with cost-push inflation.

11 Incomes policies

Keynesians (after J. M. Keynes, see Chapter 39) see costs as being the main determinants of prices and the most important element in costs is considered to be wages. They therefore suggest that the best way to control inflation is to control wages. Wage controls, such as the various **incomes policies** which were pursued in the 1960s and 1970s, should therefore be imposed at point A in Figure 29.2 to keep the wage increases at or below the rate of increase of productivity. Such policies can be either:

- Voluntary
- Statutory

The results of such policies are however inconclusive and their effects on inflation appear to be only temporary.

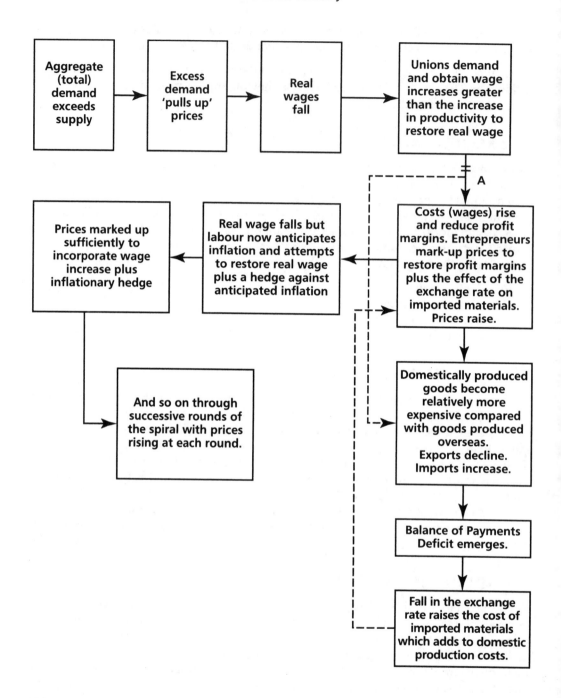

Figure 29.2

12 Monetarists view

Monetarists consider that inflation is due solely to the over expansion of the money supply by governments and that attempts to control inflation by any means other than the strict control of the money supply will be doomed to failure (see Chapter 43 for further details).

13 The quantity theory of money

The quantity theory of money attempts to explain the relationship between the supply of money and the price level. In its most basic form it can be expressed as

$$MV = PT$$

where

M = the money supply, or stock
V = the velocity of circulation of money
P = the price level
T = the volume of transactions

The left hand side of the equation represents the total amount of money used to finance transactions in a given period and the right hand side total expenditures in that period. Both sides are therefore equal. Because velocity (V) is a residual, calculated as PT/M and is included to make both sides of the equation balance, the equation is sometimes referred to as a tautology (self evident). It is still useful however in identifying the variables which influence the value of money. Classical economic theory assumed that both V and T would be constant in the short run. Any change in the money supply (M) would therefore have an equal effect on the price level (P).

ie

$$M\bar{V} = P\bar{T}$$

If there were a substantial reserve of unemployed resources however an increase in M, with V remaining constant would result in increased output and therefore transactions, with P remaining unchanged.

There is much controversy however over whether or not V is in fact constant. If V varies then it is quite conceivable that an increase in M could be offset by a reduction in V leaving the price level (P) unchanged. During deep recessions such as that of the 1930s, spending was greatly reduced, which did in fact result in a reduction in V. During periods of hyper-inflation one of the characteristics is a rapid increase in V as people spend their cash balances as quickly as possible before they lose their value. More recent adaptations of the quantity theory will be discussed in the chapter on monetarism (Chapter 43).

14 Purchasing power parity

In an open economy such as Britain's it is not possible to isolate the domestic inflation rate from inflation in the rest of the world and inflation can be transmitted through the relative exchange rates. This is the **purchasing power parity** theory which holds true in the long run although there may be deviations from it in the short run. There is therefore a transmission mechanism through which inflation can become internationally transmitted. It should be noted in this context that the high rate of inflation of the 1970s was by no means restricted to Britain but also appeared in most industrialised countries.

15 The evils of inflations

Inflation is generally considered to be undesirable for the following reasons:

- The longer debtors can delay repayment of debts the less they repay in real terms, therefore debtors gain and creditors lose and eventually there is a reluctance to give credit. As credit is the basis of trade, inflation eventually results in a breakdown of trading relationships.
- The reluctance to give credit results in higher interest rates.
- There is an arbitrary income redistribution between groups in society. Those on fixed incomes, non union labour, and weaker groups generally lose out to well organised, stronger groups or those who set their own incomes through commission or profits.
- The value of savings is rapidly eroded leaving the saving classes embittered.
- The dangers from inflation are by no means all economic and possibly the greatest problems of inflation arise from the social and political strains it places upon society, in particular its divisiveness between different groups within society. For these reasons most democratic governments give high priority in their economic policies to curbing it.

APPENDIX

The construction of retail price index

		Year 1 (Y1)			Year 2 (Y2)		
Item	Weights	Price	Base year index	Weighted price index	Price	Index Y2 as a % of Y1	Weighted price index
Potatoes	5	10p	100	500	15p	150	750
Milk	3	30p	100	300	39p	130	390
Meat	2	£1.50	100	200	£1.65	110	220
	10			1000÷10			1360÷10
		Base year index =		100	Year 2 index =		136

YEAR 1 = 100
YEAR 2 = 136
An increase in the retail price index of 36 percentage points.

STAGES

1 Select appropriate weights reflecting the importance of the item in the household budget.
2 Set base year index = 100. weights × index = weighted price index. The sum of the weighted price index ÷ the sum of the weights = base year index.
3 Second year index calculated as year 2 prices as a percentage of year 1 prices.
4 Year 2 weighted price index = Year 2 index × weight.
5 Year 2 index = the sum of the weighted price index ÷ the sum of the weights.
6 The procedure is continued in a similar manner for each subsequent year.

Index numbers can be used to 'deflate' data for purposes of making comparisons over time. Deflating data removes the effects of inflation so comparisons can be made in real terms. The technique is often used to make comparisons of gross domestic product over a time period, or the growth of incomes.

e.g. Real weekly earnings for 1992 at Jan. '84 prices $= \dfrac{£230.00}{32.4} \times 100 = £71.78$

The data above shows that weekly earnings have risen faster than prices in every year except 1986 when 'real' weekly earnings fell. However, the increase in income is much lower in real terms than in nominal, or money, terms.

EXAMPLE:

Year	Average Weekly Earnings(£)	Retail Price Index	'Real' weekly earnings at Jan. ' 84 prices
1984	65.75	100	65.75
1986	95.90	157.1	61.04
1988	130.00	197.1	65.96
1990	180.00	263.7	68.26
1992	230.00	320.4	71.78

Self assessment questions

1 Distinguish between cost-push and demand-pull inflation.

2 Outline what is meant by a 'wage price spiral'.

3 State the quantity theory of money and outline how it relates the money supply to the price level.

4 How is inflation measured?

5 Explain the role of expectations in generating wage inflation.

6 Why is inflation considered to be undesirable?

30

Unemployment

1 Labour

Labour is the least durable of all resources; a day's output lost due to unemployment is lost permanently and cannot be regained. Unemployment therefore has high economic costs, but in addition the costs in terms of misery and despair cannot be ignored.

2 Types of unemployment

In order to formulate appropriate policies to cure unemployment it is necessary to identify precisely the type of unemployment which is being dealt with as the policy instruments appropriate to the cure of one type may not be appropriate to another. It is usual to classify the employment as one of four types: **seasonal**; **frictional**; **structural** and **cyclical (deficient demand)**.

3 Seasonal unemployment

Some industries are highly seasonal in character and the levels of unemployment in such industries therefore also tends to fluctuate with the seasons, e.g. the hotel and catering industry in resorts, fruit picking, and the construction industry, are all affected particularly by climatic changes.

4 Frictional unemployment

This results from the frictions in the labour market which occur due to labour immobility, or the process of searching for job information. Even at what is normally deemed to be full employment there would still be an element of frictional unemployment because it takes time and resources for workers to change jobs. There may be an adequate number of vacancies but it takes time for a suitable match between those seeking employment and appropriate vacancies to be found.

5 Structural unemployment

This type of unemployment arises out of more fundamental changes in the industrial base of the economy. It is associated with the decline of 'staple' industries and the problem arises because as industries decline the skills required for them become obsolete also. This becomes a serious problem because these industries tend to be concentrated in certain **regions** and when these industries decline **regional decline** occurs as a consequence. Examples include: shipbuilding in the North West, North East, Glasgow and northern Ireland; cotton textiles in the North West; iron and steel making in south Wales and the north east, and some of the coal fields in the North West, the Midlands and the North. Vacancies may exist in the economy but they may be in different areas and involve different skills. The concentration of unemployment in the regions becomes a problem due to:

- The occupational immobility of labour – the unwillingness to abandon skills and acquire new ones.
- The geographical immobility of labour – workers are reluctant to move to vacancies elsewhere due to cultural, family and financial ties to the regions. Structural decline may result from some or all of the following:
  - Technological change.
  - The development of substitutes, e.g. the effect of man-made fibres such as nylon on the cotton industry.
  - The growth of overseas competition.

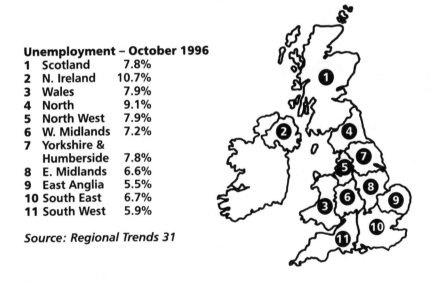

Unemployment – October 1996
1	Scotland	7.8%
2	N. Ireland	10.7%
3	Wales	7.9%
4	North	9.1%
5	North West	7.9%
6	W. Midlands	7.2%
7	Yorkshire & Humberside	7.8%
8	E. Midlands	6.6%
9	East Anglia	5.5%
10	South East	6.7%
11	South West	5.9%

Source: Regional Trends 31

Figure 30.1

6 Regional unemployment

Figure 30.1 illustrates the regional variation in unemployment rates. The reluctance of labour to move from the regions has resulted in the alternative policy of moving 'work to the workers' in the form of **regional policy**, under which governments have used a variety of measures in order to encourage firms to expand into the regions of high unemployment. (See Chapter 31).

7 Cyclical unemployment

This type of unemployment results from a general deficiency of total demand in the economy (This is dealt with in more detail in Chapter 39).

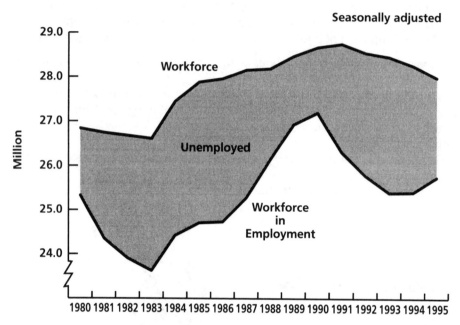

Figure 30.2

8 Unemployment trends

There were in 1992 almost as many unemployed as there were in 1984, and three times as many as in the 1950s. Three further important points to note regarding recent unemployment.

- The increase in unemployment among the young.
- An increase in the duration of unemployment.
- The period of rising unemployment has coincided with an increase in the size of the working population, as can be seen in Figure 30.2.
- A continued reduction in the numbers employed in manufacturing industry (see Figure 30.4) and an increase in those employed in non-manufacturing.

In January 1993 unemployment peaked at 3 million (seasonally adjusted) in the UK, this represented 10.6% of the workforce. A large proportion of these had been unemployed for more than a year. The highest level of unemployment prior to this had been in 1984 with approximately 13% of the workforce unemployed.

Since January 1993 the jobless total has fallen consistently and by the end of 1996 the official figure was 2 million or 7.2% of the workforce. All of the regions of the country have enjoyed a fall in unemployment with the largest being experienced in the South West, the West Midlands and the South East.

This fall in the level of unemployment has been attributed to the economic recovery that has taken place in the UK. It should however be born in mind that the official government statistics are unreliable, as the methods used for counting unemployment have been changed 31 times since 1979. Most of these changes have reduced the published unemployed total by a significant amount. This makes any comparison over time very difficult.

The result of this has been that the UK government now produces two different series of unemployment data, the claim count (the figures produced above) and the labour survey.

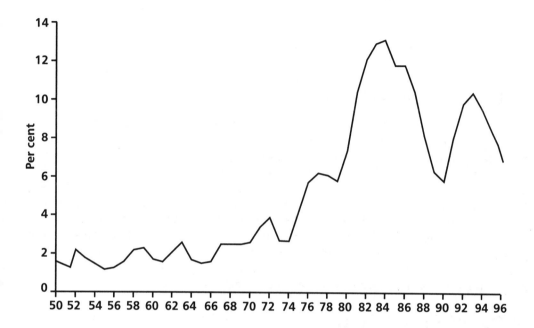

Figure 30.3 UK unemployment 1950–96

Self assessment questions

1 How does frictional unemployment occur and why is it a less serious problem than other forms of unemployment?

2 Why does structural unemployment create a problem for the regions?

3 What is meant by regional policy and why have governments in the past felt that they needed such a policy?

4 In what sense is unemployment a waste of resources?

5 As an economy develops what changes would you expect to take place within its occupational structure?

6 State the main categories of unemployment and indicate those which are the main concern of government economic policy.

31

Regional policy

1 Regional imbalances

The regional imbalance of incomes and employment which arises from the decline of the staple industries in the regions has resulted in the devising of various measures aimed at reducing these regional disparities. These measures, generally referred to as **regional policy**, attempt to encourage the growth of industry in the regions. Government intervention in this context arises from the desire for the greater economic growth which will result from a fuller utilisation of resources, both labour and capital; and a desire for greater equality of employment and incomes. Because of the reluctance of labour to move to areas of high employment measures generally attempt to influence the firm's location decision, i.e. 'bring work to the workers', by a combination of measures aimed at reducing the firm's costs if they locate in specified areas or by prohibiting through planning regulations expansion elsewhere (the 'carrot and stick' approach).

2 The regional map

The present pattern of assistance was established in the 1972 Industry Act, although regional policy originated in the 1930s and expanded rapidly in the 1960s. The extent of assistance available varies according to the designation of the area. Prior to November 1984 there were three categories of development area:

- **Special development areas (SDAs).**
- **Development areas (DAs).**
- **Intermediate areas (IAs).**

SDAs were the areas with the most serious problems of structural decline such as Merseyside, Clydeside and Newcastle, and these received the greatest assistance. The scale of assistance was less in the DAs and IAs. Northern Ireland was categorised as a **Special Development Area**, receiving additional assistance because of the unique problems of that region. In November 1984 the category of special development area was dispensed with and the map was redrawn. In 1993 a new 'map' of assisted areas was produced by the government. Once again it used a ranking of areas in terms of aid priority.

This had only two categories for assistance as with the 1984 map:

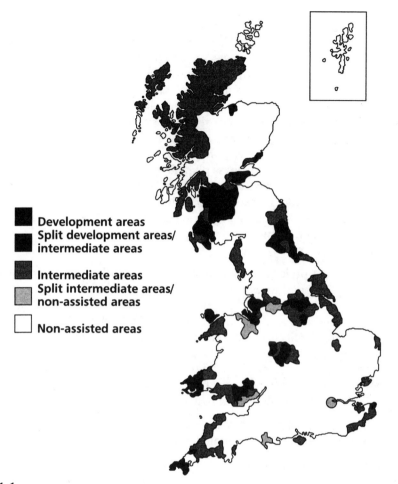

Development areas
**Split development areas/
intermediate areas**

Intermediate areas
**Split intermediate areas/
non-assisted areas**

Non-assisted areas

Figure 31.1

- Development areas.
- Intermediate areas.

Some areas were also designated as 'split' areas, these fell between the criteria used for DAs and IAs.

Another significant change was the inclusion of areas in the south east such as London (Park Royal and the Lea Valley), Clacton, Dover, Folkstone and the Isle of Wight.

The distribution of the development areas is illustrated in Figure 31.1.

3 Instruments of regional policy

The main instruments of regional policy are as follows:

Prior to March 1988 the main instrument of regional policy was the regional development grant (RDG). The RDG was a capital grant of 15% payable to firms in the development areas on investment in plant, buildings and machinery. The grants were subject to a cost per job limit of £10,000. Alternatively a job grant was made available of £3,000 for each new job created in labour intensive projects. In the 1988 White Paper, the

DTI stated that automatic eligibility for the RDG was to cease, in the 1990s it has been greatly reduced.

Capital grants were subject to the criticism that they encouraged capital intensive production when the underlying purpose was the creation of jobs. Also the grants failed to discriminate between good and bad investment; moreover the grant would be paid to firms who would have made the investment even if the grant did not exist.

To overcome some of these criticisms the government introduced in March 1988 **The Regional Initiative** with a new system of **regional enterprise grants.** These grants are given at the discretion of the Department of Trade and Industry (DTI) upon the presentation of a **business plan** by the applicant and are no longer automatically available. The grants will be provided only if the business plan meets the criteria of the DTI and the project is taking place in a Development Area or South Yorkshire.

The criteria applied include: market opportunities for the business over the next 2–3 years, the effect of the project on sales, profits and employment levels, and how the project and the business will be financed.

The grants are of two types:

- Grants for **investment** projects in most manufacturing and some service sectors. The DTI will pay 15% of expenditure on fixed assets in the project, up to a maximum grant of £15,000. Eligible costs include plant and machinery (new or second-hand), buildings, purchase of land and site preparation, and vehicles used solely on site.
- Grants for **innovation** projects which lead to the development and introduction of new or improved products and processes. The DTI will pay 50% of eligible costs, up to a maximum grant of £25,000. Work can range from feasibility studies, through the development of technical specifications, to the design and manufacture of prototypes. There is no limit on the size of projects which can be considered.

The measures introduced in March 1988, and built upon in 1993, represented a significant movement towards a more market orientated approach to regional policy.

- The provision of '**advance factories**' for sale or rent on favourable terms. These were standard factory units constructed by a division of the Department of Trade and Industry which were immediately available for firms to move into. However recently the emphasis has been on smaller units ('Busybee Workshops') in order to encourage the growth of new businesses.
- **Enterprise zones.** These represent an attempt to deal with the problems of the inner cities and go beyond what is strictly regional policy as some of them lie outside the development areas. The concept reflects the view held by the previous government that excessive controls and regulations can stifle initiative. The zones are specified areas mainly within the larger cities where special provisions apply in order to encourage industrial and commercial activity. At present there are 25 such zones in areas such as Merseyside (Speke), Midlands (Corby & Dudley), Northern Ireland (Belfast), Greater Manchester (Salford Docks and Trafford Park), Tyneside (Newcastle and Gateshead), London (Isle of Dogs). The main incentives in the enterprise zones are as follows:
  - Exemption from development land tax for 10 years.
  - 100% capital allowances (for corporation and income tax purposes) for commercial and industrial buildings.
  - Exemption from rates on industrial and commercial property for 10 years.

- Simplified and relaxed regulations for planning procedures.
- Simpler and speedier administration of remaining controls, and government requests for statistical information is to be kept to a minimum.
- **Regional selective assistance.** This is a variety of further grants available for capital and training costs where it can be shown that jobs will be created.
- **Industrial development certificates (IDCs).** These represented a form of administrative control on industrial development outside the assisted areas. An IDC was required for all new factories or extensions, and by refusing to grant an IDC for anywhere outside a development area pressure could be exerted to ensure that development took place within the development areas. The use of IDC's as a policy instrument was abolished as it was seen as interference by the government in the market mechanism, (see 5).

4 The European Union (EU)

In the 1990s the EU has become a significant part of the UK's regional policy. The European Regional Development Fund makes loans to central and local government for spending on capital and infrastructure projects. The European Social Fund also provides funds for the regeneration of areas with particular social problems which usually originate from high levels of unemployment.

This has provided new capital for the regions in the UK and a whole range of new initiatives. Three areas of the UK – Northern Ireland, the Highlands and Islands and Merseyside qualified for £2 billion of expenditure from the EU's structural funds over the period 1994–97. This money is not given to individual firms but made available to the government.

5 The free market approach

The **free market approach** to the regional problem suggests that any interference in the location decisions of firms will lead to location decisions which are non optimal and therefore inefficient. The firm makes its location decision on the basis of cost minimisation and any interference with this process, it is suggested will result in a location being chosen which is not the best one in terms of economic efficiency.

Advocates of the free-market approach suggest that the **regional problem will solve itself if left to market forces**. Regional unemployment merely indicates a labour market disequilibrium with an excess supply of labour at the prevailing wage rates and all that is required is a reduction in wages which will then be reflected in lower product prices and equilibrium will be re-established in the labour market. Labour and capital should be free to make their own decisions regarding location and if unemployment is high in a region then wage rates will be lower and some labour will be attracted to other more prosperous regions by the higher wage rates. Also at some point in time the lower wage rates in the declining regions will begin to attract firms who realise that by locating there they can reduce their wage costs and ultimately increase their profits. Eventually this movement of labour and capital will re-establish an equilibrium situation with full employment. If labour is unwilling to move then there must be some other advantages which equalise the employment disadvantages; the same is also true of firms who are unwilling to move voluntarily into the regions.

The market approach is generally advocated by those who believe that government intervention in the market should be minimal if economic efficiency is to be achieved.

Advocates of the free market approach also suggest that there are further burdens imposed by government intervention in the form of taxation, subsidisation, and the imposition of bureaucratic controls.

6 The arguments against the free market approach

Opponents of the market approach however point to a number of weaknesses in that principle:

- **The time scale involved** in the re-establishment of a new equilibrium situation may be very lengthy as the comparative advantage in production between regions is likely to change only slowly.
- **Social costs** may be imposed in both the areas of expansion and of contraction. In the declining regions as labour departs there will be costs imposed by the underutilisation of existing facilities such as schools and hospitals which will fall into decline as the regional income falls. In the expanding areas there will be a shortage of such social facilities with a high level of demand for those facilities which do exist. There are also likely to be the problems of inner-city decay and falling property prices in the declining regions, with shortages of accommodation and rapidly rising prices in the areas of growth. There may also be additional costs from congestion as roads and transport facilities are used more intensively in the growth areas. The disparity in house prices between the North of England and the South-East are a case in point.
- The market solution ignores the **hardship and suffering imposed** upon those involved, which may be so extreme that governments may find it politically unacceptable.
- As labour leaves the declining region the population falls, reducing the size of the potential market for new firms in the region. The departure of labour and firms also reduces local expenditure, and therefore incomes, resulting in further unemployment in the ancillary industries such as retailing and distribution. This further decline in incomes is referred to as the regional multiplier and makes it less likely that firms will locate in the declining regions. The opposite is the case in the expanding regions where the **regional multiplier** sets in train a circle of rising incomes and prosperity and is likely to be a factor in attracting firms to the more prosperous regions.
- The assumption that the labour market operates in a frictionless manner must also be questioned in the light of **nationwide collective bargaining.** Nationwide collective bargaining has the effect of reducing regional wage differences. Where national representatives of a trade union negotiate a national wage rate for their membership then the sensitivity of wage rates to regional differences in employment will be reduced.

7 Regional policy effectiveness

The effectiveness of regional policy is difficult to quantify, however, many studies indicate that regional unemployment is worse in the absence of policy

An official paper, 'The Movement of Manufacturing Industry in the UK, 1945–65' which was updated in 1981 showed that during the period 1945–81 the South East lost 1,647 manufacturers and the West Midlands 334. During the same period 586 manufacturers were gained in Wales, 365 in the North, 354 in East Anglia and 316 in the South

West. This clearly shows the success of regional policy.

A 1986 DTI paper estimated that 784,000 jobs were created in the assisted areas between 1960 and 1981. By the end of 1981, even after a hard recession 600,000 jobs remained. This of course ignores the cost of these jobs and the social costs and benefits involved.

In contrast the market based approach of the 1990s showed the regional unemployment differentials widening and a decrease in the participation rates of the depressed areas.

Regional differences in employment and income are still substantial despite assistance. The South East also appears to have a greater comparative advantage in the modern growth industries, especially since the opening of the channel tunnel.

8 Inner city programmes

The problem of the inner cities has been the focus of the greatest attention since the late 1980s. Inner city areas, particularly in the North of England, frequently have very high levels of unemployment, inferior housing, poverty, declining public servlces and a poor environment generally. The reasons for this deterioration are complex but the decline of manufacturing industry has been a major factor, also the age of the housing stock and the development of new business areas in more pleasant areas with better access to motorways. Many initiatives have been used by the government to assist the inner cities and some of the main schemes are listed below. A point which should be noted is that several of the schemes rely on partnerships between central and local government and private industry.

- **The Urban Programme,** implemented by the Department of the Environment, allocates money to local authorities and community groups. The money is spent on training schemes for the unemployed, factory renovation, small factory units and provision of community centres.
- **Enterprise zones** (discussed above under regional policy) are directed primarily at the inner city areas.
- **Task forces**, established by the Department of Employment provide special help to the most badly deprived areas, some of which have suffered rioting and public disorder. The task forces consist of small teams of civil servants based in deprived areas who draw aid from existing programmes and from the private sector and local authorities and concentrate the assistance into these areas.
- **Urban Development Corporations (UDCs)** have been playing an increasingly important role in the inner cities. They have extensive powers and can buy and sell land, build factories and offices; they can renovate sub-standard property, convert property to alternative uses, e.g. warehouses into flats or offices. One of their main objectives is the attraction of private capital back into the inner cities with the idea of making the environment more attractive generally in the hope that new industries will develop in addition to housing. The dockland developments in London and Liverpool are notable examples of the work of two UDCs.
- A number of local authorities established local employment initiatives, for example economic development units to co-ordinate policy initiatives to gain the maximum effect, and enterprise boards which invest directly in property and business.

9 The future

In reality the choice lies not between the two extreme views of the free market and the planned location approach, but in the selection of the most appropriate mix. In recent years less emphasis has been placed on regional policy with a move towards a more market-orientated solution despite the increasing contribution of the EU. There is however still an important role for the policy for the regions.

Self assessment questions

1 Why is there a 'regional problem'?
2 What are the main instruments of UK regional policy?
3 Outline the market approach to the regional problem.
4 What are the main problems involved with the market approach to the regional problem?
5 Discuss the problems created by the tendency of labour to be immobile. What measures can government adopt in order to resolve these problems?

Section H

International dimensions

Containing the following chapters:

Chapter 32 – International trade

Chapter 33 – Balance of payments

Chapter 34 – Exchange rates

Those elements of economies that determine how and why countries trade with one another.

This section should enable students to:

- *Understand* why countries trade with one another.
- *Explain* how the balance of payments account is calculated.
- *Contrast* the different exchange rate systems.
- *Evaluate* the benefits to the UK of the ERM.

Keywords to consider :

opportunity cost; comparative cost; comparative advantage; absolute advantage; terms of trade; protectionism; current balance; visibles; invisibles; balancing item; foreign exchange markets; purchasing power parity; floating exchange rate; fixed exchange rate; par value; devaluation; revaluation; J-curve effect; effective exchange rate; European Monetary System (EMS); European Exchange Rate Mechanism (ERM).

32

International trade

1 Reasons for trade

Nations engage in international trade for a variety of reasons:

- Due to **climatic differences** some goods would not be available in many parts of the world without trade. For example, coffee grows prolifically between the tropics, but not elsewhere. This is true of many natural commodities.
- **Natural resources** are not evenly distributed throughout the world, for example many countries have no coal or oil reserves whilst others have a surplus over their domestic requirements.
- **Skills and technology** are also not distributed evenly and whilst some countries have a high level of technological development others have a much lower level, both will therefore tend to produce goods of a different nature.
- Because factors of production and natural resources tend to be **immobile** it is more convenient to specialise in the production of those goods in which there is a natural, or acquired advantage, and trade the surplus not required for domestic consumption for those goods which cannot be produced.

2 Specialisation and trade

Although it was stated above that certain crops would not grow naturally in some regions of the world, it is not true that they could not be grown given sufficient diversion of resources to their production. For example, bananas can be grown quite successfully in heated greenhouses in the UK, but the cost would be very high and therefore the output would only be available to the wealthiest people. It is far more efficient for each country to use its resources in the production of those goods in which they have a cost advantage and trade with other nations to obtain those goods which are not produced. For example, the UK has an advantage over the West Indies in the production of machinery whilst the West Indies for climatic reasons can grow an abundance of bananas. It is therefore more efficient for Britain to **specialise** in the production of machines and trade with the West Indies for bananas. Both countries then enjoy the **gains from trade** which result from **specialisation**.

Specialisation and trade increase world output and enables everybody to enjoy a higher standard of living than would be otherwise available. A wider variety of goods are made available to more people.

3 The law of comparative advantage

The **law of comparative costs** shows that countries can gain from specialisation and trade provided that there is some difference in the **relative costs** of producing those goods. The **opportunity cost** of producing a good domestically may be too high, for example the growing of bananas in the UK quoted above.

To illustrate the law of comparative costs, suppose there are two countries X and Y. Both produce just two goods, beef and cars. Both countries have an equivalent amount of capital and labour but X has abundant grasslands and suitable climate for beef production whilst Y has less favourable climate and agricultural conditions but a more highly skilled workforce. There are no unemployed factors in either country. When both countries are using their resources equally to produce both goods output is as follows:

Country	Beef (Units)	Cars (Units)
X	1000	200
Y	200	1000
Total production before specialisation	1200	1200

If however each country specialises in the production of those goods at which they are most efficient, i.e. X specialises in beef and Y in cars, then output is as follows:

Country	Beef (Units)	Cars (Units)
X	2000	NIL
Y	NIL	2000
Total production after specialisation	2000	2000

(Note: It was originally assumed that each country was using half of its resources in the production of each good, therefore if country X could produce 1000 units with half its resources logically it could produce 2000 with all its resources.)

The **net gains** from specialisation are 800 units of beef and 800 units of cars (note: in specialising X gave up the production of 200 cars and Y the production of 200 beef units leaving a **net** gain of 800 of each). In this example each country specialised in the production of goods in which they had a **comparative advantage.**

4 The principle of absolute advantage

If one country is more efficient in the production of both goods, i.e. has an **absolute advantage** then it may still be worthwhile engaging in trade if one country specialises in the production of those goods in which its disadvantage is least; referred to as **least comparative disadvantage,** and the other country those goods in which the **comparative advantage is greatest.**

Suppose that country X was more efficient in the production of both beef and cars, and the positions before specialisation are as follows:

Country	Beef (Units)	Cars (Units)
X	1000	600
Y	900	200
Total production before specialisation	1900	800

Specialisation is still worthwhile as X's comparative advantage is greatest in car production, i.e. three times as efficient whereas X is only 1.1 times more efficient in production of beef. Therefore if X specialises in cars and devotes nine-tenths of its resources to car production and one tenth to beef production, whilst Y specialises in beef, total production will be as follows:

Country	Beef (Units)	Cars (Units)
X	200	1080
Y	1800	NIL
Total production after specialisation	2000	1080
Gain	100	280

5 Gains from trade

Using the same example the **gains from trade** can be illustrated by the use of production possibility curves (or boundaries) as in Figure 32.1. The production possibility boundaries are linear because it is assumed the diminishing returns do not occur as resources are transferred from one use to another. In the figure the lines Y–Y and X–X are the production possibility boundaries of both countries prior to specialisation and trade. The line T–T is the total production possibility boundary for both countries after specialisation and prior to trade. Although specialisation has brought gains in total production trade must occur. The **terms of trade**, i.e. beef: cars, must lie between the two sets of (internal) domestic opportunity cost ratios which are:

    In   X   1.6 : 1   (beef : cars)
         Y   4.5 : 1   (beef : cars)

Hence the terms of trade must lie between 1.6 and 4.5: 1, for example 3:1.

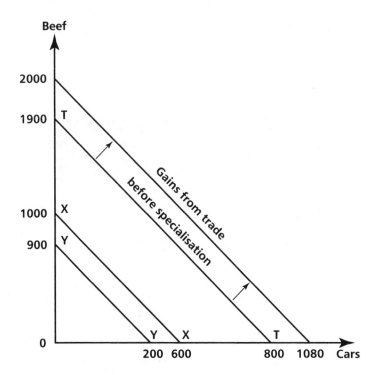

Figure 32.1

If the terms of trade are 3:1, X can trade 1 car with Y and receive 3 units of beef in return, whereas to transfer resources domestically X would only gain 1.6 units of beef. Conversely Y can gain 1 car in exchange for 3 units of beef by trading, whereas to gain 1 car by transferring resources domestically it would give up 4.5 units of beef. Both countries will therefore gain from specialisation and exchange providing the terms of trade lie between the two domestic (non trading) opportunity cost ratios.

Trade will continue as long as the **domestic opportunity cost ratios in the two countries are different.** Trade would cease when it cost more in terms of resources for X to import beef than to produce it. If X could produce beef more cheaply in terms of cars than Y by transferring resources to beef production then trade would cease.

Trade theory must be qualified however to allow for the fact that there may be some loss of efficiency when transferring production from one good to another. Also, transport costs will be incurred, which may outweigh a marginal cost advantage.

6 Terms of trade

The **terms of trade** refer to the rate at which one nation's goods can be exchanged for those of others. In the example above it was 3:1. In reality physical goods are not exchanged but prices are paid in various currencies. The terms of trade are measured by means of a **terms of trade index** which is calculated as:

$$\frac{\text{index of export prices}}{\text{index of import prices}} \times 100$$

The base year of the index is 100. An improvement in the terms of trade is said to be **favourable** and shows as an increase in the index, indicating that a given volume of exports can be exchanged for a greater volume of imports. A fall in the index is said to be **unfavourable** as a given volume of exports can only be exchanged for a smaller volume of imports. The terms of trade index has important implications for the UK's performance as a trading nation.

Table 32.1 shows the UK terms of trade 1981–1995.

TABLE 32.1	
YEAR	TERMS OF TRADE (1990=100)
1981	105.9
1982	104.3
1983	102.6
1984	101.5
1985	101.9
1986	96.1
1987	96.7
1988	98.6
1989	98.8
1990	100
1991	100.2
1992	101.4
1993	103.5
1994	102.2
1995	98.9

Source: Economic Trends

7 Trade restrictions

Despite the gains from free international trade, nations have frequently attempted to restrict the amount of trade in order to protect their domestic economies from the effects of foreign competition. The competition may be from lower cost producers due to either, or both, greater efficiency and lower wage costs. Such an attitude is referred to as 'protectionism' and restrictions on trade may take a variety of forms:

- Tariffs – taxes on imports, generally referred to as duties.
- Quotas – physical limits on the quantities of specified goods which can be imported.
- Subsidies – to domestic producers to reduce their prices below those of foreign competitors.
- Exchange control regulations – limit the amount of foreign currency available to pay for imports.
- Physical controls – a complete ban or embargo.

8 Arguments for trade restrictions

The arguments generally put forward in favour of restrictions on trade are:

- To protect a new or developing industry – the 'infant industry case'.
- To assist in the elimination of a balance of payments deficit.
- To protect the domestic economy against unemployment caused by too many imported goods.
- To protect strategically important industries such as iron, steel and shipbuilding.
- To protect the domestic economy from 'unfair' competition, in particular 'dumping' where excess production is sold abroad at cost in order to cover marginal costs only, and allow profits to be made on the domestic market; or where 'cheap' labour is being used (e.g. child labour).

9 The costs of protection

Protecting domestic industries from competition in order to ensure their survival is a dubious argument. In the long run protection from competition results in a loss of efficiency and inventiveness, and when eventually industries have to face international competition again they will be weak and ill-equipped to do so.

The costs of protection however are generally borne by consumers who are forced to pay higher prices and have a restricted choice of goods. Also, trade is possibly the best way of forging links between countries and promoting international co-operation. Attempts to interfere with trade generally result in some form of retaliation which may lead to a disastrous trade war where everybody loses.

10 Changes over time

It cannot be assumed that because a country has a comparative advantage in the production of a particular good that it will retain that advantage indefinitely. The centres of comparative advantage in production tend to change over time, particularly with changes in technology and the growth of capital resources, for example, Britain's comparative advantage in the production of cotton textiles has shifted towards the cotton producing countries. Changes in comparative advantage can be a major cause of **structural unemployment** (see Chapter 30).

Self assessment questions

1 Distinguish between an absolute and a comparative advantage.

2 What are the gains from trade?

3 What are the 'terms of trade'?

4 How is the 'terms of trade index' calculated?

5 Why might nations impose restrictions on trade?

6 What are the main arguments against restrictions on trade?

7 What forms may restrictions on trade take?

33

Balance of payments

1 Recording transactions

The balance of payments in the accounting sense is a record of all the transactions of the UK with the rest of the world. Like all accounting balance sheets the balance of payments taken as a whole **must** be in balance; what is more important however is the performance in the component sections.

Table 33.1 illustrates the summary balance of payments accounts for the UK for 1995.

TABLE 33.1	
	£ m
1.Visible balance (trade balance)	-11,550
2.Invisible balance	+4,880
3.CURRENT BALANCE	-6,670
4.Net Transactions in U.K. Assets and Liabilities	+4,798
5.Balancing Item	+1,872
(note (3) + (4) + (5) = NIL)	

The figures shown are net figures, i.e. the figure after imports (inflows) are offset by corresponding exports (outflows).

2 The current balance

The part of the accounts which receives most attention is the **current balance**. The current balance has two components, **visibles** and **invisibles.**

● The **visible balance** comprises of the import and export of **goods.** Until the 1980s Britain rarely had a surplus on visibles, however after the advent of North Sea oil a surplus on visible trade was regularly achieved although by the mid 1980s the trade balance had again deteriorated.

- **Invisibles** refers to trade services and to transfers. These include:
  - Shipping.
  - Civil aviation.
  - Insurance.
  - Banking.
  - Tourism.
  - Interest and profits.
  - Government transfers, e.g. military and diplomatic expenditure.
  - Private transfers.

Britain has generally had a substantial surplus on invisible trade, sufficient to outweigh the deficit on visibles. Although on occasion the deficit on trade has been so great that even after allowing for invisibles there was a substantial **deficit on current account**. Table 33.2 illustrates how a trade deficit can become a current account surplus after the inclusion of invisibles.

TABLE 33.2	
	£m
VISIBLE TRADE	
Exports	2500
Imports	3300
Trade deficit	- 800
INVISIBLE TRADE	
Exports	1900
Imports	1000
Invisible surplus	+ 900
CURRENT ACCOUNT SURPLUS	+ 100

The current account is generally taken as being the main indicator of the nation's performance in international trade.

3 Transactions in UK assets and liabilities

Transactions in UK assets and liabilities refers to the increases or decreases in the UK assets and liabilities during that period. It refers only to new transactions in that period and not the total stock of UK external assets or liabilities. This section therefore records the increase or decrease in the following:

- Foreign assets, including foreign currency held by UK residents and the UK government.
- Liabilities of the UK to the residents of foreign countries. They represent an increase or decrease in the ownership of UK assets which are held by overseas residents which may be individuals, firms, or governments, and include holdings of sterling. In the

presentation of the accounts it is important to note that an increase in the external assets held by UK residents is indicated with a negative (–) value and an increase in external liabilities by a positive (+) value.

A deficit on current account may be offset by a surplus on the capital transactions, i.e. a net asset inflow. This may imply however an increase in future invisible outflows when the remittance of profits and interest overseas has to be made.

Official financing refers to the changes which take place in the reserves if the deficit (or surplus) on the current account is not matched by a surplus (or deficit) on the capital transactions. If, for example, there is an overall deficit then it must have been met either from the official reserves which would have been reduced, or foreign currency borrowing from abroad. A surplus would increase the reserves or be used to repay earlier loans. This is included under the assets section of the accounts.

4 The balancing item

As stated earlier the balance of payments taken as a whole must balance in the accounting sense because every transaction has a double aspect; as in accounting every debit must have a matching credit. For example, if a UK firm sells goods to a foreign firm then the value of the export is a credit (+) in the current account, however the payment for the export represents a debit (–) in the deposits held by the foreign firm in UK banks.

The sum of the current balance and the net transaction balance must therefore be zero. In reality however due to various errors and omissions this may not be the case and the **balancing item** is added to the net transactions balance of the capital account, which is known with a higher degree of certainty, in order to ensure that the account balances. Eventually the source of some of the errors is found and the adjustments to the accounts made later. Concern has been expressed over recent years regarding the size of the balancing item and its implications for the reliability of the accounts.

5 Equilibrium/disequilibrium

Reference to **equilibrium** or **disequilibrium** in the balance of payments usually refers to the **current account**. Equilibrium is generally taken to refer to the fact that exports are equal to imports. This definition has to be qualified however, and before it is truly meaningful should include discussion of:

- The time period involved.
- The exchange rate – if the exchange rate is freely floating then in theory equilibrium in the balance of payments will always be attained in the long run. (See Chapter 34).
- The exchange rate may be managed in order to manipulate transactions in such a way as to make them balance.

6 Balance of payments deficit

A deficit in the balance of payments means that in the short run the nation is enjoying a higher material standard of living than it would otherwise do. Such a situation can however only be maintained for as long as there are adequate reserves. In the absence of bottomless reserves no country can run a balance of payments deficit indefinitely.

7 Policies to correct a deficit

Policies to correct a balance of payments deficit include:

● A reduction in the exchange rate to make exports cheaper and imports dearer.
● Import controls – which may result in 'retaliation'.
● Expenditure 'dampening policies' – reducing the level of domestic demand for all goods including imports. This has high costs in terms of domestic output and therefore employment.
● Expenditure 'switching policies', intended to shift domestic expenditure from imports to domestically produced goods. An example here is raising the price of imports relative to domestic goods by imposing duties.
● Subsidies or aid to exporters.
● Increasing the domestic rate of interest in order to attract capital inflows.

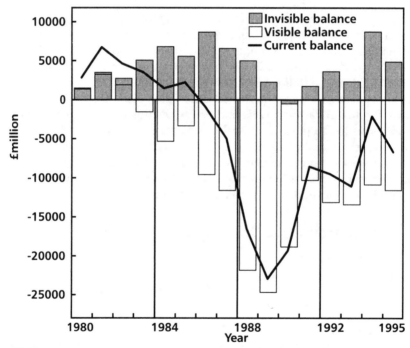

Figure 33.1

8 Recent trends

Figure 33.1 illustrates Britain's balance of payments 1980 to 1995.

Quite clearly there has been an improvement in Britain's current account balance from the large deficits of 1989 and 1990. Economic recovery is part of the reason along with an increase in exports of cars in particular. Many of these are cars produced by foreign owned manufacturers such as Nissan, Toyota and Honda.

At the same time imports have grown and services have under performed compared to Britain's major competitors. The outlook for the rest of the 1990s is therefore not as good as the trend would indicate.

Self assessment questions

1 Distinguish between visibles and invisibles.

2 How is the current balance obtained?

3 Does a deficit on the balance of payments necessarily imply a reduction in the standard of living of the nation?

4 How is the total currency flow obtained?

5 In what ways may a deficit on the balance of payments be financed?

6 Discuss the arguments for and against import controls in the UK.

7 What policies can a government adopt in order to correct a balance of payments deficit?

34

Exchange rates

1 The price of currency

The exchange rate refers to the rate at which one currency can be exchanged for another, e.g. pounds for deutschmarks, or dollars. As we are discussing how many dollars etc. we can obtain for a pound then it is the same as discussing the **price of foreign currency**. In the rest of this discussion reference will be made only to the rate of exchange between dollars and pounds (sterling), there are of course rates of exchange between all currencies and the analysis of them is identical.

Exchange rates are important because they determine the prices at which UK goods will be sold abroad, and the price at which foreign goods will be sold in the UK. They therefore have a direct effect on the balance of payments and the domestic economy.

2 Changes in the value of the pound

If the exchange rate between pounds and dollars was originally £1 = $2, and then on the international market began to be exchanged at £1 = $1.50 we would refer to a **fall** in the **value of the pound** relative to the dollar, and the price of UK goods selling in America in dollar prices would fall. If the rate of exchange became £1 = $2.50 we would refer to a **rise** in the **value of the pound** relative to the dollar and the dollar price of UK goods in America would rise.

3 The determination of exchange rates

As mentioned above, the exchange rate is really the price of foreign currency and as is the case with other goods, price is determined by supply and demand. In the absence of intervention by governments therefore, exchange rates are determined by the demand for, and supply of, currencies. The price of the pound in terms of the dollar will depend upon the demand for the pound by holders of dollars and the supply of pounds will be from holders of pounds who want to buy dollars. The demand for pounds is derived from the demand by overseas residents for British goods and who require pounds to pay for them. The supply of pounds is derived from the demand by UK residents for goods from overseas and who require foreign currency to pay for them. In exchanging pounds for foreign currency, in this case dollars, the supply of pounds is increased. The demand for, and supply of, pounds takes place on the **foreign exchange markets**, and the **equilibrium exchange rate** will be where demand and supply are equal. In Figure 34.1 the equilibrium exchange rate is where the demand and supply for sterling are equal. Clearly the value of a nation's currency depends ultimately upon its overseas trade performance. A balance of payments surplus would therefore indicate a high demand for pounds in order to pay for UK goods, the exchange rate would therefore be high relative to other currencies. A deficit would imply an excess supply of pounds and a weak currency.

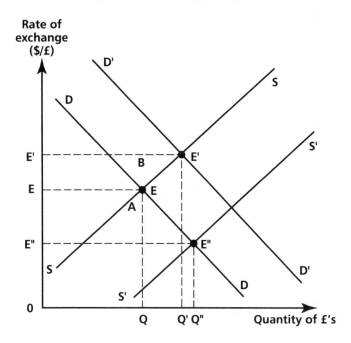

Figure 34.1

4 Changes in demand

In Figure 34.1 the shift in the demand for sterling from DD to D'D' has caused an increase in the equilibrium exchange rate relative to dollars from E to E'. Such a shift could be caused by:

- An increased preference amongst US citizens for British goods.
- An increase in incomes in the United States.
- Capital inflows to the UK.
- Speculation.

5 Changes in supply

An increase in imports into the UK from the USA would increase the supply of pounds, shown in Figure 34.1 as the shift in the supply curve from SS to S'S', with a consequent reduction in the equilibrium exchange rate from E to E''.

6 Changes in the value of the pound

A fall in the value of the pound will, ceteris paribus:

- Raise the price of imports.
- Reduce the price of exports.

An increase in the value of the pound will, ceteris paribus:

- Reduce the price of imports.
- Raise the price of exports.

7 Purchasing power parity theory

This explains the equilibrium exchange rate between two currencies in terms of the price levels in the two countries. It states that the value of one currency relative to another depends upon the relative purchasing power of the two currencies in their domestic economies, i.e. the exchange rate will be determined at the point where the purchasing power of a unit of the currency is the same in each country. The theory can be expressed as follows:

$$\textbf{The price of the pound in dollars} = \frac{\textbf{US price level}}{\textbf{UK price level}}$$

This has important implications for the relationship between exchange rates and inflation. Although short-run deviations from purchasing power parity are possible, in the long run the theory probably does hold true.

8 Floating exchange rates

Floating, free or flexible exchange rates refer to an exchange rate system such as that described above where the equilibrium rate of exchange is determined by the forces of demand and supply on the foreign exchange market. The following characteristics of floating exchange rates should be borne in mind:

- A businessperson who enters a contract with an overseas supplier for delivery of goods at a future date with payment in foreign currency upon delivery never knows exactly how much they will have to pay as the exchange rate may be subject to fluctuation in the intervening period. Some argue that this tends to act as a deterrent to international trade. It is possible however to safeguard against currency fluctuations by buying currency ahead on the forward exchange market.
- In a free exchange rate system the action of speculators will tend to stabilise the currency around a long term trend as they buy the currency when it is weak and sell it when it is dear.
- Under a flexible exchange rate system the balance of payments should be self correcting. A deficit results in a fall in the exchange rate which reduces the price of UK exports and therefore demand increases. At the same time the increase in the price of imports should reduce some of the demand for imports. Eventually a balance of payments equilibrium should be re-established.

9 Fixed exchange rate

Fixed exchange rate systems are intended to remove the uncertainty associated with flexible rates. The fixed exchange rate system was introduced at the Bretton Woods conference in 1944 and was effective from 1947. The system was intended to bring stability to world trade and to stimulate its growth. The **International Monetary Fund** (IMF) was also established in order to assist countries with balance of payments difficulties. The fixed exchange rate system was finally abandoned in 1973.

Each currency was given a **par value** in terms of the dollar, e.g. £1 = $2.80 and the central bank of each country (in the UK the Bank of England) agreed to intervene on the foreign exchange markets in order to maintain the value of its currency 1 % either side of the par value, widened to 2¼% either side of par in 1971. In Figure 34.2 the par value is £1 = $2.40. As a result of an increase in imports the supply of pounds shifts from SS to S'S'and equilibrium shifts to E' with a new exchange rate at $2.00. However the central bank intervenes and buys pounds with gold or foreign currency shifting the demand from DD to D'D' with a new equilibrium at E'' and the exchange rate returns to par value at $2.40. Had the exchange, rate risen to £1 = $3.00 the Bank of England would have intervened and sold pounds in order to increase the supply and return to the par value. An essential component of such a scheme is large reserves of gold and foreign currency. Under the scheme member countries could draw reserves from the IMF for this purpose when their currencies came under pressure.

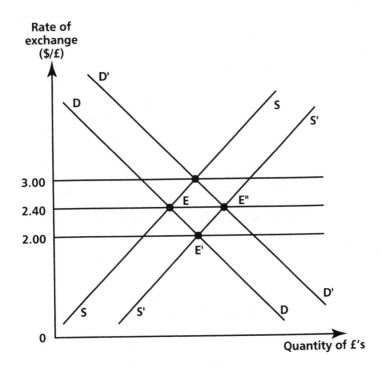

Figure 34.2

10 The advantages and disadvantages of a fixed system

The major **advantage** claimed for fixed exchange rates is that they eliminate uncertainty from international trade.

The alleged **disadvantages** of fixed exchange rates are:

- If the original rate is set too high, i.e. above the equilibrium rate, then it will be difficult to achieve a balance of payments equilibrium.
- Domestic policies for managing the economy are dominated by the need to maintain the external value of the currency.
- Fixed exchange rates are subject to extreme speculative pressures. The speculator has 'everything to gain and little to lose'. If he anticipates a **devaluation** of the sterling exchange rate and sells pounds, this can only add to the pressure for devaluation; after devaluation he can buy the pounds back at a lower rate. Even if the devaluation does not occur he is no worse off. In the event of an anticipated revaluation the purchase of pounds can only add to the pressure for revaluation, again if it does not come about the speculator has little to lose. The pound came under extreme pressure from speculators in the 1960s and early 1970s when the overvalued pound resulted in a series of balance of payments deficits.

11 Devaluation

Devaluation refers to the deliberate reduction of the exchange rate relative to other currencies in a fixed exchange rate system, the objective being to make exports more competitive terms of foreign currency whilst imports become more expensive. Under the fixed exchange rate system this was allowed where a nation was subject to recurring balance of payments difficulties. The UK devalued sterling in 1949 and in 1967. **Revaluation** refers to the decision to raise the par value of the exchange rate. Devaluation will not necessarily result in an improvement in the balance of payments however.

- If the demand for exports is **inelastic** then the devaluation may not raise total export earnings, and the desired improvement in the balance of payments will be even more difficult to achieve if the demand for imports is also **inelastic**.
- If other trading nations retaliate with a successive round of devaluations then the advantage gained from the devaluation will soon be lost.
- There must be sufficient excess capacity in the domestic economy to meet the increased demand for exports.

12 J-curve effect

The initial impact of a currency depreciation or devaluation may well be to cause a deterioration in the current account. In a manufacturing economy such as the UK this occurs because raw materials have to be imported at a higher cost than previously and in larger quantities if more goods are to be manufactured for export. Eventually the effect of the depreciation results in a higher level of exports, and domestic goods are substituted for imports, the current account then moves into surplus. This effect, known as the **J-curve effect**, is illustrated in Figure 34.3.

The depreciation at M initially results in a deterioration of the current account. At point N the effect of the depreciation begins to feed through to exports and the current account starts to improve, moving back into surplus at Q.

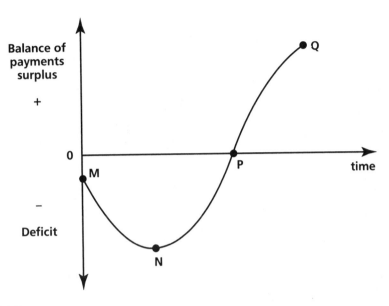

Figure 34.3

13 Depreciation and appreciation

Under a fixed exchange rate system devaluation tends to become confused with issues such as national pride, under a floating rate the exchange rate adjusts automatically to equilibrium with the domestic economy being less sensitive to changes in external demand. Under floating exchange rates a fall in the exchange rate is referred to as a **depreciation** and an increase in the exchange rate as an **appreciation**.

14 Effective exchange rate

The discussion of exchange rates so far has been in terms of the rate between the pound and the dollar, in reality of course the pound will be appreciating in terms of some currencies whilst depreciating against others, for example it may weaken against the yen and at the same time strengthen against the franc. In order to evaluate the overall change in the value of sterling a measure known as the effective exchange rate is used. The **effective exchange rate** (EER) shows the movements in sterling relative to a weighted average of the currencies of the UK's major trading partners. The movements in sterling are therefore measured against a 'basket' of other currencies and the importance (weight) of these currencies in the basket is determined by the amount of trade we conduct with that nation, i.e. it is 'trade weighted.' Recent movements in the sterling exchange rate and the EER are shown in Figures 34.4 and 34.5.

%

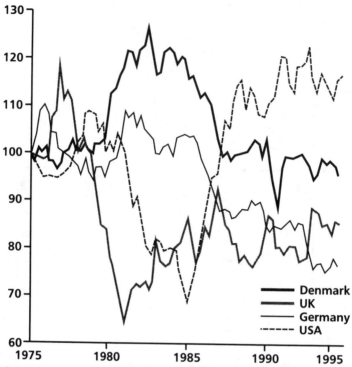

Figure 34.4
Real effective exchange rate, four countries 1975–95 (%, 1975 = 100%)

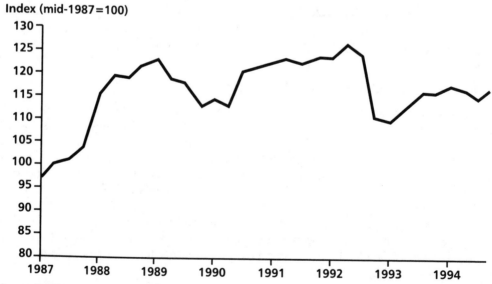

Figure 34.5
UK real effective exchange rate 1987–95

15 The end of the fixed exchange rate system

The devaluation of sterling in 1967 was the first crack in the fixed exchange rate system. Following this other currencies came under successive bouts of speculative pressure, and later with the onset of world recession, inflation, and the oil price crisis of 1973/74, the system became increasingly unstable. Despite various attempts to restore it, in particular the Smithsonian Institute agreement in 1971 and the attempt to establish a European Monetary System, sterling was allowed to float in June 1972 effectively signalling the end of the Bretton Woods system.

16 The EMS

In 1979, member states of the EU established the **European Monetary System (EMS)**, with the objective of creating a European zone of monetary stability as a preliminary step towards full **European Monetary Union (EMU)** and eventually a single currency.

17 The ERM

The **Exchange Rate Mechanism (ERM)** was established to link the currencies of the member countries by restricting exchange rate movements within agreed bands as a means of achieving the desired monetary stability. It is therefore a fixed exchange rate system similar to the Bretton Woods scheme.

Britain joined the ERM with effect from 7th October 1990 at the parity of £1 = DM 2.95 with the value to be maintained within a 6% band on either side of the par value. The value of the pound was to be maintained by the Bank of England, in conjunction with the other central banks of the EMS members, buying and selling pounds. If intervention on the money markets failed then interest rate policy was to be used as the next stage, and as a last resort application could be made for a realignment.

Fixed exchange rate systems inevitably mean that internal economic policy becomes dominated by the need to maintain the external value of the currency, and hence there is some loss of control over domestic policy decisions. The government's medium term financial strategy emphasised control of the money supply as its policy objective and the EMS emphasised the exchange rate.

This conflict over policy objectives impaled the government upon the horns of a major dilemma. As the UK economy slid into recession in 1991 pressure mounted for reductions in interest rates; this, together with a loss of confidence in the UK economy, resulted in the selling of sterling which drifted toward the bottom of its permitted range. By August 1992 the pound appeared hopelessly over-valued against the D-mark, the balance of payments was heavily into deficit and the domestic recession was deepening. In such a situation it would normally be expected to have a depreciating currency and reductions in interest rates. The commitment to the ERM however ruled out these options, and the risk of even higher interest rates mounted. On 16th September 1992 ('Black Wednesday') there was massive selling of sterling resulting in large scale intervention by the Bank of England to the tune of £13 billion of foreign currency and an increase in interest rates to 15%, without a recovery, resulting in the suspension of Britain's membership of the ERM the same day.

18 'Black Wednesday' and beyond

1993 saw further volatility, the Spanish peseta and the Portugese escudo were devalued further. The Danish krone experienced speculation as did the Belgian franc. This nearly destroyed the ERM. The result was that the ERM finance ministers declared 15% bands of fluctuation instead of the 2.25% bands. Although the ERM survived in principle the bands were so wide that they were thought to be rather meaningless.

Britain's view was to wait and see. However many believe, that rather than the 16th September 1992 being 'Black Wednesday' it did in fact produce beneficial effects for the UK. The large devaluation produced an export-led recovery and at the same time the government was allowed to use its monetary policy with greater effect, freed from the constraints of membership of the ERM.

19 EMU – The future

The crises of 1992 and 1993 seemed to signal the end of the EMU but in 1994 it returned to the political agenda. European Union leaders are preparing for a single currency, already named as the 'Euro', and predictions are that it will start in 1999. There has been debate and argument over the conditions for entry and France and Germany's commitment has been questioned.

Britain has negotiated an 'opt-out' agreement which requires the agreement of a future British government, with a majority. In return Britain has agreed not to prevent or influence other EU members joining a single European currency.

Self assessment questions

1 Distinguish between fixed and floating exchange rates.

2 Why was the fixed exchange rate system introduced?

3   What are the major disadvantages of fixed exchange rates?

4 Distinguish between a devaluation and a depreciation of a currency.

5 In what circumstances would devaluation result in an improvement in the balance of payments?

6 In the absence of official intervention in the foreign exchange market, what factors are likely to influence changes in a country's exchange rate?

7 Examine the courses of action open to a country faced with a deficit on its balance of payments.

8 On a given day the demand for, and supply of, sterling in the foreign exchange market are as follows:–

Price of sterling (in francs)	11.50	11.80	12.10	13.00
Sterling demanded (£ million)	25	22	20	17
Sterling supplied (£ million)	15	17	20	22

Exchange rates

(a) What will be the equilibrium exchange rate?

(b) Britain's trade figures show a deficit, and demand for sterling falls by £5 million. What is the new equilibrium exchange rate?

(c) In these new circumstances the British authorities decide to peg the exchange rate at £1 = 12.10 francs. What steps must they take?

(d) If the exchange rate was successfully pegged at £1 = 12.10 francs, would sterling be over-valued or undervalued?

Section I

Containing the following chapters:

Chapter 35 – Defining the money supply.

Chapter 36 – The banking system & the control of credit.

The many measures of acceptable exchange and the system used to safeguard and control these acceptable means of exchange.

This section should enable students to:

- *Understand* the role of the Bank of England.
- *Explain* how banks create credit.
- *Contrast* the different measures of the money supply.
- *Evaluate* the value of the money market to the economy.

Keywords to consider:

narrow money; broad money; PSBR; Bank of England; reserve banks; fiduciary issue; money market discount market; money at call; lender of the last resort; treasury bills; clearing banks; commercial banks; bank credit multiplier; liabilities; assets.

35

Defining the money supply

Before we consider the policy instruments which may be utilised by government in the control of the money supply (Chapter 38) we need to define precisely what we mean by the money supply. It is suggested that students re-read the section on money in Chapter 3 before commencing on this chapter.

1 A definition

Money can be defined as anything which is generally acceptable in return for goods and services, however in an advanced economy such a definition is not sufficiently precise for operational purposes. The main definitions used in the UK are M0 and M4. M0 is generally referred to as a 'narrow' definition of money and M4 as a 'broad' definition. The components of these definitions are approximately as follows:

- M0 = Notes and coins in circulation with the public + banks' till money + banks' operational balances with the Bank of England.
- M4 = Notes and coins in circulation with the public + private sector sterling time bank deposits + building society deposits.

(Note that sight bank deposits are generally referred to as current accounts and time deposits as deposit accounts).

Prior to 1987 the main definitions in use were M0, M1, sterling M3 (£M3) and the measures of private sector liquidity PSLI and PSL2. The main measure for targeting purposes between 1976 and 1987 was £M3, but the targeting of £M3 was abandoned because it was always outside the growth range targeted and also its relationship to money GDP was never clear. In March 1987 two new broad definitions were introduced M4, and M5 as a new measure of private sector liquidity. The exact composition of the main monetary aggregates is given in Figure 35.1.

Main monetary aggregates

Narrow money

'Narrow money' refers to money balances which are readily available to finance current spending, that is to say for 'transactions purposes'.

M0

Notes and coin in circulation with the public
plus banks' till money
plus banks' operational balances with the Bank of England

Broad money

'Broad money' refers to money held for transactions purposes and money held as a form of saving. It provides an indicator of the private sector's holdings of relatively liquid assets – assets which could be converted with relative ease and without capital loss into spending on goods and services.

M3

Notes and coin in circulation with the public
plus private sector sterling sight bank deposits
plus private sector sterling time bank deposits
plus private sector holdings of sterling bank certificates of deposit

M4

M3 plus private sector holdings of building society shares and deposits and sterling certificates of deposit
minus building society holdings of bank deposits and bank certificates of deposit, and notes and coin

M5

M4 plus holdings by the private sector (excluding building societies) of money market instruments (bank bills, Treasury bills, local authority deposits), certificates of tax deposit and national savings instruments (excluding certificates, SAYE and other long-term deposits)

Figure 35.1
Source: EPR No 195

2 Money aggregates

The definitions above are often referred to as monetary 'aggregates' as they aggregate together various forms of 'money'.

- **Narrow money** refers generally to money held predominantly for spending immediately or in the near future on goods and services, i.e. for transactions purposes.
- **Broad money** refers generally to money held for transactions purposes and as a store of value. When we say that it provides a guide to liquidity, we mean that it provides an indicator of the private sectors' holding of relatively liquid assets – i.e. assets which could be converted with relative ease into spending on goods and services without capital loss.

3 Changing measures

It would appear that the introduction of M0 in March 1984 was a consequence of the difficulty in achieving targets for monetary growth utilising broader definitions such as M3. Broad measures give an indication of the growth of liquidity in the economy whilst narrower definitions give a better idea of how money is being used for transactions as opposed to saving.

Because of institutional changes which take place in the economy it becomes necessary to adjust the definitions, particularly the broader ones, from time to time. The introduction of M4 in May 1987 reflects the fact that the distinction between building societies and banks had become increasingly blurred and that building society deposits are increasingly used for transactions rather than just savings. Also the building societies now offer a wide range of banking services, such as cheque book facilities and cash points, and since the 1986 Building Societies Act they have been able to extend their lending beyond lending for house purchase and can grant loans and issue credit cards. At the same time the banks have greatly expanded their mortgage lending. The trend for building societies to become PLC's and gain full bank status has confused the situation even further. These developments make it sensible to concentrate on measures of broad money like M4 which include the liabilities of both banks and building societies rather than measures such as M3 which cover only those of the banks. M5 is a broad 'liquidity' aggregate and is an excellent measure of those assets which constitute a temporary abode of purchasing power. M4 has totally replaced £M3 as the main focus of attention in terms of broad money.

4 A summary

Narrow and broad definitions can be summarised as:

Narrow = M0
Broad = M3, M4, M5.

The composition of the main monetary definitions is summarised in Figure 35.2

5 The PSBR

The **public sector borrowing requirement (PSBR)** refers to the deficit between the income and expenditure of the public sector (in particular central and local government). It arises because governments have generally failed to balance their budgets (see Chapter 39) i.e. their expenditures have been greater than their incomes from taxation and other sources. This deficit is usually financed by debt sales (government bonds etc.) to the 'non bank' private sector, borrowing from the banking system, borrowing from overseas, or by issuing more cash (notes and coin) to the public. There is a close relationship between the PSBR and the money supply, which will be explored more closely in Chapter 43.

6 Control of the money supply

If we consider, for the purposes of our discussion, control of the money supply to refer to the M4 definition, we can identify those variables for which policies will be required in the control of the money supply:

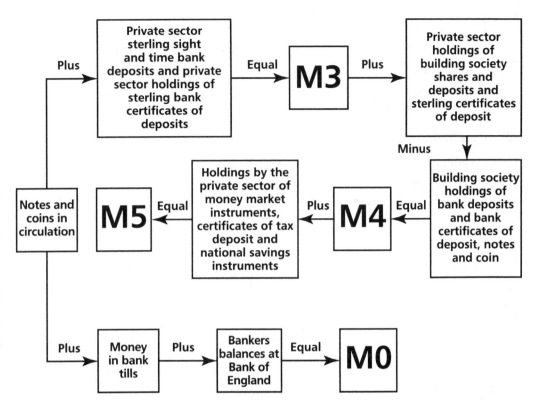

Figure 35.2 Composition of the main monetary aggregates

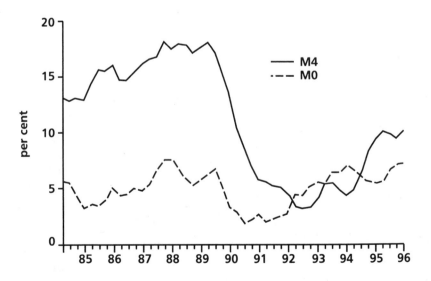

Figure 35.3 Broad and narrow money growth 1980–1996

- Bank lending to the private sector (credit policy).
- The control of the size of the PSBR.
- The sale of more public sector debt to the non-banks (debt management policy).

In the UK, between 1987 and 1990, public sector income exceeded expenditure, this budget surplus is referred to as public sector debt repayment (PSDR) as it is available for repayment of the national debt.

Self assessment questions

1 Distinguish between 'broad' and 'narrow' definitions of money.

2 Define M0, M3 and M4.

3 What are the components of an increase in M4?

36

The banking system & the control of credit

In this chapter we will discuss the structure of the UK banking system, the role of the Bank of England, the process by which the commercial banks can create credit and the way in which this credit creating ability is controlled by the Bank of England.

1 The Bank of England

The Bank of England (referred to as 'The Bank') is the institution in the UK which is vested with the control of the banking system and, jointly with the Treasury, the implementation of the government's monetary policy. Banks which undertake these responsibilities are referred to as **central banks** or **reserve banks** and are found in most industrialised countries.

Since its founding in 1694 the Bank of England has always been closely associated with government policy, a fact which was explicitly recognised when it was taken into public ownership in 1946.The Bank is managed by a board of directors, known as the Court, which consists of a governor, deputy governor and 16 directors, all appointed by the crown. For accounting purposes the Bank is divided into two functions each producing its own balance sheet.

- **The Issue Department** is responsible for the notes in circulation and their issue.
- **The Banking Department** is responsible for the other functions of the Bank of England and the commercial banks.

2 The Bank Charter Act

The **Bank Charter Act of 1844** allowed the note issue to exceed the stock of gold backing the issue. Notes not backed by gold are known as the **fiduciary issue**. Since 1931 when the 'Gold Standard' was abandoned, the whole of the note issue has been fiduciary. It is no longer backed by gold and neither is it convertible into gold, its backing now being confidence in its value.

3 The Bank's traditional responsibilities

The responsibilities of the Bank of England can be summarised as follows:

- It acts as banker to the government, and as such it keeps the accounts of the government departments. In order to ensure that the government always has sufficient finance for its expenditure it manages the government's short term borrowing requirement through the Treasury Bill issue and by making advances. It also manages the longer term debt of the public sector, maintains the stock register, pays dividends, and conducts new issues.
- It is also responsible for providing financial advice to the government.
- It is responsible, together with the Treasury, for implementing the government's monetary policy.
- It is the 'bankers' bank'. The commercial banks maintain their balances in current accounts with the Bank. It also provides them with advice and assistance.
- The Bank is the sole authority responsible for issuing notes in England and Wales.
- The Bank acts on behalf of the government on the foreign exchange market when intervention is felt to be necessary to support the pound.
- It acts as 'lender of last resort' to the banking system. If there is a problem of liquidity in the banking system the Bank will give assistance.
- The Bank participates in the activities of such international agencies as the International Monetary Fund and the International Bank for Reconstruction and Development (IBRD).
- The Bank also acts as banker to foreign central banks.
- An important role is the supervising of the banking and financial institutions in order to ensure their stability and efficient operation. When part of the system is in difficulty the Bank will provide support so as to prevent any undermining of the stability of the system as a whole. The major institutions take advice and leadership from the Bank partly because of its pre-eminent role in the system, but also because in the final analysis it may be essential to their survival. The fall of BCCI saw the Bank of England investigating and producing new guidelines for all banking and financial institutions.

4 Changes in financial supervision

May 1997 saw the biggest overhaul of financial supervision for many decades.

The newly elected Labour government changed two major aspects of the Bank of England's responsibilities.

- The Bank was given sole responsibility for the rate of interest, the Bank Rate, without government interference.
- The supervisory function of the Bank was removed with the intention of setting up a

new 'super-regulator'. This body would combine the functions of all of the previous supervisory bodies such as the SIB, PIA etc.

5 The money market

The **money market** is a general term used for a variety of financial institutions and includes:

- Discount houses
- Commercial banks
- Merchant banks (also known as 'accepting houses').
- The foreign exchange market.

6 The discount market

The discount market comprises of the eleven institutions which are members of the London Discount Market Association (LDMA). The original function of discount houses was to provide cash immediately, less a discount, to holders of bills of exchange which were not due for payment until after three months or longer. The discount houses are now recognised as occupying a central role in the financial system. They act in an intermediary role between the Bank of England and the commercial banks. The Bank of England utilises the discount market to implement its money market operations as part of its overall monetary policy.

To the commercial banks the discount market provides a form of investment which has the two desirable characteristics of being both **highly liquid** (i.e. can easily and quickly be repaid), and **safe**. Because the commercial banks can call in this money at very short notice it is referred to as **money at call**. The discount houses use these funds to invest in short-term assets such as Treasury bills and commercial bills.

Should the discount houses find themselves short of funds, for example if the banks call in their investments, then the discount houses can borrow from the Bank of England against suitable collateral. Because the terms of such lending, such as interest rates and duration of the loan, are so severe, the Bank of England is referred to as the **lender of last resort.** These stringent conditions are imposed because the arrangement is not intended to be part of the everyday operations of the Bank of England but as a true last resort.

This last resort borrowing facility is extended only to the discount houses. In return for this privilege the discount houses are expected to tender (offer to buy) each week the full issue of Treasury bills on offer. Normally other institutions will also want to buy them so the discount houses will only be required to buy a part of the issue, but in the event of there being a deficiency of demand the government can be assured that all the issue will be taken up and can therefore be certain of meeting its short-term borrowing requirement.

The Bank of England does not deal directly with the commercial banks, and the discount houses play an intermediary role between them. The Bank of England does not lend directly to the banks but does lend to, or buy bills from, the discount houses. In this way the Bank of England increases the stock of balances at the central bank which is available to the commercial banks. If the commercial banks run short of balances they call in their 'money at call' from the discount houses. These funds have however been reinvested in various short term assets and in order to meet their commitments the discount houses will be forced to utilise the services of the 'lender of last resort' – the Bank of England. By borrowing from the Bank of England the discount houses pass on these central bank balances to the commercial banks. The discount houses could be said to act as a 'buffer' between the Bank of England and the banking system.

7 Authorised institutions

Following the **1987 Banking Act** any institution wishing to carry on a banking role now requires to be authorised by the Bank of England. These banks, known as **Authorised Institutions,** are expected to provide information to the Bank on a regular basis and to respond to directives when given. The Bank also lays down criteria for the capital adequacy of the Institutions. The Act provides legal support to the supervisory role of the Bank of England over the banking system.

8 Treasury bills

Treasury bills are issued each week by the Bank of England on behalf of the government and are one of the means by which the government covers its short term borrowing requirement. The amounts vary between £5,000 and £1 million and are normally issued for a period of 91 days after which they are redeemable.

9 Government stocks (gilts)

The government also raises revenue through the sale of longer dated (or undated) securities. These are sold by the Bank's broker on the securities market, and as they are less liquid than Treasury bills they tend to be purchased outside the banking sector as well as within it. Government stocks can be bought and sold also on the secondary market (i.e. retraded after being acquired) and as they carry a fixed rate of interest the yield will vary inversely with the price.

10 Retail banks

Retail banks are those banks offering retail banking services to both the business and personal sector through a branch network. The main feature of these commercial banks is the money transmission function through cheques etc. The settlement of drawings by cheque or by other means is carried out through the banks Clearing House or banks Automated Clearing Services.The retail banks at January 1991 were:
Allied Irish Banks plc.; Bank of England, Banking Department; Bank of Ireland; Bank of Scotland; Barclays; Clydesdale; Co-operative; Coutts and Co.; Girobank; Lloyds; Midland; National Westminster; Northern Bank; Royal Bank of Scotland; TSB; Ulster Bank; Yorkshire Bank.

Much inter-bank indebtedness is self cancelling. For example, many of the cheques drawn on Barclays by Lloyds can be offset against cheques drawn on Lloyds by Barclays. This offsetting is carried out by the Clearing House and at the end of the day only the net indebtedness which is left is adjusted through the commercial banks' current accounts at the Bank of England.

11 Functions of commercial banks

One of the main functions of the commercial banks is to accept the deposits of their customers. Deposits can be held in one of three, ways:

- **Current accounts (sight deposits)**: These accounts do not earn interest and may be subject to charges for transactions. They are normally held for their convenience as a means of payment by cheque and they can be withdrawn on demand.
- **Deposit accounts (time deposits)**: These accounts earn interest and cannot be transferred by cheque. For large withdrawals a period of notice may be required, although today most banks show a degree of flexibility over this.
- **Large deposits:** Larger deposits attract a higher rate of interest. For deposits of about £50,000 or more a **certificate of deposit (CD)** may be issued. These have a maturity of between 3 months and 5 years and as they are **negotiable instruments** they can be traded. The banks find them a useful means of raising large sums of money for fixed periods; holders of CD's find them useful as they can be sold if funds are required immediately.

12 Liquidity v profit

Commercial banks like all companies need to earn a profit for their shareholders. This requirement however creates a dilemma for banking operations. Banks also have obligations to their depositors to pay them upon demand and to safeguard their deposits. When a customer makes a deposit with a commercial bank that deposit will be reinvested either in loans or on the money market, or elsewhere; but what is important is that the customers believe their deposits are safe. If customers collectively feared for the safety of their deposits and demanded them all back at the same time the bank would be unable to pay them out and in the absence of assistance from the central bank, may collapse. This is referred to as a 'run on the bank' and was common during the recession in the USA during the late 1920's. In order to be able to pay on demand the banks need to maintain a percentage of their total deposits in the form of cash (the cash ratio) and some in the form of assets which are easy to liquidate ('money at call'). The commercial banks have found that they can operate effectively on a cash ratio of about 8% which is sufficient to meet the everyday demands for cash. The desire to make profit, however, conflicts with the need to maintain liquidity in a system based almost entirely upon confidence, as the more profitable investments tend to be less liquid. Also profits are higher the more risky the investment, but a high level of risk may result in a loss of confidence. The art of successful banking is therefore to maintain a balanced 'portfolio' of investments. Bank investments therefore contain a range of investments from very low to modest risk, and with varying degrees of liquidity. Table 36.1 lists the assets held by the London clearing banks (May, 1995).

Prior to 1971 the banks were required to maintain 28% of their assets in investments which were highly liquid, this was referred to as the 'liquidity ratio', and included an 8% cash ratio; both of which were abandoned in 1971. For operating purposes however banks still require a cash ratio and some of their assets in investments which are easy to liquidate. Because of the large proportion of transactions which are now carried out by cheque the banks tend to maintain a smaller cash ratio, as can be seen from Table 36.1

TABLE 36.1

The Sterling assets of the London clearing banks (May 1995)

	£mn	Per cent
Notes and coin	3,620	0.05
Balances with the Bank of England	1,571	0.23
Treasury Bills	9,424	1.39
Other bills	14,013	2.08
Money at call with the London discount market	6,474	0.96
Other market loans	175,075	25.8
Advances	405,120	59.87
Banking department lending to central government	1,581	0.23
British government stocks	15,616	2.30
Other investments	44,104	6.52
	676,688	

13 Credit creation

Banks have a powerful ability to **create credit**, and as credit can be considered as a form of money in that it facilitates the purchase of goods, governments need to exert some degree of control over this credit creating ability.

This ability to create credit arises from the fact stated above, that the banks only require a small fraction of their total deposits in the form of cash; just sufficient to meet the daily demands of their customers. This cash ratio is generally a percentage of total deposits and for purposes of illustration we will assume it is 10% (although in reality it could be much smaller). With a cash ratio of 10% a deposit of £50 would be used as the basis for creating £450 in credit money (i.e. £50 is 10% of £500 and £450 + £50 = £500). This is made possible by the fact that when a bank makes an advance to a customer the customer's account is credited and he will then probably use a cheque to obtain the goods he requires, the recipient of the cheque will then redeposit the cheque into the banking system, which because of the operation of the clearing system has a similar effect to that of redepositing the cheque with the same bank. In Figure 36.1, 'A' has deposited £50 with his bank. With a cash ratio of 10% the bank creates credit for 'C' by crediting his account with £450. 'C' uses this to buy goods for £200 from 'D' and £250 from 'E', paying them both by cheque. These cheques are eventually redeposited with the bank, and even if 'E' and 'D' draw some cash, statistically it will be unlikely to be of such an amount that it could not be met from the £50 initial deposit and still leave sufficient for the average cash demand of 'A'. As stated earlier it does not matter if the cheques are deposited with a different bank because of the clearing arrangements, and as they do not draw cash against each other they operate in a similar manner to a single bank.

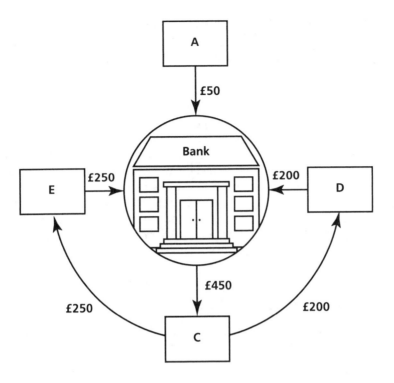

Figure 36.1

14 Credit multiplier

The process of credit creation is referred to as the **bank credit multiplier**. In order to explain this process further it is necessary to appreciate that a cardinal rule of banking is that they must maintain an **equality between their assets and liabilities** on their balance sheets. It should also be noted that as far as a bank is concerned **deposits** appear as a **liability** on the balance sheets as they have a liability to repay the customer, and **advances** (loans) appear as **assets.**

In order to simplify the explanation of the process of credit creation we will assume initially that the economy's banking system consists of a single bank only. Because of this all credit, also referred to as **created deposits**, will be deposited with the same bank. If we also assume a 10% cash ratio for ease of calculation we can illustrate the process in Table 36.2.

TABLE 36.2				
	LIABILITIES (£)		ASSETS (£)	
Period I	Initial deposits	25,000	Notes and coin	25,000
Period 2	Initial deposits	25,000	Notes and coin	25,000
	Created deposits	<u>225,000</u>	Loans (credit)	<u>225,000</u>
		250,000		250,000

In period 1 the bank has attracted initial deposits from its customers of £25,000. Operating on a cash ratio of 10%, which is considered to be sufficient to meet the average withdrawal, then loans can be advanced to the extent of £225,000 (9 × 25,000). These loans will eventually be spent, probably by cheque, and as we have assumed a single bank they will be redeposited with the same bank, and in period 2 they then show on the liabilities side of the balance sheet in the form of **created deposits.** It should be noted that initial deposits of £25,000 have served to create credit nine times greater (£225,000). This **multiple expansion of credit** is also referred to as the **bank credit multiplier.**

Dropping the assumption of a single bank economy makes little difference to the ability to create credit. In a multi-bank system such as the UK the only difference is that the initial cash deposits are divided between the various banks, but assuming the same cash ratio is maintained the same **total** amount of credit will be created. Even if the different banks were not equally successful in attracting deposits only the final distribution will be affected and not the total amount of credit. As mentioned above, although we have a multi-bank system it operates in a similar manner to a single bank system through the operation of the clearing system.

15 Limits to credit creation

The ability of the banks to create credit is powerful, but not unlimited. Limitations to credit creation are as follows:

- An over extension of credit would increase the proportion of bad debts which would undermine both profitability and confidence.
- The need to maintain liquidity in a system where confidence is paramount.
- Controls exerted over the banks by the Bank of England as part of the government's monetary policy (see Chapter 38).

16 The principles of banking

The principles of sound banking can be summarised as:

- The balancing of profit and risk so as to maintain confidence and at the same time produce an adequate return.
- Maintain confidence by demonstrating both integrity and soundness.
- To maintain adequate liquid assets in order to ensure that withdrawals can be met.
- To ensure that assets are equal to liabilities on the balance sheet.

Self assessment questions

1 What are the main functions of the Bank of England at present?

2 What role does the discount market play in the financial structure?

3 Describe the function of the bankers' clearing house.

4 Outline the process by which banks can bring about the multiple expansion of credit.

5 What are the principles of sound banking?

6 What are the characteristics of a liquid asset?

7 To what extent do balance sheets of commercial banks reflect their function?

Section J

Policy instruments

Containing the following chapters:

Chapter 37 – Taxation

Chapter 38 – Monetary policy

Those economic instruments which are available for the government to use in order to change aspects of the economy.

This section should enable students to:

- *Understand* how the Bank of England controls the money supply.
- *Explain* how the UK tax system operates.
- *Contrast* the effectiveness of each of the instruments at the government's disposal.
- *Evaluate* the extent to which taxation is a disincentive to effort.

Keywords to consider

equity; certainty; efficiency; convenience; direct tax; indirect tax; PAYE; regressive tax; proportionate tax; progressive tax; marginal rate of tax; negative income tax; corporation tax; property tax; council tax; Laffer curve; quantitative controls; qualitative controls; special deposits; open market operations; interest rate policy; funding.

37

Taxation

1 Origins of taxation

Taxes were originally-levied for the purposes of raising **revenue**, in a modern economy; however, they are also used as a means of regulating the level of total (aggregate) demand (see Chapter 39), redistributing incomes and wealth, and regulating markets.

2 'Canons' of taxation

Adam Smith stated that the four 'canons' (principles) of taxation were as follows:

- **Equity**
- **Certainty**
- **Efficiency**
- **Convenience**

Equity refers to the principle that taxes should generally be seen to be fair.
Certainty refers to the principles that the taxpayers should know their tax liability in advance and that the government should know their revenue in advance.
Efficiency refers to the principle that a good tax will be economic to administer and the costs of administration should be a small proportion of the tax revenue.
Convenience refers to the principle that taxes should be levied at a time and place convenient to the taxpayer.

3 Additional criteria

In a modern economy there are a number of additional criteria for an efficient tax system.

- **Neutrality** – Taxes should as far as possible be neutral, i.e. not distort the price mechanism. The way in which resources were allocated prior to the introduction of the tax should be the same afterwards. Direct taxation is generally held to be superior in terms of neutrality than indirect taxation. The cost to the economy in terms of resource misallocation, which is incurred as a consequence of indirect taxation, is referred to as the excess burden of indirect taxation. The excess burden is greatest the more indirect taxes change the relative prices of goods.

- **Stabilisation** – Taxes should be efficient from the point of view of their use in regulating the level of aggregate demand in the economy (see Chapter 39). It is useful if a small tax change has a significant effect on demand, this however may conflict with the neutrality principle.
- **Incentive/disincentive effect** – The extent to which the tax is an incentive or disincentive to work, save, and invest.
- **Flexibility** and **stability** – The speed with which tax laws can be changed, and those changes implemented.
- **Redistribution of income and wealth** – The effectiveness of the tax system in creating a more equal distribution of income and wealth.

4 PAYE

Pay As You Earn (PAYE) income tax is an example of a tax which conforms closely to each of the four principles. The tax rates are **progressive** so the higher paid pay a higher tax rate than the lower paid. Tax rates are published and the tax rate made known to the taxpayer. The tax is efficient as the collection of the tax is the responsibility of the employer, who deducts it from incomes and pays it to the Inland Revenue. It is convenient for the taxpayer as it is deducted at source by the employer.

5 Direct taxes

These are borne by those responsible for paying the tax and are levied on either incomes or wealth and are collected by the Inland Revenue. Direct taxes include:

- Income tax: levied on personal income.
- Corporation tax: levied on company profits.
- Inheritance tax: chargeable on gifts, including property, transferred upon death or within seven years of death.
- Capital gains tax: levied on the increase in the value of assets between their acquisition and sale.
- National insurance contributions; although not formally regarded as a direct tax are a direct deduction from income.

6 Indirect taxes

Taxes on goods. The incidence (burden) of the tax may be passed on through higher prices to the buyer of the goods. The distribution of the tax incidence is related to the relative elasticities of demand and supply.

In Figure 37.1(a) a per unit sales tax of a–b shifts the supply curve from S to S^1, the vertical distance being the equivalent of the tax. The price to the consumer increases to p^2, in this instance the incidence of the tax is borne equally by the producer and the consumer, i.e. the consumer pays $p^1 - p^2$ of the tax and the producer pays $p^3 - p^1$, because the elasticity of demand and supply are approximately unity. The tax revenue is represented by the rectangle p^3p^2ba and the producers revenue is the rectangle $OP^3 aQ^2$. The triangle abc is referred to as **'deadweight loss'** and is a loss to society as a whole. In Figure 37.1(b) demand is inelastic and as a result more of the tax burden is passed on to the consumer, here the consumer pays $p^1 - p^2$ of the tax and the producer absorbs only p^3p^1. (Students should also experiment with different supply elasticities). Indirect taxes include:

- Value added tax (VAT): a percentage tax on consumer expenditure.
- Excise duties: are duties levied on domestically produced goods. They are generally specific taxes in that they are charged in the form of a sum per unit, e.g. petrol duty is levied on each gallon Other goods subject to excise duties include cigarettes, beer and spirits. These goods are subject to additional taxation because they tend to be in inelastic demand so that the tax does not reduce consumption significantly and the yield of

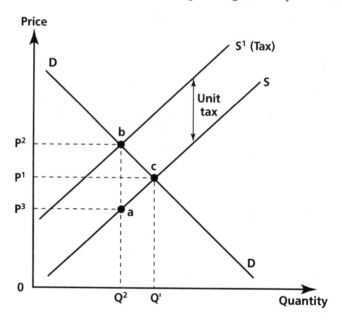

Figure 37.1(a)

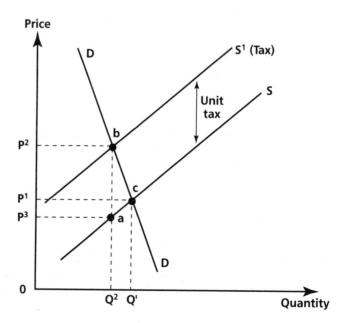

Figure 37.1(b)

the tax is maintained. Such goods may also bear additional tax because there may be an element of 'paternalism' in that governments may wish to curb excess consumption.
- Customs duties are taxes placed on imported goods. These may be imposed both for revenue purposes and for the protection of domestic industries. (See Chapter 32)
- Motor vehicles duties.
- Petroleum revenue tax (PRT) levied on the profits from obtaining oil and gas within the UK or its territorial sea. This has become an increasingly important source of revenue as a consequence of North Sea oil discoveries.

7 Regressive taxes

Regressive taxes are taxes which fall more heavily on the poor than the rich and therefore contravene the equity principle. Indirect taxes are generally held to be regressive. For example, if the duty on a bottle of whisky is £3, for a person earning £30 the tax rate is 10% of income but for a person earning £300 it is only 1% of income. A lump sum tax on income is the most regressive form of income tax. (See Figure 37.2)

8 Proportionate taxes

Proportionate taxes are a constant percentage of income, e.g. 10% of income. Corporation tax is an example of a proportionate tax in the UK as it is levied on companies as a percentage of profit. If it is accepted that the marginal utility of money declines then

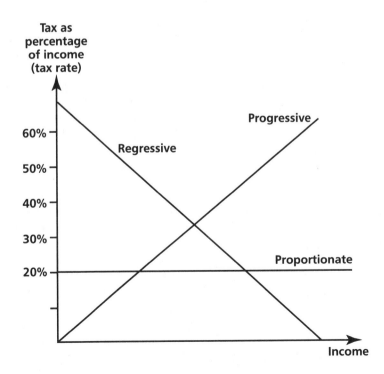

Figure 37.2

proportionate taxation of incomes is inequitable as the sacrifice of 10% of income by a person on a low income is a greater sacrifice than it is to somebody on a high income. (See Figure 37.2)

9 Progressive taxes

Progressive taxes are taxes where the tax rate increases as income rises and different 'slices' of income are taxed at different rates. As a consequence the proportion of income paid in tax becomes greater the higher the income. Progressive taxes therefore fall most heavily on higher incomes and are generally held to be the most equitable method of taxation. It has long been an accepted contention that taxation should be related to **ability to pay** on the grounds of **equity** (fairness) between individuals. This inevitably leads to consideration of the **tax rate** and two approaches can be identified.

- **Equality of sacrifice**: that the total burden on the nation should be equalized between individuals.
- **The benefit principle:** that people should be taxed according to the benefit they receive from the tax system.

Progressive taxation of incomes can be justified on the grounds of **equality of sacrifice**, given the assumption that the **marginal utility of money declines,** e.g. taking £1 in tax from a person earning £100 per week does not involve the same sacrifice of utility as taking £1 from a person earning £1000 per week. The major disadvantage which is claimed for the progressive taxation of incomes is that they operate as a **disincentive** to work and effort. (See 15)

10 The disincentive effect and the marginal rate of tax

The disincentive effect of progressive taxation will be greater the greater the marginal rate of taxation, i.e. the steeper the rate of progression. The disincentive effect can therefore be reduced by having wider tax bands and a lower rate of progression. The average rate of tax is defined as the total taxes paid divided by income, and the closer the average rate (or effective rate) of tax is to the marginal rate the lower will be the disincentive effect.

Figure 37.3 illustrates marginal and average rates of tax. The marginal rate of taxation is steep, hence an increase in income from Y to Y^1 results in a substantial increase in tax paid on the additional income $(Y–Y^1)$ which may in theory act as a disincentive to work harder in order to increase income from Y to Y^1. The marginal and average tax rates are wide apart indicating the marked disincentive effect of this tax structure. Table 37.1 illustrates the income tax rates for 1976–77, 1985–86, 1988/89 and the rates introduced in the November 1996 budget. The simplified tax structure introduced in March 1988 was intended to create a simple two rate tax system which reduced the highest rates of tax, increased the starting point for everyone, and reduced the marginal rate for the majority of tax payers. In the 1997/98 tax structure the basic rate of income tax is 23% with a single higher tax rate of 40% for taxable incomes over £26,100 and a starting rate of 20% for the first £4,100 of taxable income. In Table 37.1 the move towards fewer, broader tax bands is clear as is the decrease in the basic rate of tax:

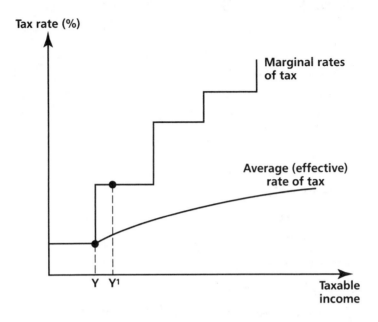

Figure 37.3

An additional measure has been to gradually reduce the basic rate of tax and reduce the rate at which people begin to pay tax.

The changes in the structure are intended to remove the disincentive to work purported to be inherent in a progressive tax structure and to give greater incentives to those on higher incomes Care must be taken when comparing the four periods due to the effect of inflation on money incomes between the three periods.

In particular for those on low incomes consideration of the disincentive to work has to include consideration of the whole **tax system** including the receipt of benefits. For an unemployed worker the taking of a job may mean loss not only of unemployment benefit but benefits such as free school meals for children, rent subsidies etc.; the loss of these benefits can be considered as a form of **implicit tax.** The loss of benefits combined with positive income tax payments may act as a disincentive to the unemployed to take lower paid jobs, referred to as the **unemployment trap**. The ratio of unemployment benefit and/or supplementary benefit relative to post tax earnings is referred to as the **replacement ratio.** In theory a rise in the replacement ratio would result in an increase in unemployment and act as a disincentive to the unemployed to take low paid jobs; the evidence, however, is that the replacement ratio has in fact fallen over the last ten years and cannot therefore be a contributory factor to unemployment, although some commentators such as Professor Minford suggest that if the analysis is applied to the non unionised sector of the workforce only, then a substantial disincentive effect is evident. (See Chapter 44). Wider tax bands at the basic rate represent one measure aimed at overcoming this affect; others include reduced benefits or the use of negative income tax systems.

TABLE 37.1

	1976/77
Income	Tax Rate %
0 – 5,000	35
5,001 – 5,500	40
5,501 – 6,500	45
6501 – 7,500	50
7,501 – 8,500	55
8,501 – 10,000	60
10,001 – 12,000	65
12,001 – 15,000	70
15,001 – 20,000	75
20,001 and over	83

Max 83% where total income after subtracting personal allowance and reliefs exceeds £20,000.

	1985/86
0 – 16,200	30
16,201 – 19,200	40
19,201 – 24,400	45
24,001 – 32,300	50
32,301 – 40,200	55
40,201 and over	6-

	1988/89
0 – 19,300	25
19,301 and over	40

	1997/98
0 – 4,100	20
4,101 – 26,100	23
26,101 and above	40

11 Negative income tax

Negative income tax systems guarantee a minimum income with benefits given as a right to all those below the minimum. As income increases towards a break-even point the size of benefit diminishes, and as the income recipients pass through the break-even point they become positive tax payers. In order to remove any disincentive effect the transition from being a recipient of benefit to a net taxpayer should be as smooth as possible. In Figure 37.4 the minimum income (or poverty line) is O–G, meaning that an individual earning no income would receive benefit payment O–G. As employment income rises benefit payments fall hence a person earning income M would receive benefit M–N (OL) thus total income is OMN. The break-even point is at E beyond which income recipients become positive tax payers. The positive tax rate EA is quite steep and may act as a disincentive to employment at the marginal income E or above. For example, if a person received a gross income of OY net income would be Y^1 (OY–XY). One suggested way of overcoming this is to have initially a lower positive marginal tax rate such as E–B, before moving to high marginal tax rates. In the example quoted this would leave a net income Y^2 if gross income was OY (Y^2 = OY - YZ). Various schemes have been suggested but they all claim the advantages of certainty, benefit being given as a right, ease of calculation, the concentrating of help where it is most needed, and the reduction of disincentives to take employment. The evidence regarding the disincentive affects of income tax is however inconclusive and it is possible that income taxes may in fact make some individuals actually work harder in order to maintain their post-tax incomes.

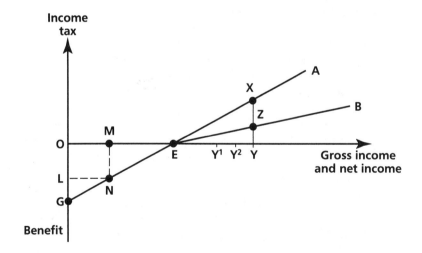

Figure 37.4

12 Corporation Tax

Corporation tax is a tax on company profits. Treating companies and shareholders as different entities enables the authorities to pursue different policies for the company and personal sectors of the economy. The **classical system** of corporation tax which was used in the UK up to 1973 taxed retained profits at a different rate to dispersed profits (dividends). One of the objectives of this policy was to use the tax system to influence the level of retained profits and therefore investment and consequently was not a neutral tax. Since April 1973 the **imputation system** has been used and under this system all profits whether distributed or not, are subject to the same corporation-tax rate, but part of the tax is 'imputed' to shareholders, and collected from the company at the time of payment of dividends. The 1984 budget reformed corporation tax by reducing the main rate from 52 per cent to 35 per cent by 1986, the reduction of the small companies rate to 30 per cent, and the phasing out over three years of stock relief, of first year capital allowances for plant and machinery and initial allowances for industrial building. For 1997/98 the main rate was 33% with the small company rate at 23%.The reason for making these changes was the belief that the old system of allowances subsidised and encouraged investment projects with low rates of return and that the new system would improve the business environment by taxing profits less and relaxing the amount of subsidation of investment.

13 Property tax

In the UK the traditional **property tax** has been the **rates**. The idea of rates is that they are a local tax used to provide local provision of goods and services by local authorities. Rates together with grants from central government were the main sources of revenue for local authorities. Rates were payable on the 'rateable value' of property which, was in principle equal to the yearly rent which could be obtained on the property. The actual amount payable, however, depended not only on the rateable value but also on the rate in the pound charged by the local authority which was calculated by dividing the sum to be raised to cover expenditures by the yield of a one pence rate to give the tax rate (or poundage).

Although rates were administratively easy to collect and difficult to avoid they were subject to the criticism that they were inequitable because they were not related to income and were therefore a regressive tax, i.e. they contravene the ability to pay principle. Also they were not paid by everyone within the household. A further criticism was that rates lacked buoyancy in that they did not rise automatically with income and the periodic substantial revaluations which this necessitated proved highly unpopular with rate payers. Business rates were criticised on the grounds that they were related to local authority expenditure plans rather that profitability.

The argument that rates were regressive may however not be as strong if wealth is taken as the basis and property size is taken as an indicator of wealth.

In response to the criticisms of rates the UK government replaced rates with a 'community charge' which was a flat rate poll tax on every adult in the local authority jurisdiction. The community charge was introduced in March 1989 in Scotland and March 1990 in England and Wales. The principle underlying the charge was that it would make local authorities more responsive to the wishes of the local community in their expenditure and would be more like a charge for the services received than a lump sum tax. It proved to be the most short-lived and costly tax ever to be introduced. The tax proved to be highly unpopular due to its regressive nature resulting in massive non-payment. This coupled with the difficulties and costs of administration and the political unpopularity resulted in the abandonment of the 'poll tax' and its replacement from April 1993 with a new council tax. The cost of the community charge fiasco to the Treasury has been estimated at £7 billion per year.

14 Council tax

The council tax is based on property capital values, determined by approved estate agents/valuers, making use of a system of banding. The valuer determines which of eight bands of predetermined value a property falls in. A different rate of tax determined by the local authority is then applied to each band. The household rather than the individual will be the tax unit, with single person households receiving a 25% discount, and a rebate system maintained for those on low incomes.

- The council tax can be characterised as a combination of property tax, or old rating system, with a per capita element being retained. An element of progression is achieved through the valuation of property.
- The council tax, as a property tax, is strong administratively, but weak on efficiency and equity and unclear in terms of accountability.
- A problem exists due to the fact that in the south-east almost everyone will reside in property in one of the highest bands, whilst in the north there will be a far greater concentration in the lower bands. Consequently the tax provides little recognition of ability to pay within some areas and may be perceived by many as being another flat rate tax like the community charge.
- The provision of discounts to single householders requires authorities to carry out checks and set up a register, a costly exercise which is potentially as unpopular as that associated with the community charge.
- The valuation of property also has the potential for causing disruption. Householders have the right of appeal against valuations, and as many properties were valued before the fall in property values many appeals and protests were caused.

15 The Laffer curve

The discussion relating to taxation as a disincentive to effort is a supply-side concept that owes much to the worth of Arthur Laffer. His work produced the **Laffer curve** (see Figure 37.5) which argues that if taxes rates are zero then tax revenues will also be zero. Equally if tax rates are 100% the tax revenue will also be zero because individuals will refuse to work or will work illegally.

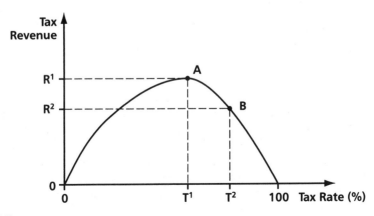

Figure 37.5

Between these rates lies an ideal rate of tax, T^1, where tax revenue will be maximised. Individuals will not feel the need to decrease their work or find ways of avoiding paying tax, tax avoidance.

The policy implication is that if a country's tax rate is at T^2 and it is reduced to T^1, then tax revenue will actually increase. This reasoning has formed the basis of the tax changes that have occured in the UK since 1979.

16 The national debt

When governments fail to cover all their expenditure from taxation they finance the deficit by borrowing. The cumulative total of outstanding debts owed by successive governments is referred to as the **national debt**. The major part of the debt is in the form of different government securities some of which is long term debt and some short term. Much of the debt is held by institutions such as banks, insurance companies and pension funds, and much of the debt is marketable in that it can be bought and sold on secondary markets such as the stock exchange and the money market. The debt has tended to grow most rapidly during wars when it is impossible for governments to finance all of their expenditure from taxation. Growth of the debt is not in itself a bad thing provided its growth rate is not significantly faster than the rate of growth of gross domestic product.

Self assessment questions

1 State the four principles of taxation.

2 Distinguish between direct and indirect taxation.

3 Distinguish between regressive and progressive taxation.

4 Why is progressive taxation considered to be more equitable than proportionate taxation?

5 What is the national debt?

6 How does the unemployment trap arise and how would a negative income tax system attempt to overcome the situation?

38

Instruments of monetary policy

1 Control of credit money

From our previous discussion it is evident that one of the main components of the money supply is credit money. If the government is to control the money supply it is therefore essential that it has some means of controlling the ability of the commercial banks to create credit.

In the period prior to 1971 credit creation was controlled in two ways:

- **Direct controls**. Direct controls were either of the **quantitative** type or the **qualitative** type.
  - **Quantitative controls** took the form of **ceilings** on the amount of credit which the main banks could create, and on hire purchase terms.
  - **Qualitative controls** were instructions regarding the composition of bank lending, i.e. those sectors of the economy to which the banks could lend, for example, preference to finance for exporters, or finance to be used for investment purposes.
- The other main instrument of control during this period was that the banks had to observe a 28% liquidity ratio, i.e. they had to hold a stock of specified liquid assets equal to 28% of their deposits, including an 8% cash ratio.

The main emphasis during this period was on direct controls.

2 Competition and credit control

In 1971 a new system of controls over credit creation was introduced, known as **Competition and Credit Control (CCC)**. These measures were intended to encourage greater competition in the monetary system and at the same time rely more heavily on market forces as a method of control, rather than direct controls. The new system of controls emphasised short term interest rates and the composition of the banks' balance sheets. The new regulations introduced a 12½% **reserve asset ratio** whereby all banks were to hold certain specified assets whose value was not to fall below 12% of their **eligible liabilities**. The **reserve assets** included:

- Balances with the Bank of England (other than special deposits).
- Treasury bills.
- Money at call with the London discount market.
- Gilt edged stock with less than a year to run to maturity
- Local authority and commercial bills eligible for rediscount at the Bank of England.

Most of these assets originate in the public sector and are therefore under the control of the Bank of England, and any reduction in their availability would mean that the banks would be forced to reduce the level of their deposits in order to maintain the 12½% ratio, and this would therefore restrict their ability to create credit. Some commentators suggest that the purpose of the 12 ½% ratio was primarily intended to ensure that banks continued to invest on the traditional money markets and that the fractional reserve aspect was intended to be of secondary importance, but this secondary role became increasingly prominent. These regulations were abandoned in August 1981.

3 Special deposits

Special deposits constituted a further instrument of control. These were first introduced in 1960 but became more important after the introduction of CCC. Special deposits are called in from the banks by the Bank of England and are held in a special account. While they are held by the Bank of England they do not form part of the banks' current assets (They are in fact 'frozen'). As these balances cannot be drawn upon like the commercial banks' normal Bank of England balances, they cannot be included as reserve assets. Special deposits therefore reduce the liquidity of the banks and in so doing restrict their ability to create credit.

4 Supplementary special deposits

By 1973 it became apparent that the level of interest rates was not in itself sufficient to control the growth of the money stock and in December 1973 an element of direct control was reintroduced in the form of the **supplementary special deposits scheme,** known generally as **'the corset'.** Under the scheme the Bank of England set a target rate of growth for each bank's interest bearing deposits. If the actual rate of growth of deposits exceeded the target rate a deposit had to be made in an account with the Bank of England. These deposits received no interest and grew progressively larger the more the banks exceeded the target growth rate for deposits. The effect of this 'corset' was similar to that of the ceilings imposed before 1971. The corset was however by-passed as credit was diverted into uncontrolled channels, a process referred to as 'disintermediation'; and also by the raising of funds through the issue of commercial bills – known as the 'bill leak'. The failure of the corset resulted in its abandonment in 1980, ordinary special deposits were however retained.

5 Open market operations

Open market operations are the means by which the Bank of England influences the stock of financial assets and thereby indirectly the lending of the banks. If the Bank of England's broker sells government securities on the market purchasers of these securities pay by cheques drawn on their banks in favour of the Bank of England. When these cheques are presented for payment the banks' deposits are reduced at the Bank of England. This reduces the liquid assets of the banks and to restore the ratio of assets to liabilities the banks are forced to reduce the amount of lending. When the Bank of England enters the market to purchase securities and pays for them with cheques drawn on itself it has the opposite effect as these cheques will be deposited in the sellers' bank accounts increasing the commercial banks' asset base and enabling them to create additional credit. To summarise:

- The **sale** of bonds **reduces** the money supply.
- The **purchase** of bonds **increases** the money supply.

6 Interest rate policy

Creating a reduction in liquidity by the use of open market operations also allowed the Bank of England to pursue its **interest rate policy**. In order to restore liquidity the banks would be forced to 'call in' money from the discount market (see Chapter 36). As the discount market would have this money invested in Treasury bills, bills of exchange and commercial loans, it may have to turn to the 'lender of the last resort' – the Bank of England. The rate at which the Bank of England was prepared to lend to the discount market was known as **minimum lending rate (MLR)**. An increase in MLR would reduce the profitability of the discount houses' operations and they would be forced to adjust their interest rates to restore their profitability, and all other interest rates, on bank loans, mortgages, hire purchase etc. would follow suit.

In 1981 however the Bank of England ceased declaring an official MLR but could still intervene to influence short-term interest rates. Control over short-term rates is now achieved by the Bank through its own market operations, by varying the supply of funds the general level of interest rates can be pushed up or down. The supply and demand for funds will determine the general level of interest rates whilst market forces are free to determine the pattern of interest rates between different institutions. The current objective of UK monetary policy is to keep inflation low and the Bank will raise short-term interest rates whenever it thinks inflation will rise significantly.

7 Funding

Funding operations refer to the practice of managing the government's debt in order to influence the money supply. These operations involve the replacing of maturing debts with longer-term securities in order to reduce the amount of liquidity in the economy, or vice versa to increase liquidity. A secondary consequence of such activities is ,however, to influence bond prices and therefore interest rates.

8 Abolition of CCC

Competition and credit control and its main provision the 12½% reserve asset ratio, was abandoned in August 1981 and was replaced by a new system of controls which were intended to give the government tighter control over the monetary aggregates (M0 and M4).

9 The 1981 monetary control arrangements

The main provisions of the new regulations introduced in August 1981 were as follows:

- All institutions in the monetary sector with eligible liabilities of over £10 million were required to hold ½% of eligible liabilities in non interest bearing balances at the Bank. The eligible reserve asset ratio and 1½% cash ratio were abolished. These new balances were intended to provide the Bank with the funds to conduct its open market operations.
- MLR was suspended. Money market operations were to be conducted with reference to a narrow band for short-term interest rates. MLR was however re-activated in January 1985 as a temporary measure in response to a sterling crisis. The purpose of this was to make indications of interest rate changes less visible and therefore less of a politically sensitive issue.
- Eligible banks were required to hold an average of 6% (now 5%) but never less than 4% (now 2½%) on a daily basis, of their eligible liabilities in secured money with the discount houses. This was intended to ensure that the traditional channels for such funds continued to be used.
- The Bank retained its function as 'lender of last resort' to the discount market but through the channels of open market operations.
- In order to give the Banks open market operations more impact and to widen the bill market, the number of eligible banks was increased.
- The banks were still to maintain their operational balances at the Bank for everyday clearances and also to enable the Bank to monitor the relationship between MO and the broad monetary aggregates.

The new arrangements introduced in 1981 meant that in future open market operations would operate solely upon the level of short-term interest rates and would allow more flexibility in interest rate policy. This implies that interest changes were considered to have importance as an instrument of money demand management. Short-term interest rates were to be determined by a combination of official influence and market forces. However under these new arrangements market forces would have the greater influence in the determination of short-term rates, whilst the Bank would influence only very short-term rates by its dealings with the discount market. Generally, however, interest rates were to be market determined.

The Bank's influence was to operate through an 'unpublished band of interest rates', which were essentially short term; by means of its dealings with the discount market. Should the Bank want to see a rise in short-term interest rates it would lend at a rate above market rates and because of its pre-eminent position in the money market this would tend to determine the short-term rate operating in that market. As discussed earlier, the relationship between interest rates and the money supply is complicated. However, despite this the Bank would still attempt to influence short-term rates because of their effect on the demand for credit, and therefore the money supply.

The three main policy instruments currently utilised for the control of the money stock are:

- **Fiscal policy** – controlling the supply of money through the reduction of the PSBR.
- **Funding** – sales of public sector debt to the non-bank private sector to offset the effects of the PSBR on the money supply.

- **Open market operations** – to influence short-term (and so long-term) interest rates and the demand for money.

Control of interest rates are now the main policy instrument by which government attempts to influence the demand for money.

10 Monetary growth targets

Since 1976 governments have followed the policy of announcing **targets** for the growth of the money stock, from 1976 to 1981 for M3 only, but in 1982 also for M1 and PSL2. In March 1984 the Treasury announced that monetary targets would be set for five years ahead rather than three as previously and would include a target for M0. Problems have been encountered in the past in achieving targets due to the difficulty of estimating the demand for bank lending; for example, other objectives were sometimes given priority over control of the money stock, and other factors which resulted in an increase in the stock of money, for example one of the main elements in the creation of money is the public sector borrowing requirement – was not under the direct control of the Bank of England. The persistent failure of the government to meet the target growth rates for the broad monetary aggregates has resulted in their abandonment and in the March 1988 budget a target growth rate for the narrow definition M0 only was announced. In 1993 the government specified a range for the annual growth of M4 of 3–9%. An outline of the way in which monetary targets have changed since 1980 is given in Appendix 1, Chapter 43.

Methods of monetary control have tended to reflect the prevailing attitude towards the importance of the role of money in the economy. In the era of the 1950's and.1960's following the Radcliffe Report money was not perceived as being a particularly important instrument of policy, but as this perception changed during the 1960's the money supply was seen as being increasingly important, a development which was reflected to a limited extent in the changes introduced in competition and credit control 1971. Throughout the 1970s, with the growing acceptance of the ideas of the 'monetarist' school of thought, money was viewed with growing importance and came to be seen by many as being the most important of economic variables; culminating in the 1981 monetary control arrangements.

Self assessment questions

1 Distinguish between qualitative and quantitative controls over bank lending.

2 What are special deposits?

3 What was the 12 ½ % reserve asset ratio introduced in the 1971 competition and credit control regulations?

4 How does the Bank of England utilise open market operations in order to influence the money supply?

5 How does the system of monetary controls introduced in 1981 operate?

Section K

Demand management

Containing the following chapters:

Chapter 39 – The Keynesian model

Chapter 40 – Demand management in practice

Chapter 41 – The accelerator .

Chapter 42 – Interest rate determination and investment

The control of the aggregate level of demand in an economy through the use of fiscal and monetary policy

This section should enable students to:

- *Understand* Keynes' theory and the significance of the multiplier
- *Explain* the accelerator principal
- *Contrast* Keynesian policies with the monetarist view.
- *Evaluate* the effectiveness of demand management policies.

Keywords to consider

full employment; voluntary and involuntary unemployment; consumption function; savings function; marginal propensity to consume; marginal propensity to save; average propensity to consume; average propensity to save; aggregate monetary demand; multiplier; marginal propensity to import; marginal propensity to tax, incomes policy; Phillips curve; accelerator; net present value; discount rate; discounted cash flow; internal rate of return; marginal efficiency of capital; transactions demand; precautionary demand; speculative demand; liquidity preference.

39

The Keynesian model

1 The general theory

The idea that governments should attempt to manage the economy in order to achieve full employment owes much to J.M (Lord) Keynes. His book 'The General Theory of Employment Interest and Money' (1936) (referred to as 'The General Theory') was probably the most influential work on economics of the twentieth century and was used as the basis for managing the economies of the western world for the thirty years following 1945. This text attempts to do no more than explain in simple terms some of the ideas involved in the Keynesian model of demand management and it is recommended that you supplement it at a later stage with reading from a more advanced text.

2 Classical ideas

In order to understand Keynes' contribution it is useful to very briefly outline how economists before Keynes, referred to loosely as the 'classical economists', viewed the working of the economy. This is not an attempt to analyse the ideas of any particular economist but merely an overview of how the economy was considered to operate Classical economists believed that two essential principles prevailed:

- That the quantity theory of money operated (see Chapter 29).
- That Say's law of markets applied.

Say's law of markets is usually expressed as 'supply creates its own demand', or more literally that 'production creates the market for goods'. If these two principles are accepted it implies that the following points also apply:

- Prices and wages are flexible.
- Savings and investment are always brought into balance by movements in the interest rate, and all savings are therefore reinvested.

If we accept these principles then over-production of goods and unemployment become impossible, the economy will always tend towards equilibrium and by definition **equilibrium in the economy coincided with full employment**.

If we consider the process by which equilibrium was considered to be established, in very simple terms, we can see that prolonged periods of involuntary unemployment were not possible. In a situation where high unemployment did exist competition for jobs would depress wage rates until they became so low that entrepreneurs would take on additional labour. The very act of producing the extra output would, according to Say's law, generate sufficient purchasing power in the economy for its consumption. Also, according to the quantity theory, money balances were held only for making transactions.

It was not possible therefore for a situation of deficient total demand to exist. Savings could not exceed investment except in the short-run because the rate of interest would fall, deterring some saving whilst encouraging investment until they came into equilibrium, and vice versa if attempted investment exceeded savings.

The essential point was that in the absence of government intervention the economy would always tend back to the **full employment equilibrium**. Any unemployment which then existed was **voluntary** and occurred because workers were not willing to work at the prevailing market equilibrium wage rate.

3 Keynes' theory

The experience of the prolonged depression of the 1920s and 1930s and the failure of the economy to move automatically back to a situation of full employment caused Keynes to question the fundamental principles of the classical economists. Keynes argued that there was no longer an automatic tendency for the economy to move back to full employment because of changes which had taken place in the structure of the economy which made invalid some of the classical assumptions. In particular:

- Wages were no longer flexible in a downwards direction due to the growth of trade unions.
- The direct quantity theory relationship between money and prices was no longer valid.
- Saving and investment are carried out by distinctly different groups and there is no reason why what firms are **planning** to invest is necessarily the same as what they are **actually** able to invest. Also, what individuals are planning to save is not necessarily the same as what they actually manage to save. An increased desire to save by the whole community actually reduces consumption, and, therefore incomes, resulting in less actual saving (known as the **paradox of thrift**). It was possible therefore for **planned investment and savings to differ, and that equality between savings and investment is brought about not by changes in the interest rate but fluctuations in income and therefore employment**. As there was no tendency for the situation to change during the 1920s and 1930s the economy could be assumed to be in equilibrium **but with a high level of unemployment**. What Keynes argued was that a modern economy could be in equilibrium with **any** level of unemployment and stay there indefinitely. It was in fact **demand** which was deficient and the only way to achieve full employment was for the government to intervene and raise the level of demand thereby shifting the equilibrium point of the economy to coincide with the full employment level. Keynes' essential contribution was **the possibility of a less than full**

employment equilibrium, and the need for government intervention to manage the level of demand in order to achieve full employment.

4 The Keynesian model

Our initial analysis of the Keynesian model assumes that there is **no taxation or government activity, a closed economy (i.e. no imports or exports) and no changes in the price level.** As a consequence **all income** must be either **consumed** or **saved**. These simplifying assumptions will be dropped later.

5 The consumption function

The **consumption function** refers to the relationship between consumption (C) and income (Y). In the Keynesian model income is considered to be the most important determinant of consumption, i.e.

C = f(Y).

where f = function of, or depends upon, income

C = consumption
Y = income

If we drew a scatter diagram of an individual's consumption at different levels of income we would expect consumption to increase as income increases. This is illustrated in Figure 39.1 by the observations plotted on the diagram. A line of best fit drawn through the observations, i.e. C–C, is referred to as the **consumption function**. It can be observed that it is composed of a constant, a, and a slope or gradient, b, and if we assume a linear relationship (i.e. b is a constant) then the consumption function can be expressed as:

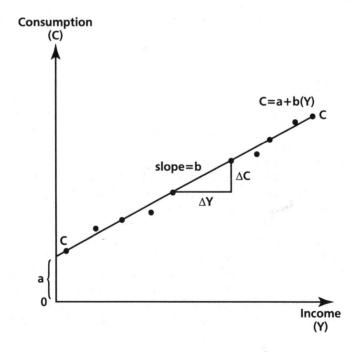

Figure 39.1

$$C = a + b(Y)$$

Where there are deductions from income in the form of taxation then consumption will depend upon the amount of **disposable income**, i.e.

$$C = a + b(Yd)$$

where Yd = disposable income.

6 The savings function

A 45° line drawn from the origin indicates the points where **consumption and income are exactly equal**. This is illustrated in Figure 39.2(a) where the 45° line has been superimposed onto the consumption function. At the equilibrium point E all income is consumed. Below E consumption exceeds income and there is 'dis-saving', for example, selling assets or living on earlier savings. Above E consumption is less than income and the area between CC and the 45° line represents savings. Ye is the equilibrium level of income. Figure 39.2(b) illustrates the **savings function** which corresponds with the pattern of con-

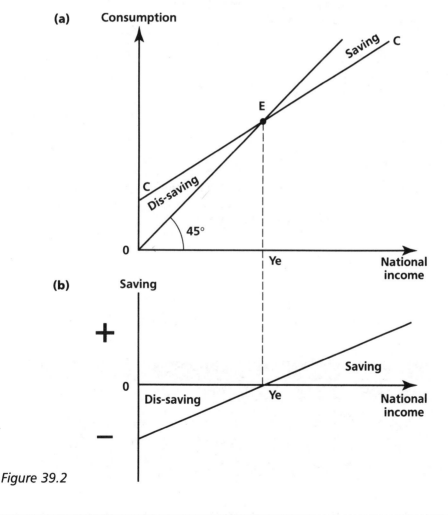

Figure 39.2

sumption and saving in 39.2(a). When income is below Ye saving is negative, and above Ye it is positive, and because of the relationship between consumption and saving both diagrams produce the same equilibrium level of income. Clearly it is **income** which determines **consumption** and **saving**.

7 The marginal propensity to consume and save

The marginal propensity to consume (MPC) refers to the amount of each additional unit of income which is consumed. It is calculated as:

$$\frac{\Delta C}{\Delta Y}$$

where C = consumption
Y = income
Δ = small change

It is the MPC which determines the shape of the consumption function, i.e. b in the formula C = a + b(Y).

The **marginal propensity** to save (MPS) refers to the amount of each additional increment of income which is saved. It is calculated as:

$$\frac{\Delta S}{\Delta Y}$$ where S = consumption

Because income can only be either consumed or saved then:

MPC + MPS = 1

8 APC and APS

The **average propensity to consume (APC)** and the **average propensity to save (APS)** refer to the distribution of **total** income between consumption and saving and can be calculated for **every** level of income. They are calculated as:

$$APC = \frac{C}{Y}$$

$$APS = \frac{S}{Y}$$

Table 39.1 illustrates the calculation of both the MPC and the APC.

TABLE 39.1				
Year	Income (Y)	Consumption (C)	MPC = $\Delta C/\Delta Y$	APC = C/Y
1996	1000	800		0.8
			150/200 = 0.75	
1998	1200	950		0.79

9 Total consumption

The consumption behaviour described so far referred to the individual, however by **aggregating each individual's consumption function** we can produce a similar consumption function for the economy as a whole relative to **national income**. There will also, therefore, be an MPC, MPS, APC and APS for the economy as a whole. From this point on therefore we will be referring to **total consumption (TC)** and **national income (Y)**.

10 National income equilibrium

Bearing in mind our assumptions regarding the closed economy and absence of government we can develop our conditions for national income equilibrium. In our analysis so far we have assumed that the only expenditure is consumption (C). However we know from our national income analysis that investment (I) is also an element in total expenditure. It is reasonable to assume that investment, like consumption, rises with income, therefore in Figure 39.3 an investment schedule (I) has been added. Aggregating the consumption and investment schedules produces the combined C + I schedule, to produce the equilibrium level of income Ye. In the lower Figure 39.3(b) this can be seen to be the

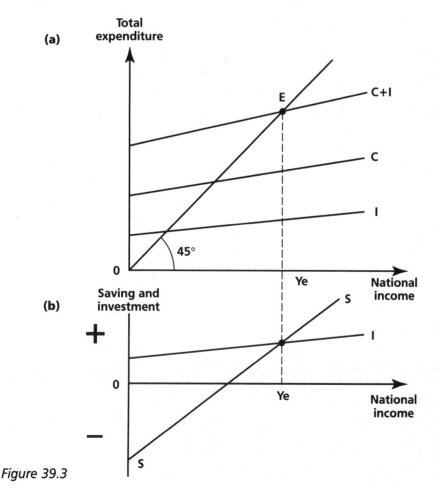

Figure 39.3

same point as the intersection of the saving and investment schedules. The equilibrium condition for national income is therefore the point where the C + I line intersects the 45° line; which is the same as saying that equilibrium is where income equals planned expenditure (E), i.e.

Y = E

at which point, as we can see from 39.3(b)

S = I Planned

11 Equilibrium and the circular flow

The equilibrium condition for national income S = I can be easily illustrated by the use of circular flow diagrams, as in Figure 39.4. In period 1 firms are paying out factor incomes (national income) of £100m to households. The chain of re-spending is not complete however because only £80m goes directly back to firms in the form of consumption because there are **leakages** from the circular flow in the form of savings which amount to £20m. This would not matter if the **injections** in the form of investment into the circular flow were also £20m.

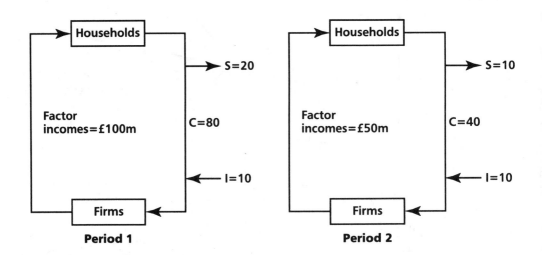

Figure 39.4

However, firms are only planning to invest £10m, therefore total receipts by firms are reduced and they will be unable to pay out the same amount in factor payments in period 2. In period 2 factor payments to households fall to £90m, i.e. **national income falls**. Incomes continue to fall until households are no longer planning to save more than firms are attempting to invest and when savings and investment are again equal at £10m equilibrium is established with national income = £50m. Had planned investment exceeded savings national income and therefore savings, would have risen until savings had risen sufficiently to match investment, again establishing equilibrium where S = I. (Assuming the MPC remains constant at 0.8).

12 Keynes and equilibrium

According to Keynes therefore it was **fluctuations in national income and therefore employment which brought about equilibrium between income and expenditure, and this equilibrium could be at any level of employment.**

13 National income and equilibrium

The equilibrium condition can also be explained in terms of national income analysis. From Chapter 28 we know that in equilibrium income (Y) is equal to expenditure (E).

therefore Y = E in equilibrium

As all income is either consumed (C) or saved (S), then

(1) Y = C + S

and as expenditure in our closed economy is either consumption or investment (I), then

(2) Y = C + I

As C can be eliminated from both equations 1 and 2, as it is common to both sides, we are left with the equilibrium condition

S = I

14 The three sector economy

We can now drop our assumption of no government activity and introduce the third element of total demand **government expenditure** (G). When government expenditure is added to the private expenditures of consumption and investment we can derive what is referred to as **aggregate monetary demand** (AMD), alternatively referred to as **effective demand.**

AMD = C + I + G

Figure 39.5 illustrates the separate C, I and G schedules, which together constitute the aggregate monetary demand curve of C + I + G, giving the equilibrium of income and expenditure at E (income Ye).

As we have discussed earlier however there is in the Keynesian model no reason why the equilibrium point E should coincide with the full employment level of income. In Figure 39.6 equilibrium E produces level of income Ye but the level of income consistent with full employment is Y', and equilibrium point E', unemployment is therefore present. The deficiency of AMD at the full employment level is E'–G, known as the **deflationary gap**. The problem is therefore how to shift the equilibrium level of income from E to E', the full employment level.

15 Changing equilibrium

Shifting equilibrium output from E to E' could be achieved by an increase in investment, but this would be unlikely to occur autonomously (independently), as firms facing a depressed level of sales would have little incentive to invest. What Keynes argued was

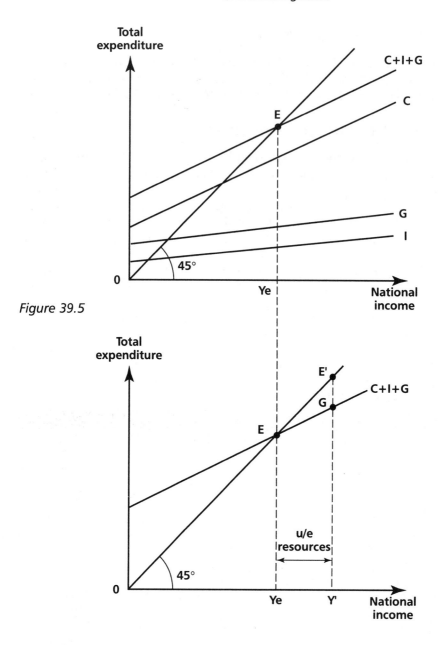

Figure 39.5

Figure 39.6

that governments should intervene in the economy and raise the level of their own expenditures, on for example public works projects, and boost the level of AMD to the full employment level. The increase in G would therefore represent an **injection** into the circular flow of income.

16 The multiplier

One essential point of the analysis is that the increase in G will not have to be as large as the required increase in AMD because of the **multiplier** process of re-spending. The simplest way to explain this re-spending process is to imagine an area of the country which has suffered high levels of unemployment and recession over a sustained period. The government then decides to build a major highway between two towns in the region and spend many millions of pounds on the project. The contract is placed with a construction company; however, before they can proceed they have to place orders for new construction equipment and materials, the suppliers of this equipment and materials have to employ additional labour to produce it, this labour is now in receipt of wages and proceeds to spend them, local businesses find they are selling more and place orders for additional supplies, the suppliers of which take on fresh labour and so on. In addition the construction firm will take on new direct labour for construction purposes, these workers will now make increased expenditures with local traders. A cycle of re-spending is started and each pound spent by the government will have an effect on final demand which is some multiple greater than itself. This is referred to as the **multiplier process**.

How large this multiplier process is depends upon how much is re-spent at each round, which is a function of the MPC and MPS of the income recipients. If they spend a high proportion of their incomes the multiplier will be larger than if a large proportion is saved at each round. The higher the MPC therefore the greater is the multiplier. This can be illustrated in Table 39.2 where the original government expenditure is £50, with an MPC of 0.7 and MPS of 0.3.

TABLE 39.2			
Spending round	Income (£)	Consumed (£)	Saved (£)
1st	50	35	15
2nd	35	24.50	10.50
3rd	24.50	17.50	7
4th	17.50	12.00	5.50
5th	12.00	8.40	3.60
6th	8.40	5.88	2.52
7th	5.88	4.10	1.78
8th	4.10	2.88	1.22
9th	2.88	2.00	.88
10th	2.00	1.40	.60
11th	1.40	.98	.42

The process continues until the amount of re-spending reduces to an infinitely small amount, and the total amount of income generated, or the multiplier effect, will be £166.66. This consists of the original £50 of government expenditure, referred to as autonomous expenditure; plus the re-spending generated at each successive round, referred to as **induced expenditure**.

17 The multiplier coefficient

The multiplier refers to the amount by which final income will be raised by any increase in government spending (or investment). The multiplier coefficient (usually represented by k) can be calculated by the formula

$$k = \frac{1}{1 - MPC}$$

or the reciprocal of the MPS. (The mathematically inclined will identify Table 39.2 as a geometric progression, the sum of which is the formula.)

In order to illustrate, let us assume that national income is £2000m and the government raises its expenditure by £50m, the effect on income is calculated as follows:

$$
\begin{aligned}
\text{National income} &= \text{£2000m} \\
\Delta G &= \text{£50m} \\
MPC &= 0.7 \\
\text{therefore } k &= \frac{1}{1 - 0.7} = 3.33 \\
50 \times 3.33 &= 166.67
\end{aligned}
$$

New national income = **£2166.67m**

(Note it is only the injection of £50m which is subject to the multiplier.)

18 The multiplier illustrated

The multiplier is illustrated in Figure 39.7. The economy is originally in equilibrium at E with income Y'. The full employment level of income is Yf, unemployment is Y'–Yf. An increase in G (ΔG) raises the AMD curve from E to the full employment equilibrium E' (income Yf). It should be noted that the increase in G is only about one third of the increase in Y, due to the effect of the multiplier. The effect of the multiplier can be estimated as

$$\frac{\Delta Y}{\Delta G}$$

19 Consumption and the multiplier

As the size of the multiplier is dependent upon the MPC, and we know that the MPC is the same as b in the formula for the consumption function $C = a + b(Y)$, which is the slope of the curve, then graphically the steeper the slope of the AMD curve the greater the multiplier effect. In Figure 39.8 the increase in income from Y' to Yf was achieved by a much smaller increase in G when the AMD curve is steeper than when it has a shallow slope, this is because the steeper slope has a higher MPC (b) than the shallow slope, and the multiplier is correspondingly greater.

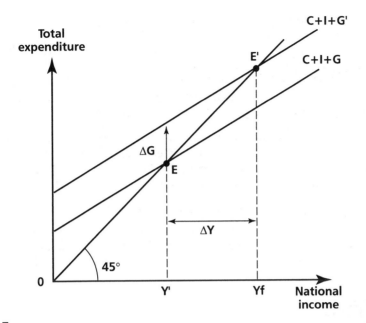

Figure 39.7

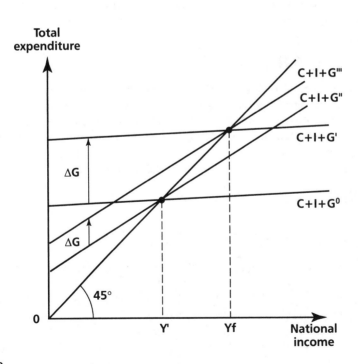

Figure 39.8

20 An open economy

We can now **drop our assumption of a closed economy** and allow for the effects of **imports** and **exports** in the form of the balance of payments surplus or deficit.

So far the only **injections** into the circular flow have been **investment (I)** and **government expenditure (G)**. We can now add a third, **exports (X)**, as selling goods abroad is an injection of purchasing power into the domestic economy.

The only **withdrawal** from the circular flow so far has been **saving (S)**. However, as we have introduced government expenditure we must also allow for the effects of **taxation (T)**; and as we now have an 'open' economy, for the effects of **imports (M)** which reduce purchasing power in the domestic economy.

Total injections		= Investment	+	Government expenditure	+ Exports
ie J	=	I	+	G	+ X
Total Withdrawals	=	Saving	+	Taxation	+ Imports
i.e. W	=	S	+	T	+ M

21 Equilibrium

The **equilibrium condition** for national income now becomes

injections = withdrawals or

$$J = W$$

which is identical to our previous closed economy condition of S = I except that savings and investment are no longer the only injections and withdrawals from the circular flow.

22 MPM and MPT

In addition to the marginal propensities to consume and save we now have to accommodate the fact that some of any increment to income will be taken in **taxation** and some will be spent on **imports**, we therefore need to include in our analysis:

The marginal propensity to import (MPM) which is the amount of each increment to income which is spent on imports.

The marginal propensity to tax (MPT) which is the amount of each increment to income which is taken in tax (the tax rate).

Note that the **MPC + MPS + MPM + MPT = 1**.

23 The circular flow revisited

We can illustrate the principle again by the use of simple circular flow diagrams. (See Figure 39.9)

Diagram A represents an economy in equilibrium as the factor payments to households are received back by firms therefore **withdrawals are equal to injections**, i.e. J = W at £40m. It should also be noted that there is a balance of payments equilibrium (X = M) and the government has a balanced budget (G = T). Unemployment is however unacceptably high and it is estimated that the full employment income is £120m. In order to achieve this increase in income the government increases its expenditure by £8m which after the multiplier effect raises national income by £20m, a multiplier of 2.5. The government has achieved its full employment objective but note that this is only at the cost of 'trading-off' other equally desirable objectives.

A deficit has emerged on the balance of payments (i.e. imports = 12, exports = 10).

The government now has a deficit on its budget (taxation = 24, government expenditure = 28). This implies an increase in the **public sector borrowing requirement** which may have an inflationary impact on the price level.

There may be a fall in the exchange rate as a result of the balance of payments deficit which may add further inflationary pressure.

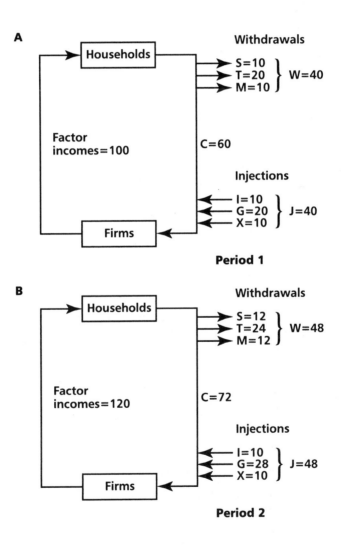

Figure 39.9

24 The new numerical multiplier

The multiplier (k) is now calculated by the following:

$$k = \frac{1}{1 - MPC}$$

$$\text{or} \quad \frac{1}{MPT + MPM + MPS}$$

e.g. MPC = 0.6
      MPM = 0.1
      MPS = 0.1
      MPT = 0.2

$$\text{therefore } k = \frac{1}{1 - 0.6} = \frac{1}{0.4} = 2.5$$

$$\text{or } k = \frac{1}{0.2 + 0.1 + 0.1} = \frac{1}{0.4} = 2.5$$

25 AMD

It is now possible to allow for an increase in AMD by an increase in either, or all, of the injections G, I or X. We will continue to assume however that the easiest of these variables for the government to manipulate is its own spending. Aggregate demand now however includes the effect of the **balance of payments deficit or surplus (X–M)**, hence our AMD schedule now becomes:

AMD = C + I + G + (X - M)

For brevity we will now identify the C + I + G + (X - M) line as AMD.

26 Injections and withdrawals

Previously we also utilised saving and investment functions, as these were the only withdrawals and injections, we can however follow the same analysis utilising an **injections function (J)** which represents I + G + X and a **withdrawals function (W)** representing S + T + M. It is not unreasonable to assume that all these functions rise with income and, as we have already established equilibrium is where J = W.

27 Equilibrium illustrated

We can illustrate the shift to a new equilibrium by utilising 45° line analysis as before or by using injections and withdrawals functions. In Figure 39.10 the economy is equilibrium at E with income Y below the full employment level Yf. In order to achieve full employment the government increases its expenditure, but it could be any of the injections G, I or X, i.e. ΔJ. This has the desired multiplier effect and shifts the AMD line to E',the size of the multiplier effect being

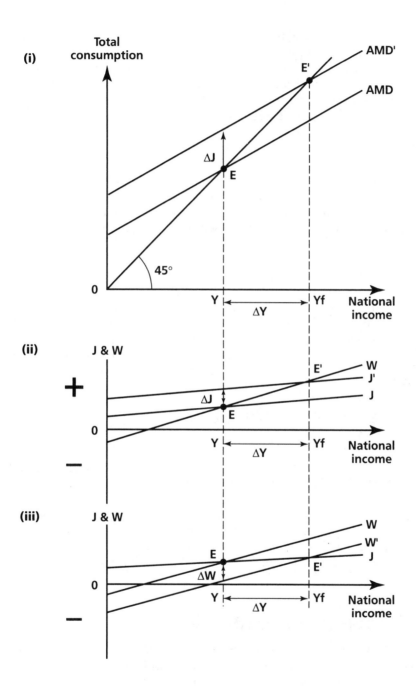

Figure 39.10

$$\frac{\Delta Y}{\Delta J}$$

and new equilibrium E' is at the full employment level of income Yf. In 39.10 (ii) this is represented as a shift in the injections function (J).

Original equilibrium is at E where J = W, the increased injections (ΔJ) shift J to J' and income rises until a new equilibrium is established where J = W again at E', and income Yf. The horizontal shift in Y being greater than the increase in G (i.e.ΔJ) due to the multiplier effect, which can again be estimated as

$$\frac{\Delta Y}{\Delta J}$$

Exactly the same result could have been achieved by reducing withdrawals and in Figure 39.10 (iii) this is represented by a shift of the withdrawals function (W) down from W to W' whilst injections remain constant. Income rises as a consequence and continues to do so until J = W again at E' and income has risen from Y to Yf. The size of the multiplier effect being

$$\frac{\Delta Y}{\Delta W}$$

With the inclusion of the additional variables it is evident that there are other policy instruments available to the government in addition to its own expenditure which can be used to boost the level of demand, for example reductions in direct or indirect taxes, encouragement to private investment or assisting exports. It is more likely in fact to be a 'policy mix' rather than total reliance on a single policy instrument.

28 Fiscal and monetary policy

Policy measures are generally referred to as being either **fiscal** or **monetary.**

- **Fiscal policy** generally refers to changes in **government expenditure** and **taxation.**
- **Monetary policy** generally refers to the control of the money supply (open market operations etc.), control of the banking system, and interest rate policy.
- **Direct controls** operate directly upon the policy objective, e.g. incomes policy.
- In reality the distinction between fiscal and monetary policy is not quite so straightforward, for example the PSBR is one of the most important influences on the money supply but arises as a **consequence** of the level of government expenditure (fiscal policy).

29 The 'downward' multiplier

In the analysis so far we have assumed that the multiplier is utilised to increase AMD during a period of deficient demand. The process could be reversed and in a period of excess demand the inflationary pressures reduced by selecting the appropriate policy mix of reduced government spending and increased taxation to produce a 'downward' multiplier effect. Experience indicates however that Keynesian policies have been less successful in dealing with inflation than unemployment.

30 The government budget

Prior to Keynes the annual budget was similar to a book-keeping exercise whereby the sources of tax revenue and how the government intended to spend it was outlined, and there was generally a belief that as far as possible the budget should balance. The implication of Keynes' analysis was that the government should deliberately aim for an unbalanced budget.

- In a situation of deficient demand and recession the government should spend more than it gathers in tax revenue and run a **budget deficit.**
- In a situation of excess demand and inflation a government may in theory attempt to gather more in taxation than it spends and run a **budget surplus**. During the post-war period budget deficits were the norm however a budget surplus was established in the UK between 1987 and 1989. As the budget surplus is available for debt repayment it is referred to as the **public sector debt repayment (PSDR).**
- A further possibility is the **balanced budget**. For a balanced budget government revenue is equal to its expenditure. This may be politically attractive to governments, particularly so when it is still possible to have a multiplier effect. The multiplier effect with a balanced budget is referred to as the **balanced budget multiplier**. (This concept is developed further in Appendix 2).

31 The Keynesian approach

Keynes advocated that the increased government spending could be financed by the government borrowing from wealth holders. The additional income created would generate sufficient tax revenue to repay the borrowing, and those finding employment would now be taxpayers rather than receivers of benefits. The process would not be inflationary provided domestic output could grow sufficiently rapidly. The additional borrowing does however imply an increase in the PSBR.

Keynes' ideas were first tried in the USA with the 'New Deal' in 1933, where projects such as the Tennessee Valley Authority scheme were undertaken. Most countries however based the management of their economies on Keynesian principles in the period following 1945 until inflation became the overriding concern during the mid 1970s, and the emphasis changed towards the control of the money supply as being the most important policy instrument.

Self assessment questions

1 What is the consumption function?
2 What is the marginal propensity to consume and how it calculated?
3 State the equilibrium condition for a closed economy with no government sector.
4 State the components of aggregate monetary demand in an open economy with government activity.
5 State the equilibrium conditions for an open economy with taxation and government spending.
6 Given an MPC of 0.8 calculate the size of the multiplier.

7 Discuss the affects of an increase in government expenditure on the level of aggregate demand.

8 The businessperson should be aware of the multiplier effect because of its importance in their business operation. Explain why this is so.

Appendix 1

Where fiscal policy involves a change in direct taxation the analysis of the multiplier is slightly different to that for government expenditure. Using b = MPC for brevity the effect of a change in government expenditure was given above as

$$\Delta Y = \frac{1}{1-b}\Delta G$$

and the multiplier coefficient was therefore:

$$\frac{\Delta Y}{\Delta G} = \frac{1}{1-b}$$

An increase in taxation, however, will reduce the level of disposable income for any level of national income, shifting the AMD curve downwards as it reduces the level of consumption spending. The downward shift in consumption, however, will be less than the increase in taxation because some of the tax increase will be absorbed by reduced saving. Changes in government spending and investment therefore have a pound for pound effect on AMD, whilst changes in taxation have an effect which is a fraction of their magnitude. A change in taxation changes AMD by the fraction (-b) of the tax change only as (1–b) is absorbed in reduced savings. This fraction (-b) multiplied by the full expenditure multiplier [1/(1–b)] gives the multiplier for the effect on equilibrium income of a change in taxation, i.e.

$$\left(\frac{1}{1-b}\right)$$

Hence for the effect of a change in taxation we have

$$\Delta Y = \frac{1}{1-b}(-b)\Delta T$$

and the tax multiplier is therefore:

$$\frac{\Delta Y}{\Delta T} = \frac{-b}{1-b}$$

It is important to note therefore that impact of policy measure on the economy may vary because the multiplier effects may vary.

Appendix 2

The **balanced budget multiplier** arises because, as outlined in Appendix 1 above, the negative tax multiplier is always less in value than the government spending multiplier. In order to assess the combined effect of an increase in government expenditure financed from an equivalent increase in taxation the two multipliers are added together:

$$\frac{\Delta Y}{\Delta G} + \frac{\Delta Y}{\Delta T} = \frac{1}{1-b} + \frac{-b}{1-b} = \frac{1-b}{1-b} = 1$$

i.e. The **balanced budget multiplier = UNITY (1)**, hence a £1 increase in government expenditure financed from a £1 tax increase will increase national income by £1.

Demand management in practice

1 Policy objectives

The objectives of economic policy can be stated as:

- **full employment**
- **stable prices**
- **balance of payments equilibrium**
- **economic growth**

In achieving any one of these objectives governments may have to accept a deterioration or 'trade-off' in one or more equally desirable policy targets.

2 Keynesian policies

The use of Keynesian policies in the 1950s and 1960s prevented any return to the mass unemployment of the 1930s, the era was, however, characterised by what has been referred to as 'stop-go' policies as governments attempted to achieve their policy targets, but found them difficult to achieve simultaneously. Following Beveridge (1944) full employment was generally accepted to be about 3% unemployment. As unemployment rose above this figure measures would be taken to expand the economy by appropriate fiscal policy measures (government spending and taxation) in order to increase the level of economic activity and reduce unemployment. The increase in demand however also had the effect of increasing imports because not all of the additional demand was met from domestic output, and also of raising the price level which made UK exports less competitive, consequently a balance of payments deficit emerged. This put downward pressure on the exchange rate and under its commitment to maintain the exchange rate the government would be forced to intervene and use the foreign exchange reserves in support of sterling. The achievement of the full employment objective had been at the cost of price stability and the balance of payments. In order to stabilise the price level and eliminate the deficit on the balance of payments the government would then introduce deflationary policies in order to dampen down demand, the rate of price increase would stabilise and an improvement in the balance of payments would be achieved at the cost of higher unemployment, hence the reference to 'stop-go' policies. One of the arguments against the 'stop-go' cycle was that it created a climate of uncertainty and therefore interfered with investment plans and reduced long term growth prospects. The period also saw repeated attempts to introduce **incomes policies** which were intended to keep the rate of wage increase within the increase in productivity in order to allow the economy to be run closer to full employment whilst avoiding the inflationary effects. Unfortunately during the most stringent periods of incomes policy costs rose due to non wage factors, e.g. oil in 1973/74.

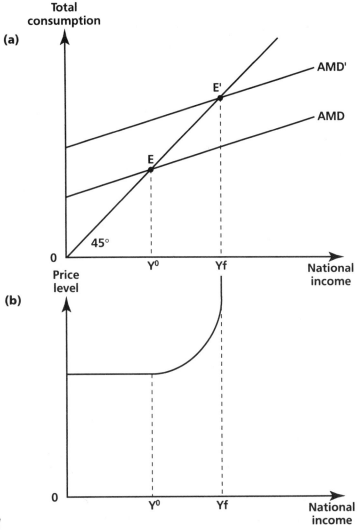

Figure 40.1

3 AMD and the price level

The Keynesian model outlined in the previous chapter ignored any effect the increase in AMD may have had on the price level. In Figure 40. 1(a) equilibrium is shifted from E to E', the full employment level, by an appropriate fiscal policy mix. In the lower diagram (b) however, it can be seen that prices are relatively stable until full resource utilisation is approached when they begin to rise progressively. At full employment output cannot be raised further and the rate of increase becomes almost vertical. Where there are unemployed resources therefore a reflation of the economy through fiscal policy would initially raise real output and employment with a modest rise in the price level, but as full employment is approached further increases in demand result only in a rise in the rate of inflation.

4 The Phillips curve

The 'trade-off' between inflation and unemployment was formalised in the **Phillips curve**. A.W. Phillips (1958), using data covering the period 1861–1957, identified a close correlation between the rate of change of money wages and employment. As wages are the most significant influence on prices the Phillips curve can also be expressed as the relationship between inflation (rate of change of prices) and unemployment, as illustrated in Figure 40.2. On the curve rates of inflation can be identified for each level of unemployment. Stable wages should be achieved at 5½% unemployment. The employment target of 3% would be associated with a modest level of inflation, and as employment is reduced below this there is ever accelerating inflation. Very high levels of unemployment such as x may even be associated with falling prices (y). Note that as the curve approaches full resources utilisation it becomes progressively steeper, hence at low levels of unemployment further reductions become more costly in terms of inflation. The Phillips curve was very accurate in predicting wage increases over the period 1958–1966,

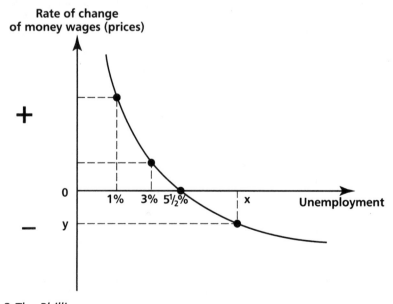

Figure 40.2 The Phillips curve

however the concept of the Phillips curve took a severe blow during the period 1974/75 when unemployment actually rose to 5½% but rather than price stability price increases of over 20% were being recorded. (This is discussed further in Chapter 44).

5 The monetarist view

Monetarists (see Chapter 43) suggest that the budget deficits resulting from demand management policies and the increase in the public sector borrowing requirement that this implies, results in an increase in the money supply and as a consequence leads to inflation.

The use of government spending described in the Keynesian model is also criticised on the grounds that the government expenditure would merely replace or '**crowd out**' an equivalent amount of private expenditure. Keynes suggested however that the multiplier effect would generate a sufficient increase in total expenditure to prevent this.

Crowding out may however happen as a result of the increase in interest rates which result from the budget deficit. In order to raise the necessary debt finance the government issues debt instruments (Treasury bills and gilts) which compete with the private demand for finance and raises the interest rate. The increase in the interest rate may reduce any private investment expenditures which are interest rate elastic (i.e. sensitive to interest rate changes). This implies that total expenditure may not increase by as much as the traditional multiplier suggests.

6 Slumpflation

The new phenomenon which arose in the mid 1970s of rising unemployment and simultaneously rising prices, referred to as **slumpflation** or **stagflation** suggested that the previously accepted relationships had broken down and were difficult to accommodate within orthodox demand management policies. In particular the Keynesian tradition of demand management and the relationships explicit with the orthodox Phillips curve came under attack. Some of the criticisms of the Keynesian model have been outlined above but these and the criticisms of the Phillips curve will be discussed in more detail in later chapters.

Self assessment questions

1 Outline the 'stop-go' cycle.
2 Discuss the relationship between increases in aggregate demand and the price level.
3 What are the implications for the relationship between prices and employment contained within the Phillips curve?
4 Why was the period of the mid 1970s referred to as an era of 'stagflation'?
5 How might government spending 'crowd-out' private spending?

41

The accelerator

1 A definition

The **accelerator** is a **capital stock adjustment process** which relates changes in the capital stock to the **rate of change of national income**.

2 Derived demand

The demand for capital is a **derived demand**, as capital is not demanded for its own sake, but for what it will produce, it therefore reflects changes in consumer demand which is itself dependent upon income. The accelerator principle suggests that any change in income (consumption) will be reflected in a magnified form in the output of the capital goods industries.

3 The accelerator principle

In order to illustrate this principle we will assume that in the production of brake cylinders for cars there is a fixed ratio between output and the number of lathes required (capital stock). If we assume that 10 lathes are required to produce 1000 cylinders and each lathe lasts for 10 years, as long as demand remains constant at 1000 cylinders each year the firm will just replace the one lathe which wears out each year. However if as a result of an increase in income demand rises to 1100 cylinders, an increase of 10%, the firm will now have to order 2 lathes, 1 replacement machine plus 1 to provide the additional capacity, therefore the demand for lathes, and therefore the output of the lathe industry, has risen by 100%. A 10% increase in consumption has resulted in a 100% increase in the output of the capital goods industry, i.e. an 'accelerated effect' If income continues to rise at 10% per annum then the output of both industries will continue to grow; however, if eventually consumption ceases to grow and the firms supplying brakes and other components to the car industry find they have sufficient capital to meet current demand, investment demand will return to replacement demand and in the example the demand for lathes would return to 1 each year, a 50% fall in the output of the lathe industry, again an accelerated effect of the change in consumption but this time operating in reverse. A reduction in investment demand can therefore occur as a result merely of a failure of consumption to increase. If consumption actually declines then the firm may find it has excess capacity and may not even replace its worn out machines. This 'naïve' accelerator provides one explanation for the pronounced cyclical upturns and downturns in the output of the capital goods industries.

4 A numerical example

The accelerator principle is illustrated here using the same example but with data to make the relationship clearer.

TABLE 41.1

	Year	Brake cylinders	Lathes	Gross investment (replacement plus net investment)	Net investment	
Phase 1	Year 1	1000	10	1	0	
	Year 2	1000	10	1	0	
	Year 3	1000	10	1	0	
Phase 2	Year 4	1100	11	2	1	100% increase in lathe production
	Year 5	1200	12	2	1	
Phase 3	Year 6	1300	13	2	1	100% decline in lathe production
	Year 7	1300	13	1	0	
Phase 4	Year 8	1200	12	0	0	Lathe production fallen to zero – disinvestment

Gross investment includes replacement investment plus net investment. Only net investment increases the capital stock and it is possible to have gross investment but no net investment. The demand for brake cylinders depends upon consumption (or income). The demand for the latter is derived from the demand for brake cylinders. In Phase 1, assuming the firm replaces one lathe each year, then gross investment is one lathe per year which consists only of replacement investment to replace the one lathe worn out. In year 4, income rises and the consumption of brake cylinders rises to 1100 – requiring a capital stock of 11 lathes. Gross investment now consists of one replacement plus one new machine, i.e. a 100% increase in the output of the capital goods industry. There is no problem as long as incomes continue to rise throughout phase 2; however in phase 3 income ceases to rise so investment falls back to replacement investment as the existing capital stock is sufficient. In phase 4, year 8, income falls slightly and there is dis-investment with the worn out machine not being replaced. Note that merely a failure of income to rise at the previous rate was sufficient to cause a 50% downswing in the fortunes of the capital goods industry. These violent upturns and downturns in the fortunes of the capital goods industry are referred to as the accelerator.

5 The accelerator relationship

The 'naïve' or simple accelerator can be expressed as follows. If we assume a direct relationship between income (GDP) and the stock of capital required to produce it, then

$$K = \alpha Y$$

where

K = the stock of capital
Y = income (GDP)
α = the coefficient (ratio) which relates the level of capital stock to the level of output.

Changes in the stock of capital are the same thing as investment therefore $\Delta K = I$, and

$$I = \alpha \Delta Y \quad \text{(or alternatively } I = \alpha \Delta C)$$

6 Dampening factors

In reality the accelerator effect may not be as extreme as suggested in the example and the effect may be dampened by a number of factors.

- Firms will not automatically increase investment at the first sign of an increase in sales, they may prefer to wait until they become convinced that the increase in sales is permanent. They may rationalise that some loss in sales in the short-run is less expensive than a bad investment decision.
- There may be some excess capacity in the industry which can be utilised before new investment becomes necessary. It may even be possible to use existing capacity more intensively, for example by working extra shifts. Although this may raise costs it may still be cheaper than re-investing to meet a temporary increase in demand.
- The capital goods industries may not be able to respond quickly to an increase in demand and it may take a considerable time for them to adjust their own capacity.

The accelerator may therefore be subject to considerable time lags. In order to incorporate these lags several other accelerator models have been developed, these lagged accelerator models can be found in most more advanced texts.

7 The accelerator and the trade cycle

The accelerator principle may explain the upper and lower turning points of the trade cycle. If as a result of an increase in income there is an increase in investment and a growth in the output of the capital goods industries the additional investment will generate a multiplier effect on incomes and a further rise in consumption and further new investment. The accelerator and multiplier interact with each other in an upward spiral. Eventually however the full employment ceiling will be reached and output cannot increase, or at least slows down. As the rate of growth of incomes slows down, or ceases, the accelerator effect operates in the opposite direction and the stabilising of consumption has a magnified downward effect on the capital goods industries. The reduction in investment has a downwards multiplier effect on consumption and multiplier and accelerator interact in a downward spiral into recession. If the economy has been in a prolonged recession with low levels of consumer demand, firms will eventually have to make a choice between reinvesting to replace worn out plant or going out of business. As plant becomes worn out or obsolete and firms are forced to reinvest they set the upward spiral in motion again. This of course is a highly simplified outline of the process, but does provide one explanation of the upper and lower turning points of the trade cycle.

Self assessment questions

1 What is the 'driving force' behind the accelerator principle?

2 Outline the relationship between changes in consumption and the output of the capital goods industries.

3 What factors may dampen the accelerator effect?

4 Examine how the interaction of the multiplier and the accelerator may cause trade cycles or fluctuations in the national income.

42

Interest rate determination and investment

The marginal productivity theory of interest rate determination was discussed earlier (Chapter 24) and should be referred to at this point. In this chapter we will briefly outline the Keynesian view of interest and money.

1 Discount rate and net present value

We will consider first the relationship between interest rates and the firm's investment plans. A firm considering any investment proposal will attempt to estimate the addition to profits which will be forthcoming from the investment project. These additions to profit will not however be made in a single time period but will be received over several years. In order to estimate the net benefit of the investment it is necessary therefore to estimate the **net present value** of the future returns by means of a **discount** factor. To explain this more simply, imagine the alternatives of £100 received today or £100 received in 1 year's time with a current interest rate of 10%. If the £100 received today had been invested for 1 year it would have been worth £110, alternatively we would only need to invest £91 today for it to be worth £100 in 1 year's time. Hence £100 in 1 year's, time is worth only £91 today. In other words future income receipts are worth less than present income receipts. For this reason estimates of future income receipts from an investment project have to be discounted by an appropriate **discount rate** in order to find the **present value**, the process being similar to compound interest in reverse. The discount rate represents the **opportunity cost of capital,** which is in fact the **rate of interest**; as the outlay involved in the project could have been invested and have earned interest with zero risk. The present value of the annual inflows is summed and compared with the cost of buying the machine (C), if the present value is greater than the cost the net present value will be positive and the project goes ahead, and vice versa.

2 Discounted cash flow

This process, referred to as **discounted cash flow**, can be represented as:

$$NPV = \frac{Y_1}{(1+r)} + \frac{Y_2}{(1+r)^2} + \frac{Y_3}{(1+r)^3} + \ldots \frac{Y_n}{(1+r)^n}$$

The income or yield from the investment (Y) is discounted each year by the appropriate discount rate (r) over the relevant number of years (n). The discount rate is simply the percentage rate expressed as a decimal, i.e. if the percentage rate is 6% then r = 0.06, so in the first year (I + r) = 1.06, in year 2 the discount factor is $(1.06)^2$ and so on. Normally however it is unnecessary to calculate this as tables are available, or more commonly today the calculation is carried out by computer, utilising one of the investment appraisal packages available. Discounted cash flow is normally represented by the following formula:

$$NPV = \sum_{i=1}^{n} \frac{Y}{(1+r)^n}$$

where   NPV = Net present value
    Y = Income or yield from the investment
    Σ = sum of
    n = number of years the project will last
    r = discount rate

The discount factor can be found from a standard NPV table, an extract from which is given below in table 42.1

TABLE 42.1						
Present	Value of £1					
Year	1%	2%	3%	4%	5%	6%
1	0.990	0.980	0.971	0.961	0.952	0.943
2	0.980	0.961	0.943	0.925	0.907	0.890
3	0.971	0.942	0.915	0.889	0.864	0.840
4	0.961	0.924	0.889	0.855	0.823	0.792
5	0.951	0.906	0.863	0.822	0.784	0.747

Whenever the result of the calculation produces a negative outcome a project should not go ahead as the investment is not producing a return greater than the opportunity cost of the capital, which would earn more in an alternative financial investment such as the bank. Alternatively if the choice is between two projects then the one which yields the greatest NPV should be chosen. For example, supposing a firm can invest £20,000 in either of two alternative investments or could leave the capital in the bank earning 6% per annum. The income (or yield) from the sale of the output from the two projects is estimated as follows.

YEAR END AMOUNT £s					
	Year 1	Year 2	Year 3	Year 4	Year 5
Project A	- 20,000	4,000	5,000	6,000	8,000
Project B	- 20,000	8,000	6,000	5,000	4,000

(Note that the - 20,000 in Year 1 indicates the capital outlay.)
The capital inflows and outflows are then multiplied by the appropriate discount factor to find the NPV of both projects.

PROJECT A					
	Year 1	Year 2	Year 3	Year 4	Year 5
Outflow (£s)	- 20,000				
Inflow (£s)		4,000	5,000	6,000	8,000
Discount factor (6%)	0.943	0.890	0.840	0.792	0.747
NPV	-18,860	3,560	4,200	4,752	5,976
Cumulative NPV	-18,860	-15,300	-11,100	-6,348	-372
NET PRESENT VALUE = -£372					

The project should be rejected as it yields a negative NPV.

PROJECT B					
	Year 1	Year 2	Year 3	Year 4	Year 5
Outflow (£s)	- 20,000				
Inflow (£s)		8,000	6,000	5,000	4,000
Discount factor (6%)	0.943	0.890	0.840	0.792	0.747
NPV	-18,860	7,120	5,040	3,960	2,988
Cumulative NPV	-18,860	-11,740	-6,700	-2,740	248
NET PRESENT VALUE = £248					

This project should be accepted as it yields a positive NPV i.e Project B offers a greater return than Project A. Note that this is despite the fact that the total income over the 5 years is identical (£23,000) - it is the timing of the income which is crucial.

3 Internal rate of return

An alternative approach based on exactly the same principles as those outlined above is referred to as the **internal rate of return (IRR)**. This can be summarised as

$$PV = \sum_{i=1}^{n} \frac{Y}{(1+x)^n}$$

where $\quad$ x = IRR

The firm estimates the value of x (the internal rate of return) which produces a present value equal to the cost of the machine, i.e. finds that x which produces PV = C. The firm will rationally invest in the machine whenever the **internal rate of return is greater than the rate of interest,** i.e. x is greater than r.

4 The marginal efficiency of capital

The internal rate of return is also referred to as the **marginal efficiency of capital (MEC)**. It will pay a firm to invest and increase its stock of capital up to the point where the MEC is equal to the interest rate.

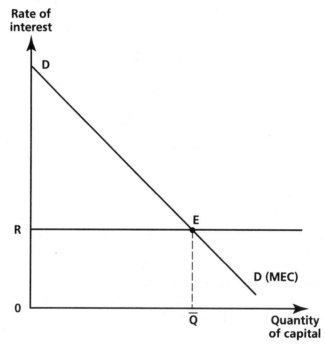

Figure 42.1

If however the stock of capital is increased, relative to other factors, then like the other factors of production it will be subject to **diminishing marginal productivity**. As a consequence the MEC declines as the capital stock is increased, and if represented diagramatically it slopes downwards to the right and constitutes the firm's **demand curve for capital.** It slopes downwards because the most profitable investments will be undertaken first and further investments will be less profitable as marginal productivity declines, and will therefore only be undertaken at lower rates of interest. The profit maximising firm will be in equilibrium regarding its capital stock when the **marginal efficiency of capital is equal to the rate of interest,** i.e.

$$MEC = R$$

In Figure 42.1 the firm is in equilibrium at E with capital stock $\bar{Q}$ when the rate of interest is R.

The firm would only increase its stock of capital if either the rate of interest fell, or the MEC of capital increased; through for example the introduction of new technology.

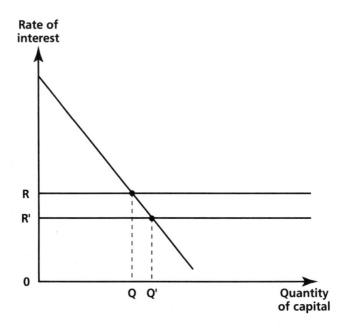

Figure 42.2

In Figure 42.2 a fall in the rate of interest from R to R' raises the firm's optimal stock of capital from Q to Q'. An increase in the rate of interest would have the reverse effect.

In Figure 42.3 the MEC of capital has increased as a result of the introduction of new technology with greater productivity this has shifted the MEC curve outwards from MEC to MEC' raising the firm's optimal capital stock from Q to Q' at R rate of interest.

In both cases if the firm changes its capital stock to the new optimal level then the change in the capital stock, i.e. Q to Q' represents **net investment.**

5 The demand for money

We have so far taken the rate of interest as given, however in order to consider how the rate of interest is determined it is necessary to consider the demand for money. The demand for money does not refer to the demand for money for spending on goods, but the demand for the actual stock of money to hold as money balances. It will be recalled from Chapter 39 that according to 'classical theory' money was only held for purposes of

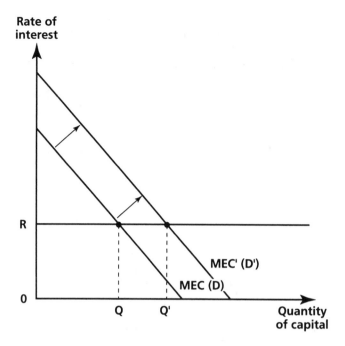

Figure 42.3

making transactions and bridging the time period between income receipts, however Keynes added the possibility of the demand for money as an asset, i.e. speculative balances. Three 'motives' for demanding money balances are identified as:

- **Transactions demand** – as in classical theory transactions balances were needed to bridge the gap between receipts and expenditure. The size of such balances is dependent upon:
  - **The length of time** between receipts and expenditure.
  - The **size** of receipts and expenditure. Transactions balances would vary with income and **not** rates of interest.
- **Precautionary demand** – money will be held for the purpose of meeting unforeseen emergencies. This motive was not included in classical theory where perfect certainty was assumed. Keynes grouped transactions and precautionary balances together into a single sum which varied directly with the **level of income**.
- **Speculative demand** – the speculative motive was Keynes' innovation. In order to understand this motive it is necessary to ask, why should people hold money balances over and above those described above when money is an asset which yields no return at all? The answer to this is that if other financial assets, in particular bonds, are likely to fall in price then losses on bonds can be avoided by holding money instead. The motive for holding speculative money balances is therefore to avoid losses in a declining securities market. In order to understand this more clearly it is necessary to consider the relationship between bond prices and the rate of interest. In this context Keynes was referring to undated government securities (referred to as 'gilts' or 'consols'). These bonds pay a fixed annual sum and are bought and sold on the securities market, their price therefore varies with demand and supply. For example, if an undated security has a nominal value of £200 and pays £10 per annum, the nominal interest

(or coupon) is 5%. However, the actual yield or earnings yield, expressed as a rate of interest, will vary inversely with the market price of the security.

Normal			
Price	£10 annual payment expressed as % of nominal price	Market price	(Earnings yield) = Rate of interest
£ 200	5%	£400	2½%
£ 200	5%	£200	5%
£ 200	5%	£100	10%

For example, it can be seen that as the market price rises to £400 the fixed annual payment of £10 represents the equivalent of an earnings yield of 2½% rate of interest and when the price falls to £100 the rate of interest rises to 10%. The market price and rate of interest, i.e. earnings yield, on fixed interest bonds is therefore **inversely related**.

6 Liquidity preference

Speculative money balances vary therefore with the anticipated gains or losses on the securities market, and the extent to which individuals prefer holdings of money to other financial assets is referred to as **liquidity preference**. Bearing in mind the relationship between security prices and interest rates above we can make the following assumptions.

- When security prices are high (and interest rates are low) speculators will expect bond prices to fall and therefore a capital loss to be made. They will therefore attempt to avoid such losses by holding speculative money balances. Low interest rates therefore imply a high liquidity preference. Note also that the opportunity cost of holding money is lower.
- When bond prices are low (and interest rates therefore are high) speculators will anticipate a rise in bond prices and therefore a capital gain. They will attempt to take advantage of the capital gain on bonds by holding bonds rather than money balances. High interest rates therefore imply a low liquidity preference. Note also that the opportunity cost of holding money is higher.

7 Expectations

It is important to note the importance of speculators' expectations about the future course of interest rates. Each individual is assumed to hold their expectations with complete certainty, although there may be disagreement between individuals about the future course of interest rates.

8 The liquidity preference curve

If each individual's liquidity preference is added together a **liquidity preference curve** can be drawn, which represents the **demand for money**. The liquidity preference curve relates the total demand for money to the rate of interest. Although each individual may have different expectations of future events, by adding them all together we obtain the smooth liquidity preference curve in Figure 42.4.

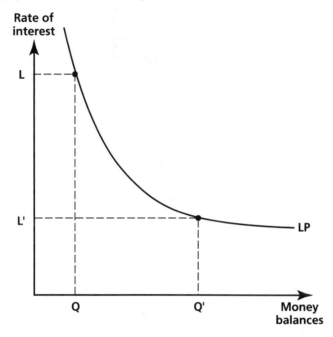

Figure 42.4

In Figure 42.4 when the interest rate is L bond prices will be low and a rise in bond prices, and therefore capital gains, will be anticipated and speculative balances will be zero, only transactions and precautionary balances being held, i.e. Q. When the rate of interest is low at L' and bond prices are high capital losses are anticipated and larger speculative money balances are held, i.e. Q' in order to avoid capital losses on bonds. The horizontal portion of the liquidity preference curve is referred to as the **liquidity trap**. In this portion of the curve the demand for money is infinitely elastic with respect to the interest rate. Reductions in the interest rate, in this portion only, increases people's desire to hold cash balances. The implication here is that any attempt to achieve internal expansion through increased investment brought about by lowering the interest rate would fail, because any increase in the money supply created in order to reduce the rate of interest would be held in the form of cash balances, making it impossible to use interest rates (monetary policy) to expand the economy.

9 Money supply

The **supply of money** at any point of time is fixed by the monetary authorities and is therefore independent of the rate of interest. In Figure 42.5 the money supply is therefore the vertical line MS. The rate of interest is determined where the demand for money (LP) intersects the supply (MS), at interest rate R.

Changes in the interest rate could occur as a result of:

- A shift in the liquidity preference curve as a result of anticipated changes in bond prices.
- A shift in the money supply curve by the authorities changing the supply of money. Note that an increase in the horizontal portion, the liquidity trap, would leave interest rates unchanged and would be held entirely in the form of additional money balances making monetary policy weak and ineffectual.

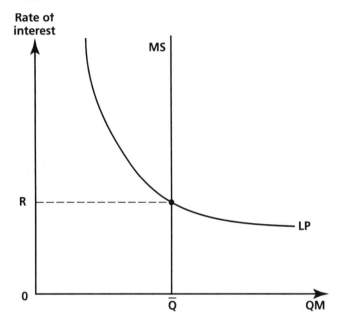

Figure 42.5

10 Changes in money supply

According to conventional liquidity preference theory an increase in the money supply in the 'normal' range of the liquidity preference curve will result in a reduction in the rate of interest which should increase the firm's optimal stock of capital and therefore result in an increase in investment. In Figure 42.6 the authorities increase the money supply from Ms to Ms' and as a consequence the rate of interest falls from R to R'; the effect of this on investment is shown in Figure 42.7, where the fall in the interest rate from R to R'increases the firm's optimal stock of capital from Q to Q'. This increase in investment would not occur if the demand for money was perfectly elastic as in the 'liquidity trap' situation (see section 8 above).

Further as Keynes suggested, firms' investment plans depend also upon their view of the future. If their expectations of future sales were pessimistic a lower rate of interest may not be sufficient inducement to undertake investment and national income would remain unchanged. It was for precisely this reason that Keynes advocated the use of government expenditure. The way in which the increase in the money supply is financed may also be important, because, as is explained in the following chapter, if the increase in the money supply is a result of an increase in the public sector borrowing requirement, a consequence of this may be a rise in the price level and a return to a higher level of interest rates with at best only a temporary effect on the level of investment and output. Conventional liquidity preference may also fail to operate during a period of inflation because bonds are only one example of a portfolio of assets which may be held as an alternative to money, and during a period of inflation other assets such as houses and land may offer a better hedge against inflation than bonds which will have low prices, because a high yield will be required in order to compensate for inflation.

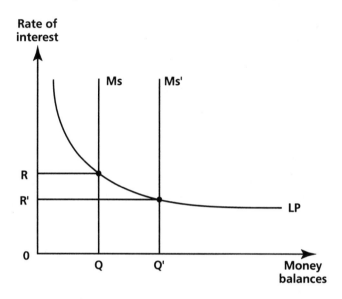

Figure 42.6

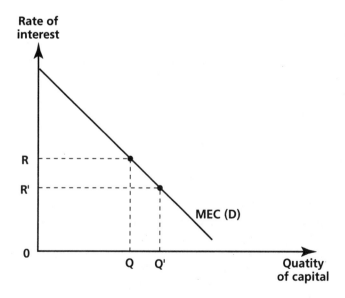

Figure 42.7

11 Sales expectations

Keynes, it should be noted, suggested that the investment decisions by firms were only marginally influenced by interest rates, the major factor being **sales expectations**. Firms would invest if they expected the future level of demand and therefore profits to be high.

12 Different views

In classical theory the rate of interest brings equality between savings and investment; however in Keynesian theory savings and investment are brought into balance through changes in income operating through the multiplier process.

Keynesian theory emphasises the effect of interest rates on real activity through the effects on investment, and through the multiplier effect, on income.

Monetarists (see Chapter 43) stress the effects of interest rates on the money supply and inflation.

13 The interest rate spectrum

The interest rate here refers to the basic rate of interest on government undated bonds. There is of course a whole spectrum of other interest rates, e.g.
- Building societies
- Hire purchase
- Bank deposit accounts
- Private tenders etc.

Each will have a different rate of interest which is determined by factors such as:

- The duration of the loan.
- The degree of risk, in particular the credit-worthiness of the borrower.
- The amount of collateral available.
- The purpose and nature of the loan.

Self assessment questions

1 What is meant by the marginal efficiency of capital?
2 How does the firm determine its optimal stock of capital?
3 Discuss why the speculative demand for money varies with the rate of interest.
4 What is meant by liquidity preference?
5 How does liquidity preference and the money supply determine the rate of interest?
6 What is meant by the net present value of an investment?
7 How is the internal rate of return calculated?
8 What is the affect of an increase in the money supply on the, firm's demand for capital?

Section L

Supply-side economics

Containing the following chapters:

Chapter 43 – Monetarism and inflation

Chapter 44 – The natural rate of unemployment and the Phillips curve

A view of macro economics that suggests that the output of the economy is influenced by the growth of the supply of the factors of production and technology

This section should enable students to:

- *Understand* the causes of inflation
- *Explain* the concept of the natural rate of unemployment
- *Contrast* the original Phillips curve with the long run Phillips curve
- *Evaluate* the success of the UK government's MTFS

Keywords to consider :

natural rate of unemployment; quantity theory of money; medium term financial strategy; permanent income hypothesis; expectations; adaptive expectations; rational expectations;supply factors; free market system; government intervention; fiscal drag.

43

Monetarism and inflation

1 A definition

The expression 'monetarist' is a general term used to describe those economists who believe that the money supply is the most important factor in determining the level of expenditure and prices.

2 Monetarist origins

The monetarist concepts have their origins in classical economics, however their revival in modified form owes much to Professor Milton Friedman. Friedman and Schwartz (A.J.) analysed data in the USA between 1867 and 1960 and demonstrated a close correlation (relationship) between changes in the money supply and the rate of change of money GDP, and therefore prices, after a time lag of about 18 months. Friedman suggested therefore that there was a strong causal relationship between the supply of money and inflation.

3 Friedman's views

Friedman states that 'inflation is always and everywhere a monetary phenomenon', meaning that inflation is always due to an excessive growth in the money supply. Several historical examples are quoted such as the influx of gold from S. America into Europe in the 16th Century, the gold finds in California in 1849, and those in Australia and S. Africa in the late 19th and early 20th centuries: all of which were followed by a rapid rise in prices. Friedman suggests that those examples have their modern counterparts in the budget deficits of the second half of the 20th century.

4 Causes of inflation

As inflation is caused only by increasing the money supply the implication is that as only governments can print money, then only governments cause inflation. Only governments therefore can cure inflation – by keeping a tight control over the supply of money. Governments can always obtain the resources they require by increasing the supply of money which raises the price level. The increase in the price level reduces real incomes which enables the government to acquire a greater share of the available resources. This is identical to the effect of taxation, hence Friedman refers to expansion of the money supply as 'taxation without representation'.

The increase in the money supply arises from the budget deficits which governments maintain in order to pursue fiscal policies which will maintain aggregate demand at levels consistent with full employment. Governments are pressed to maintain high levels of expenditure but they are unwilling to raise taxation in order to pay for it and so resort to deficit financing. (See Chapter 39). As suggested above, this is a hidden form of taxation due to the effect on the price level and therefore real incomes.

5 The money supply

At this stage it is worth reiterating exactly what we mean by the money supply. The most important definition in this context is the broader definition M4 which it will be recalled from Chapter 35 is defined as:

Notes and coins in circulation + current and deposit accounts held by all UK residents in sterling in banks and building societies.

The money supply therefore includes not only notes and coin but also the banks' ability to create credit. An important element of controlling the money supply is therefore control of the banksí ability to create deposits.

It will be recalled from Chapter 35 that an increase in the government's budget deficit implies an increase in the public sector borrowing requirement (PSBR). The PSBR is financed by borrowing through the sale of gilts to the public and by the taking up of short term public sector debt (bills) by the banks which increases the asset base of the banks as these securities constitute bank reserve assets.

This enables the banks to undertake the multiple expansion of credit, which represents an increase in M4; the majority of which is comprised of bank deposits. Figure 43.1 illustrates the link between government expenditure and the money supply.

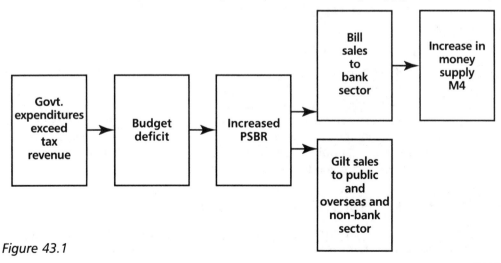

Figure 43.1

The government may attempt to sell as much of its debt as possible outside the banking system, to the public or other financial institutions, but in order to do this it will have to increase interest rates in order to attract them. To prevent an increase in the money supply by this method therefore implies a higher level of interest rates.

6 The natural rate of unemployment

Monetarists consider that the main reason for the increase in the money supply, and therefore inflation, is the commitment of governments to full employment. Governments have attempted to keep unemployment below the **'natural rate' of unemployment** (see Chapter 44) and in order to achieve this have incurred ever increasing budget deficits, with the consequent growth in the money supply. Any attempt to keep unemployment below the natural rate will therefore result in ever increasing inflation (see Chapter 44).

7 The quantity theory of money

Essentially the monetarist view represents a return to the **quantity theory of money** (see Chapter 29). It will be recalled that the quantity theory stated that

$$MV = PT$$

where M = Money supply
V = the velocity (or speed) of circulation of money
P = the price level
T = the level of transactions

The level of transactions (T) can be assumed to be the equivalent of the real level of economic activity or output.

The debate between monetarists and Keynesians hinges around V, monetarists suggest it is a constant and therefore is predictable. Keynesians argue that it varies in an unpredictable manner with changes in interest rates (see liquidity preference theory, Chapter 42). If we accept the monetarist contention that V is constant then any increase in M will result in an increase in the value of PT, and monetarists argue that the effect will fall on P (the price level) rather than T (real output), and will therefore be **inflationary, i.e. excessive growth of the money supply will increase money GDP (prices) rather than real GDP (output).**

8 The Keynesian view

It will be recalled from Chapter 39 that in Keynesian economics an increase in the money supply will influence income only **indirectly** through the reduction in the interest rate stimulating investment which would raise income through the multiplier effect. If there were unemployed resources in the economy output and real income would be raised; if there was full employment the price level would increase. In Keynesian economics therefore changes in the money supply affect the economy in an unpredictable and indirect manner and is therefore not a good policy instrument.

9 The transmission mechanism

The monetarist transmission mechanism through which increases in the money supply result in higher expenditure is quite straightforward. Money is considered to be an imperfect substitute for other financial assets and is held for its own sake. When there is an increase in the money stock the immediate effect is that people find they are holding higher money balances in relation to their holdings of other assets than they desire. They therefore attempt to reduce their money balances and increase their holdings of other assets – a kind of 'portfolio' adjustment. Some of these additional money balances will be used to purchase other forms of financial assets; however, some will be used to purchase goods and services which are also considered to yield a return to the purchaser. The increased expenditures will result in higher prices.

10 Monetarist views

Monetarists believe that fiscal policy is a destabilising influence on the economy and should be avoided. This is because of the long and variable time lags between the implementation of a policy and its effect upon the economy. For example, a reflationary policy taken during recession may take two years to take effect, by which time the economy may be growing autonomously and the effect of the policy becomes inflationary. In Figure 43.2 the trade cycle the economy would follow with no intervention is indicated by the continuous line, the broken line indicates the pro-cyclical effect of government intervention in the monetarist version.

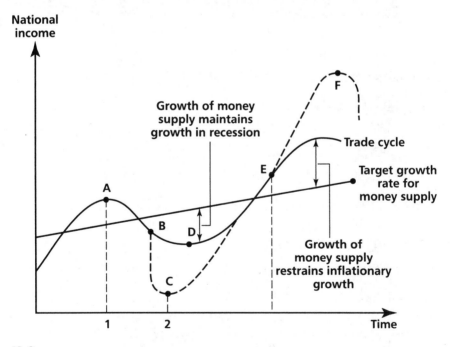

Figure 43.2

For example, the economy is on the growth or 'boom' stage of the cycle and anti-cyclical measures are taken at time period 1 to dampen down any inflationary growth tendencies. These measures do not come into effect until point B when the economy was on the down-turn anyway causing the recession to go deeper, to point C, than it would have done in the absence of such intervention, i.e. point D. Reflationary measures taken at C in time period 2 come into effect, after say 18 months, at point E when the economy is in the up-turn causing an inflationary period of excess growth to point F, and so on in a pro-cyclical manner exaggerating the upswings and downswings, rather than dampening them down in the anti-cyclical manner intended.

They believe that intervention in the economy should be minimal and that a simple monetary rule should be followed. A target rate of growth for the money supply should be announced which is consistent with the rate of growth of real output (GDP), illustrated in Figure 43.2. Attempts by the workforce to gain wage increases which are not consistent with the rate of growth of the money supply can only result in higher unemployment. Workers are expected to learn from their experiences and as reduced monetary targets are announced they will revise their expectations of inflation downwards and settle for lower wage increases. The slow growth in the money supply is sufficient to maintain growth during the down-turns in the economy and restrain inflationary or excess growth in the up-turn. Eventually the economy should stabilise around its 'natural growth rate.

11 The medium term financial strategy

Table 43.1

	PSBR (£bn)	PSBR as a percentage of GDP
1984/5	10.2	3.1
1985/6	6.8	2.0
1986/7	3.4	0.85
1987/8	−3.0	−0.75
1988/9	−14.5	−3.0
1989/90	−7.8	−1.5
1990/1	−0.8	0.1
1991/2	13.8	2.2
1992/3	36.3	6.0
1993/4	45.4	7.0
1994/5	34.4	5.2
1995/6	21.5	4.5
1996/7	23.8 (f)	3.5 (f)

(f = forecast)
Note that a negative PSBR implies a budget surplus

The 1979 Conservative government embraced the monetarist doctrine which was embodied within the 1980 **medium term financial strategy (MTFS)**. The MTFS contained two key elements:

- A set of declining targets over a four year period for the growth of £M3.
- A plan for the reduction of the PSBR as a proportion of GDP from 4.8% in 1979/80 to 1.5% by 1983/84.

Little success was achieved in hitting the targets for the broad monetary aggregates however the attempt to reduce the PSBR as a percentage of GDP met with more success with a budget surplus being attained by 1987/88.

The stages in the development of the MTFS are summarised in Appendix 1.

The implication of the adoption of the MTFS was a switch of emphasis away from maintaining full employment to the control of inflation. The effect of the policy was thought to be more expensive in terms of unemployment the more slowly workers revise their expectations of inflation, and therefore wage demands, downwards in the light of announced targets for monetary growth. In this context it is important that the government should be seen to be achieving its targets, which is not easy given the nature of broad aggregates such as M3 and M4.

12 Criticisms of the MTFS

- One of the major criticisms of this strategy is that reductions in the money supply fall not on the price level (P) but on real output (T). The resulting decline in real output and activity results in high unemployment. It is this induced recession which critics suggest controls the price level rather than by any direct effect of the money supply on prices.
- The results of research, such as that of Friedman, is criticised because the demonstration of a close correlation between the money supply and changes in GDP is not necessarily causal, and if GDP was growing the money supply could be expected to grow in line with it.
- Keynesians suggest that if GDP is growing, attempts to control the money supply will be by-passed by the development of alternative forms of money.
- The empirical research of Friedman and Schwartz for the UK economy has been criticised by Hendry (D.F.) in an article published by the Bank of England[1]. Hendry suggests that Friedman's research in dealing with statistical evidence shows a lack of rigour and that his assertions are 'devoid of empirical support.'

13 Monetarist recommendations

Monetarists advocate a reduced role for the state:

- They believe that intervention through Keynesian type demand management policies are ineffective in reducing unemployment and result in inflation.
- The production of as many goods and services as possible should be carried out by the private sector which is believed to be more efficient and more able to respond to consumers' needs.

---

[1]Assertion Without Empirical Basis: An Econometric appraisal of *Monetary Trends in the United Kingdom* – M. Friedman and A. Schwarz. By David F. Hendry and Neil R. Ericsson. (B. of E.)

14 The monetarist experiment

In the UK the Conservative government which took power in 1979 embraced the monetarist doctrine which found expression in the medium term financial strategy, which as stated above, set targets for monetary growth and in order to secure these it was necessary to contain the level of public expenditure in real terms. The objectives of this policy were firstly the control of inflation and secondly to reduce the proportion of the economy's resources consumed by the state sector, ie to prevent the state from 'crowding out' private production. By 1987 a degree of success could be claimed in the control of inflation, however, much of the impact of monetary policy seemed to have fallen on the level of output and employment. The size of the public sector had been reduced, standing at about 45% of GDP, a figure comparable with many other industrialised nations. The use of public expenditure targets expressed in cash terms however, in order to constrain the growth of public spending in real terms, became discredited as targets were persistently overshot. Public expenditure also rose faster than expected due to public demand for better health services, education, welfare benefits and law and order, as living standards rose. Instead of aiming to cut public expenditure the 1986 Autumn Statement from the Treasury (and in the 1987 Public Expenditure White Paper Cm 56) stated that the objective was to reduce public spending as a proportion of national income, which clearly implied that an increase in real terms was acceptable provided that it was less than the rise in real GDP. This change of emphasis together with the virtual abandonment of targets for monetary growth was taken by many commentators to mean the end of the Monetarist experiment in the U.K.

Following the 1988 budget the broad monetary aggregates were abandoned for targeting purposes as the outcomes were seldom within the targeted range and the narrower definition M0 was adopted as the main monetary indicator. The rise in inflation to 8% during 1989/90 resulted in a tightening of monetary policy but with reliance on interest rates as the main policy instrument; interest rates rising to 15% by the end of 1989. The economy was slow to respond to the rise in interest rates and the increase worsened the recession. Monetary policy was relaxed in 1991 as interest rates fell to 10.5% with further decreases in 1992 to 7% and 1993 to 6.5%.

In 1993 the government specified a range of 3–9% for maintaining the growth of M4 . Interest rates rose in 1995 only to fall again in 1996 to below 6%.

Self assessment questions

1 What is meant by 'taxation without representation'?

2 Describe how an increase in the PSBR implies an increase in the money supply.

3 How is the commitment to 'full employment' connected with increases in the PSBR?

4 What assumptions are implied by monetarists regarding the velocity of circulation of money (V)?

5 Outline the monetarist transmission mechanism by which increases in the money supply result in higher expenditures and prices.

6 Outline the monetarist rule for the growth of the money supply.

7 Why was is it considered necessary to announce targets for monetary growth?

8 Why have governments experienced difficulty in achieving targets set for the growth of broad monetary aggregates?

Appendix 1

The medium term financial strategy (MTFS) was introduced in 1980 in the belief that by setting targets for the growth of the money supply, the money supply, and therefore inflation, could be controlled. Targeting the money supply however proved to be far more difficult in practice, largely because there is no unique definition of money and furthermore there is no means by which the money supply can be directly controlled. Since its introduction therefore the exact nature of the MTFS has frequently been changed. Targeting the money supply is one thing but hitting the target is another. When the government responded by changing the target many commentators accused them of resorting to 'moving the goal posts'. Targets for the growth of the money supply have been expressed in various forms since 1980, but can be summarised as follows:

1980-82   The only target was sterling M3 (£M3)

1982-84   M1, £M3 and PSL2

1984–88   MO and £M3

1988–90   MO only

1993–present M0 and M4

The measures of money published by the Bank of England have also changed over the period, and the only measures now published (June 1990) are as follows (read in conjunction with Chapter 35):

MO	Cash in circulation plus commercial bank operational deposits at the Bank of England
N1B M1	Cash in circulation plus non-interest bearing private sector sight deposits with banks
M2	Cash in circulation plus retail deposits with banks, building societies and the National Savings Bank
M4	Cash in circulation plus all private sector sterling bank and building society deposits
M5	M4 plus private holdings of money market instruments and national savings instruments

The exercise has lost much of its credibility because, as indicated above, when monetary targets do not behave as the government wishes them to they are simply replaced by different targets or their importance is reduced by taking into consideration some other indicators. For example, the Chancellor said in his 1984 budget speech that he would 'take account of other indicators of broad money in particular PSL2'. It was just as well that PSL2 was not targeted because it grew by 14.4% over the year.

During the first 3 months of the 1985 target period £M3 grew by 4.4% which is an annual rate of 19%. The immediate reaction to the overshoot was to announce in the Economic Progress Report May 1985 that the presentation of the figures would be changed.

The change is in fact entirely sensible but the timing was unfortunate and it does seem that overshoots are no longer regarded with alarm; the government merely tries to present the figures in as palatable a way as possible. The change actually reduced the growth in £M3 from 19% to 12% which was still 3% above the target. In a highly significant speech at Loughborough University on 22nd October 1986 the Governor of the Bank of England, Mr. Leigh-Pemberton questioned the ability of governments to control M3 and therefore the usefulness of setting broad monetary targets, 'which may even become counter productive serving to undermine confidence .... '

By 1988 targeting for the broad monetary aggregate had been abandoned and the March 1988 budget contained a target for the narrow definition M0 only. The key points of the MTFS announced in the 1988 budget were as follows:

- The broad aim of policy is the steady reduction of inflation, over the medium term, by reducing the growth of total spending power in the economy, as measured by the cash value of national output (money GDP).
- The growth of M0 to be kept within the range 1–5% in 1988-9.
- Interest rate decisions to be based on a continuous and comprehensive assessment of monetary conditions to maintain downward pressure on inflation.
- A balanced budget to be the norm, for the medium term.

The actual trends for M0, M4, GDP and the PSBR are shown below

TABLE 1					
MONEY GDP, MONEY SUPPLY AND THE PSBR					
Year	90-91	91-92	92-93	93-94	94-95
Money GDP[1]	4.2	4.5	4.2	6.0	5.3
M0[2]	3.0	2.5	5.6	7.3	5.2
PSBR[3]	-0.6	13.8	36.3	45.4	35.9
M4[4]	5.8	3.6	4.6	4.6	9.9

[1] Percentage change on previous year.
[2] and [4] percentage change on previous year.
[3] £ billion, cash.

Appendix 2

The monetarist consumption function and the permanent income hypothesis

This appendix is optional for A level students but would be useful to more advanced students.

The permanent income hypothesis

Post-war cross sectional data on the consumption function has consistently provided a poor fit to that forecast on the basis of long-run time series data. Friedman's **permanent**

income hypothesis provides one possible solution to this problem. The central theme of Friedman's theory is that **planned or permanent consumption** is proportional to expected or **permanent income**. Permanent income itself is dependent upon the individual's stock of wealth and subjective rate of interest (not market rate). Permanent income can be viewed as the annual flow of income generated by the individual's estimated stock of wealth at a rate equal to the rate of interest. Alternatively, it is the annual flow of resources that could be spent by the individual without disturbing his estimated stock of wealth. Both permanent income and permanent consumption differ from measured income and consumption by amounts Friedman calls **transitory income** and **transitory consumption**. Current measured consumption (C) is the sum of transitory consumption (CT) and permanent consumption (CP), and current measured income (Y) is the sum of transitory income (YT) and permanent income (YP). The relation can be summarised as

(Measured) $C = CP + CT$
(Measured) $Y = YP + YT$
$CP = kYP$ (k = factor of proportionality)

Friedman also assumes that there is no systematic relationship or correlation between permanent income and transitory income, between consumption and transitory consumption.

Monetarist consumption function

Friedman's version of the consumption function therefore differs significantly from the simple relationship between consumption and disposable income described in Chapter 39. In this version of the consumption function consumption depends upon total resources available. Resources are assumed to include income from non-human wealth (i.e. property) plus income from human wealth (future earnings). The relationship described above between permanent consumption (CP) and permanent income (YP) is the basis of the consumption function which can be summarised in the equation:

$CP = k (i, w, u) YP$

- The subjective rate of interest, i, at which the consumer can borrow or lend (not the market rate)
- The relative importance of property and non property income, symbolised by the ratio of non-human wealth to income (w)and
- The factors symbolised by the portmanteau variable u determining the consumer's tastes and preferences for consumption versus additions to wealth.

Consumption here refers to the **flow of services** which goods yield over their lifetime, not the initial expenditure, since utility is derived from their services, not from the expenditure. For example a refrigerator will yield a service to the purchaser over its lifetime, say 10 years; in this sense it is therefore 'consumed' over 10 years.

The essential point is that changes in income that are believed to be temporary do not cause the individual to revise his estimates of permanent income. Also unexpected or transitory changes in consumption spending cause no alteration or modification to permanent consumption expenditures.

The MPC out of transitory income is zero.

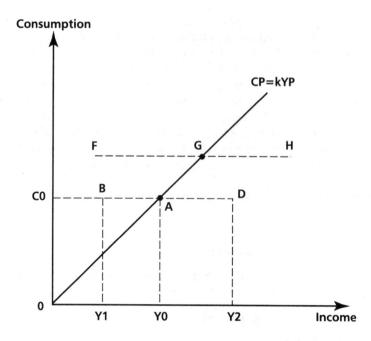

Figure 43.3

Transitory income

The implication is that sudden or 'windfall' changes as a result of government fiscal policy may not have the predicted effect upon levels of consumption. Thus the multiplier effect of a tax reduction will be much lower than originally thought (or zero). The concept of transitory income provides one explanation for the poor fit of post-war consumption data to estimated consumption. This is illustrated in Figure 43.3.

Permanent consumption function is plotted through the origin, i.e. CP. Suppose income falls from Y0 to Y1 and households perceive this fall to be transitory with no change in YP. Since there is no correlation between CT and YT and because permanent income has not changed, measured consumption will therefore not change. Thus for the fall in measured income from Y0 to Y 1 measured consumption remains constant at C0. The same is true of an increase Y0 to Y2, giving the same consumption C0. Observed points from data would trace the line BAD. A consumption function fitted to these observations would not be the 'true' consumption-function. An increase in income which persisted long enough to be considered as permanent would result in a move from A to G, but there would then be a new 'short run' consumption function FGH. Successive points such as A and G produce the long run consumption function. The discrepancy between long run and short run observations is therefore explained by the fact that cross section, or short run data are observing short run consumption functions as BAD and FGH, whilst long run data are observing points such as A and G on the long run function.

44

The natural rate of unemployment & the Phillips curve

1 The monetarist view

The concept of the **natural rate of unemployment** is closely associated with the monetarist school of thought, and has much in common with the classical view of the labour market. It differs from the Keynesian view in that it considers unemployment from the **supply** side of the economy rather than as resulting from deficient demand.

2 The labour market

The labour market is considered to be like any other market where the equilibrium price, which in this instance is the wage rate, is determined by demand and supply. The amount of labour demanded by employers will depend upon the level of real wages.

$$\text{Real wages} = \frac{\text{Money wages}}{\text{Prices}} = \left(\frac{W}{P}\right)$$

The higher the real wage the lower the demand for labour, and vice versa. The total supply of labour will increase as the real wage rises and fall as the real wage falls. Provided the market operates smoothly then an equilibrium real wage will be established where the demand and supply for labour is equal. Any unemployment remaining when the labour market is in equilibrium is referred to as the **natural rate of unemployment.**

In Figure 44.1 DD is the demand curve for labour which slopes downwards reflecting the declining marginal productivity of labour. SL is the supply curve which slopes upwards indicating that at higher real wages more labour will be supplied. The labour market is in equilibrium at E with real wage $(W/P)^2$ and QL^E labour. If the real wage was above the equilibrium wage, for example at $(W/P)^1$ the quantity of labour demanded would fall to QL^1 but QL^2 would be supplied, there is therefore an excess supply of labour at this higher real wage and QL^1–QL^2 will be unemployed at the prevailing real wage rate. Full employment could be restored by reducing real wages, for example by cutting money wages, this would increase the demand for labour and eliminate some of the excess supply returning the labour market to equilibrium at E. The implication is that unemployment such as QL^1–QL^2 is caused by real wages being too high and therefore the cure is to accept cuts in real wages. It follows therefore that any unemployment existing at the employment level QL^E is **voluntary** and occurs because workers are not willing to work for a low enough wage. The residual unemployment that exists at the equilibrium employment level QL^E is referred to as the **natural rate of unemployment** and is the unemployment which remains when the labour market is in equilibrium.

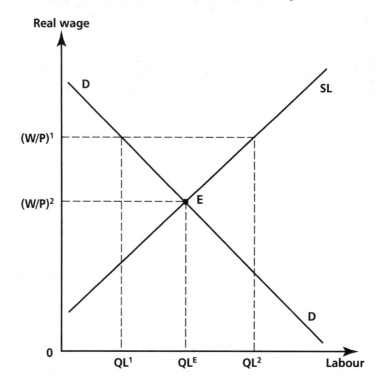

Figure 44.1

Advocates of the natural rate consider that full employment as defined in the post-war era (3% in the UK) was a political objective rather than an economic concept. The natural rate of unemployment is the level the labour market would tend towards if wages were flexible and in the absence of artificial 'frictions' or obstacles.

3 The natural rate of unemployment

The natural rate of unemployment cannot be defined as some percentage of the labour force as it is not a constant. It depends upon a number of factors which are liable to change:

- Technology and innovation.
- Comparative advantage and international trade.
- The degree of occupational and geographical mobility.
- Information regarding job opportunities.
- Restrictive practices imposed by trade unions.

4 Frictions in the labour market

If unemployment is persistently high and above what may be considered the natural rate, according to this theory it is because the labour market is being prevented from operating smoothly and efficiently by the existence of 'frictions' or obstacles to supply. There are two main sources of such frictions which are suggested:

- The high level of benefit paid to the unemployed which prevents them from taking low paid jobs. Professor Minford suggests a combination of reduced benefits and lower taxation as an incentive to the unemployed to take lower paid jobs. He suggests this disincentive effect is felt most strongly in the non-unionised sector of the workforce.
- The power of trade unions to resist reductions in real wages and impose minimum wage rates prevents people from obtaining jobs at lower pay which they might otherwise take.
- Both are areas which are highly controversial politically.

5 Breakdown of the Phillips curve

Monetarists suggest that any attempt by governments to keep the level of unemployment below the natural rate will result in ever accelerating inflation. This has important implications for the Phillips Curve which it will be recalled from Chapter 40 implied a stable 'trade-off' between prices and employment. Governments could select a level of inflation and engineer the appropriate level of unemployment. However the Phillips curve relationship started to break down towards the end of the 1960s and by the mid 1970s seemed to have broken down altogether, underpredicting the inflation rate by about 20%. Table 44.1 shows the change in retail prices and unemployment over the period 1962 to 1995.

By 1976 instead of 5% unemployment giving the predicted wage stability it was associated with inflation of almost 25%. It was possible that the relationship had broken down altogether. An alternative suggestion was that the curve had shifted to the right, to PC2 in Figure 44.2, so that 5½% unemployment was now associated with 25% inflation, and stable wages would now only be achieved at much higher levels of unemployment, such as y.

The implication is that policies designed to stabilise inflation by reducing expenditure would now result in much higher unemployment levels than previously. Various reasons have been put forward for this apparent breakdown in the Phillips curve relationship but the fact that governments resorted to incomes policies at that time would suggest that they considered that wages and therefore costs were the most important factor. The view that cost increases were responsible operates within the traditional framework of the Phillips curve and has two main elements:

The first is that prices rose due to cost-push inflation. This was associated with an increase in trade union militancy whereby trade unions were able to gain pay increases

TABLE 44.1

Year	Unemployment (UK Excl. N. Ireland)	Change in Retail Prices (%)
62	1.8	2.6
63	2.2	2.1
64	1.6	3.3
65	1.3	4.8
66	1.4	3.9
67	2.2	2.5
68	2.3	4.7
69	2.3	5.4 (Av 3.53)
70	2.5	6.4
71	3.3	9.4
72	3.6	7.1
73	2.6	9.2
74	2.5	16.1
75	3.9	24.2
76	5.2	16.5
77	5.7	15.8
78	5.6	8.3
79	5.3	13.4 (Av 12.4)
80	6.7	18.0
81	10.4	11.9
82	11.7	8.6
83	12.4	4.6
84	12.6	5.0
85	13.1	6.1
86	11.41	3.4
87	10.0	4.1
88	7.8	4.9
89	6.0	7.8 (Av 7.44)
90	5.6	9.5
91	7.9	5.9
92	9.6	3.7
93	10.2	1.6
94	9.3	2.5
95	8.2	3.4 (Av 4.43)

for their members which were greater than the rate of increase of productivity. Firms' costs would then rise and as a consequence prices would also rise. The increase in prices would reduce demand, resulting in increased unemployment and the simultaneous rise in prices and unemployment implies a worsening of the terms of the trade-off, and therefore the shift to the right of the curve to PC2 (Figure 44.2). If the government then attempts to increase aggregate demand in order to reduce unemployment there will be a further rise in inflation from a point such as x in Figure 44.2 to a point such as z with its high rate of inflation. This explanation sees the ability of trade unions to gain wage increases for their members above the rate of productivity increase even when unemployment is high, and the market power of firms to pass on these increases as being the main reason for the shift.

This explanation also incorporates the external cost increases, such as the oil price rises and the commodity price boom of 1970s, as being of major significance in the process.

It also includes the possibility of higher benefits making the unemployed more selective about which jobs they take and an unwillingness to accept the lowest paid jobs.

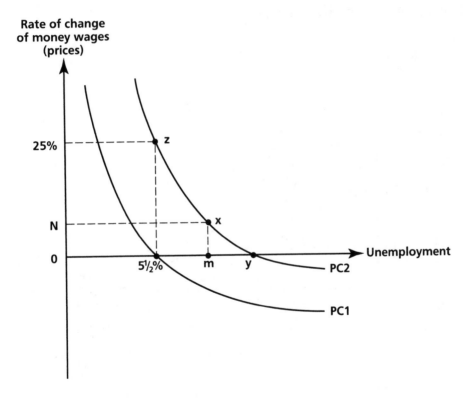

Figure 44.2

Footnote to Table opposite:
[1]. The basis of compilation of unemployment statistics was changed in March 1986 reducing the figure by approximately 50,000.

6 Expectations

Friedman criticised the original Phillips curve on the grounds that it assumed that the **anticipated** rate of inflation was given, and also that the effect of **expectations** on inflation had been omitted; in which case the stable Phillips curve relationship was only a very **short-run phenomenon**. In the longer run there was no stable relationship and **any attempts by government to reduce unemployment below the natural rate would result in accelerating inflation and the return of unemployment to the natural rate.** The orthodox Phillips curve assumes that workers suffer from a 'money illusion', i.e. the belief that an increase in money wages is the same as an increase in real wages. However if we assume that workers learn from their past experiences of rising prices they will begin to base their behaviour on what they **anticipate** the rate of inflation to be and begin to bargain in **real** terms, i.e. they see through the money illusion. Workers will only offer themselves for employment if they believe their **real wage** will rise. The greater the anticipated rate of inflation the greater the increase in **money** wages workers will demand in order to maintain the value of their real wage.

7 Long run Phillips curve

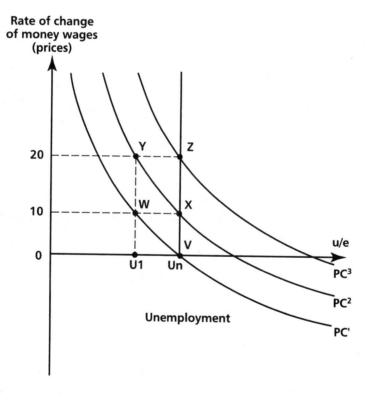

Figure 44.3

According to Friedman the long run Phillips curve is **vertical** at the **natural rate of unemployment**, i.e. there is no long run trade-off between inflation and unemployment.

For each level of anticipated inflation there will be a different Phillips curve. In Figure 44.3 the three curves indicated represent different expected inflation rates. Un represents the natural rate of unemployment. If the government believes this rate of unemployment to be too high and attempts to reduce it to Ul by expansionary fiscal and monetary policies the economy moves to point W with 10% inflation. This increase in the price level reduces real wages making labour more attractive so firms employ additional labour and expand output and then pass on the wage increase in the form of higher prices. The workers accepting employment did so because they believed their real wages had risen. At point W however they realise that they have over estimated the increase in their real wage. As workers experience the 10% inflation rate they begin to anticipate inflation of 10% and the Phillips curve shifts to the right to PC2 which is consistent with 10% inflation. As workers are interested only in the **real wage** and this has now fallen due to inflation to what it was originally, unemployment returns to the natural rate at point X as workers leave those jobs where the real wage has not risen and search for jobs with a higher real wage. At point X inflation is 10% and unemployment has returned to Un. At X if the government wishes to reduce unemployment again to Ul by expanding demand it will result in a 20% inflation rate at point Y and then shift to PC3 as workers learn to anticipate a 20% inflation rate. Again the same process is followed with a return to the natural rate at Z, the same level of unemployment but with a 20% rate of inflation. There is therefore no long term trade-off, workers are temporarily 'fooled' into thinking their real wages have risen by governments pursuing expansionary policies, but unemployment returns to the natural rate accompanied by accelerating inflation. The 'actual' Phillips curve is the vertical line V–Z. The implication being that in the long run that governments cannot permanently reduce unemployment below the natural rate by using fiscal and monetary policy, it can however have a choice of the rate of inflation, which will be stable at the natural rate. The incorporation of expectations into the analysis provides one explanation of the observed behaviour of the Phillips curve.

8 Adaptive expectations

The way in which people formed their expectations in the previous analysis suggests that people's adjustments to rising prices takes time. This implies that they form their expectations about future prices by projecting their past experience of **actual prices**, with most weight being given to the most recent past, i.e. it is a model which contains a series of lagged responses with declining weights given to the responses as they are more distant in time. It is therefore referred to as the **adaptive expectations** model. This approach does allow for the possibility of demand management policies if the size of the lags could be estimated and appropriate weights selected, although Friedman would suggest that this possibility was unlikely because of the extreme variability of the lagged responses.

9 Rational expectations

A third school of economic thought developed in the 1970s, the new classical (or neo classical) economists. The new classical economists take a more extreme view than the monetarists regarding the ability of governments to influence the level of economic activity through stabilisation policies. The central tenet of their argument is that real variables such as output and employment cannot be influenced by systematic demand management policies in either short-run or the long-run, and they include both **fiscal** and

monetary policy measures in this conclusion. Stabilisation measures of either a fiscal or monetary nature are incapable of influencing either employment or output. This conclusion is based upon the rejection by the new classical economists of the way in which price expectations are formed in both the Keynesian model and the adaptive expectations model of the monetarists. These formulations of price expectations are rejected because they both assume that expectations in the labour market of current and future price levels are based solely upon past experience of price levels. This assumption is criticised as being naïve in the extreme and they ask why should rational economic agents forming an expectation of future price levels rely only upon past levels of prices, and particularly if such behaviour resulted in them being systematically in error whenever there is a shift in aggregate demand – from the point of view that they will persistently fail to realise that such shifts are accompanied by increases in the price level? If people operate on this basis then they are going to be systematically in error which is clearly not rational. Putting it simply, people generally learn from their experience so there is no reason not to expect them to do so in the labour market.

The new classical economists propose **a rational expectations model** which suggests that when people form views about the future they will take into account **all available information** regarding the variable being predicted, and will use this information intelligently, i.e. they will understand the effect of this information on the variable they are attempting to predict. In particular they will understand the relationship between demand management policies and the price level and will adjust their behaviour accordingly. For example, if the government systematically reacts to an increase in unemployment by expansionary fiscal and monetary policies people will anticipate the increase in prices and the effect of budget deficit on future interest rates and taxes, and adjust their own consumption behaviour to accommodate them, thus making ineffective the policy measures. Although individuals are assumed to be rational however, the model does not preclude the possibility of them not having perfect information and where they do have imperfect information they may make mistakes in predicting the price level and such mistakes may cause short-run deviations in output and employment from the natural rate which would exist with full information. This would be the case for any unanticipated changes in the level of demand, the implication is however that the effects of any systematic policy measure by government will be anticipated and will be wholly ineffective as a consequence. The rational expectations model therefore casts severe doubts upon the effectiveness of demand management policies.

10 Supply-side economics

The **new classical** economists stress the importance of **supply factors** in determining the growth of output. As discussed above, these economists cast doubt upon the ability of changes in aggregate demand to significantly change output and employment. These economists, sometimes referred to as **supply side** economists, accept the classical view that output is determined by **real variables** and therefore **stress the importance of the growth of supply of the factors of production** and **technological change**. They also place more emphasis on the **role of interest rates in investment**. Supply side economists, like the classical economists, also stress the superiority of the **free-market system** and believe that **government intervention** in the economy should be reduced to a **minimum**. The main points in the **supply side** argument are as follows:

- The growth of output is mainly determined by the **growth of the supply of the factors of production and technological change.**
- The supply of labour is affected significantly by the **incentive to work**, in particular the post-tax real wage, hence they stress the importance of rates of personal taxation and benefits. In the long-run changes in population are also important.
- The **supply of capital** is determined by the incentives to save and invest, in particular the **post-tax returns** to **saving and investment.** In this instance they stress the importance of **rates of interest** and **personal and corporate taxation.**
- **Government intervention** in business activity through regulations and taxation has **reduced investment** and **labour productivity,** and therefore growth of output has been lower than it would otherwise have been.

11 Fiscal drag

Supply side economists are opposed to attempts to achieve higher growth rates through the expansion of aggregate demand in the Keynesian manner. They suggest that such policies may actually reduce growth because the inflation which it generates reduces the return from investment and the incentive to work. The incentive to work is reduced by the combined effects of inflation and progressive taxation. As nominal (money) incomes rise due to inflation the income recipient is moved into a higher tax bracket (or into taxation). At the same time as the tax liability is increased the real income may be unchanged, or even be lower, resulting in a reduction in real post-tax income. The consequence of this **fiscal drag** is a reduction in the incentive to work. In order to reduce this dis-incentive to work a combination of lower benefits and lower direct taxation is suggested (see Frictions in the labour market, paragraph 4).

Self assessment questions

1 Account for the apparent shift in the Phillips curve which took place in the 1970s.

2 Why is 'money illusion' necessary for the operation of the orthodox Phillips curve?

3 Outline the relationship between the natural rate of unemployment and inflation.

4 What is the rational expectations model and why does it cast doubt on the effectiveness of demand management policies?

5 What factors do the new classical economists stress as important in determining the rate of growth of output?

6 What is fiscal drag?

Section M

A macro economic view that incorporates both the real
and the monetary sectors of the economy

This section should enable students to:

- *Understand* how the IS-LM & aggregate demand/supply
  models are constructed
- *Explain* what is meant by supply-side policies
- *Contrast* the Keynesian and monetarist views using the
  IS-LM model
- *Evaluate* the effectiveness of monetary policy in different
  situations

Keywords to consider

real sector; monetary sector; interest elasticity; money supply line;transactions balances; crowding out effect; wealth;
wealth effect; fiscal policy; monetary policy; liquidity trap;
aggregate demand; aggregate supply; short-run aggregate
supply curve;

45

The IS-LM and aggregate demand/supply models

1 Real and money sectors

The methods used to analyse national income, in particular the use of 45° lines and the aggregate demand curve, are subject to the criticism that they ignore the monetary and assets sector of the economy. The IS-LM model attempts to overcome this by incorporating both the **real** and **monetary** sectors. (This Chapter may be considered as optional by professional and 'A' level students but the model is becoming more widely used as a tool of analysis and would be necessary reading for undergraduate students).

2 The IS curve

The IS function represents the **real** sector of the economy, i.e. goods and services, and the **IS curve** indicates the combinations of **national income and interest rates at which desired investment demand is equal to desired savings.**

The IS curve can be derived algebraically or geometrically. Figure 45.1 illustrates the geometrical derivation using four quadrants. The analysis assumes all prices are constant, with a closed economy.

Figure 45.1 consists of four quadrants which are read anti-clockwise, from 45.1(a) to 45.1(d).

Quadrant 45.1(a) relates the quantity of investment to the rate of interest and is therefore the demand curve for capital, or marginal efficiency of capital curve (see Chapter 42).

In Quadrant 45.1(b) the 45° line represents the equilibrium condition for the closed economy, derived in Chapter 39, of **saving = investment (S = I)**. The horizontal axis measures the amount of investment demand corresponding with that in 45.1(a) and the appropriate amount of savings for equilibrium can be identified by reading it off from the 45° line, as the 45° line will produce an equal reading on both axes.

Quadrant 45.1(c) incorporates the savings function derived in Chapter 39. Savings are assumed to be positively related to income so the savings function slopes upwards, the steepness of the slope being dependent upon the marginal propensity to save. The equilibrium quantity of savings is projected from 45.1(b) to 45.1(c) where the level of national income necessary to generate the required level of saving for equilibrium can be established.

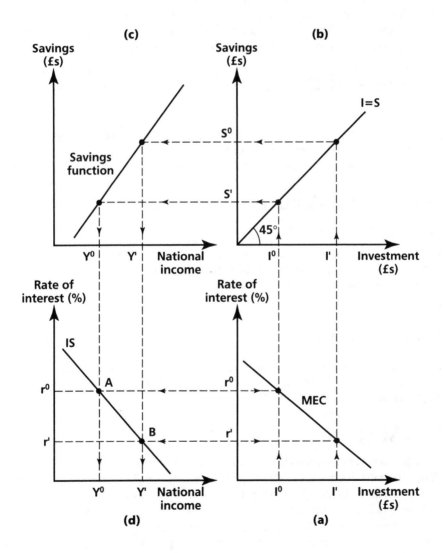

Figure 45.1

Quadrant 45.1(d) shows the derivation of the IS curve. The horizontal axis shows national income and corresponds with that in quadrant 45.1(c). Projecting down from 45.1(c) to 45.1(d) and where this coincides with the appropriate rate of interest from 45.1(a) produces one unique point on the IS curve where the combination of the rate of interest and national income will produce equality between desired saving and desired investment. By sequentially deriving numerous points such as A and B the IS curve can be derived.

3 Adjustments to the IS curve

Government expenditure can easily be incorporated into the model by horizontally adding it to the MEC curve in quadrant 45.I(a) and shifting the curve to the right, i.e. I + G.

In order to incorporate taxation a similar adjustment is made to the savings function in 45.1(c), where taxation shifts the curve to the left, i.e. S + T.

In neither case is the fundamental analysis altered, and the IS curve will be assumed here to incorporate both government expenditure and taxation.

4 The slope of the curve

The **steepness** of the **slope** of the IS curve is determined by:

- The **interest elasticity** (sensitivity) of **investment**. The more sensitive is investment to the rate of interest the **flatter** is the IS curve.
- The **marginal propensity to save (MPS)**. The higher the MPS the steeper the IS curve.

5 Shifts in the IS curve

Shifts in the IS curve result from:

- Changes in **government expenditure**. An **increase** in government expenditure will shift the IS curve to the **right**, and a **reduction** to the **left.**
- Changes in the **rate of income tax**. An **increase** in tax will shift the curve to the **left**, and a **reduction** to the **right**.

6 The real sector

The IS curve **represents the real**, or **goods and services sector of the economy**, and as it represents equilibrium then the aggregate demand for goods and services will be equal to aggregate supply at all points on the curve.

7 The LM curve

The LM curve represents the **monetary sector** of the economy and can also be derived by utilising a four quadrant diagram. The derivation of the LM curve is illustrated in Figure 45. 2

Quadrant 45.2(a) indicates the **demand for speculative money balances** relative to the rate of interest. The resulting relationship is downward sloping representing the inverse relationship between asset prices (bonds) and the rate of interest (see Chapter 42).

Quadrant 45.2(b) is referred to as the **money supply line.** Projecting upwards from 45.2(a) to 45.2(b) we obtain the size of speculative money balances, and if we assume that the only other significant money balances are **transactions balances**, then given a fixed

supply of money the difference must be the **transactions balances** which can be identified on the vertical axis of 45.2(b). The greater the speculative balances the smaller are the
transactions balances and vice versa and the sum of the two will be equal to the fixed
money supply as the line intersects both axes at the same total value. It therefore indicates
the distribution of the money supply between the two types of money balance, and given
the level of speculative balances in 45.2(a) it indicates the level of demand for real transactions balances which is consistent with monetary equilibrium.

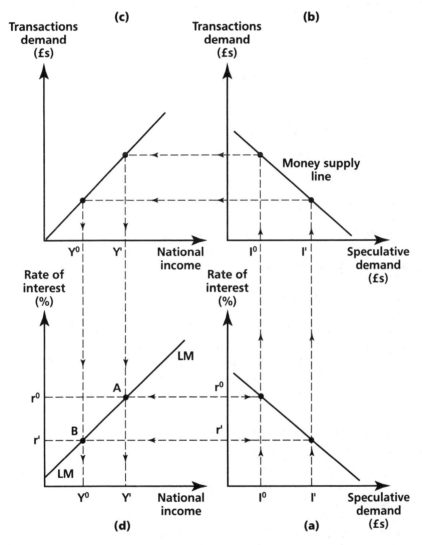

Figure 45.2

Projecting this level of transaction demand horizontally to quadrant 45.2(c) the level of
national income required to generate that level of transactions demand can be identified.
The transactions demand function slopes upwards with income as these balances will
need to be larger as income rises in order to maintain the larger number of transactions.

Quadrant 45.2(d) has the rate of interest on the vertical axis and national income on the horizontal axis. The level of national income from 45.2(c) is projected down and where this coincides with the appropriate rate of interest a single point on the LM curve is identified. Starting with different interest rates and following the process around the quadrants produce numerous such points which can be connected to give the LM curve.

8 The slope of the LM curve

The steepness of the **slope** of the LM curve depends upon:

- The **interest elasticity** (sensitivity) of the **speculative demand** for money. The greater the interest elasticity the flatter the curve.
- The **sensitivity** of the **transactions demand** for money to changes in national income. The more sensitive the demand the steeper the LM curve.

9 Shifts in the LM curve

Shifts in the LM curve occur as a result of changes in the **supply of money.** An increase in the money supply shifting the LM curve to the right, and reductions shifting it to the left.

10 The monetary sector

Each point on the LM curve indicates a rate of interest and level of national income for which the total demand for money is equal to the total supply of money and as such represents **equilibrium in the monetary sector.**

11 The IS-LM model

The complete IS-LM model combines both the IS and LM curves and the intersection of the two curves represents the combination of the rate of interest and national income which **simultaneously produces equilibrium in both the monetary and real sectors of the economy and therefore the economy as a whole.** This unique equilibrium point is illustrated in Figure 45.3, with interest rate r^0 and national income Y^0.

12 Fiscal and monetary policy

The IS-LM model can be used to illustrate the effects of either fiscal or monetary policy. An increase in government expenditure will have the effect of shifting the IS curve to the right. This is illustrated in Figure 45.4.

In Figure 45.4 the increase in government expenditure shifts the IS curve from IS to IS'. If we assume that the rate of interest **remains constant** then income shifts from Y^0 to Y'', this is the full multiplier effect discussed in Chapter 39. Incorporating the monetary effects of the increased expenditure indicates that the increase in income will be associated with an **increase in the interest rate**, and income will rise only to Y^1 with an increase in the interest rate to r^1. The rise in the interest rate 'crowds out' some private expenditure and the increase in income is less than it would have been if the rate of interest had remained constant. The 'crowding out effect' therefore **reduces the size of the multiplier.** The rise in interest rates results from:

- The need to offer higher rates of interest on government bonds in order to attract the public to buy them.
- The increased demand for money as income rises.

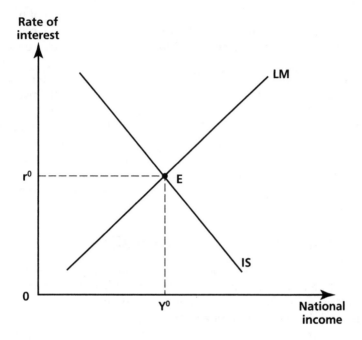

Figure 45.3

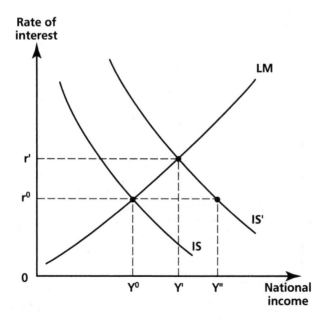

Figure 45.4

13 The wealth effect

It is also necessary to consider the affect of the change in private **wealth** which may occur as a result of a budget deficit financed by the issue of government bonds.

- A budget deficit will normally involve an increase in the holding of bonds by the public. This represents an increase in private **wealth**, which results in greater consumption out of any given income, in which case the **wealth effect** augments the multiplier effect.
- The increase in wealth however, will also have an affect on financial markets. It is argued by monetarists that where the government's deficit is financed by the issue of bonds there may be a further level of crowding out. This occurs as a result of the fall in bond prices which accompanies the rise in interest rates mentioned above. The fall in bond prices reduces the wealth of bond holders who then increase the level of their savings in order to regain their previous levels of wealth, this **wealth effect** further reduces private expenditures and dampens the multiplier effect.
- Whether the net result of these two influences is expansionary or contractionary will depend upon their relative strengths.

14 Monetary policy v fiscal policy

The debate over the advocacy of monetary policy (monetarists) relative to fiscal policy (generally Keynesians) can be analysed by utilising IS-LM curve analysis and making different assumptions about the relative slopes of the curves.

Monetarists assume that the demand for money has zero interest elasticity, i.e. is inelastic, the LM curve is therefore very steep, or vertical. Investment is assumed to be interest elastic and the IS curve therefore has a shallower slope.

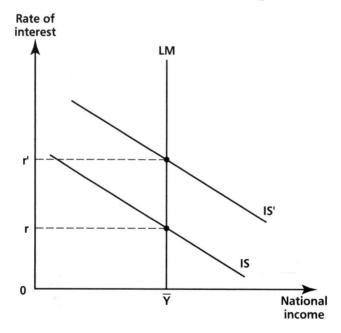

Figure 45.5

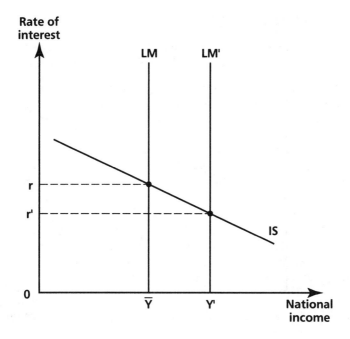

Figure 45.6

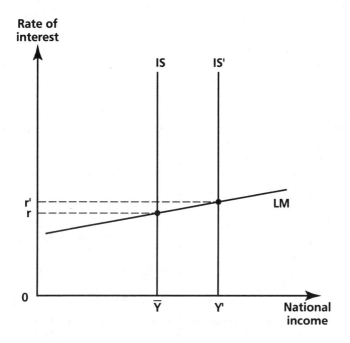

Figure 45.7

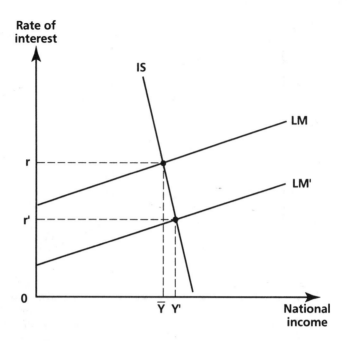

Figure 45.8

In Figure 45.5 an increase in government spending shifts the IS curve to IS' but due to the inelastic money demand income remains unchanged at Y and the impact falls upon the rate of interest which rises to r'. **fiscal policy** is **therefore ineffective**. Alternatively **increasing the money supply** as illustrated in Diagram 45.6 shifts the LM curve to the right and has a **powerful effect upon income**.

Keynesians assume that the demand for money is interest elastic (see Chapter 42) and the LM curve therefore has a shallower slope. Interest rates are assumed to have little effect upon investment demand which implies that the IS curve is steeper. The relative slopes are illustrated in Figure 45.7 and 45.8.

In Figure 45.7 an increase in government expenditure shifts the IS curve to IS' increasing income from $\bar{Y}$ to Y', **fiscal policy therefore has a powerful effect upon income**. Figure 45.8 illustrates an increase in the money supply which shifts the LM curve from LM to LM' leaving income only slightly changed at Y', the impact falling upon interest rates. **Monetary policy is therefore an ineffective policy instrument** for generating changes in income.

In the extreme case, which Keynes referred to as the liquidity trap, the demand for money becomes infinitely elastic and all increases in the money supply are held in the form of speculative money balances. This is represented by the horizontal portion of the LM curve. A–B, in Figure 45.9. In the liquidity trap increases in the money supply (LM[1], LM[2]) would be totally ineffective, and changes in income could only be brought about through the use of fiscal policy.

The interest elasticity of the demand for money is an empirical matter and there appears to be little evidence to support the extreme cases. In the 'normal' case illustrated in Diagram 45.3 both fiscal and monetary policy have a role to play.

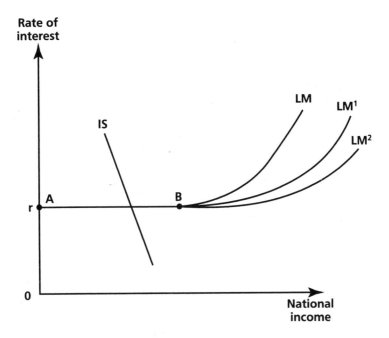

Figure 45.9

15 The aggregate demand curve

A technique which has become increasingly used as a method of macro-economic analysis is the **aggregate demand and supply model.** It is important to note here that the **aggregate demand curve** (AD curve) used in this method of analysis is not the same thing as the aggregate monetary demand (AMD) curve described in Chapter 39. The AD curve can be derived graphically from the IS-LM model, with the price level as an endogenous variable. Figure 45.10 illustrates the IS-LM model in the upper section A and in the lower section, B; the AD curve which is derived from it. The initial equilibrium level of national income is Y with interest rate r where the IS curve and LM curves intersect at E. For this analysis the money stock is held constant and the price level is allowed to vary. The LM curve is associated with the price level P, this is identified with point Z on the lower section, B, at the locus of price level P and income Y. The price level is now allowed to rise to P while the money stock is held constant, which reduces the real stock of money and thereby shifts the LM curve upwards to the left to LM'. The new equilibrium is at E' with income Y'. This can be plotted in section B to produce point W. A further rise in the price level to P^2 shifts the LM curve further to the left to LM^2, and following the same procedure point X can be derived. By following the same process numerous points such as XWZ can be identified, and by joining them together the AD curve is derived. The AD curve like the demand curve described earlier in market analysis slopes downward to the right and relates price to quantity (real national income or output). Because the AD curve is derived from the intersection of the IS-LM curves however, all the points plotted along it represent simultaneous equilibrium in both the goods and assets market, given that autonomous expenditure and the nominal money supply are held constant. Changes in either autonomous expenditure (C, I, G or X) or in the nominal money supply, will shift the AD curve; increases shifting it to the right and vice versa.

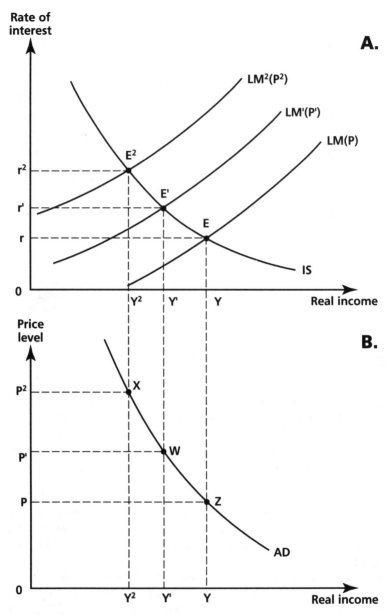

Figure 45.10

16 The aggregate supply curve

The aggregate supply curve (AS) is simply the relationship which exists between the price level and the amount produced in the economy. The concept is the same as that illustrated in the lower section of Figure 40.1 which related the level of output to the price level. The AS curve is assumed to slope upwards to the right as firms' marginal costs rise as output is increased.

17 Equilibrium

Figure 45.11 illustrates the combined AD and AS curves with initial equilibrium at E, with price level P and real income (output) Y. The government generates a shift in the AD curve to AD^1 by policy measures, operating on the level of demand, either a reduction in taxation, increase in government expenditure, adjusting the exchange rate, or by an increase in the nominal money stock. The shift to AD^1 raises income to Y^1 and the price level to P^1. It should be noted that the full Keynesian multiplier would have raised income to Y^2 (E–A), however, the new equilibrium is at E^1, the size of the multiplier being reduced by the rise in the price level. This analysis assumes that firms respond to the shift in the AD curve by raising real output because along the AS curve the money wage remains constant and if the price level increases real wages fall which results in an increase in real output and employment.

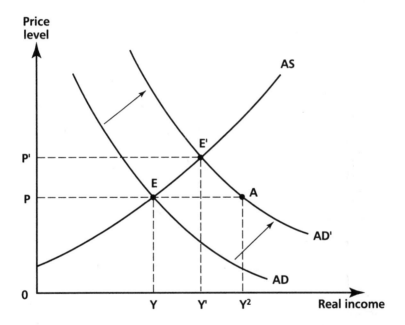

Figure 45.11

18 Short run and long run aggregate supply

With this method of analysis it is essential to consider more closely the characteristics of the AS curve. As a first step it is useful to distinguish between the **short run aggregate supply curve (SRAS)** and the **long run aggregate supply curve (LRAS)**.

Previously it was stated that the money wage remained constant along any particular AS curve and as a consequence any rise in the price level reduced real wages thus increasing real output along the curve. If however workers refuse to accept a reduction in real wages at this level of income and instead demand an increase in the money wage raising money wages in response to the rise in the price level, income and output cannot remain at Y^1 (Figure 45.11). In Figure 45.12 initial equilibrium is at point E^1 with price level P and output Y. Expansionary government policy then shifts the AD curve upwards to AD^1 with a new equilibrium at E^2 with output Y^1 and price level P^1. The rise in the price level reduces the real wage but the money wage is unchanged. With lower real wages firms increase employment and output. If however workers over time manage to raise their money wages, and hence their real wage also, the AS curve, which it will be recalled is associated with a constant money wage; shifts upwards to AS^1. As a consequence output and employment fall back to Y with equilibrium at E^3 and price level p^2, The money wage and price level have both risen in the same proportion which means that the real wage is back to its original level. Because firms now face the original real wage real output falls back to its original level but at a higher price level. Output is higher in nominal (value) terms but there is **no long run effect on real output, the only effect has been on the price level**. the long run as curve is therefore vertical, as indicated by the LRAS curve in Figure 45.12.

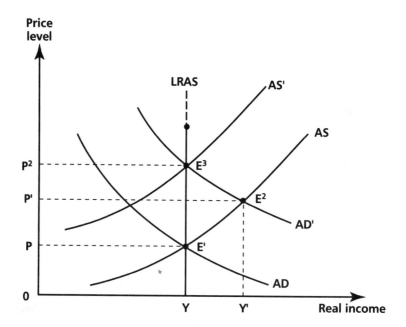

Figure 45.12

19 Adjustment lags

The time period over which the increase in real output can continue depends upon how quickly the money wage adjusts to the increase in prices. The length of this adjustment lag is closely associated with the role of expectations. In the rational expectations model expectations adjust instantaneously hence in the neo-classical model there is no distinction between the SRAS curve and the LRAS curve with no increase in output only the price level.

20 The wage-price spiral

The wage-price spiral discussed in Chapter 29 can also be illustrated by the use of AD and AS curves. The government may attempt to counteract the tendency for output and employment to return to its original level by giving a further boost to aggregate demand. In Figure 45.13 original equilibrium is at E with price level P and output Y, as in the analysis above AD is shifted to AD^1 raising output to Y^1 and the price level to P^1. Eventually however the money wage adjusts and the economy moves back as the AS curve shifts to AS$'$ on to the LRAS curve. As unemployment rises the government responds by boosting aggregate demand again and there is a move to a new equilibrium at E^3, but the economy again moves back to the LRAS curve with real output at Y and price level P^3. The succession of points such as E, E^1, E^2, E^3, E^4, represent the wage price spiral. At E^4 real output is the same as at E but with the price level at P^4. Output has risen only in nominal terms, unemployment is the same, but the price level (inflation) is much higher.

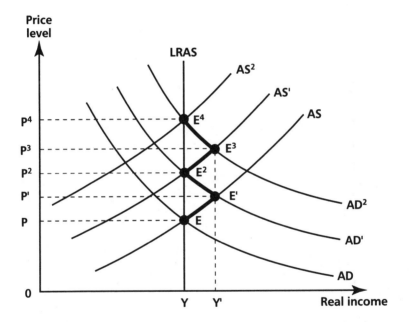

Figure 45.13

21 The Keynesian view

The Keynesian version of the AS curve is illustrated in Figure 45.14. In this version the AS curve is referred to as an L shape. Along the horizontal portion of the curve AD can be increased expanding output and employment with no conflict with the price level. When the full employment level of output is reached however any further increase in AD will lead to rising prices.

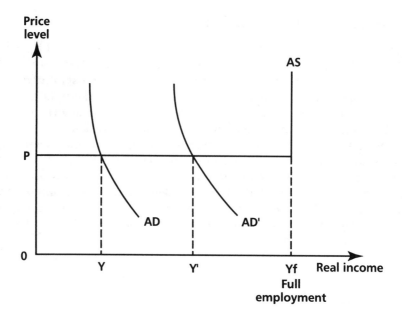

Figure 45.14

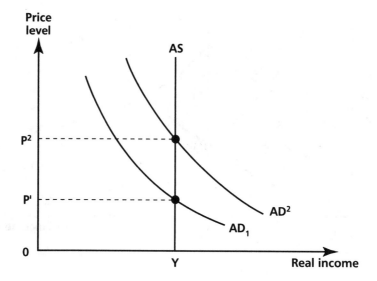

Figure 45.15

22 The neo-classical view

The extreme monetarist or neo-classical version is the vertical AS curve illustrated in Figure 45.15. In this version there is no scope for changes in AD to raise output, even in the short-run, the only affect of such policies will be to raise the price level, i.e. inflation.

23 Limitations

The implications of these models is crucially important as they indicate the limits to which governments are able to influence the economy through their policy measures. The superiority of any particular theory is however ultimately an empirical matter.

Self assessment questions

1 What does the IS curve represent?

2 What does the LM curve represent?

3 What is represented by the intersection of the IS and LM curves?

4 Explain the difference between the monetarist and Keynesian viewpoint by utilising IS-LM curves.

5 Under what circumstances would monetary policy be totally ineffective?

6 Explain the relationship between changes in money wage and shifts in the AS curve.

7 Distinguish between the Keynesian and neo-classical versions of the AS curve.

8 What is meant by supply side policies and why have they received more emphasis in recent years?

Section N

Growth and the economy

Containing the following chapter:

Chapter 46 – Economic growth and the UK economy.

The ways in which the UK economy has developed during the last decade and the problems encountered

This section should enable students to:

- *Understand* how economic growth is measured
- *Explain* the sources of growth
- *Contrast* the importance of the various factors that contribute to growth in the UK
- *Evaluate* the performance of the UK economy over the last decade

Keywords to consider:

capital; labour; investment; capital formation; net investment; incremental capital-output ratio; production function; technological change; research & development; product innovation; product diffusion; labour quality; working practices; public sector investment; manufacturing decline; competitiveness;

46

Economic growth and the UK economy

1 A definition

Economic growth refers to the increase in the economy's productive capacity. It is usual to express this in terms of the growth of gross domestic product (GDP).

Care must be taken in comparing GDP figures over time and making assumptions regarding economic growth from them for three reasons:

- Comparisons must take account of inflation and therefore can only be made in 'deflated' data, i.e. data at constant prices.
- An increase in GDP from a position of unemployed resources and deficient demand to one of full employment does not constitute economic growth as there has been no growth in productive potential. When comparisons between different time periods are made it is important therefore that the level of resource utilisation is similar.
- Even when GDP is growing, living standards may decline if the population growth is more rapid (see Chapter 23). Per capita GDP is the relevant measure and is calculated as:

$$\text{Per Capita GDP} = \frac{\text{GDP}}{\text{Population}}$$

2 The benefits of growth

Economic growth is generally considered to be desirable by governments because it enables them to achieve other policy goals which are considered desirable. Increased GDP implies higher incomes and therefore a higher standard of living in terms of material goods. Higher incomes also imply higher tax revenues for the government which should facilitate an improved level of provision of public services such as education, health, and other social services. The greater the rate of economic growth the more rapid the increase in living standards, as conventionally defined, will be.

3 British growth

The main cause of concern for the British economy has not been just the slow rate of growth which has been apparent but the fact that the growth rate has been slow relative to other industrial countries. Figure 46.1 indicates the UK's growth rate from 1967 to 1994 relative to other industrialised countries.

Britain's relatively poor performance is even more pronounced when the average figures over the period are considered. Japan averaged a growth in real per capita GDP of 4.3% per annum between 1967 and 1994, Germany 2.5% and the USA 2.4%. The UK over the same period averaged a growth in real per capita GDP of only 1.9%.

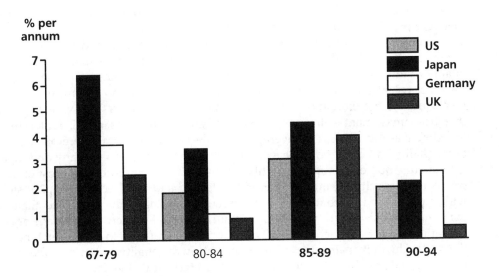

Figure 46.1

4 Sources of growth

In order to establish why growth rates differ it is necessary to identify the sources of economic growth. Economic growth is generated by an increase in both the **quality** and **quantity** of the nation's productive resources, in particular labour and capital.

- **Labour**
  - The **quantity** or **supply** of labour depends upon trends in the growth of working population, hours worked, the length of holidays and net migration.
  - The **quality** of labour is determined by the resources and facilities available for

training and education. Not only is the level of provision important but also the extent to which the skills being taught are appropriate to the needs of the economy as technological change takes place. The extent to which the labour force is willing to adapt to changes in technology and adopt new working practices is also an important factor. Investment in **human capital** has been identified as one of the major factors in generating economic growth.

- **Capital**
  - The size of the nation's stock of capital is an important factor in determining labour productivity. The more capital which is available per worker the greater will be labour productivity, referred to as the **capital:labour ratio**. The larger the proportion of GNP which a nation devotes to **investment** the greater will be the stock of capital. This **gross capital formation** is a major determinant of economic growth, however the precise stock of capital at any point in time is difficult to calculate due to the unreliability of the estimates of depreciation. Increasing the amount of capital per unit of labour is referred to as **capital deepening** whilst increasing the capital stock to keep abreast of increases in the size of the working population is referred to as **capital widening**. **Gross investment** refers to **new investment plus replacement investment** whilst **net investment** refers to **new investment** only. It is therefore possible to have gross investment without net investment.
  - The **quality** of the capital stock is of major importance, and in particular the extent to which it embodies the most recent technology, an element which is difficult to quantify but is of major importance in generating growth. The assumption is that the most recent machines incorporate the recent scientific and technical developments and are therefore more productive than older machines. This view suggests that gross investment is the most important figure even if most of it is replacement investment as this reduces the average age of the capital stock and therefore increases its quality and efficiency. The example of countries such as Germany and Japan is frequently quoted in support of this argument. These countries lost most of their productive capacity during the Second World War and replaced their capital stock with new equipment containing more recent technology which enabled them to make more rapid growth than countries such as Britain where the average age of the capital stock was much greater. This is sometimes referred to as the 'catching up' theory. Productivity gains due to improvements in the quality, rather than the quantity, of capital are said to result from **embodied technical change**.
  - The **incremental capital – output ratio (ICOR)** refers to the increase in output relative to the increase in capital (net investment) over a period. Figure 46.2 shows that the ICOR for the UK between 1964 and 1980 was considerably lower than in the other countries shown which suggests that regardless of the absolute proportion of GDP devoted to investment in the UK which was not significantly lower than the main trade competitors (see Figure 46.3), the quality of the investment decisions have not been particularly good. One reason suggested for this is that the tax system, through high rates of corporate taxation and investment allowance reduced the post tax rewards from investment whilst at the same time subsidising inefficient investment. Changes in the tax system since 1984 have been designed to introduce a more competitive climate for investment decisions by removing allowances and reducing the rate of corporation tax (see Chapter 37).

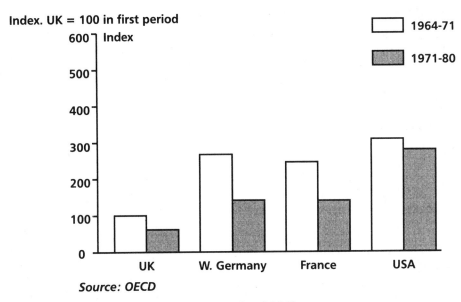

Index. UK = 100 in first period

Source: OECD

Figure 46.2 Incremental capital – output ratios (ICOR)

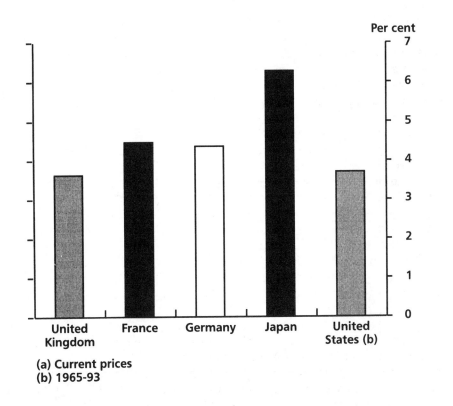

(a) Current prices
(b) 1965-93

Figure 46.3 Gross investment as a percentage of GDP

5 Production function

The importance for growth of not only increasing the amount of capital per worker (**capital deepening**) but also of incorporating the most recent technology (embodied technical change) can be illustrated by means of a simple **production function**. In this production function output (Q) is considered to be a function of capital (K), labour (L) and technological change (T)

i.e. $Q = T(t) f (K, L)$

Technological change is taken to depend only on time, and is neutral in that it affects the marginal productivity of both factors of production (K and L) equally. In Figure 46.4 the production function is plotted against output per worker, i.e. q= %. and the capital/labour ratio, i.e. $K = $ %. On production function PFN⁰ technology is assumed to remain unchanged and the declining slope of the production function reflects the assumption of diminishing returns to increases in capital per worker. When the capital/labour ratio is increased from k^0 to k^1 output per worker increases from q^0 to q^1. However, when there is embodied technical change the production function shifts upwards to PFN¹, the new capital incorporating improved technology, as a consequence the same increase in the amount of capital per worker, k^0 to k^1 increases output per worker from q^0 to q^{11}, which is substantially greater. This analysis emphasises that the growth of output per worker depends upon two factors.

- Capital deepening as the capital/labour ratio increases.
- Embodied technical change capital – capital investment should incorporate the most recent technological advances.

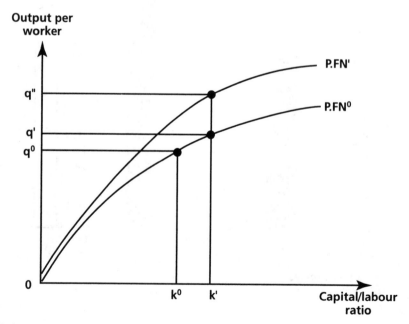

Figure 46.4

6 Technology; a source of economic growth

Denison[1] analysed the sources of economic growth in the United States over the period 1929–1969. The results of his analysis are shown in Table 46.1.

TABLE 46.1		
Total factor input		1.40
LABOUR	1.05	
CAPITAL	0.35	
Output per unit of input		1.82
Growth in national income		3.22

[1] Denison, E., 'Accounting for United States Economic Growth: 1929–69' (Brookings Institutions)

As shown in the table, national income grew at an **annual** rate of 3.22 per cent. Of this 3.22 per cent 1.40 per cent was attributable to the **growth of total factor inputs**, labour and capital and 1.82 per cent to the **growth of output per unit of factor input**. Of the growth due to increases in the **quantity** of factor inputs 1.05 per cent is attributed to the **growth of labour** input and 0.35 per cent to the **growth in capital**. Of the 1.05 per cent attributable to growth in labour input 0.49 per cent resulted from improvements in the educational attainments of the labour force. Growth in output per unit of input accounts for 1.82 per cent of growth, which is 57 per cent of total growth. Of this 1.82 per cent Denison attributes to advances in knowledge, i.e. **technological change. Economies of scale** resulting from increases in the scale of production accounted for 0.43 per cent of annual economic growth. These results illustrate the importance for economic growth of improvements in both the **quality** and **quantity** of factor inputs.

Changes in technology are the result of **research and development** and because technological change is so important for economic growth governments are generally keen to encourage high levels of research and development. They can do this either by undertaking research and development itself and making the results available to firms, or they may encourage firms to undertake it themselves by giving grants or other financial aid.

Technical change may apply to production techniques or to products. In both cases research and development are important, but in the case of new producers **market research** is also important. In the case of production techniques there are two important stages: **process innovation** which refers to the application by a firm of a new production technique, and **process diffusion** which is the application of the same technique by other firms. Product development also consists of two stages: product innovation which is the introduction of a new product by a firm, and product diffusion which is the introduction of similar new products by other firms. One criticism of UK firms, particularly in the field of micro electronics has been that they are technically very competent and achieve high levels of **invention** but fail to **innovate** new processes and products.

Firms introduce new technology into their production processes with the intention of reducing their costs. If reduction in costs is used merely in order to increase profitability by utilising more capital intensive production then the consequence will be a reduction in the amount of labour employed. However, if the firm uses its cost advantage to gain a larger market share and as a consequence greatly increases its output it may be able to maintain an unchanged labour force. The employment effects of new technology are one of the major issues facing society today.

The most significant technological change possibly in this century has been the advance in electronic **micro-technology** and in particular the advances in **micro computers**. The diffusion of this new technology into all areas of manufacturing and administration has been both extensive and rapid. It is now possible for large areas of production to be controlled by computers with them actually controlling the automatic tooling which performs the task, for example the use of robotics in motor car manufacture, referred to as computer aided manufacture (CAM). The use of computers has also spread significantly into the area of design with use of computer aided design (CAD). One area very significantly influenced by the application of micro computer technology is that of business administration. Many office functions are now performed by micro computers, for instance the storage and retrieval of information once performed by numerous clerks with filing cabinets can now be performed on a vast scale by a single operator with a micro computer. The routine typing of business letters can be performed by word processors as can the maintenance of routine accounting systems. The new technology has also influenced the way in which many businesses organise their management systems, for instance, in most firms the function of stock control, purchasing, production planning and distribution were treated as separate functions because of the sheer volume of information, which could only be handled by dividing it between specialised functions. Micro computers however provide the capacity to handle these vast amounts of data, and by utilising a common data base these functions are integrated into a single system, referred to as materials requirements planning (MRP). Newspaper publishing provides an example of the extent to which the nature of production in an industry can be changed by the advances in technology. Newspaper copy was originally written by the journalist who passed the copy to typesetters who set the typeface, the page layout also required careful design and finally the printing process employed large numbers of printers. Technology now enables the page to be printed directly from the journalist's copy, typed on a visual display unit, which can also be used to design the page layout. The printing machines are fully automatic and controlled by computer. As a consequence Express Newspapers were able to dispense with 5000 printing workers and move to a new plant employing only 500 journalists and electricians in the early 1980s.

Such changes clearly have profound employment implications. A permanently higher level of unemployment may be an inevitable consequence as technology takes over from labour. Many skills have become obsolete, increasing long term unemployment and creating the need for large scale retraining programmes. Semi-skilled employment has become scarcer as such tasks are generally easier to automate. Attitudes towards work may have to change, in particular towards the length of the working week, earlier retirement, the possibility of work sharing, and more part-time employment.

Some observers take a more optimistic view of employment prospects and suggest that although jobs will continue to be lost as a consequence of the new technology, many more will be created as new industries develop to take advantage of the technology, and with more leisure time there will be a growth in the leisure and service industries.

In future years it is unlikely that the majority of people will be able to pursue a career for life and attitudes towards career change may have to change. There is also the problem of income distribution, as the numbers displaced from work grow the income disparity between the employed and unemployed will grow unless the tax system is used for redistribution of income, in the form of unemployment benefit, for pensions, and to pay for education and retraining. Without income redistribution the ultimate question becomes – when all the goods are produced by robots, who will be able to buy them?

7 Other sources of economic growth

In the long run therefore it is the **supply of the factors of production** which determine economic growth. However, for the reasons stated above, the prospect of economic growth is attractive to governments and various measures have been adopted in the UK in the hope of achieving higher rates of growth. In planned economies it is less difficult to achieve a diversion of resources away from current consumption to investment and capital accumulation for future growth, but in a mixed economy with an electorate to appeal to resort has to be made to less direct means of stimulating growth. Measures which governments can utilise include:

- **Improvements in labour quality** by increasing the provision of education, and training of an appropriate type, in particular youth training.
- **Use of the tax system** in order to encourage investment, including allowances against tax for investment and depreciation. Differential rates of corporation tax on retained profits and dividends have also been used in the hope that lower rates on retentions would encourage a higher level of retentions and thereby increase investment (the extent to which such a policy is successful is however controversial).
- Keeping **interest rates low** and allowing tax relief on interest in order to reduce the cost of borrowing and improve the viability of investment projects.
- The encouragement of **research and development** by providing facilities and grants, and dispensing information from government sponsored research.
- Encouraging the acceptance of **new working practices** and **new technology** into industry by discussion with employer groups, trade unions and government sponsored bodies.
- The use of **public sector investment** as a source of growth. In particular capital spending on projects such as railway electrification and motorway construction.
- Maintaining a high level of domestic demand by the use of appropriate fiscal and monetary policy, although this may have costs in terms of inflation and the balance of payments which may in themselves damage long run growth prospects.

8 Government intervention

Governments have not however been particularly successful at improving growth rates. This is due largely to the problem of quantifying the relationship between the variables which are thought to influence growth and the amount of growth which changes in these variables actually generates. A further problem is that in a mixed economy too much intervention by government in order to achieve the growth objective may appear as a move towards central planning, hence the preference for indirect incentives. Britain's only attempt at planning for growth, in the form of the National Plan in 1965, attempted to stimulate growth by announcing a target growth rate of 4% per annum for 1964–1970, but was abandoned during its first year when an actual growth rate of only 2.4% was achieved. Failure was largely due to the problem discussed in Chapter 40 of achieving growth, balance of payments equilibrium, and price stability, simultaneously. During the period up to the early 1970s however, the main way in which governments in the UK attempted to achieve higher rates of growth was by maintaining a higher level of aggregate demand by pursuing expansionary fiscal policies in the Keynesian tradition of demand management.

The high rates of inflation experienced after the mid 1970s caused doubts to arise regarding the ability of governments to simultaneously control the level of inflation and maintain high levels of employment. The advent of the 'neo-classical' school of thought saw a fundamental questioning of the ability of governments to influence the growth of output and employment through demand management policies and placed more emphasis on the supply of the factors of production, both their quality and quantity, and more emphasis on the role of the free market.

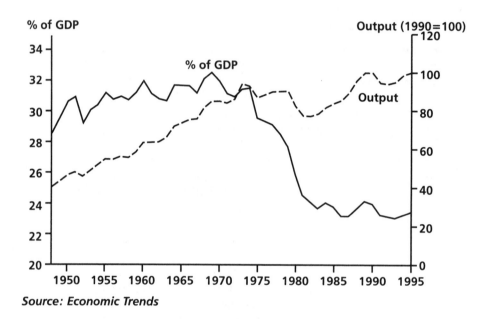

Source: Economic Trends

Figure 46.5

9 The decline in manufacturing

The report of the **House of Lords Select Committee on Overseas Trade** (HL 238,1985) associated Britain's low rate of growth with the **decline in the manufacturing sector.** Manufacturing output declined from 28 per cent of GDP in 1972 to 21 per cent in 1983, with the downward trend continuing. The trend of manufacturing output relative to GDP between 1950 and 1995 can be clearly seen in Figure 46.5. The decline in manufacturing output resulted in a reduction in manufactured exports which taken together with increased import penetration resulted in a deficit in the balance of trade in manufactures. This deficit on trade has however been compensated for in the balance of payments current account by the surplus on oil, with the advent of North Sea oil. The problem for the economy however will emerge when the North Sea oil reserves become depleted in the next decade and can no longer finance the trade deficit. The effect oil has had upon the balance of payments in the period 1985–95 can be seen from Figure 46.6(a) and (b): Figure 46.6(a) includes the export and import of oil whereas (b) shows only the situation with respect to oil.

The decline in the manufacturing sector of the UK economy has been accompanied by the growth of the service sector, over 60 per cent of GDP being derived from the service sector. The House of Lords report however suggested that sustained economic growth could not be based solely upon the service sector because it is itself totally dependent upon the growth of the manufacturing sector to use those services which it provides. Also, services are no substitute for manufacturers in overseas trade as only 20 per cent are tradable overseas. Sustainable growth therefore is only possible with a favourable trade balance in manufactures. Britain's balance of trade in manufactured goods over the period 1979–1995 is illustrated in Figure 46.7.

Balance on trade in goods 1985-95

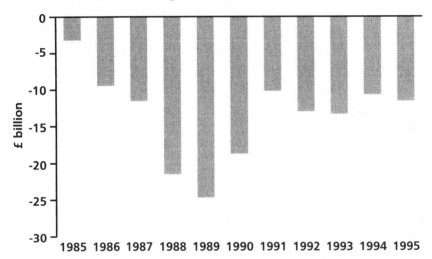

Figure 46.6(a)

The House of Lords Report identified the following reasons for the decline in manufacturing:

- The problem of being the **first industrial nation** developed on the basis of large overseas markets which have been eroded as other countries industrialised.
- **Lower rates of gross investment** than in competing countries. The reasons suggested for this included – lack of confidence placed by firms in the future, low profitability, high capital taxation, and high interest rates. Also other European countries and Japan needed to invest more rapidly than Britain after the Second World War in order to replace the capital assets which had been destroyed. Not only has investment been lower in the UK than in comparable countries but that investment has also been less effective in that the extra output from a given unit of additional capital has been lower, i.e. the incremental capital to output ratio (ICOR – see Figure 46.5). Reasons suggested

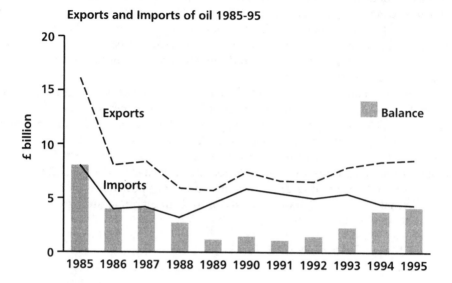

Figure 46.6(b)

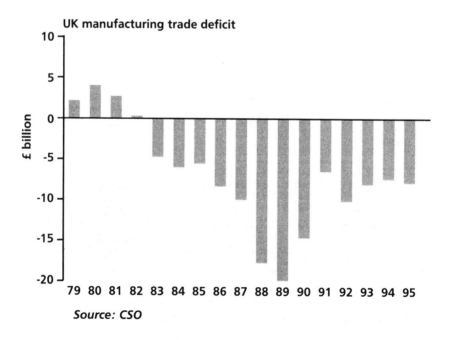

Figure 46.7

for this included – insufficient emphasis on new products embodying new design and technology, too much investment in property and industries with lower productivity than manufacturing.

- **Cultural factors** were also identified as a reason for poor performance. Such factors, sometimes referred to as **X-inefficiency** lead to sub-optimal investment decisions and include; poor management, inadequate skills, and widespread resistance to change. Cultural factors extended to include a tendency to see manufacturing in an unfavourable light, to the extent that qualified people sought employment in other areas than manufacturing, associating success and achievement with other areas of employment.

- The **lack of investment** in earlier years has resulted in a situation where the **average age of Britain's capital stock is older than in most of our competitors'** and therefore incorporates less new technology. In order to compete prices have to be reduced which squeezes profits and in turn leads to even less investment. A vicious circle of uncompetitiveness and low growth.

- A number of **non-price factors** were also identified which affected the competitiveness of UK products in overseas markets. Some of these factors related to the product, such as; quality, reliability, suitability; and other factors were related to their marketing, such as; delivery times, after-sales service, sales representation, arrangements for marketing and quotations in inconvenient formats, e.g. Ex Works.

- **Poor price competitiveness** was identified as a major factor in Britain's poor overseas trade performance. Price competitiveness is influenced largely by factors such as poor labour productivity, wage rates, and the sterling exchange rate. UK competitiveness in manufacturing and overall is illustrated in Figure 46.8.

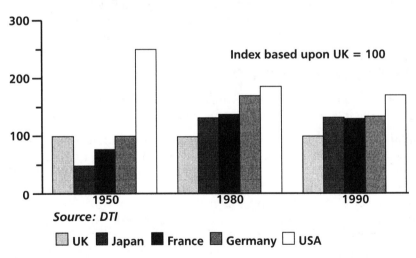

Figure 46.8

- The **high level of the sterling exchange rate**, particularly in the period after 1978 was seen as being a major factor in reducing UK price competitiveness. The rise in the exchange rate was attributed to two main factors, **North Sea oil** and **government policy**. The demand for North Sea oil kept the exchange rate at a higher level than would be justified by trade performance alone, hence it did not reflect underlying trends in the manufacturing sector. The government's medium term financial strategy kept **interest rates higher** than they would otherwise have been, resulting in capital inflows which put further upward pressure on the exchange rate. Government policy was also responsible for reducing domestic demand which had further exacerbated the decline in the manufacturing sector.

The report concluded that if Britain was to achieve success in manufactured trade, it would need a new sense of national purpose and improvements in all the areas of weakness outlined above. In particular the report called for a new national attitude towards manufacturing and trade, greater price and non price competitiveness, government macro-economic policies which favour manufacturing industry and are applied consistently, more government support for innovation and exports, more appropriate education and training, greater stability in the exchange rate, lower interest rates, a tax regime which favours manufacturing industry, improvements in both the quality and quantity of investment; and a greater inclination at all levels of society to purchase British manufactures. The process of 'de-industrialisation' is a major problem for the UK economy.

A further report appeared in 1994, the '1994 Competitiveness White Paper', as it became known, was the government's response to criticisms regarding their failure to address the issue of the manufacturing sector preferring to develop the financial sector. The white paper included schemes to deliver work related education, stimulate apprenticeships, help small and medium sized firms and reward imaginative manufacturing schemes.

The credibility of these proposals received a massive blow when in August of 1994 it was leaked that the government intended to axe some of the major parts of the DTI's aid to industry, especially the budget for regional selective assistance (RSA).

10 The drawbacks of growth

It is by no means universally accepted that economic growth is beneficial to society. Critics point to the following costs of economic growth:

- Deterioration of the environment through urban sprawl and industrialisation.
- The growth of environmental pollution to the atmosphere and rivers etc.
- High rates of innovation making skills redundant and forcing unwanted change or obsolescence onto people.
- The faster 'lifestyle' engendered by growth may bring in its wake illness and a reduced 'quality of life', e.g. heart attacks, ulcers, higher crime rates and suicide rates; which are all characteristic of urban industrialised societies.
- It may be argued that higher levels of consumerism are not necessarily synonymous with a better 'quality of life' and as quickly as 'wants' are satisfied then new wants can be created by the large corporations utilising skilful advertising. Constantly attempting to strive to new levels of 'satisfaction' can itself be a cause of stress in individuals, although it must be pointed out that most of the world's starving millions

would welcome the opportunity to enjoy at least some of the benefits of economic growth. Possibly the greatest challenge to economists in the remaining years of this century and into the 21st century will be how to achieve this growth in a responsible manner and ensure an acceptable distribution of its benefits.

11 UK growth

The slow growth rate exhibited by the UK economy in the post-war era saw a rapid improvement during the latter half of the 1980s, reaching a peak in 1988 of 4.7%. UK growth during this period compared favourably with the growth rates of the other industrial (G7) economies. The increase in growth was however accompanied by rising inflation, and a deterioration in the balance of payments as rising incomes and consumer spending caused imports to rise more rapidly than exports. 1990 however, saw the onset of recession as the rate of growth declined as a consequence of the government's counter-inflation policy of high interest rates, which restricted demand in the economy. The situation is illustrated in Figure 46.9. Despite some reductions in the rate of decline of GDP the UK economy stubbornly refused to exhibit signs of growth with the economy remaining stagnant well into 1993, despite government attempts to revive the economy through successive reductions in interest rates and the apparent evidence of 'green shoots'. Interest rates were reduced from a base rate of 15% in 1990 to 6% in January 1993, the lowest rate for 15 years with little, if any, effect on either the housing or consumer markets. Recent trends in interest rates are illustrated in Figure 46.10.

The problems of the UK economy were compounded by the decline of some of the other G7 economies in the period 1990–94, as can be seen in Table 46.2, making it even more difficult for the UK to achieve export led growth.

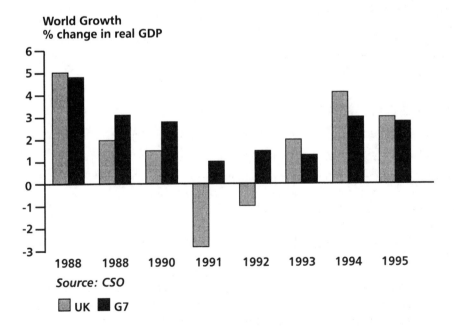

Source: CSO

■ UK ■ G7

Figure 46.9

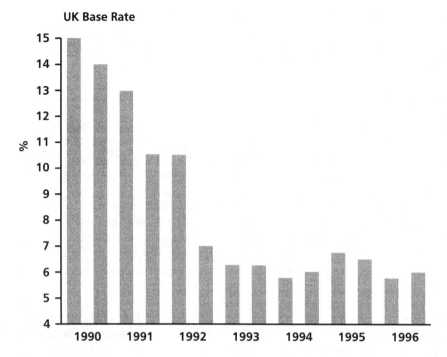

Figure 46.10

TABLE 46.2				
Growth of real GDP (%)				
	1967–79	1980–4	1985–9	1990–4
US	2.9	1.8	3.1	2.0
Japan	6.4	3.5	4.5	2.2
Germany	3.7	1.0	2.6	2.6
France	4.1	1.5	3.1	1.1
Italy	4.3	1.7	3.1	1.0
UK	2.5	0.8	4.0	0.5
EU	3.8	1.2	3.2	1.4

12 Inflation in the UK

Inflation has been a persistent problem for the UK, particularly as the rate of inflation has generally been higher than that of its trading partners making it more difficult to export to them. Following the 1988 peak in growth there was a substantial rise in inflation rates. This was due to the peak in growth and subsequent high growth rates being fuelled by a rapid increase in consumer spending. This 'consumer boom' was generated by a steady rise in real incomes, tax reductions in the March 1988 budget, a rapid rise in the money supply, as indicated in Table 46.3, and a decline in the savings ratio. Another contributory factor to the measured rate of inflation was the use of the interest rate as a counter inflation instrument. The rate of interest has a perverse effect in that it increases the cost of mortgages, which are included in the retail price index and therefore increases the rate of inflation. The 'underlying rate' of inflation is a measure of inflation which excludes mortgage interest payments (RPIX), and is considered to be a better measure for making international comparisons.

The rate of inflation rose to 10.9% in November 1990, however with the onset of recession the rate declined and by July 1993 stood at 1.2%, the lowest rate since 1964, whilst the underlying rate stood at 2.8%. The headline rate of inflation for July 1993 was lower than the European Union average of 3.3% and the G7 average of 2.7%. The fall in the rate of inflation during the period of recession was the result of reduced demand which lead to price cutting by business, and falling business costs. The reductions in the interest rates have resulted in an exaggerated fall in the RPI measure of inflation through the effect on mortgage payments, which have declined significantly. The underlying rate has fallen more slowly because, as stated earlier, they are excluded from this measure. Table 46.3 shows the rate of inflation in the UK over the period 1988 to 1996.

TABLE 46.3

	1988	1989	1990	1991	1992	1993	1994	1995	1996
Money supply growth									
M4 /annual %) increase	15.0	18.5	18.2	12.0	5.4	2.9	6.0	4.85	10.0
Interest rates									
(Base rates)	13.0	15.0	14.0	10.5	7.0	6.2	5.8	6.6	5.75
Retail prices									
(Annual % increase)	4.9	7.8	9.5	5.9	3.8	1.6	2.5	3.4	2.8
Earnings per head									
(Annual % increase)	10.2	9.1	9.7	8.0	6.1	4.1	3.8	3.2	4.0

13 Savings behaviour

Experience of the 1960s and 1970s suggest that the growth of income is a significant influence upon savings behaviour. In 1969 the savings ratio (the ratio of personal savings to personal disposable income) was 8.1, this rose to 15.4 in 1980, before declining again as the rate of growth of incomes declined. By 1988 the savings ratio had declined to 5.

The reasons for the high level of the savings ratio in the 1970s and its decline in the 1980s are difficult to isolate. It is more convenient to consider the two periods separately.

- In the 1970s it is suggested that inflation was a major influence with the peaks in inflation and savings coinciding. One reason for this correlation is that inflation eroded the real purchasing power of the individual's liquid assets, and the level of savings was then increased in order to restore wealth to its previous level.

- The decline in the savings ratio, particularly in the latter half of the 1980s, is thought to be a consequence of the increased availability of credit and the more aggressive marketing of credit by financial institutions. A further influence may also be that the rise in property values increased the wealth of individuals to such an extent that they felt less need for savings and therefore increased their consumption. The reduction in the savings ratio together with the increased availability of credit were important elements in the UK consumer 'boom' of the late 1980s.
- The savings ratio rose from 5% in 1988 to around 11% in 1992. This increase may be attributed to a number of factors. One factor is the increased fear of unemployment, another is the high level of indebtedness incurred by consumers in the late 1980s, and also the reduction in wealth suffered by home owners due to the fall in property prices and the attempt by them to restore their net wealth to the previous levels. The increase in savings is a reflection of the lack of consumer confidence in the economy. The continued fear of unemployment and the failure of the property market to return to the boom of the early 1980s has continued to keep savings at a high level, despite low rates of interest, in the mid 1990s.
- Savings have been encouraged with the conversion of many building societies to banks and the incentives that have been on offer.

14 The 90s recession

The recession of the early 1990s is the longest since 1945 and the deepest for 60 years. This recession is also different from other recessions in a number of key aspects.

- The worst hit areas in terms of unemployment were the south-east of England, the south-west, and East Anglia rather than the traditional areas of the north of England, Scotland, Wales and Northern Ireland.
- The recession brought to an end the boom in house prices, particularly in the south-east of England. House prices in England declined between 1991 and 1993, and in the south-east, where the rise in prices had been greatest during the boom, prices declined by over 10%. Many home owners were left in a situation were they owed more on their mortgages than their property was worth, a situation referred to as **negative equity**. This not only makes it more difficult for people to move house causing stagnation in the housing market, but creates a reluctance to borrow which reduces consumption.
- The very high level of business failures, significantly higher than in earlier recessions, with 65,000 recorded failures during 1992.

15 Unemployment

Unemployment rose to a peak of 3.29 million in 1986 and then fell every month between 1986 and mid 1990, however the government's anti-inflation policy of high interest rates began to slow down the rate of growth and unemployment began to rise again. Between May 1990 and February 1993 the seasonally adjusted figure for unemployment rose from 1.66 million (5.8% of the workforce) to a peak of 2.96 million (10.6% of the workforce), after which it fell each month to a total of 1.93 million in November 1996.

The largest impact of unemployment, as in the two most recent earlier recessions, fell on the manufacturing sector. Recent trends in unemployment are illustrated in Figure 46.11 below.

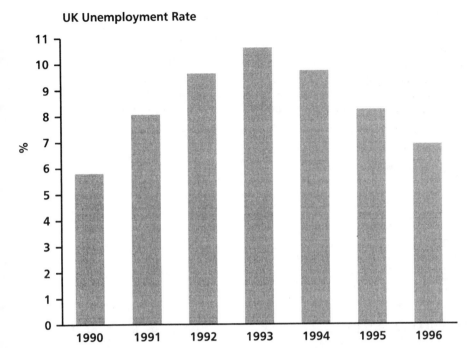

UK Unemployment Rate

Figure 46.11

16 PSBR/PSDR

During the second half of the 1980s the government was successful in its objective of reducing the ratio of public expenditure to GDP This achievement was partly due to the reduction in unemployment and the subsequent reduction in social security spending. The ratio of general government expenditure (GGE) to GDP stood at 39.5% by 1990. The government's success in reducing the percentage of GGE enabled it, by 1987, to convert the public sector borrowing requirement (PSBR) into the public sector debt repayment (PSDR) i.e. from budget deficit to budget surplus. During 1991 however a PSBR re-emerged growing rapidly to a massive £45 billion for 1993/94 which is approximately 7% of GDP, with GGE rising to 45% of GDP. Recent trends in the PSBR are illustrated in Figure 46.12. This growth in the PSBR is a consequence of the deepening recession which resulted in increased government expenditure on social security benefits whilst government receipts from taxation fell. How to fund this PSBR without damaging the potential for growth in the economy is a major problem for government economic policy.

17 The balance of payments

The rapid growth in consumer demand between 1986 and 1989 resulted in a widening of the current account deficit to £8 billion with a deficit of £14 billion on the non-oil account. The deterioration in the balance of payments continued during 1989 and the deficit for 1989 stood at £20.3 billion, the highest ever recorded, amounting to 4.5% of GDP. This was mainly due to the deterioration in visible trade as imports rose more rapidly than exports. Consumer demand slowed down during 1990 reducing the size of the deficit, however as the recession deepened instead of the balance of payments improving as may normally be expected, after 1991 the deficit grew to £11.2 billion for 1993. The improvement shown in 1994 was again reversed in 1995 with a deficit of £6.0 billion. Britain's trade position reflects the underlying weakness of the manufacturing sector but in recent years the trade in invisibles has also weakened. Figure 46.13 illustrates recent trends in the current account deficit.

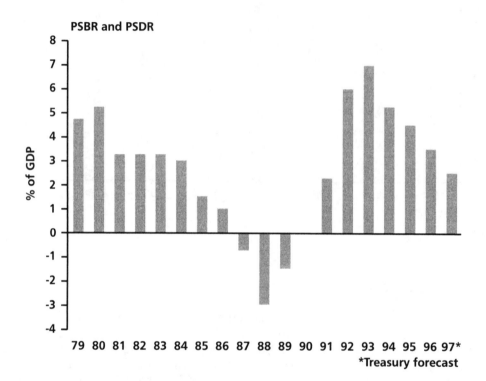

Figure 46.12

The fall in the value of sterling following Britain's withdrawal from the European Exchange Rate Mechanism (the ERM) should have made British exports more competitive but it is doubtful whether British industry was strong enough to take advantage of this.

Following the decline in sterling during 1986 and increases in productivity which reduced per unit labour costs manufacturing output increased significantly. These productivity gains substantially improved the profitability of UK companies and made a genuine contribution to the improved growth rate of that period.

With the onset of recession in 1991 output and therefore profits fell; however, profit margins stood up to recession surprisingly well. This is due to the ability to constrain cost, particularly labour costs, and substantial improvements in labour productivity. This rise in productivity can be clearly seen in Figure 46.14

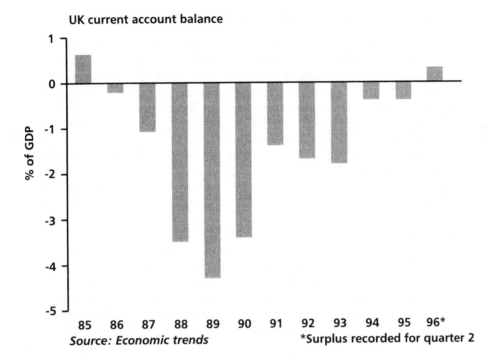

Figure 46.13

Figure 46.14

18 Interest rate movements

The government's response to the growth in consumer demand and the subsequent rise in inflation and deterioration in the balance of payments was to attempt to reduce the growth in demand by increasing interest rates. The economy however was slow to respond to higher interest rates subsequently requiring further increases. Interest rates were increased from 9 to 15% in eleven successive increases during the second half of 1988 and 1989. Interest rate increases however affect investment demand as well as consumer demand and by the final quarter of 1990 the UK economy entered recession. The depth of the recession was made worse by Britain's membership of the ERM. Sterling was over-valued against the other member currencies making exports dearer and imports cheaper, and the need to maintain the value of sterling within the mechanism forced the government to keep interest rates at an artificially high level, up to 15% just prior to leaving the ERM.

Following Britain's withdrawal from the ERM the value of sterling fell against other major currencies and the government was able to reduce interest rates to 6%. Interest rates have remained below 7% with only mild fluctuations. This has resulted in a steady increase in growth and a rise in employment. Retail sales began to pick up towards the end of 1995 whilst the underlying inflation rate (RPIX) has remained within 0.3% of the target rate of 2.5%. The growth in manufacturing has been quite marked towards the end of 1996 leading to an improved export performance.

It has been suggested that the 'feelgood' factor has returned. The weak recovery that began in 1992 has begun to translate itself into better living standards. However the upward pressure on consumer spending in the first half of 1997 caused fears of an increase in the rate of inflation, consequently the Bank of England exercised its new independence over interest rate policy and raised interest rates three times in succession to a base rate of 6.75% in July 1997, the highest rate in the G7 economies. The higher level of interest rates resulted in an appreciation in the value of sterling against other major currencies in the order of 25%. This in itself could have a deflationary impact upon the UK economy, but may also have an impact upon export performance.

Self assessment questions

1 Account for the relatively poor performance of the UK economy in the post-war era.

2 Although economic growth is generally considered desirable, what are its disadvantages?

3 Identify the main sources of economic growth.

4 Summarise the main trends in the UK economy between 1985 and 1995.

Glossary of economic terms

Accelerator Coefficient. The amount of additional capital required to produce a unit increase in output in the accelerator model.

Accelerator – Multiplier Model. A model which explains the fluctuations in the trade-cycle through the interaction of the accelerator principle and the multiplier.

Accelerator Principle (The). A capital stock adjustment process which proposes that the level of investment varies directly with the level of income (output).

Ad Valorem Tax. Indirect taxes which are a 'proportion of value'.

Advanced Countries. Industrially advanced countries with the highest levels of national income per head.

Aggregate Monetary Demand (AMD). The total demand for goods and services in the economy. Assumed to consist of the demand for consumption goods (C), plus investment goods (I) by firms, plus the demand by government (G), plus the demand for exports (X) minus imports (M). As aggregate demand determines the level of output (income) it also determines the level of employment. It is central to the Keynesian model of demand management. Therefore AMD = C+I+G+(X–M).

Aggregate Supply. The total supply of all goods and services available from domestic production plus imports to meet aggregate demand.

Arbitrage. The practice of buying in one market at a low price and reselling in another market at a higher price. Eventually the practice will eliminate the price difference between the two markets. May occur with the switching of short term funds between financial markets with different interest rates or exchange rates.

Autonomous Investment. That proportion of total investment not determined by economic factors, such as the rate of interest, but by factors such as technical innovation.

Average (Total) Cost. The total cost of production divided by output to give the average cost of production per unit.

Average Propensity to Consume (APC). The proportion of national or individual income which is used for consumption purposes.

Average Propensity to Save (APS). The proportion of national or individual income which is saved, i.e. not used for consumption. It is the complement of the APC and therefore measured as 1–APC.

Balance of Payments. An account summarising the UK's transactions with the rest of the world. Divided into two sections: the current account and the capital account. The current account is composed of visible trade (goods) and invisible trade (services). The capital account consists of flows of funds for investment purposes and loans. There may be a surplus or deficit on the current account.

Balanced Budget. Refers to the budget of the central government which is said to balance when the receipts from taxation are sufficient to meet the government's expenditure. Since 1945 UK budgets have generally been in deficit.

Balanced Budget Multiplier. The proposition that even when an increase in government expenditure is exactly matched by an increase in taxation it is still possible to have a multiplier effect on national income

Bank of England. The central bank of the UK. Established in 1694 and nationalised in 1946 and given independence in 1997. It is responsible for implementing the government's monetary policy and acting as banker to the government. It is also responsible for the issue of bank notes and coins through the issuing department.

Barriers to entry. Characteristics of a market, either economic or technical, designed to raise the costs of firms wishing to enter that market and so deter them from entering.

Beveridge Report. Prepared by Lord Beveridge in 1942 on social insurance and allied services at the request of the government. It contained a plan for social security based on three aspects; a health service, child allowances, and full employment.

Birth Rate (Crude). The average number of live births occurring in any year for every 1000 of the population.

Black Economy. That part of a country's economic activity which is not officially recorded as part of the national income. Referred to as 'black' as it is untaxed. Currently about 10% of gross domestic product in the UK.

Brandt Report. The report of the commission of inquiry into the problems of the developing countries under the chairmanship of Herr Willy Brandt. Published in 1980 entitled 'North-South: A Programme for Survival'.

Bretton Woods Conference. Bretton Woods, New Hampshire 1944, a conference to consider proposals for the settlement of post-war payments problems. Resulted in the system of fixed exchange rates, the IMF and the IBRD.

Budget Deficit. Occurs when the central government's expenditure exceeds revenue from taxation, the deficit covered by borrowing. Advocated by Keynes (J.M.) as part of the process of demand management. The normal situation in the UK in the post-war period.

Budget Surplus. When central government revenue exceeds expenditure. In the UK a surplus, established 1987, is referred to as public sector debt repayment (PSDR).

Built-In (Automatic) Stabilisers. Features in a modern tax and benefit system which tend to automatically dampen down fluctuations in income and employment. For example, as incomes rise recipients move into higher taxation brackets which dampens down inflationary tendencies. As unemployment rises the increase in welfare benefits automatically increases, maintaining the level of aggregate demand.

Capital. The stock of physical assets utilised in the act of production which are themselves the result of production. Generally taken in economics to be buildings, plant and machinery, i.e. physical goods or real capital.

Capital Expenditure. The purchase of fixed assets such as plant and equipment.

Capital Formation. Net (new) investment in fixed assets, i.e. additions to the stock of capital.

Cartel. A group of firms within an industry who collude to regulate prices and/or output in their own interests, thereby reducing or eliminating competition .

Central Bank. A feature of all developed economies, it is the instrument by which governments implement monetary policy and control banking and credit creation. In the UK also a bankers' bank and 'lender of last resort' to the discount market.

Clearing Banks. Banks which utilise the London bankers clearing house for the settlement of claims among themselves. Generally taken to be the same as the commercial banks.

Closed Economy. A simplifying device for purposes of national income analysis by which an economy is assumed to have no imports and no exports, i.e. no foreign trade.

Cobweb Theorem. A model in which the quantity currently supplied depends upon the price which prevailed in the previous market period. Usually applied to farm commodities, it explains the wide fluctuations in price and output which may occur in agricultural markets.

Common Agricultural Policy (CAP). The system of intervention in agricultural markets within the EC designed to maintain farm incomes and encourage output. 'Intervention prices' are maintained by the commission for each commodity by buying and storing surplus production.

Complementary Goods. Goods are complementary when a reduction in the price of one of the goods results in an increased demand for both goods, for example a reduction in the price of cars increases the demand for both cars and petrol.

Consumer Surplus. The surplus of utility which consumers receive resulting from the difference between the market price they actually pay for a good and what they would be prepared to pay rather than go without it.

Consumption Function. The relationship between aggregate consumption expenditure and aggregate disposable income in an economy. A central feature of the Keynesian model, in which consumption is assumed to be a function of income.

Consumption Goods. Goods purchased by consumers for final consumption rather than for the production of further goods. May be single use, e.g. ice-cream or durable, e.g. refrigerators.

Corporation Tax. A tax on the profits of companies.

Cost-push Inflation. Inflation which arises from increased cost factors such as the price of materials or labour. It is independent of the level of demand.

Currency Appreciation. An increase in the exchange rate of one currency relative to others in a regime of flexible exchange rates. In a fixed exchange rate system referred to as revaluation.

Currency Depreciation. A fall in the exchange rate of one currency relative to others in a regime of flexible exchange rates. In a fixed exchange rate system referred to as devaluation.

Cyclical Unemployment. Unemployment which results from the downward fluctuations in the trade cycle.

Death Rate (Crude). The number of deaths occurring in any year for every 1000 of the population.

Deflation. A reduction in the general level of prices brought about by monetary and fiscal policies designed to reduce the level of economic activity.

Demand. The desire and ability of consumers to purchase an amount of a particular good or service.

Demand Curve. A curve which relates the prices of a commodity to the quantity the consumer is willing to purchase. Conventionally price is shown on the Y axis and quantity on the X axis. The demand curve slopes downward from left to right reflecting the 'law of downward sloping demand '.

Demand-pull Inflation. Inflation which results from aggregate demand in the economy exceeding the full employment output of goods and services. If aggregate demand exceeds aggregate supply prices will rise, if these price rises are sustained the result is inflation.

Demand Shift. An increase or decrease in the quantity demanded at each price as a consequence of a change in factors other than price e.g. taste, preferences, incomes. Represented by a shift in the entire demand curve upwards to the right in the case of an increase, and downwards to the left in the case of a decrease.

Depression. A severe downturn in the trade cycle characterised by high levels of unemployment, in particular the UK 1929 - 1933.

Developing Country. A country with a low level of GNP per head, which has not reached the stage of industrialisation.

Development Areas. Those areas in the UK which because of their high levels of unemployment are deemed by the government as qualifying for special assistance e.g. development grants.

Discount Market. Also referred to as the money market, consists of the banks, discount houses, and accepting houses. The market deals in Treasury bills, bills of exchange, and short dated bonds. It is important to the authorities for its role as an intermediary between the Bank of England and the banking system.

Diseconomy. The long-run tendency for average cost of production to rise after reaching a minimum point. Generally due to problems of administration and co-ordination.

Disposable Income. Personal income, after the deduction of taxation and receipt of benefits, available for spending or saving.

Division of Labour. The breaking down of a task into its simplest components in order to facilitate specialisation of labour and/or mechanisation. The basis of surplus production and the exchange economy.

Dumping. The sale of excess production at the marginal cost of production in export markets in order to increase profits in the domestic market or to eliminate competition.

Durable Goods (Consumer). Consumer goods such as refrigerators which are not consumed immediately but over a period of time. More accurately it is the service or utility which they yield which is consumed.

Economic Growth. Refers to growth of national income which is generally taken to imply rising living standards.

Economic Rent. The return to a factor in fixed supply which is considered to be a surplus the size of which is determined by the price of the factor. Where there are transfer earnings it is the surplus payments over the transfer earrings.

Economies of Scale. As the scale of production increases with successive increases in plant size there is a tendency for average costs per unit of output to decline due to the economies of large scale production.

Elasticity of Demand (Price). The degree of responsiveness of quantity demanded to changes in price. In response to a price change therefore total revenue may increase, stay unchanged or fall. Measured by the formula

$$PED = \frac{\text{percentage change in quantity demanded}}{\text{percentage change in price}}$$

The resulting coefficient of elasticity will be, < 1 (inelastic), = 1 (Unitary), or > 1 (Elastic).

Elasticity of Supply (Price). The degree of responsiveness of quantity supplied to changes in price. The coefficient of elasticity of supply is measured as:

$$PES = \frac{\text{percentage change in quantity supplied}}{\text{percentage change in price}}$$

Entrepreneur. The name given to an individual in economics who manages and owns his own business, thereby providing the capital and enterprise, accepting all the risks, and receiving all the profit as a reward.

Equilibrium. An important concept in economics referring to a situation where opposing forces are in balance and there is no further tendency to change. In a market equilibrium would exist when the quantities demanded by consumers was exactly equal to the quantity supplied by producers at the prevailing price.

European Monetary System (EMS). An attempt by the EU to establish a system which would keep the fluctuations between the currencies of the member countries within narrow bands.

European Union (EU). Established by the Treaty of Rome in 1957 for the purposes of creating a customs union. The objective of the treaty was to eliminate obstacles to the free movement of goods, labour and capital between the member countries; to establish an external tariff, and a common agricultural policy (CAP). The basic idea is to form a large trading bloc to compete with other large blocs such as the USA and USSR. The original 6 member countries had grown to 13 by 1987.

Exchange Rate. The price of a currency expressed in terms of another currency, which is also the rate at which the currencies can be exchanged.

Excise Duties. Taxes levied upon goods for domestic consumption.

Externalities. An externality exists when the production or consumption of a good by one party imposes costs or benefits upon another party, but will not be included in the decisions of the party creating them.

Factors of Production. The essential requirements necessary for production to occur, namely, land, labour, and capital. These are combined by enterprise to produce economic goods.

Fiduciary Issue. Paper money not backed by gold. The fiduciary issue is backed only by confidence in the currency unit. The note issue is now entirely fiduciary.

Fixed costs. Those costs of production which in the short run do not change with output, e.g. rent, rates, interest.

Fixed Exchange Rates. A system whereby a group of trading nations agrees to maintain a par value for their own currency relative to the others through intervention on the foreign exchange markets. Such a system was operated by the IMF members from 1947 to 1973.

Flexible Exchange Rates. A system whereby the rate of exchange is determined by the market forces of supply and demand.

Frictional Unemployment. Unemployment which results from the time lag between labour becoming unemployed and locating a suitable vacancy. It may exist therefore during periods of high employment and can be a consequence of job changing.

Friedman, Milton. Professor of Economics at Chicago University and a leading exponent of monetarism.

Full Employment. In terms of gross domestic product it is a measure of the output which the economy is capable of when all its resources are employed. For labour it is taken to mean that everyone who desires a job at the current wage rate is employed and only frictional unemployment remains.

Funding Operations. The process of changing the structure of the national debt by converting short term debt to long term debt.

General Agreement on Tariffs and Trade (GATT). Established in 1948 with the objective of reducing tariffs and other barriers to trade, and to encourage free-trade between the 88 members. Replaced by the World Trade Organisation in 1995.

Gilt-edged Securities. British government securities with fixed rates of interest, traded on the Stock Exchange.

Gold and Foreign Exchange Reserves. Stock of gold and foreign currency held by a nation for the settlement of international indebtedness if required to do so.

Gross Domestic Product (GDP). The total output of goods and services produced by the economy over a year, expressed as a monetary value.

Gross National Product (GNP). Gross domestic product plus income earned from overseas investment owned by UK residents less income paid abroad to foreign residents.

Horizontal Integration. The merging of different firms at the same stage in the manufacturing process.

Import Duties. Taxes imposed on imported goods. May be ad valorem (according to value) or specific (per unit).

Import Quotas. A form of import control whereby only certain quantities of specified goods may be imported.

Imports. The goods and services which enter a country from overseas sources for domestic consumption.

Income Tax. A tax on incomes. In the UK deducted by employers at source and paid to the Inland Revenue; referred to as Pay-as-You-Earn income tax (PAYE).

Incremental Capital-Output Ratio (ICOR). The ratio of net investment to the change in output over a given period, i.e. the additional output gained from new investment.

Inflation. A generalised and sustained rise in the price level or a fall in the value of money.

Inflationary Gap. The excess of aggregate monetary demand over aggregate supply measured at the full employment level of national income.

Interest. The reward for foregoing current consumption.

Interest, Rate of. The price of borrowed money. The price a borrower must pay a lender to compensate for foregone consumption.

International Bank for Reconstruction and Development (IBRD). Known also as the 'World Bank'. Established at the Bretton Woods Conference 1944 with the purpose of encouraging capital investment for the reconstruction and development of its member countries either by making loans from its own funds or by the direction of private funds to suitable projects.

International Monetary Fund (IMF). Established at the Bretton Woods Conference 1944 and effective from 1947. The purpose of the fund was to encourage international co-operation on trade and payments. Was responsible for the management of the fixed exchange rate system which operated from 1947 to 1973, and provided a fund to assist member nations with temporary balance of payments difficulties.

Investment. Expenditure on capital goods.

J-Curve. Name given to the observation that following a currency depreciation the balance of payments generally deteriorates before eventually improving. If graphed the trend looks like a letter J.

Keynes, John Maynard (1883-1946). Author of *'The General Theory of Employment, Interest, and Money'* (1936). His writings formed the basis of the post-war economic policies of demand management, i.e. The 'Keynesian Model' in which governments utilise their own expenditure in order to manage the level of demand.

Kondratieff Cycle. After the economist M.D. Kondratieff, the proposal that there are long term cycles in the trade cycle with peaks and troughs every 50-60 years.

Laffer Curve. After Professor Arthur Laffer, a curve relating tax revenue to the tax rate.

Lender of Last Resort. An essential feature of the role of a central bank is the provision of a facility for loans to the banking system when required to do so, in the UK through the medium of the discount market. This lending is done on the central bank's own terms which enable it to influence the general level of interest rates and the money supply.

Liquidity. The ease with which an asset can be converted into money.

Liquidity Preference. The extent to which individuals desire to hold their wealth in the form of money rather than other assets such as bonds.

Long-run. The period of time in which the firm can adjust all its factors of production, both variable and fixed.

Macroeconomics. The study of the aggregate performance of the whole of gross national product and the price level.

Marginal Cost. The additional cost resulting from a small (or single unit) increase in the output of a good.

Marginal Product. The increase in total output resulting from a small increase in one factor of production whilst all the other factors are held constant. Can be applied to labour, land, or capital i.e. marginal productivity of labour etc.

Marginal Propensity to Consume (MPC). The proportion of each additional unit of income which is devoted to consumption. As not all income is normally consumed the value of the MPC is usually less than one. The size of the MPC determines the slope of the consumption function and plays an important part in the multiplier process.

Marginal Propensity to Save (MPS). The proportion of each additional unit of income which is devoted to saving. As income is either consumed or saved it has a value of 1 - MPC.

Marginal Revenue. The change in a firm's total revenue which results from the sale of one additional unit of output.

Marginal Utility. The increase in total utility gained by increasing the quantity consumed of a good by one unit.

Marginal Utility, Law of Diminishing. As successive units of a good are consumed the extra utility received from each additional unit tends to diminish. Underlies the theory of demand.

Microeconomics. The study of individual economic units, consumers and firms and the ways in which they make their decisions. The central concept is the role of the market.

Minimum Lending Rate (MLR). The rate of interest at which the central bank is prepared to lend to the banking system in its role as 'lender of the last resort'.

Monetarism. The school of macroeconomic thought that suggests that the money supply is the most important factor in determining the level of expenditure and prices.

Money. Anything which is generally accepted in exchange for goods, or in settlement of a debt.

Money Supply. The quantity of money which exists in an economy at any single time. As there is no single definition of money different definitions may be utilised for operational purposes such as M0, M4 etc.

Monopoly. A market in which a single seller controls the entire output of a good or service.

Multiplier (The). A measure of the effect on national income of a change in one of the components of aggregate demand. A central element in the Keynesian model of demand management, generally referred to in terms of investment or government expenditure. Calculated as:–

$$\frac{1}{1 - MPC}$$

where MPC = marginal propensity to consume.

National Debt. The cumulative total of outstanding debts owed by successive governments

National Income. The aggregate or total income of the nation which results from economic activity, measured in monetary terms, over a specified time period - usually a year.

Net Investment. Gross expenditure on capital formation less investment to replace worn out plant and equipment

Oligopoly. A market which is dominated by a few large sellers i.e. there is a high degree of concentration in the market.

Open Market Operations. The purchase and sale of securities by the central bank on the open market in order to influence the stock of financial assets and thereby indirectly the lending of the banks.

Opportunity Cost. Cost defined in terms of the value of the alternatives which have been foregone in order to achieve a particular objective.

Optimum. The best outcome which can be achieved from a given set of variables.

Organisation of Economic Co-operation and Development (OECD). Established in 1961, the organisation's aims are the encouragement of economic growth and high employment among the member countries, to assist in the economic development of the less advanced member and non member countries, and the expansion of multilateral world trade. The organisation functions through a number of committees and publishes a regular statistical bulletin.

Organisation Of Petroleum Exporting Countries (OPEC). A group of fourteen countries who are the major producers and exporters of crude oil. Established in 1960, it attempts to fix prices and production quotas for crude oil exports.

Participation Rate. The proportion of the population who are of working age and are part of the labour force.

Per capita income. Income per head of population. i.e.

$$\frac{NY}{population}$$

Phillips Curve. The empirical proposition put forward by Professor A.W. Phillips in 1958 that there was a significant inverse relationship between the level of unemployment and the rate of change of money wages.

Precautionary Motive. Money held for the purpose of meeting unforeseen expenditures.

Prices and Incomes Policy. Government policy aimed at regulating the rate of increase of wages and prices in order to control inflation.

Privatisation. The sale of government holdings in nationalised industries to the private sector.

Productivity. The rate at which output flows from the use of factors of production. Often used in terms of productivity to mean efficiency.

Public Sector Borrowing Requirement (PSBR). The deficit between the income and expenditure of the public sector, in particular central and local government. Usually financed by debt sales to the 'non bank' private sector, borrowing from the banking system, borrowing from overseas, or by issuing more cash to the public.

Quantity Theory of Money. A theory of the relationship between the supply of money in an economy and the price level.

Rate of Return. Net profit as a percentage of capital employed in a business. An important measure of business efficiency.

Real Income. Income measured in terms of the goods and services it will actually purchase.

Real Wages. Money wages deflated by an index such as the retail price index to give the actual purchasing power implied.

Reflation. Policy measures designed to raise the level of aggregate demand closer to the full employment level of national income.

Rent–see Economic Rent

Retail Price Index. An index used to express current retail prices in terms of a base year. The index is based on a weighted average of typical consumer expenditure patterns.

Saving. Desisting from using income for current consumption, as income which is not consumed must be saved. Note that this is not investment, it only becomes investment when the saved funds are used to acquire an asset.

Seasonal Unemployment. Unemployment which arises from the seasonal nature of some types of work such as the holiday related industries.

Short-Run. The time period during which the firm can adjust only its variable factors of production, such as labour.

Social Cost. Occur when actions by one party create costs which are borne by others or by society as a whole.

Special Deposits. Cash deposits by the clearing banks with the Bank of England in response to a directive by the Bank in order to restrict credit creation.

Special Drawing Rights (SDRs). Used by the IMF to finance international trade. Countries with balance of payments difficulties could draw up to 125% of the quota they contributed to the fund, but with increasingly severe conditions regarding their domestic economic policies imposed upon them.

Speculative Motive. Money balances held for the purposes of avoiding losses on a declining securities market. An innovation to monetary theory by J.M. Keynes to explain liquidity preference.

Structural Unemployment. Arises out of fundamental changes in the industrial base of the economy. Generally associated with the decline of 'staple' industries concentrated in the regions, hence also related to the 'regional problem'.

Supply. The quantity of goods or services which a producer is willing to put on to the market at the prevailing price during a particular time period.

Supply Curve. A curve illustrating the relationship between the market price of a good and the quantity supplied. The convention is that price is shown on the Y axis and quantity on the X axis. Supply curves generally slope upwards to the right.

Supply-Side Economies. A view of macroeconomics which emerged during the 1970s but with much in common with the classical tradition of economics. Supply-side economists take the view that output is determined by real variables and therefore stress the importance of the growth of the supply of the factors of production and technological change. They also suggest that fiscal and monetary policy cannot influence real output in the long run.

Tariff–see Import duties

Terms of Trade. The ratio of the index of export prices to the index of import prices. If export prices rise more quickly than import prices the index rises and represents an improvement in the terms of trade and vice versa.

Trade Barrier. A term used to describe any restriction on international trade imposed by government.

Transactions Demand for Money. The demand for cash balances to finance normal expenditures between receipts of income.

Transfer Earnings. The returns to a factor of production which are just sufficient to keep it in its current use. Any excess over transfer earnings is economic rent.

Transfer payments. Income transfers between different groups in society. For example from the employed to the unemployed, or students in the form of grants. Deliberately excluded from national income calculations as to include them would result in 'double counting'.

Treasury Bills. One of the means by which the government covers its short term borrowing requirement. The bills have a maturity of 91 days after which they are redeemable with interest. The amounts vary between £5000 and £1 million and are issued by tender to the money market.

Unemployment, Natural Rate of. The unemployment which remains when the labour market is in equilibrium. Such unemployment is therefore considered voluntary in the sense that the unemployed labour is not willing to work for a sufficiently low wage. Associated with the monetarist view.

Utility. The satisfaction derived from the consumption of a good or service.

Value Judgement. A statement of opinion which cannot be validated by appeal to the facts.

Vertical Integration. The merging of firms at different stages of the production process, either backwards towards the source of raw materials or forwards towards the retail stage.

World Trade Organisation. Established to monitor world trade and encourage free trade. Set up in 1995 to replace GATT.

Yield. The income from a security as a percentage of its current market price.

Index

Market research, 361
Marris, R., 126
Marshall, A., 190
Memorandum of Association, 73
Merit goods, 187
Migration, 157
Minford, P., 329
Minimum efficient scale, 118
Minimum lending rate, 271
Mishan, E.J., 186
Monetarism, Chp. 43, 316–322
Monetarists, 204
    and consumption function,
      App. 2, Chp. 43, 324–326
    and employment, Chp. 44
Monetary Base Control, 271
Monetary Policy, 293
Monetary Sector Analysis, Chp. 43,
    341–353
Monetary Sector Equilibrium, 342
Money, 21–22
Money at call, 251
Money illusion, 332
Money market, 250
Money supply, Chp. 35, 207, 347
Money supply – effects of, 343, 352
Money supply targets, 273
Money precautionary demand for, 309
    speculative demand for, 309, 341
    transactions demand for, 309, 341
Monopolies Commission, 129 et seq
Monopolies and Mergers Act, 129
    et seq
Monopolistic Competition, Chp. 17
Monopoly, Chp. 15
Monopoly – natural, 183
Monopoly profits, 108
M.T.F.S., 323–324 App. l, Chp. 43
Multi-national, 71
Multiplier, App. 1, Chp. 39, 285 et seq

N
National Debt, 281
National Expenditure, 190 et seq
National Income, Chp. 28
    definition, 190
National Income per capita, 196
National Income (real), 191
Negotiable instruments, 252
Neo-classical economists, 333–334
Net National Product, 192
Net Present Value, 304
New Deal, 293
Nominal Income, 201
Non-price competition, 117

O
Office of Fair Trading, 130
Oligopoly, 115–119
Open market operations, 270
Opportunity Cost, 2
Optimum population, 157
Organisational slack, 128
Ostentation goods, 28, 33
Output method, 194
Output optimum, 88
Overdraft, 78–79
Over populated, 158

P
Pareto optimum, 183
Pareto V, 183
Partnership, 72–73
Partnership Act, 72
Par value of currency, 235
P.A.Y.E., 259
Per capita income, 196
Perfect competition, Chp. 14
Permanent Income
    Hypothesis, App. 2, Chp. 43
Phillips, A.W., 298
Phillips Curve, 298
Phillips Curve – adaptive
    expectations model, Chp. 44, 331
Planning envelope, 91
Poll Tax, 275, 266
Population, Chp. 23, 154 et seq
    ageing, 154
    bulges, 157
    census of, 154
    increasing, 157
    decreasing, 157
    Malthus theory of, 159
    natural increase of, 156
    optimum, 157
    pyramid, 156
    total, 154
    working, 154
P = MC, 99–100
Price consumption curve, 175
Price discrimination, 110
Price leader, 116
Price mechanism, Chp. 27
Price rigidity, 115
Price target, 60
Price theory, Chp. 6
Process diffusion, 361
Process innovation, 361
Pro cyclical, 319–320
Producer surplus, 181
Product differentiation, 118, 120